I SEE THAT
YOU ARE DOWN,
BUT WHEN ARE YOU
GOING TO GET UP?

T0381055

SHAWN M^CDOWELL

Trafford
PUBLISHING™

Order this book online at www.trafford.com/07-0445
or email orders@trafford.com

Most Trafford titles are also available at major online book retailers.

Note for Librarians: A cataloguing record for this book is available from Library
and Archives Canada at www.collectionscanada.ca/amicus/index-e.html

Printed in Victoria, BC, Canada.

ISBN: 978-1-4251-2041-2 (sc)

ISBN: 978-1-4269-3203-8 (e-book)

*We at Trafford believe that it is the responsibility of us all, as both individuals
and corporations, to make choices that are environmentally and socially sound.
You, in turn, are supporting this responsible conduct each time you purchase a
Trafford book, or make use of our publishing services. To find out how you are
helping, please visit www.trafford.com/responsiblepublishing.html*

*Our mission is to efficiently provide the world's finest, most comprehensive
book publishing service, enabling every author to experience success.
To find out how to publish your book, your way, and have it available
worldwide, visit us online at www.trafford.com/10510*

www.trafford.com

North America & international
toll-free: 1 888 232 4444 (USA & Canada)
phone: 250 383 6864 ♦ fax: 250 383 6804
email: info@trafford.com

The United Kingdom & Europe
phone: +44 (0)1865 722 113 ♦ local rate: 0845 230 9601
facsimile: +44 (0)1865 722 868 ♦ email: info.uk@trafford.com

10 9 8 7 6 5 4

DEDICATION

I dedicate this book to our Great God and Father and to the Number One Son our Lord and Savior, Jesus Christ. Please accept this book as a small down payment on the promise I made to You as a young boy. As a Torch Bearer for Jesus Christ, striving to be a reflection of His Light on Earth, I now pass it forward to those who seek Your Face, Your Love and Your Guidance out of the darkness.

I humbly offer this book of my life to You in order make a difference for the betterment of all of Your beloved children of the world in desperate need of your Love and Eternal Grace. In Jesus name, we say with the utmost of gratitude, Amen.

ACKNOWLEDGEMENT

I wish to acknowledge and give thanks to my ancestors and predecessors in the struggle for humanity, to the many people who sacrificed their lives in order that I may live. First and foremost, thank you Big Frank Wilkins for helping me to become a man may you Rest In Peace. I wish to thank my mother Brenda, my sisters Monya and Shay, for without their love and support I would not be here today. I also wish to acknowledge Neeko, Tyree and Saijee, whom I love with all my heart and am so very proud to have as my sons.

I wish give special thanks to my teachers Mrs. Crawford (OH & AL), Mr. Sminchek, Mr. Grass, Mr. Hoffman, Mr. Francil and Mr. Noser, whose instruction, support and guidance shaped my mind and character which gave me the confidence to pursue my dreams, goals and ambitions. Over past twenty years, I have traveled the world with the opportunity to meet great and wonderful people from all walks of life. However, there are a few that I can call and consider my true friends to the end.

To my main men Rick, Mike, Scott, Carlos, Bobby, Eric, Donny, Roger, Ralph, Robert, Richard, Bob, Alistair, Aubrey and Brad, each of you in your own way made me the man I am today and without your friendship and support, this book would not been possible.

Last but not least, I wish to give thanks to those detractors, haters, naysayer's and deceivers who sought to bring me down and place me into harms way. For as the saying goes "That which does not kill you makes you stronger", you unknowingly gave me untold strength and power to light the Eternal flame that will carry me forward for the remainder of my life.

PREFACE

In Gods infinite love, wisdom and grace the universe and its divine matrix known as the Game of Life came into being. Through the experiences gained from this physical playing field, humanity has the opportunity to create and recreate itself. Life is very much like a box of chocolates whereby our choices allows us to taste and savor every flavor of our experience and thus become a greater and grander version of our eternal self.

Our total existence consists of the elements of mind, body, and spirit, which provide the means by which we come to grow and evolve. The various experiences that we face in life affect how we react to what occurs in our surrounding environment. These experiences come from many sources, such as our relationships with family, friends, associates, and even strangers.

These relationships ultimately affect our ability to love, learn and grow as individuals. The choices and decisions we make along our life's journey will dictate the quality of the experience we will attain. Most of us tend to make our choices and decisions unconsciously, not based in a state of true awareness. Through the conscience thought process, one can tune their spirit towards God's universe in order to enhance the quality of one's life experience.

The hardships we come to endure in life are the result of our lack of understanding as to how pure the process of the Game truly is. The ability to trust our own judgment and ability to make informed decisions depends upon the quality of our internal filtering system. These filters (mind, body, & spirit) provide the means by which we each process the various internal and external stimuli coming in from our surroundings.

In order to make sound decisions and choices, it is required that the individual have the skills and ability to think clearly and logically. Most of our parents and current forms of education do not teach children at an early age how to think independently using the power of the conscience mind. Author's such as L. Ron Hubbard with his book "Dianetics" and the Dale Carnegie series of books on the power of positive thinking have been in circulation for decades.

Many of the concepts are far too complicated for children and many adults. Many people, based on their religious convictions, summarily reject the concepts espoused by the authors. This is due partly to the unwillingness of many individuals to acknowledge they have problems and issues within their life, which require efforts on their part to change behavior patterns that no longer serve them.

The path to spiritual enlightenment requires that decisions be rooted in more than just the five senses of touch, taste, sight, smell, and sound. The process also requires the use of intuition, considered the sixth sense otherwise known as the Holy Spirit. The Holy Spirit is essentially God's Positioning System to help guide us through life's trials and tribulations. If concrete information is not readily available, then one must consider other means to derive at a particular decision. It is imperative to weigh and consider the many variables, causes, and effects that may occur if a specific course of action is undertaken.

Utilizing and tapping into the power of the Holy Spirit is similar to playing chess. Expert chess players first study the chessboard in order to anticipate the many potential moves available to their opponent based on the current placement of the chess pieces. Any movement on the chessboard produces a series of possible counter movements. If the player can foresee these possibilities, the greater the chance the player can anticipate and execute a counter-move to thwart their opponent.

All decisions start within the mind with the creation of thought, taking into consideration the possible outcomes of a particular decision. The individual can then project a feeling or an emotion to that choice selected. These feelings are then manifested into words and finally into a subsequent series of actions. By using one's intuition and the process of elimination will help determine the choice best suited that will produce the highest or greatest good.

There is not one creation brought into existence in which God's Spiritual energy was not present. Through spiritual inspiration, every song ever sung, poem ever written, and invention ever created came as the result of the individual connecting their inner spirit to the Divine matrix. The power of thought is a by-product of spiritual energy expended.

All that we come to experience in life serves a greater purpose, no matter what the occurrence. Be it the pain and anguish over the loss of a loved one, or the scars caused by the emotional or physical abuse endured as a child. There is a direct correlation between utilizing the God given power to exercise our free will to make conscience-based decisions and the resultant outcome experienced. These decisions will affect the quality of life we live and the love we seek.

Through our decision and choices, we elect to play certain roles throughout our lives. Some may choose the role of the saint or the sinner, the hero or the villain, or the healer or the killer. In either case, God places no judgment in this life upon the person and the role one chooses to play. For if life is truly a treasure and free will is a gift given unconditionally by God with love, do what you choose with the treasures given to you. However, with the gift of life comes great personal responsibility and accountability based upon the choices one makes.

The hand of God touches all that occurs under the sun, for there is nothing that is required from us that He does not already own. For the Creator was, is, and will forever be at the center of all that occurs in the universe. This provides the framework for God's unconditional love for us no matter what we choose to do. Unfortunately, there are those of this world whom are not as forgiving. For the indiscretions or choices you commit today, may come back to haunt you tomorrow.

For the young woman who has many sexual partners and contracts a disease or ends up pregnant, or to the young man who commits a crime and does prison time. In either case, each exercised their own free will to engage in their chosen behavior. However, the price of exercising that freedom can be quite high. Be prepared to deal with the consequences and ramifications of your actions. As long as you are willing to pay the costs for being the boss for what you say and do in life, all praises be unto you no matter what you choose to do.

The world and the universe are but a grand stage, whereby at the mere change of a thought and mind state, we can change the role we elect to play in life. How willing we are to embrace our new chosen role shall determine the quality of the experience. This in turn will affect the manner, tone, and tenor of the interrelationships of those around us.

Once the scene starts, then it becomes incumbent upon the individual to know their role and to play it well. The Divine matrix of the universe operates on a myriad of physical laws and principles, well documented throughout human existence. The universe in which we live operates on several principles, one being the principle of relative perspective.

Just as the dial on a thermostat, life is all but a matter of degrees of choice that separate one experience from another. Nothing exists in the universe that does not have an identical but polar equivalent energy. Such examples of duality are good and evil, love and hate, hot and cold, etc. You cannot know one without the other, for the existence of both provides the mechanism for allowing the individual to choose that which it desires to experience.

A person may not be able to stop the rain from falling or the sun from shining, but you can decide to seek shelter from or dress for either weather condition. The Game of Life also operates on the physical principle that for every action there is an equal but opposite reaction. Otherwise known as the Law of Compensation, "reaping what we sow", or "what goes around, comes around".

Contained within the laws of science and mathematics, both known, and those yet to be uncovered are spokes. They provide the medium by which the exchange of energy travels within the Divine matrix. From these spokes and other influences, our relationship to the environment and the truth contained within it is connected. To some extent, common threads of relative truth connect even the spokes of the many world religions.

However, note the use of the word relative. There is nothing absolute in the universe and what is true today, can upon a new discovery or passage of time becomes rendered false tomorrow. At one point in man's existence, the relative truth of the time was that the world was flat. Another truth that prevailed during ancient times was that the earth was the center of the universe.

It was an act of heresy by the practicing religions of the time for a person to believe or speak otherwise. Bold individuals such as Copernicus and Christopher Columbus came forth willing to risk their lives to disprove the prevailing myths and religious truths of the times. By their willingness to take a leap of faith, the human race was able to grow and evolve from its existing state of being and belief in only what one's eyes could see.

In the movie "On Any Given Sunday", Al Pacino gave a pre game speech to his team. In this speech, he spoke metaphorically of football being similar to the game of life. Football as is life, is a game of inches whereby two teams wage a fierce battle for control over the line of scrimmage. In the game of life, the opposing forces of our choices come together on the playing field of our life's existence.

We each through our thinking and pondering the many options available wage a continual daily battle to determine the path best suited. The path chosen as a result shall determine the outcome of our experience. In football as in life, all of the inches we need for our personal growth are all around us. During the course of playing the game, if one hesitates or moves a second too fast or too slow, the player misses an opportunity to grow.

If we fail to take chances or risks and stretch the limits of our capabilities, when the ball of opportunity is tossed, we may fumble the opportunity to improve upon our abilities. By being spiritually in tune with God, the probability of catching the pass and crossing the goal line increases. Many times over the course of history, humanity has come close to scoring the cosmic touchdown.

However, due to the collective choices of the human race, mankind continually fumbles the ball of spiritual evolution in the red zone. As a result, forward progress towards crossing over into the next level of our spiritual evolution becomes a dream denied. Many highly advanced ancient civilizations have graced our planet over the many millennia. Civilizations such as the Mayans and Aztecs, the Inca's and Egyptians, Greek and Romans fielded great teams. As the result of the choices and decisions made by the collective cultures, much of their knowledge and wisdom were lost to future generations. As a result, their respective cultures went the way of the dinosaur and became extinct.

Over the many millennia, God has sent many great teachers, master players of the Game of Life. Each in their own way, attempted to assist humanity to recognize those inches that surround us and to take full advantage of them. They have come in the form of philosophers, scholars, writers, poets, scientists, and spiritual leaders such as Jesus, Gandhi, Buddha, Albert Einstein, Charles Dickens, Shakespeare, Aristotle, Socrates, Plato, Muhammad, Moses, and countless others.

"Truth Seekers" throughout history have been subjected to the scorn of those blissful in their ignorance. Those who wrap themselves within a cocoon of self-righteousness, caged by their pious, dogmatic and legalistic viewpoints. In time, many of the messengers lost their lives due to simply sharing and speaking their truth with the masses. In many instances the very same individuals, who called out to the heavens hoping to have their prayers and concerns addressed, were the very same ones duplicitous in the killing of the heaven sent messenger.

I will offer anecdotal commentary on many social issues and problems I have encountered in my life. By utilizing a combination of plain talk, clichés, and metaphors, I shall attempt to drive home my points to the reader. I will offer no placebos or candy coated pills, as I shall open the book of my life story with both great hope and reservation. Through my observations, it appeared to me that the only instances whereby people consider changing their behaviors occur when their own physical being is threatened.

Some perhaps only consider changing the current methods and approaches used in their life after experiencing some catastrophic and traumatic loss. I wrote this book with the hopes that perhaps someone can learn and lessen their pain from the experiences I have gained thus far. I will tell the whole truth as I remembered it, showing how the decisions and choices I made unconsciously affected the quality of the life I came to experience.

The major "demon" in my life to date has been my inability to trust others, which manifested itself into displays of anger and rage. These by products of fear were deeply embedded in my subconscious and thus affected my choices in life as well as my ability to trust others. As a result, my anger reduced my capacity to love myself as well as diminishing the means to love others as well.

Mistrust is as toxic as cyanide, and there are many instances throughout history where mistrust can result in the deaths of millions. Ignorance and fear breeds suspicion, from which the Spanish Inquisition and Salem Witch Hunt were born. The Nazi's "Final Solution" to the McCarthy era hunts for the "Red communist scourge" and today's War on Terror are but a few examples of the power fear can have upon a nation.

At one point in time in my life, I was one of the billions upon billions of wandering souls lost in sea of darkness and despair. Through this book, I hope to be a beacon of light to all those seeking the safety and comfort of the shores of Gods love and eternal wisdom. We are on the verge of another Great Depression of both spiritual and psychological proportions. Our collective spirit and state of mind is currently in flux, with a strong undercurrent of major social dysfunction.

From the moment Christ was crucified, a crack in the fabric of the human spirit was formed which has continued to grow. It is this crack, which has distorted the reflection of His Light throughout the soul of mankind. A crack, which has created more than 24,000 different Christian sects and denominations, let alone other religious belief systems. A crack which refracts and distorts His True Likeness, and therefore repels those who would otherwise seek His light through the physical lens of those of us who lips profess one thing, but whose actions move in contradiction to His Word. As a result, many people seeking a relationship with Jesus have become disengaged, and thus turn away from the body of Christ.

The collective spirit of the human race is in need of healing. In order for the collective spirit to become whole and the crack sealed, healing is required to repair the damaged soul of each individual . As with a mesh woven chain, the overall strength of the chain is only as strong as the weakest links. The time has come for the human race to take a quantum leap forward in our societal and spiritual evolution.

"I SEE THAT YOU ARE DOWN, BUT WHEN ARE YOU GOING TO GET UP?' chronicles the trials and tribulations I encountered during my transition from boyhood to manhood through the transformative powers of Christ and the Holy Spirit within us all. We are far more than our parental DNA, and far greater than the product of our environment. We have far more in common within the human experience than we are willing to accept. The three primary causes of conflict chronicled throughout history have been based upon racial division, religious intolerance, and those who seek to control the resources of this planet God created for us all to share.

As a student of history and follower of the teaching of Jesus Christ, I have come to understand that there is nothing new under the sun. Unless we all strive to live a balanced life whereby our mind, body and spirit work in unison to bring forth inner peace, inner turmoil will bring forth external conflict into our environment. A PARADIGM SHIFT IS OCCURING, WHICH IS AWAKENING THE COLLECTIVE SPIRITUAL CONSCIOUSNESS. In addition to attaining spiritual awareness, people must also be intellectually and socially aware to avoid being misled down the path of self-destruction mankind has traveled for far too long.

We as a species are once again at the crossroads, whereby we will collectively choose whether we travel the path of self-destruction or the path of enlightenment. It is my hope that by sharing the lessons and experiences I have acquired in this life will help individuals as well as mankind itself, finally cross the goal line into the next level of spiritual consciousness.

CHAPTER ONE

As with all stories, I will start from the beginning. I was born on August 27, 1962 in the city of Mansfield, Ohio. Like so many children, I was born to a teenage mother. Her fraternal grandmother reared her, having lost her own mother due to a serious illness. She grew up in Cleveland during the 50's and early 60's.

My biological father from all accounts was what we term today as a "player". His grandparents, who were quite elderly at the time, raised him. He was able to smooth talk his way and manipulated his grandparents into doing his bidding. He received the best of clothes, putting forth little effort on his own to attain material items. Because of his rearing, he grew up becoming a spoiled, self indulgent, manipulative, and irresponsible boy. Being given all that his heart desired by his grandparents, he could attract the attention of teenage girls.

My mother said he fancied himself as the high school Casanova, and at first was not interested in him. He had a reputation of being "nickel-slick", but I suppose, as with so many teenage girls, the attraction to the "bad boy" is a hard one to resist. My great grandmother spotted trouble with him right out of the gate, and disliked the fact that my mother was seeing him.

Like so many tens of millions, my birth came as the result of two teenagers involved in having unprotected sex. I am sure neither of them gave any consideration as to how their behavior may affect their present and future lives. My great grandmother and great aunts were very angry towards my mother, whom that had hopes she would enter nursing school. After receiving pressure to abort the pregnancy, my mother decided to move to Mansfield to give birth to me.

Her maternal grandmother Suzie had taken her in. During the summers of her youth, my mother would spend her break from school there. She had come to know and date a local boy there. Upon her arrival, she reunited with him and rekindled their relationship. He chose to ask for her hand in marriage, in part to give me his last name and to avoid the stigma placed on babies born out of wedlock. Until I reached the age of ten, I thought of this man as my biological father.

He was a truck driver, and was a member of the army reserve. Therefore, for the next year or so, we moved around and finally settled in a rental property. My mother worked as a housekeeper, whereby her maternal grandmother would care for me during the day. Times were difficult, but the two of them managed to get by.

A few years later, my middle sister Monya was born. My recollections of life during the early years are amazingly vivid. I can remember one instance where my mother left me alone to go next door to the neighborhood store. In my mind's eye, she was gone too long, so I decided to walk out of the front door and go to my granny's house.

I could not have been much more than four years of age at the time, and in order to get to my great grandmother's house I had to cross a major thoroughfare. I remembered walking through the back door of my granny's house. She was a small woman, with snow-white hair. The house always smelled so good, from the variety of foods she prepared. The house was a duplex, in which several of her children resided in the home in addition to herself.

I supposed that sometime afterwards, my mother discovered I was not there. In a panic, she looked all over the apartment and up and down the street for me. She stated that she gathered up my sister, and proceeded to granny's house crying. When she arrived, I was laying across granny's lap eating a cookie. I do remember the look my mother gave me, a combination of relief and downright anger.

Nevertheless, granny saved me from an ass whipping and calmed my mother down. My great grandmother was the matriarch of the family. Granny held every major holiday function at her home, and no one got out of pocket with her around. I do remember feeling so much love around during that time. Her family was very important to her and she gave us all the love she had to give.

Things were becoming difficult for my mother and stepfather. At the time, truck drivers did not make much money so things were always tight. We ate most of our meals at my granny's house, and groceries were seldom in our own apartment. Many young married couples lack sufficient income during the early stages of the relationship and my family was no different. The lack of money and the financial strains it brings began to take a toll upon my mother. As I would come to find out later in my life, a secret hidden from me at the time contributed to the disintegration of their marriage.

My mother's fraternal grandmother decided to come to Mansfield for a visit. Almost two years had passed since my mother left Cleveland, and the ill will that my great grandma Annie displayed toward my mother diminished. She was never fond of my stepfather. God gave women a keen sense of instinct and I suppose as with most mothers, she had an intuitive vibe about him that was far from favorable. I noticed that he seemed to be more absent during her visit, but as a child, my sense of reason was rather limited.

During her stay, I remember my great grandmother taking my sister and me to Woolworth's, a now defunct department store. She bought us clothes and shoes that we needed. In the beginning, I remember being somewhat reluctant to get close to her. She was a very stern, no nonsense type of woman. She grew up in the south during the time of Jim Crow, and sad to say, I never asked her much about her life growing up during that era.

As the days worn on, I began to warm up to her. As was stated before, she raised my mother from a small child. She was a domestic housekeeper and nanny to a Jewish family who lived in suburban area of Cleveland. She was definitely no stranger to hard work or hard times. She was married at one time, and had two daughters and one son who was my mother's father. She divorced my great grandfather due to his infidelity, and ultimately taken on the responsibility, as do so many women of raising her children as a single parent.

Going through such a painful ordeal, tends to harden and jade most women's perspective about men. Moreover, I am sure that the hurt and pain she endured affected her outlook on my mother's relationship. Before her returning back home to Cleveland, I remember an argument she had with my stepfather. I cannot totally recall what caused the argument, but it must have related to his drinking and mistreatment of my mother. They were shouting at one another, and eventually he stomped out of the house in anger. This was a common occurrence in our house.

It was not until many years later that I discovered what the true source and cause for my stepfather and mothers divorce. We had taken my great grandmother to the bus station and said our tearful good bye's. I really became close to her over the years, and I am sure that she deep down really regretted the anguish she caused my mother during the time of her pregnancy. I do not believe she ever directly apologized to my mother for her actions, she attempted to redeem herself by doing all she could for my sister and I.

As time marched on, the relationship between my stepfather and mother worsened. He began to drink more heavily, and shirk his responsibilities to his family. There were many times I recall that the only thing in our refrigerator was beer, lunchmeat and bread. Our lives were certainly a reflection of the times. The 60's were one of the most turbulent times our nation and the world have experienced. The polarization of the races, religious conflicts, the Vietnam, and Cold wars were some of the most divisive issues confronting America. With that type of turmoil abound, it was no surprise that our life be any different.

During the year of 1968, this was a year of tragic proportions on many accounts. In addition to the deaths of Martin Luther King and Bobby Kennedy, our family experienced a great loss as well. Around the age of six, my granny had passed away. Her passing had a great impact on our extended family, which to this very day never truly recovered. Many came to rely upon my granny for her wisdom and support, which now was gone.

Power struggles began to ensue as to who would assume the leadership role she provided. Many of my relatives formed alliances against one another, which further fractionalized the family. I really loved Grandma Suzie, for other than my mother and Grandma Annie, theirs was the only love I truly knew.

This period in my life also marked the awareness of my own spirituality. Calvin's mother was a very religious woman. She was a follower of the fundamentalist apostolic faith, which practiced the tenants as espoused in the Old Testament. She was also a very mean spirited woman, and I truly hated going to her home. She had nine children, most that attained their degrees and were accomplished professionals. My stepfather for all intents and purposes was the black sheep of the family.

He was not a college graduate, and felt as though he was a failure because he did not live up to her expectations of him. I remember how he would attempt to garner favor from her, repairing and fixing things around her home, running errands, etc. However, no matter what he did, it was never good enough and his efforts to please her were to no avail.

She played favorites with her children, as well her grandchildren. Her children would compete amongst one another for her approval and affection. She had some measure of affection for my sister, but disliked me with a passion. I always wondered why, but as I became older, I came to understand.

My sister and I would periodically attend church with her, which to me was pure torture. I would sit in the pews, and pay close attention to the sermons given by the pastor. He seemed ancient, even back then as I recalled. When excited, he would tend to stutter a bit as he preached about God's unconditional love. In the next breath, he would then speak of an angry and vengeful God, who struck fear in the hearts of men. He would tell the congregation that we were all born into a life of sin, and needed to repent.

The pastor would begin to go into a tirade, hollering to the top of his lungs about how we were all doomed to hell if we did not follow the tenets as stated in the bible and accept Jesus Christ as our savior. Most of us have heard the story of Jesus, of His birth and His subsequent death for our sins. At an early age, I began to question the various opinions and statements forced upon me regarding God's word. I could remember feeling so uneasy and afraid, for it seemed to me that no matter what my good intentions; I was doomed to hell in either case.

I would looked around the congregation and see how the women of the church would nod their heads in affirmation with all that the preacher spoke. I would chuckle when some of the old women popped their grandchildren for whispering or playing while the pastor ranted and raved.

Women predominately attended the church, with very few men in attendance. Some of the outfits the women would wear would make me chuckle sometimes, especially the hats they would wear. Most wore some of the ugliest looking hats I ever saw. The church would smell of the combination of mothballs, Ben Gay, and cheap cologne worn by many of the elderly members of the congregation.

I would sometimes attend the children's bible study class, which consisted mainly on coloring or reciting the Ten Commandments. There were a few instances whereby I asked questions to the teacher. Questions such as "If Jesus loves me no matter what I do, why would

God send me to hell for doing something bad"? "If God created everything and all that He does is perfect, doesn't that mean that I am perfect too because He created me?" The typical answer was a simple "because the bible says so" or "shut up, and just believe what I am telling you".

After her statement, I felt like a fool in the eyes of my peers. From that point forward in my life, I became withdrawn and introverted. One of the most detrimental things that an adult can do to stifles a child's creativity or inquisitive nature is to berate or belittle them in a public setting. An individual should challenge any religious teaching touted as the gospel truth. For if a person lays claims to a belief and holds their beliefs to be true, then let the truth stand upon its on merit. If one's beliefs cannot bear the weight of scrutiny, then the so-called messenger should be challenged every step of the way.

In my opinion, children being relative newcomers to this realm of existence, come with an innate ability to discern and see truth with honesty as naked and pure as their own birth. The ability of children to see things as they are an essential ingredient to their spiritual growth and maturity. This is necessary because most parents and teachers fill their minds with misinformation, half-truths and false teachings passed down through generations. I was always a keen observer even in my youth. As I began to question the many things about religion and I slowly began to look for inconsistencies.

This encounter sprouted the seed of distrust and skepticism within me, especially as it related to my interpersonal relationships with people. This was the catalyst for one of my life's major themes; one that I am still coming to grips with today which is the ability to trust. As I looked around at the adults, starting with Calvin's mother, things just did not add up to me. She spent the bulk of her life and time in the church, but she was a very angry and bitter woman. I could not comprehend how someone, who spent so much time reading the bible and going to church, could be so mean and cold hearted. I knew deep down that she did not like me, and I do not believe she cared for my mother much either.

As time went by, I would beg my mother not to send me to church with her. My mother was aware of my step grandmother's dislike for her and after a while, I no longer had to spend my Sunday's in misery. My mother for all intents and purposes struggled alone in her attempts to take care of us. She had gotten a new job working on an assembly line at one of the local plants in town.

We had just moved to another house across town. Calvin continued to drink himself into oblivion. I later came to understand why. Although he did take it upon himself to marry my mother and give me his name, he truly could not come to grips with the fact that she slept with someone else other than him. Every time he saw my face, I reminded him of that fact.

So one particular day, my mother told me that she had asked him for money to buy shoes for me. He cursed her and said he refused to give her a damn thing. The proverbial straw broke the camels back as she reached the point of no return as she became totally fed up with his lack of concern towards our financial plight. She worked overtime to save up some money, hired an attorney and filed for divorce.

I remember the day he was moving out of the house. How my sister and I cried and begged him not to leave us. For all of the countless arguments, I overheard for the many times I saw my mother crying, I did not want him to leave. As he was packing up his belongings, he was sobbing too and when he drove off, I stood in the middle of the road screaming for him to come back. If parents truly knew how great an impact divorce has on the psyche of a child, many would think twice about it. Because of their divorce, I began to withdraw into myself. I would not allow myself to feel that depth of pain again. I began to close my heart emotionally to loving anyone other than my mother and sister, for I trusted them.

The issue of trust will play a major role in the evolution of my life's experience. I understand how difficult it is for someone to be in an abusive, unloving relationship. When hope is lost, despair, and depression sets in. From his experience, Calvin never really knew unconditional love from his mother, for there were always conditions.

Therefore, he could not give the gift of unconditional love to my mother, for he did not have it within to give. Although it was a noble gesture on his part to marry a woman with child, the decision was not rooted in the cement of love.

CHAPTER TWO

It was the winter of 1969, and we were going to experience the first Christmas by ourselves. My mother worked a lot of overtime at the plant to provide a great Christmas holiday for us. Of course, my sister and I still believing in Santa Clause were both attempting to be on our best behavior. I pestered my mother for a Hot Wheels set, and had I known then what I know now, I never would have asked for it. Every African American male, who received a Hot Wheels set, came to believe that a massive conspiracy between Mattel and parents existed.

Receiving a whipping with a willow tree branch was bad enough. Disguised as a toy for boys, the plastic tracks and curves became lethal weapons in the hands of a parent. A spanking with hot wheel tracks was a very painful experience and if a kid chose to break and run, the banked curves provided for an effective boomerang.

Almost a year had passed since the divorce, and my mother started to date a man who had two kids from a previous marriage. He was a firefighter, and co-owned a lounge. When they became serious, my mother quit her job at the assembly plant and began to manage the lounge. We later moved into a duplex house with him and his children.

My sister and I did not initially warm up to the new living arrangement, but we came to adjust to it relatively quick. Since the both of them worked a lot outside the home, we had to fend for ourselves. His daughter was a year older than I was, attempted to boss us around. Skirmishes and arguments were the order of the day, and the house reflected it. As children, the house stayed a wreck until the weekend. My mom's boyfriend would act as a field general barking orders to us to clean up the mess we made.

We really did not engage in family oriented activities, but being kids, we made our own fun. During this time, I taught myself how to cook. Those early attempts at preparing meals were bad. I had a captive audience with my sister and newly found stepbrother and sister for test subjects. I would not eat the food I prepared unless they tried it first.

If no one gagged or pushed the plate away, it was safe enough for me to eat. The relationship between my mom and her boyfriend did not last too long. I remember one Saturday that he just packed up his children and their belongings and just left. I never knew why until I became older. Their relationship ended when he cheated with one of my mother's best friends.

So once again, my sister and I were on our own. To be honest, it felt great to have the freedom to do as we so chose. My mother started working at a hole in the wall bar located a few blocks down the street. She had hired a teenager who lived a few houses down from where we were living to baby sit. The teenage girl lived with her grandmother, who was a member of the Nation of Islam.

I recall the discussions as she spoke of Allah being the one true God. The members of the nation of Islam believe that Elijah Muhammad was the last prophet, the pure embodiment of God Himself. She had pictures of him all over her home, and the house always smelled of incense.

 I would watch, as she would kneel to recite the prayers. She had a Koran, which she kept under a covered glass bowl. Before the Koran was read, one must first wash their hands and could not touch it without first receiving her approval to do so. She said that only a person of clean mind and spirit could lay hands upon it.

She told me that white people were bad, that they were the devil's disciples and were not to be trusted. I asked her why, and she gave examples of how they enslaved, beat and hung people of African decent from trees. She also stated that is was a white man, which killed Martin Luther King.

When she made that statement, I recalled how my family reacted when the news told of his death year's prior. Everyone was crying, upset, and very angry. Therefore, as listened to her comments, they made perfect sense to me. This encounter was the first time I became aware of the issue of race. Until then, I never really paid much attention to the color of a person's skin. From that moment forward, what I saw first of a person was the color of their skin. I suppose that this incident was the beginning of the stereotyping process whereby I began to judge people according to their race entered into my experience.

During my entire childhood growing up, education was always a painful experience for me. The hairs on the back of my neck still rise up to this very day whenever I pass by a school. I realize that hate is a mighty strong and powerful word, but as a kid, I truly hated going to school. As far as I could remember, I was always a fat pudgy kid and I became the subject of ridicule by some of the other children.

From kindergarten to about the beginning of the second grade, I used to loathe going to school because I knew as soon as I walked in the door; the smart alecks would chime in on me. As time past by, I began to snap back at the those who were cracking on me by talking about their mothers or selecting other hot buttons I knew would inflict pain or emotional response.

At this age, I was also a chronic bed-wetter. I internalized my emotions; therefore, I suppose they had to manifest themselves in some fashion. I would awaken soaking wet, and because we did not have a washer and dryer at the time, there was no hiding the fact from my mom. She used to get so upset with me, and the more upset she became, the more I seem to wet the bed. It was a very embarrassing time for me. Sometimes I really had to fight back the tears when I became frustrated and angry. I never allowed anyone to see me cry no matter what the circumstance.

I became quite masterful at the art of verbal jousting, with the ability to inflict great pain with the mere utterance of a word. I began to develop quite a temper too, not to the point where I engaged in physical fights, but my tongue could be as deadly as snake venom when I became angry.

My favorite subjects were history and anything related to science. As a child, I watched a considerable amount of television especially science fiction shows. I loved shows such as "Lost in Space", "Voyage to the Bottom of the Sea" and of course "Star Trek". I think that the love of science fiction fostered my desire to do well on subjects related to science.

History was another fascination of mine growing up as a kid. I had a rather active imagination, so the stories of how the Roman Empire conquered most of the known world or how the Egyptians built the pyramids sparked an interest within me.

I performed well with these subjects, but I always struggled with English and math. I perceived English as being boring and unimaginative, while I just could not grasp the concepts of mathematics. While in the second grade, our class was part of an accelerated learning program. Using a third grade level curriculum at the end of the year, all but three children received promotion from the second grade to the fourth.

I really was proud of myself and thought I was oh so smart. I did not master the math portion too well, and began to struggle with the subject throughout my entire scholastic experience. I received average grades for the most part, getting A's, and B's in science, history, C's, and D's in English and math.

Sometime during the spring of 1971, someone would enter my life that made a most profound impact upon me. My mother worked at a hole in the wall bar not far away from home. My sister and I would sometimes walk down to the bar after school, to check in with her before going home. She later began to date a man who later became my stepfather and the father of my youngest sister. He was an older man, about twelve years older than my mother. He was very large in stature, 6'4" tall weighing in excess of 360 pounds.

He wore his hair conked (processed) back, and most times wore large hats or brims in the vernacular of the day. I remember the first time I saw him and just looked in awe at how large he was. Everyone knew him as Big Frank around town. For a large man, he always dressed impeccably and he drove a Cadillac, which was his trademark.

He had he fathered several sons around town through previous relationships he had before dating my mother. Big Frank had a reputation even then which almost made him a living legend. He grew up in the South during the Great Depression, and was one of nine children.

I remember his telling us stories of his childhood growing up as sharecroppers on a small farm in Missouri. Of having, to walk five miles to school with shoes that were handed down from one of his brothers that were either too large or too small for his feet. Big Frank received little in the way of formal education; I believe he did not go beyond the sixth grade.

His stepfather had little value for education, and being of the opinion that their time spent working the farm was more important. I believe he embellished some of the stories. Most of us recall having heard how our grandparents or parents had to walk a hundred miles up hill in a blinding snowstorm on their way to school, or have nothing but a bucket of grits to eat. After a while, the relationship between my mother and Big Frank began to blossom, once again we moved out of the house we were living in to the one he shared with an older man. He did not hold a job, in the conventional sense of the word. In his earlier years when he moved to Mansfield from the South, he had taken a job at the local steel mill.

The steel mill was one of only a few places in town a black man could get a job during that time. Most of the black men were given jobs that were either quite dangerous or the most strenuous, for little pay. After a few years of working at the mill, I guess that he grew weary of the long hard hours for little pay. He left the mill in the early 60's, and embarked on his new occupation. He started in the game in the street known as hustling.

He would do most anything to make a dollar, which ranged from gambling to selling clothes and knock off jewelry. Most hustlers in the game are very charismatic individuals with magnetic personalities, and Big Frank was no exception. With his stature, he would definitely stand out in a crowd, and could sell snow shovels to an Eskimo, or sand to a Saudi.

His friends and associates was quite a color bunch of men. They ranged from gamblers, pimps, drug dealers and other hustlers like him. They had such names as L.A, Ricky Dog, Big Hank, Detroit, Three-Finger Freddie and the like.

Before the release of one of the most famous blaxplotation films ever made "Super Fly", he and his associates epitomized the life style depicted in the film. However, this was no movie but our life in the real sense of the word and world. I would look in astonishment at some of the outfits these people wore which bordered on the ridiculous.

There would be a running competition as to who would put on the most outlandish and colorful street uniform. The hairstyles consisted of either large Afro's or "blow outs" in the vernacular of the era, or some still wore their hair conked back. Some of the hats were so big; they could black out the sun and the colors they wore so bright, would blind Ray Charles more so than he already was. Long crushed velvet coats with three-piece suits to match, wide elephant sized lapels. In addition, no outfit was complete with out the high platform shoes and walking canes.

The cars they drove were an extension of their flamboyant persona's and status. I remember a song by William DeVaughn that contained a hook "Diamond in the back, Sunroof top…

digging in the scene with the gangster lean". The song depicted the lifestyle they were living at the time.

Many of the vehicles were customized with wheel kits on the trunk, or some other outlandish accessories. Gangster white walls that were 4-6"inches in width, customized vinyl tops, and the whole nine. Although the vehicle of choice was Cadillac's, a few rolled in Lincoln Continental and Mercedes Benzes.

Less than a year had passed by before my mother became pregnant with my youngest sister. A few months after her birth, he and my mother went on a trip to California. A hustler's life is a nomadic one, and where they perceive milk, honey and money to flow, like a flock of birds, will migrate towards in a New York minute. My sister and I stayed with one of my mother's co-workers from the bar for a few weeks.

She had six children of her own a continual madhouse between the kids arguing amongst themselves, or their mother arguing with their father. Their father, Floyd was a substance abuser of both alcohol and cocaine. I do not believe he was in a lucid state of mind the entire two weeks we stayed in their house. My sister and I would avoid being there as much as possible, either visiting with other kids in the neighborhood or walking a few blocks up the street from our old apartment to see old friends.

I was so happy when Big Frank and my mother came back from their trip to California. I think they were home all of two weeks before they headed off to another cross-country trip. This time, they had taken my middle sister and me to our great grandmother's house in Cleveland. I really enjoyed spending my summers there as a kid. My great grandma Annie and great aunt Ruthie lived in the same house located in Shaker Heights, a suburb of Cleveland.

My great grandma Annie had a dog-named Peppy, a rather large German shepherd. When I was younger, I remember receiving a bite on the earlobe by that dog after yanking its tail. After that ordeal, I had a measure of fear about making any visit to her home. It had taken me quite some time to get over that incident. However, in time my fear dissipated by the love I received from my great grandma Annie.

I was about to turn ten that summer, and that was on of the most enjoyable times I recall as a kid. After she would get home from work on Fridays, my great aunt Ruthie would drive my sister and me over to our Grandfather Will's house to spend the weekend. He and my grandma Liz, who was my mother's stepmother, lived in a rough section of East Cleveland.

They had four children of their own, three of which were in their late teens. My grandfather was an alcoholic, and drank a steady diet of cheap wine and malt liquor. My mother was somewhat estranged from her father, who was far from the ideal role model parent. He was very belligerent when he drank too much, and kept up much chaos and commotion in the house. He had two close friends who lived a few houses down named Willie and Bubba, who together on occasion would work painting houses.

I wanted to make some money and my grandfather brought me along to paint a two story triplex house. The day before, we went to the hardware store and purchased painting supplies. We got up at 5:00am the following morning loaded up Willies pickup truck and off we went to work. Being young and my first time painting, my grandfather and his friends took full advantage of my ignorance.

I was tasked with handling everything above the first floor, which meant I had to scrape off the old paint, mask the windows and paint the house and the trim. I guess that since I weighed less than they weigh and was so eager to help, they saw it has an opportunity to drink and socialize.

The first two days we scraped paint, and the summer sun cooked my skin to a golden brown complexion. We worked from sun up to sun down. Besides taking a periodic time out to get something to drink, I was up on that ladder the entire time. I would look down at them and at any given point in time; two of the three would be smoking and drinking.

While taking their break, the other painted slower than molasses appearing to move in slow motion. On the third day, it was time to start painting, and I thought oh how fun it would be. I painted two entire sides of the house, while the three of them painted the front and back porch area.

In the evenings, we would come back to my grandfather's house covered from head to toe in white paint. I was so tired; I would fall asleep in the bathtub as the water turned cold. At the end of the week, we had completed painting the entire house and it was time to be paid. Oh, I just knew I had a serious cut coming since I painted over half the house by myself. In my mind's eye, if I did half the work I should get half the pay. My grandfather was paid $300 for that job and he split the money with his friends three ways. As he turned to me, he reached out his hand and gave me five dollars.

My sister had just come outside, whereby she gave him a hug and he gave her a five-dollar bill. I went ballistic, mind you though I was not quite ten years old, but I was livid! I asked him in an angry voice how my sister could receive the same amount as I for doing nothing, and how could he give his buddies a third of the take for doing next to nothing.

As I stated earlier, math was one of my poorest subjects in school. However, when it came to counting money, my skills were quite good. He essentially said because they were adults and being his friends, entitled them to the share they received. I went into the house foaming like a rabid dog crying and hollering to the top of my lungs for my grandma Liz. I told her what he had done, and that I wanted to go back to my great Grandmother Annie's house. She went outside, and proceeded to chew him out in front of everyone in sight for taking advantage of me in such a manner.

He was already high from drinking all day but even in his state of drunkenness, he knew he had committed an injustice. He reached in his pocket and pulled out a twenty-dollar bill, and his two friends each gave me ten. I knew I still received the short end of the stick, but I also knew that the offer was not going to get any better. After that incident, I lost what measure of respect I had for him.

Once again, the issue of trust arose to the forefront of my experience. I stared at the forty dollars I had in my hand and the longer I stared at it; the more I became angry. Whenever I felt slighted for as long as I can remember, I was quick to temper. As a child, it did not pay great dividends to display my temper but I would just seethe at anyone who I deemed caused me harm. I started on the road of becoming more and more introverted, covering up my emotions from public view. On the exterior, all would appear well to those who looked upon me. However, buried deep within me, I harbored anger and resentment.

In becoming more introverted, I began to observe and pay keen attention to people and their behavior. I began to notice very subtle nuances in speech, the way a person would use their hands, tilt their head a certain way. When I think back, I began at an early age to size an individual up, as a means of emotional self-defense. I always had a suspicious nature, being quite leery of the motivation of others. This suspicious nature began with my own family.

Summer was almost over and my mother and stepfather had returned to Cleveland to take us back home. I had mixed emotions anytime I would have to go back to Mansfield after any extended stay elsewhere. In all honesty, I never felt as though Mansfield was my home. I always felt like a stranger or a visitor growing up there. Going back meant returning to a house I did not like, going back to chores, and returning to a life that I gained little joy in living.

School was going to start in a few weeks, and the annual ritual of clothes shopping would begin. Several reoccurring factors I would encounter every school year revolved around equity and fairness in the treatment I received from both of my younger sister's fathers. Up until recent, I was under the impression that my middle sister's father was my biological father.

I was a fat kid, which made my clothes more expensive and more difficult to find. I noticed that as the new school year would approach, my sister and I would always have to track her father down. He worked as a truck driver for one of the local dairy distributors in town. There was a bar next door to the plant, and my sister and I would walk across town in an attempt to get some money to buy clothes.

Being he was an alcoholic, more oft than not, a bar or lounge is where we would find him. He frequented three bars. My sister and I became as well known as he. The one thing I must admit is that although he drank, he never missed a day of work. He would go to work hung over looking like death warmed over but he still managed to get through the day.

When we did catch up to him, he would make up excuses as to why he could not give us money. On those occasions when he did, he gave my sister more than I did. Same thing would occur when it came to birthdays and Christmas too. At the time, I did not question why but I did notice it. The same thing would occur with my youngest sister's father, Big Frank. He saw to it that both of my sisters had a fair amount of clothes for school, but when it became time for me, I had to settle for less.

I knew money was tight, for the lack of money was always an issue in our house. I also knew how cruel kids could be when you do not have the money to buy the latest "gear". I became accustomed to the ridicule not desiring either of my sisters to go through the experience.

I understood the difficulties my mom and Big Frank had in making ends meet. Therefore, in lieu of complaining about only having three pair of pants and five shirts, I kept my mouth shut. Back then, I was not big into making a fashion statement anyway. It was more the point of not wanting to deal with the taunting and teasing from the other kids. I do remember that both of my stepfathers came through for me on both my birthday and on a few Christmas holidays. I had gotten a new bike for my birthday from Big Frank, a purple Schwinn three-speed with the banana seat. I had been riding my sister's bike, which she received for her birthday.

Now she and I would hop on our bikes and we would ride all over town. That Christmas, I had received a chemistry set that I wanted. I fancied myself as a great scientist, and I would mix a few of the chemicals in the kit to make stink bombs, or add baking soda to create a foaming test tube.

It took very little effort to put a smile on my face, and when either of my stepfathers showed any measure of attention towards me, I just ate it up. As time progressed, I continued to become more reclusive and distance myself from my emotions. My ability to mask the inner turmoil I was experiencing manifested itself outwardly. Unbeknown to my family until now, that I engaged in shoplifting.

There was an A&P grocery store a few blocks away from the house. When I felt angry or frustrated, I would walk to the store and steal small items such as candy or snacks. I would get such a rush but shortly after, I felt such guilt. As time went on, I stole more frequent and the items became larger in value. At the same time, the amount of guilt I was experiencing also became just as large. I knew it was wrong to steal and as I think back, there were times that I stole for no justifiable reason other than I could.

One day after school, I had stolen an entire Sarah Lee cheesecake from the store freezer. I went home, walked upstairs, and sat on the bed. I had plans of just wolfing the cheesecake down, but I could not take a bite. I do not know to this day, what came over me, but I had a vision of myself behind bars. I remember how I felt, walking with handcuffs being yelled at by several guards and feeling the anxiety of being trapped with no way of escape.

I never stole again after that experience, and until now, no one ever knew about it. I am sure that psychologists would say that my self-loathing and subsequent stealing was a cry out for attention. I beg to differ; for this was the first time, I applied the conscience thought process.

From a logical standpoint, there was nothing for me to gain by stealing and I consciously knew that. Through exposure to religion and the moral instruction received by my mother, I knew it was wrong to steal. It was not until I could actually project what I felt in the vision and took ownership of the emotions I experienced that I no longer desired to steal.

During the times that my mother, sister and I were, alone I had developed a very strong sense of independence. I had extreme difficulty in obeying anyone whom I did not personally like or respect. I never bought into the adage "respect your elders", as a child for I saw many adults who in my opinion were not worthy of respect.

Although they had been together for over a year, I still did not view Big Frank as someone I respected as a father figure. When it came to me, he was a strict disciplinarian. At an early age, I had already taught myself to cook, but he heaped many other chores upon my list. I had yard detail, had to sweep and mop the kitchen floors, wash dishes (my sister and I took turns), take out the garbage and in the winter, shovel the driveway and sidewalks.

The one thing I will say is that Big Frank would take the time to show me how he wanted things done first. Moreover, if I did not perform any of the tasks correctly, I received many whippings, which resulted in having to perform the chores over again. In my mind's eye, what I did was never good enough. He was never in the military, but he constantly stayed on my back for not putting forth the level of effort he perceived was lacking on my part.

I recall one event that I had not mopped the kitchen floor to his satisfaction and he whipped me. The linoleum on the floor was very old and faded, and no amount of mopping would change the way it looked. I felt as though the whipping I received was unjust and unwarranted, and I would not take another one from him.

I went upstairs, and grabbed a very large green suitcase that belonged to my mother. I packed everything I valued in it, including some apples and other snacks. I climbed up on the roof, tied two of my sisters jumping ropes together and lowered the suitcase to the backyard. I then came downstairs, pretending to take out the garbage. I never volunteered to take out the garbage.

My mother was not home at the time, so I told my sister goodbye and I took the garbage and proceeded out the backdoor. Apparently, my sister began to cry because she knew I was running away. The suitcase was heavier than I was, but I proceeded to drag it down an alleyway at the back of the house. Big Frank peered out the back door in search of me. He then proceeded out the front door as he marched down the street to cut me off before I could reach the intersection.

I dropped the suitcase and started to run from him, but he hollered ordering me to come back. I was afraid that he would hit me again and made him promise he would not. That is one thing I remembered about him, that his word was his bond. He picked up the suitcase and we proceeded home. I walked upstairs to my bedroom and as soon as my mother returned, he told her what happened.

She was so upset with me that she could not speak to me at that moment. Later on that week, as a means of appeasing him, she applied a minor punishment for my attempted getaway. I believe he actually laughed at my attempt to run away, but would never let me know about it. We were always at polar opposites of the spectrum; very rarely did we see eye to eye on many matters. This incident marked the turning point where I emotionally shut down.

Big Frank had one hell of a temper too, and he often displayed his anger. There was one instance where he and several of his associates were up late playing cards. One of his old running friends, Ragsdale had come to town and stayed at our house. During the course of the game, he was hiding cards to win the hands. One of the cards slipped out of his sleeve, and when Big Frank noticed it, he went berserk. There were five men including him, and it had taken them all plus my mother to pull him off this man.

Even in the hustle game, there are rules of the street one being you do not run game on one of your own especially when the person is your host. The fact that he ate food from our table drank liquor and slept in our home made the situation worse. He immediately packed up his belongings and left, and we never saw the man again in life. After bearing witnesses to that, I had more of a respect of what he could do to me in a physical sense, but I still did not respect him as a father figure.

 The distorted point of view I held regarding my definition of respect began from an early age. The entire persona and lifestyle associated with hustling requires the ability to deceive and to con (Vince) people in order to get something you desire from them. Respect is based upon the level of "game" one has, the amount of street credibility or toughness one is perceived to have, and the amount of accumulated material wealth a person flaunts. This was the perspective of respect I had come to believe in, until I reached young adulthood.

As in all "games", a point in time comes along where the game ends, and those participating in the game eventually become "played out". This is one of the lessons of life few can avoid and none are exempt from experiencing. My stepfather and his associates would later come to discover this fact as most often do…come to find out the lesson the hard way.

CHAPTER THREE

My mother and Big Frank decided to go into business, buying a small restaurant on Main Street. On the weekends, the traffic along the strip was heavy with partygoers and being adjacent to several bars, the location was perfect. During this time, my mother and Big Frank grew weary of living in the home we shared with the owner.

Old man McCoy worked at the steel mill in town that at the time was one of the largest employers. He was trifling in every sense of the word; he did not bath often and always left a trail of mess behind him. I guess they grew tired of it, so shortly after opening the restaurant they decided to move out. We moved to a predominately white, middle class neighborhood on the south side of town.

Our family was one of only two black families within a two-mile radius. We were very excited about the move, it was a small two-bedroom home and I slept in what was the laundry room, which led to the rear of the house. The backyard of the house was adjacent to the local cemetery. At first, living close to the cemetery did not sit very well with me. The cemetery would later become a place that I would go to relax my mind and meditate. The cemetery assisted in helping me to deal with an issue we all must face…death.

The restaurant was doing quite well, and my mother and Big Frank were gone quite a bit. My sister Monya and I would watch our youngest sister, Shay who was just a year old at the time. There were many kids in the neighborhood to play with, but there was something else in the neighborhood we had to contend with as well. Being predominately a white working middle class area, there were not many occasions for whites to interact with blacks outside their work environments. Therefore, living amongst them, we had to occasionally deal with their ignorance and prejudices.

I recall one of the first encounters we had shortly after we moved there. My sister Monya was playing tetherball with one of the girls who lived in the house behind ours. Some time after, one of the boys in the neighborhood wanted to participate in the game. He became angry, called my sister a black nigger, and attempted to hit her.

She jumped over the fence that separated the yard and came into the house crying. I proceeded to run out of the backdoor to chase him down, but he had already jetted home. The boy's family was what is termed today as "trailer park trash". His parents came from some small country town in Kentucky. His mother and father had a reputation around the neighborhood for their heavy drinking and engaging in periodic domestic disputes.

For the first few months or so, fighting these kids became a regular occurrence. One particular incident changed how the kids in the neighborhood treated my sister and me. I was playing basketball in the alleyway with one of the Bishop boys, who were part of a large family that lived on a street behind our home.

The same boy who picked on my sister happened to come by and began to call me nigger. I caught him this time, and proceeded to pound on him. I was larger than he was and I suppose the size differential was enough that one of the Bishop boys wanted to take up sides on his behalf.

So now, I am fighting two boys and I was getting the better of them both. The Bishop boy had a teenager brother, who was sixteen years old at the time. As one of the boys ran inside to get him, I took off and ran home. As I ran, I darted and made a sharp cut to the right. At that very moment, a large pointed piece of wood went flying by me that hit square along the edge of the garage. I was so mad and angry I began to cry I went in the house to get a butcher knife.

My uncle Skip was visiting at the time from Detroit stopped me as I started to run back outside. He had taken the knife from me, but I shook loose from him to go back to the fight. I grabbed a broken table that was laying in the neighbor's yard and ran in their direction. About six or seven boys were sitting at a picnic table in their driveway and when they saw me coming, they scattered like roaches.

After that incident, I had gotten the reputation as being the crazy fat black kid, which gave my sister and me a measure of credibility and respect. Things were going well for us at the time of our lives. Money was coming in from the restaurant, and it was almost time for the school year to commence. Later the same summer, tragedy had fallen upon our family.

My grandfather Will had passed away from a stroke resulting from the many years of alcohol abuse and smoking. We headed to Cleveland for the funeral, which was the first of a series of deaths that would later befall our family. I was not aware of it at the time, the relationship between my grandfather and my mother was estranged. I noticed that she did not appear to be upset at the news of his passing.

As I sat in the car, I thought and wondered about what death would be like. The kids in the neighborhood including myself would play hide and go seek in the cemetery at night. We would sometimes crawl through a hole under one of the fences, which led into the graveyard. Sometimes during the day, I would get up very early crawl under the hole and walk around looking at the headstones and mausoleums. It was very peaceful and serene to me. As most people would fear being in a cemetery, I found it a place I could come to escape from whatever was troubling me.

As we got closer to Cleveland, the mood in the car became more quiet and somber. Big Frank was a fan of the blues, and he would pop in an eight-track tape. B.B. King and Bobby Blues Bland were his favorite artists, and to this day, I can hardly stand to listen to either. Although he had several tapes, he would play the same ones repeatedly. I believe the songs "The Thrill is Gone" and "Born under a Bad Sign" were the two songs that stood out most in my mind. We finally made it to my great Grandma Annie's house to unload, and then traveled across town to my grandfather's place. When we arrived she welcomed us at the door and gave us all such a hug.

I could tell that she had been crying all day. Liz was always a sweet kindhearted woman who caught so many bad breaks in life. My grandfather fussed and fought with her so, and her children gave her so much grief. In spite of all of the hardships she experienced, she somehow managed to keep a smile on her face and love in her heart. She was one of the very few women in my life whom I held the utmost of respect. So many women who I have met in my life that came from privileged backgrounds. Few women, who were educated with careers and homes filled all of the modern conveniences, could not hold a candle to her.

Liz had next to nothing her entire life, but the love she had for her family. They would sometimes steal from her, curse her, strike out at her and not once do I recall her complain about her life. The strength of her will and character was unequaled. The house quickly filled with visitors, who were gathering to attend the wake that evening. My grandfather's two drinking partners Bubba and Willie were sitting on the couch. They both looked so sad, and I could tell Bubba had been crying earlier. They called me over, gave me a five dollar bill to run to the corner store for them to buy a pint of wine to take with them to the funeral home.

As soon as I returned, it was time to load up the vehicles and head out. When we arrived, I got out of the car and felt somewhat uneasy. As I entered the parlor, I saw his casket towards the front and proceeded to walk to it. Once there, I stood and gazed at him lying there motionless. To me, he looked as though he was sleeping with an ever so slight smile on his face. To be honest, I did not feel much of anything. The moment grandma Liz and her children came to view his body; they just broke down crying. Their tears started a wave of emotions that seem to travel across the entire place. Everywhere I turned, people were sobbing.

I took a seat and just looked around, but I could not cry. I felt bad for those who were crying, but to me my grandfather looked happy. I sat back thinking about the serenity of the cemetery back home. How peaceful and quiet it was there. I knew he was going to be buried at a cemetery so in my mind, my grandfather was going to a peaceful place.

The following day of the actual funeral service was even more dramatic. After the preacher said his words, the ushers came to close the casket lid to prepare for the trip to the cemetery. My aunt Ruthie walked up to the casket just before the lid closed and began to wail and gasp. That set off another chain reaction of tears and sobbing among the attendees.

Almost everyone was crying even Big Frank, and that was something rare for him to do. It was raining very hard that morning, as the cool rain felt great on my face. I felt somewhat bad that I did not cry, so I imagined that the clouds shed the tears that my eyes could not. We headed back to the house afterwards, with a long caravan of vehicles as far as my eyes could see. Once we arrived and went inside, I had never seen so much food. Food dishes were everywhere and a steady stream of people coming through the door with more food. The atmosphere was jovial and upbeat, as I overheard many speaking of some good times that they shared with my grandfather.

Grandma Liz was in the kitchen fixing plates and stayed constantly on the move the entire time. As the last of the visitors left, she sat down at the dining room table and just stared out into space. I think that was the first moment it actually hit her that my grandfather was gone. There would be no more staggering through the front door cussing and fussing, no more preparing his meals.

For all of the heartache and stress he brought to her life, I saw in her eyes how much she loved him. I sat on that couch at that point, and that is when the tears began to fall down my face. No one saw my tears, as I cried feeling so sad for her. There was a song by Smokey Robinson "Tear's of a Clown"; whereby he sung how he shed the tears of a clown when there is no one around.

The image of a clown always smiling to the crowd, but yet when sad would hide away his tears. I was always conscience about letting anyone see me cry and to this very day, very few have. In my mind, I associated crying in public as being weak, or allowing someone the satisfaction of getting under my skin. I did not differentiate the circumstances, whether it is hiding the hurt and pain of the ridicule received by kids, or grieving the loss of a family member.

During that summer, my mother and Big Frank decided to throw a house party, and what an affair it was. It was more of a pimp, players, and hustler's convention. They invited friends and associates from around the country, and it was a sight to see. The fact we were living in a predominately-white middle class neighborhood, I could only imagine what was going through their minds.

I was in the backyard getting the grills together for the barbecue. My mother and I were up the night before seasoning and marinating the meat for the picnic. Pork spareribs and chicken is always a mainstay at any black family barbecue, but Big Frank decided to add a new entrée…a live goat.

One of his friends bought a baby goat over the day before, and tied him up in the backyard. The goat was an attraction to the kids in the neighborhood, who thought at first it was a new pet. I felt bad for the little goat, and I honestly believe it knew its fate. It cried and bleated the whole afternoon and most of the night. Big Frank had gotten up early that Saturday morning to slaughter the goat. One of his running buddies, Big Thurman came over to lend a hand. Very rarely would you see one without the other, and I thought of them as the hustler's version of Batman and Robin.

Thurman was a close friend of my stepfather, but I always sensed a measure of jealousy from him. He admired Big Frank and his level of game, and even adopted the nickname of "Big" into his street name for added credibility. While he may have admired him, he also was envious of Big Frank. As they prepared to kill the goat, I got a nervous pitch in my stomach. As Thurman held the body of the goat, Big Frank got a butcher knife and slit the goat's throat.

Blood was flowing everywhere; they tied the hind legs up and hung the goat from the branch of the tree located in the backyard. They later skinned the goat and began to cut it up into pieces. I remember how the muscles were still twitching as they brought the goat into the kitchen. I cooked all of the meat that day, but after witnessing the slaughter of the goat, I had no appetite at all.

The party started on a Saturday and did not end until Sunday. As the partygoers began to arrive, they came in a collection of cars and outfits right out of any of the current blaxplotation movies of the time. The partygoers parked their cars lined up on both sides of the street with customized Rolls Royce, Cadillac's, Lincoln's, Mercedes Benz, Jaguars and even a stretch limousine.

The men were dressed in silk and crush velvet suits big brims and platform shoes and socks to match. The women, and there were some gorgeous women, dressed in tight fitting pants or skirts. The women masked up their faces adorned with thick eyelashes, multicolored rouge and lipstick to match whatever the outfit they were wearing. The hairdos were either Afro's gleaming with oil sheen and glitter, or long curly hairs (which more than likely were wigs. Being a young boy reaching puberty, it hardly mattered to me. Later that evening, the party was in full swing.

Every square inch of space inside and outside the house was full of people eating, drinking and smoking weed. I went from being the grill master to the DJ, playing collection of eight-track tapes and 45s on a stereophonic system we had. The men were playing cards and rolling dice for big money, and the women huddled off in various corners talking amongst themselves. My sister Monya and I made out like bandits that night, receiving money for bringing food or drink to those who requested it. When I think back to that time, it was amazing that with all of the people we had at our home, not one time did any of the neighbors complain or the cops rolled by. The local police department knew Big Frank; he even sold suits to a few of the beat cops and detectives.

I would assume that he received a special green light pass that night by the police department not to disrupt his party. He was the man that night, and I remember how great a time everyone seemed to have. Times were soon to change for the worse for our family, and this event would be the highlight of what measure of the good life we would come to experience as a family.

CHAPTER FOUR

A new school year was coming up and I was entering junior high school. Because we moved, all the kids I went to elementary school with attended a different junior high across town. However, being I spent the summer in the neighborhood, I was not a total stranger when I enrolled there. Johnny Apple seed was the name of the school with an enrollment of a little over 800 students.

I had fond memories during the three years in which I attended that school. Four teachers were my favorites, each of which contributed to forming the way I came to look upon the world around me. The first was Mr. Yurista, who was the seventh grade civics teacher at the time.

He was a white man in his late twenties, tall slender person. All of the students considered him one of the coolest in school. He did not treat us like a bunch of dumb youngsters; he truly cared about our opinions and us. The approach he used to instruct us was far from the norm for the time. Although he taught from the textbook, he also brought different perspectives for us to ponder.

School age children are taught the history of the world as seen through the eyes of western Europeans. Typically, history is written from the perspective of the conqueror not the conquered. He played the devil's advocate, by asking our opinions about how we perceived a situation in history to have looked from the other side of the coin.

On Friday's as a group, we would have discussion on a main topic in the forum of a debate. He also would allow us to bring in 45s he would play on a record player in the back of the class. Even though I was a shy kid, I would enjoy engaging in the debate and I was damn good at it too. Another one of my favorite teacher's was Mr. John Cruise the shop teacher. He was a tall, lanky lumbering man with a "butch" styled haircut. He had a deep southern accent raised in the hills of Kentucky. When he spoke, he had somewhat of a lisp, and he would spray you with a shower of saliva if you got too close.

He and another teacher, Mr. Smith taught metal and woodworking in vocational education class. Mr. Cruise was the ruler of his domain in the shop room, which was in the far corner of the basement level of the school. He was a character, as close to a live animated cartoon as you could come. Before every class, he would lay down the law about no horseplay and so on and so forth. The one odd thing was this man was missing a piece of his forefinger and his pinky finger on his left hand. Every time he would go into his safety story, he would gesture with that hand and some of the boys in class would just start cracking up.

The best part of his class is that he would treat us to one of his stories about the many exploits that occurred in his life. At the time, he may have been at the most forty years of age. This man held every occupation known to man since the age of ten. I remember one occasion whereby he told one of his great stories. Mr. Cruise told a tale regarding how he and his brother received punishment for lying to his father for taking a jar of fruit preserves. Both of them had to shovel over five acres of cow and horse manure. Typically, these tall tales would come out as a means of letting us know how soft and easy we had it in contrast to the youth of his era.

He really was a kind man through the rough exterior, taking the time to help us with our projects. I learned at an early age that a life as a carpenter was not the career path meant for me. I remember we had a project that required of us to make a candleholder. We had to draw the pattern on a piece of lumber and use an upright band saw to shape it.

The upper end was supposed to be in the shape similar to the spade on a deck of cards. By the time I got through cutting, mine looked more like the shape of a tip of a penis. The boys in class just fell out laughing, and Mr. Cruise did all he could not to just fall out of his desk in laughter. Most students were smart enough not to upset or get on the wrong side of Mr. Cruise. He stood 6'-4" weighed every bit of 260 pounds. I remember a boy was running down the hallway and he told him to stop. The boy turned around and called him out of his name. He snatched that boy up with one arm and picked him up off the floor pinned against the wall.

Every kid in the hall froze in awe. He let the kid down the hallway by one arm and marched him to the principle office. After the word spread, the boys in shop class really came to attention when he spoke. He was a very fair man though, and although he grew up in rural Kentucky where bigotry and prejudice reigned supreme, he did not tolerate any of those behaviors in his class. He treated us all with kindness and respect.

Another favorite teacher of mine was Mrs. Crawford. She was the history teacher, a middle-aged woman with glasses. She was a very classy and kind woman who would come to school early in the morning and stay late after school to help students in need. She was all about business in the classroom too.

She would write the entire outline of the subject matter we were to study for the day, and we had to keep a notebook essentially containing the notes she outlined. She taught history from more of a global perspective. As part of our year-end assignment, we had to write a ten-page term paper. Mrs. Crawford walked us through every step of the process, from writing outline cards, how to approach the process of researching our source materials. This was in the eighth grade I remind you, and she taught from a world history book that the sophomores used from one of the high schools. She never spoke down to us, and she commanded the utmost of respect.

When there were differences of opinion, she facilitated the exchange of ideas and insisted that we performed additional research to back up our position. To this day, I appreciate the lesson she taught us to seek out the truth, to question everything and never accept anything blindly as fact.

My favorite junior high teacher of all was the physical education and health teacher, Coach Carroll. He was a heavyset man, balding in his mid forties. His voice was so very distinct, if you closed your eyes he sounded exactly like John Wayne. He was a married man, and sometimes his wife would bake brownies or cookies to pass out to us. I was in his second period class, and although he did not broadcast it, our class was his favorite.

We had a cast of characters in our bunch. Most of the black kids lived across town and some were the biggest cut ups I ever came across. We used to play the "dozens" snapping and cracking on each other's relatives with no mercy. Being I was a fat kid, I did not excel much in the way of sports outside of flag football. Most of the boys in class played on the school football team, and Coach Carroll would always try to convince me to come out for the squad.

He always made allowances for me in gym class, always encouraging me to do my best. When some of the boys would start up on me, he had them run extra laps or straighten up the equipment room. Most of the kids loved the man; he had such a kind demeanor about him.

I remember one day in health class when the issue of sex became a topic of discussion. At the time, sex was a subject very much taboo in a junior high setting. However, that did not stop Coach Carroll from giving us some very sound advice. He spoke of how a good friend of his he went to high school with had a child at the age of 16. He spoke of the struggles the young man and his girlfriend had, not being able to finish high school having to work menial jobs scrapping to get by. He told us eventually his friend went into the military, but his girlfriend ended up leaving him for another man.

Coach Carroll believed that a child should have a mother and a father to love and care for the child. Being a parent of teenage children of his own at the time, coach spoke of the difficulties he and his wife had in raising theirs. Since most of us were experiencing some measure of hard times in our own families, we could relate. Whenever you needed some advice or a sound opinion, you could always count on Coach to be there to listen.

There were a few times he came out of his own pocket and bought gym shoes or shorts, gave kids lunch money. He was a good man, and I can only imagine how many lives he touched in a positive way during his tenure as a teacher. One of the most memorable times is when Coach Carroll had taken us to on a field trip for a class picnic. We were freshmen heading to high school, and it was the last time we would be together.

Where you lived determined which of two high schools you could attend. Roughly, half the freshman class would attend Mansfield Senior High, the other Malabar. I remember just before the picnic began, Coach Carroll looked around and his eyes began to well up with tears. He told us he would miss us. Coach Carroll said that of all the classes he taught over the years, that we were his favorite.

One of the boys, Kevin was one of the class clowns. He was also one of the most popular boys in school. He could mimic Coach Carroll mannerism and voice. As part of the goodbye ceremony, he did his imitation of Coach. We laughed so hard, that many began to start laughing and crying simultaneously. Attending Johnny Appleseed was one of the great blessings that God has ever given to me.

The teachers that I had come to admire truly loved their profession. They also taught me to become an independent thinker, to look at situations in life from different angles and perspectives. Teachers such as Coach Carroll and Mr. Cruise showed me that kindness and compassion comes in many colors, not just in the shade of blackness.

Growing up in a neighborhood with white kids, and going to school with black kids presented some challenges at times for me. Although the experience gave me the ability to communicate with both groups, I also developed a measure of an identity crisis. For as long as I could remember, I always had difficulty dealing with individuals of my own race. Even to this day, most African Americans I encounter either love me or hate me, with not much variation in between.

The animosity I seemed to generate from other black males puzzled me greatly. I always had the ability to get along with about everyone, but I most always had problems dealing with the so-called cool crew. Coming up, I did not wear the latest gear nor hung with the so-called brothers who were "down" or hip. Not having the money to keep up with the latest fashion trends kept me on the outside of the clique.

I was far from being the most academically gifted, but I always had a great deal of common sense. It appeared to me that a vast majority of my peers had little interest in intellectual pursuits. Displaying one's intelligence was not considered cool or hip. The more ignorant, disrespectful and belligerent one became, the more popular and accepted one would become.

I was an outsider to the "in" crowd of black kids, but for the most part, the majority of the white kids accepted me. I made some great friends and acquaintances while attending Johnny Appleseed. Those friendships helped to shape my views on issues of race and interpersonal relationships throughout my life.

Being a fat kid growing up made my adolescent years quite hellish too. I would again turn to food as my security blanket whenever I felt sad or angry. To the outside world, I was just a quiet and reserved boy. However, I had a very low level of self-esteem. Since there was no one I felt comfortable enough or trusted enough to turn to, I suffered in silence.

When my mother and Big Frank ran the restaurant, I would take one or two extra dollars from their receipts to buy extra junk food at the school cafeteria or at the corner store on the way home from school. I felt so bad stealing from them, and felt even guiltier after I consumed what I bought with the stolen money.

The restaurant Big Frank and my mother were running was starting to falter. The bulk of the reason I believe was due to my stepfather's passion for gambling. He played the numbers, today's equivalent of the daily three-digit lottery. The winning numbers were drawn by a center spread combination of numbers from the previous day's stock market closing on the DOW Jones.

The payoff for hitting a number straight on a one-dollar bet was $600. Big Frank was a self-described numerologist; he would get up at three or 4:00am in the morning light up a cigarette and stare at the floor for at least one hour. I believe that was his way of meditating and reflecting.

 Big Frank had a collection of dream and numerology books that he used to figure out the numbers he would play for that day. He stored the losing bet slips in a shoebox located in bedroom closet. I could not even to this day, begin to guess how much money he lost by playing the numbers over the years. There were a few times he won money from playing the numbers. However, his losses far outnumbered his gains. The economy during mid seventies was beginning to slow down. Everyone was tightening their belts and holding on to their hard-earned cash.

As business at the restaurant began to slow down, Big Frank began to supplement his income by trying to revive his hustle. His old clientele who during more prosperous times purchased the clothing and knock off jewelry, were holding on to their money. He was always looking for the big payday, the pot of gold at the end of the rainbow.

Eventually the restaurant closed, and Big Frank began to travel quite a lot. He would be away from home for months at a time, trying to work his hustle and make money. Times were quite hard for our family and my sister Monya and I would do odd jobs for some of the elderly people in the neighborhood to help.

My sister would be the face, knocking on doors and asking if we could cut grass, rake leaves, shovel snow or any other chore we could perform to make money. I of course was the workhorse and performed the bulk of the manual labor. Since we were small kids, my sister Monya and I were close. She was always small and petite having a heart made of gold. From the time of her birth, Monya had cared for our youngest sister Shay. Of the three of us, Monya has always been more of the caregiver of the family. She always has had a strong work ethic, and has a very charismatic personality. In a crisis, she uses her very keen sense of vision and resourcefulness to conquer any challenge she confronted.

When my mother gave birth to Shay, she developed severe back problems and ultimately had to have surgery to repair damaged disks. This affected our mother's ability to hold down a permanent job, and ultimately affected the quality of life we would experience growing as children. Therefore, my sister and I would do what we could to help. There was many times that the money we made doing odd jobs our mother would use to buy groceries or diapers. We did not mind whatsoever; it actually felt good knowing that we were able to help.

The lifestyle of hustling, pimping or gambling is very much a parasitic existence. Those playing the game depend and prey upon the weakness and ignorance of those that desire to get something for nothing. When people were making money hand over fist, times were great for us. We depended upon Big Frank for our very existence. When the economy began to take a dive, we like so many black families experience the hardships quite early. It's been said that the black community is the canary of the society at large. In the coal mining industry, miners would take canaries into the mines to gauge the amount of toxic gases, as the miners would drill for coal. Those of the society who had the least would be the first to experience any social or economic downturn affecting the nation.

There was a time that we were on the welfare system. I remember times that Monya and I would have to walk about three miles to the nearest grocery store. Our mother would sometimes send us to the store with food stamps. How I would hate pulling the stamps out from the book to give to the cashier. I felt so humiliated as the cashier would pull each stamp out one at a time appearing to move slower than a dancer under a strobe light. We would proceed to walk the distance back carrying the groceries we bought.

To make the money stretch further, my mother would make "boiled" pots of beans, stews, chili etc. I grew so tired of eating the same thing day in and day out. I remember one day I came home from school and smelled a pot of beans cooking. The look upon my face must have told the tale of my dislike. I never cared for the taste of homemade bread made from corn meal I only liked Jiffy.

When my mother said it was time to eat, I asked her what kind of corn bread she made. She cursed at me, and said it did not matter because I was going to eat what she prepared. When I replied I was not hungry, she screamed at me to come to the table and sit down. I sat there but refused to eat the corn bread. When she noticed I did not pick it up, she clocked out and proceeded to start slapping me.

I rose from the chair and raised my hand to her. I was so angry and I came so close to hitting my mom, but I pulled away. She was startled at first, but then became angrier at the fact that I would even contemplate doing such a thing. She ripped my tee shirt off my back, and I had to run upstairs to my sister's room and lock the door. I was not afraid of being hit by her, I was afraid of why I may do to her. I was very enraged, and to this day, she does not realize how close I came to hurting her.

There was one particular Christmas I recall where we received assistance from the local Salvation Army. A middle-aged woman came to our home with a couple of boxes of food and a few presents in hand. If my memory serves me, I received a pair of rubber snow boots that were a size too small, and a knit cap and gloves. I think there were a few toys consisting of a couple of white dolls for my sisters and a game or two. This was a true Charlie Brown Christmas if I ever saw one.

It is stressful enough raising children when you have all of the so-called creature comforts available at your disposal. For those who depend upon the government welfare system for assistance, providing for the needs of your children becomes much more challenging. A very different dynamic and set of problems comes into play. Many people are of the opinion that those on welfare live the life of Riley. That is the furthest thing from the truth, no one I knew that relied upon the welfare system could conceive living life high on the hog.

American society is quick to render judgment upon those who lack financial and economic means as shiftless and lazy. The meager amount of funds provided under government assistance meets a minimum level of existence, not a living and there is a great difference between the two. I can understand now as an adult how humiliating and frustrating it must be for a parent to provide for their family in such a manner. Moreover, since many individuals on welfare lack formal education and marketable job skills, one can easily be sucked into the cycle of poverty under the welfare system.

When despair and hopelessness sets in, one can understand the attraction and allure of turning to the dark side of our nature. Many individuals will choose to make ends meet by participating in the underground economy. In an act of desperation, some people engage in selling or using drugs, prostitution or gambling.

The emotional rush one attains after receiving money through ill-gotten gains is an addiction in and of itself. Many individuals link their self-esteem directly to the amount of money they have in their pockets. I can understand how addicting the lifestyle can be to those who lack hope. I know of what I speak, because I bore witness to these experiences growing up.

To this day, neither my mother nor Big Frank was aware that I knew he was engaged in selling drugs. I recall the many mornings he would walk downstairs and light up a cigarette and stare at the floor. This was his daily ritual as he tried to figure out the next move or angle as to where he could make the next buck.

For a short period, he and a few of his associates sold prescription drugs for profit. During the early and mid seventies, Valium and Quaaludes were some of the more popular drugs of choice. I do not know where he obtained them or to whom he sold them too. He kept his activities on the down low, out of our direct line of sight. It was by sheer accident that I came to find out about this other occupation.

I came downstairs one afternoon while he was assessing how much supply he had left to sell. There were prescription bottles all over the kitchen table. I startled him, because he believed I was outside playing. He never said a word to me, never tried to explain it or motion me out of the kitchen.

He just looked at me, and proceeded to count out the various pills and separate them into small bags. Never was a word uttered about what I saw, but I knew the deal. As I perceived it, he was placing himself at risk in order that we could have food on the table and a roof over our heads. My head was filled with imagined statements I could hear from people such my grandmothers, who would have rendered many judgments and opinions about the situation. As I recall, there was no Calvary riding in on white horses to assist or save us. The collective series of decisions Big Frank made up until this point in his life placed him in the predicament he faced. A predicament that limited the options he had available.

He saw no value and had little use in regards to attaining a formal education. Being forty-three years of age with a sixth grade education, the options available were few when the need to provide for the family was immediate. I do not know how long he was engaged in selling drugs. I remember a few other occasions later on throughout the years that he would sell drugs in order to supplement what we needed to get by.

During this time, my mother's half brother and his family moved from Detroit and stayed with us for a while. At one time, my Uncle Skip was the chosen one of the clan. Both he and my mother lost their mother a short time after his birth. My great Grandma Suzie raised Skip along with her other children, which were his uncles and aunts. During his high school years in the sixties', he was a promising athlete where he broke or set all types of records in both football and track.

From all accounts, he had the talent to play at the professional level. As with most children raised by the older generation, he was spoiled by my Grandma Suzie. His uncles and aunts also were a party to the spoiling, providing him with whatever he desired. Being he was a star athlete, the teachers also made accommodations for him as well. Outside of his activities on the field of play, Skip never truly developed a sense of a work ethic. He was a handsome man, and used his physical prowess to manipulate people in order to attain the things in life he desired. I thought he was the coolest man alive as a young boy; he dressed sharply and always had a good-looking woman hanging off his arm.

Many famous universities heavily recruited my uncle to play college football. Due to some rift with his high coach who refused to send game films to his college of interest, he elected to enlist in the U.S. Air force instead. After being discharged, he moved to Detroit and married some local woman he met through working for her father. She was far from the type of woman I was accustomed to seeing with him. She was not that physically attractive or appeared to be very bright.

I do not recall the entire story, but he had to leave Detroit because he stole money from one of the local hoods. So to escape the heat he was under, he moved to Mansfield with his wife and two kids until things cooled down. We were already catching hell making it from day to day. He burned bridges with our other relatives he had nowhere else to turn but to my mother.

Having nine people in a house to feed with little or no money caused much strain inside the house. There was one day while walking home from school that I found a twenty-dollar bill pressed up along a line of bushes. Little did I know that there was nothing in the house to eat, and that neither of them had a dime in their pockets.

I know now that God was looking out for us. I came home and told everyone what I found. My mom asked me to give her the twenty to buy some food. I gave it to her without question and I do not know how she did it, but we ate three days from the twenty-dollar bill. Skip fancied himself as a hustler too, but he was also a cocaine and heroin addict. The life of a hustler was tough enough, but when you have a habit such as his to support, it makes plying the trade somewhat more difficult. In between hustles, he worked for one of the local garbage trucking companies.

I really looked up to him, and wanted to be around him as much as I could. One day I asked him if I could earn some extra money by helping him on his route. He had a partner who drove the truck, so we would get up at 4:00am in the morning and start on our way. Working on a garbage truck is one of the difficult jobs I ever had. At the time, the trucks were not equipped with the modern hydraulic lift forks installed on the trucks today.

We manually lifted the garbage cans, bags and boxes of trash into the bed of the truck by hand. When we would break for lunch, my uncle and his partner would stop by a corner store and pick up a pint of cheap wine to wash down whatever he would buy for lunch. Not that there is such a thing as "clean" garbage but some of the things people placed into the garbage was just downright disgusting. People were not supposed to put items such as bricks, wood, tires or large items like couches and household appliances for curbside pickup.

For a few extra dollars, my uncle and his friend would haul the stuff away. I worked that garbage route for two weeks straight. Once again, as it came time to be paid, someone I had come to love and respect dealt me the short end of the stick. After dragging stinking heaps of garbage to the truck, having my hands and arms cut up and coming home dead tired with every muscle aching my uncle gave me twenty dollars. That amounted to two dollars a day for working ten to twelve hours a day. My days as a junior garbage man were over and I never looked at my uncle ever the same again.

This was the first of a series of letdowns and disappointments I would come to experience by the deeds of my Uncle Skip. I recall when my mother told me to mow the lawn one afternoon; I already promised to help one of my friends to deliver newspapers. My uncle overheard the conversation, and told me to go ahead and he would finish cutting the lawn. I thanked him and ran off with the friend.

When I arrived home, I stepped in the back door whereby my mother proceeded to chew me out for leaving home without completing the task. While I attempted to tell her that my uncle agreed to finish cutting the grass, she proceeds to start hitting me with a broom handle. As I attempted to run out the back door, I ran square against the edge of the door. I was semi conscience laid out on the floor, but the beating continued.

He had apparently received a call from one of the women around town that he was seeing on the side and left without finishing the job. When he arrived home, he denied that he ever offered to finish cutting the lawn for me. It was at that point that I came to see him in his true light as a conniving, lowdown, lying shell of a man. At that time of my life, the only persons

I trusted were my mom, my sister and came to trust my Uncle Skip. After standing in the presence of my mother looking me square dead in the eyes and denying what he said, added another layer of cold callousness to my heart. As the saying goes, "what goes around comes around and back around again" began to hold great meaning for my Uncle Skip.

Mansfield being a small town, word travels fast especially when it involves any measure of dirt. The word of his exploits cheating with other women, stealing from his employer and his use of drugs were beginning to catch up to him. His wife had taken the kids and headed back to Detroit. He lost his job and eventually moved out of our house after he was caught stealing from my mom and Big Frank to support his drug habit. I was happy that he left, but this would not be the last time our family would have to contend with my uncle and his exploits.

CHAPTER FIVE

Big Frank left home on another moneymaking scheme. One of the few qualities that I came to admire about him was that no matter what obstacle life placed before Big Frank; he would continue to pursue his goal. After the failure of the restaurant, Big Frank bought a run down semi truck to try his hand in the long hauling business. He enlisted the husband of one of his nieces to drive it for him. The truck spent more time in the garage under repair than on the highway. The trucking venture was short lived.

Since he loved the blues so, he came to know several of the more popular blues artists of the time. He thought that everyone loved the blues as much as he did; so on a few occasions he would work his hustle to make enough money to book a blues cabaret. He would rent one of the local union halls in town, buy posters and promote the artists. He would book a few of the blues artists such as Little Milton and Bobby Blues Bland.

He would spend so much time money and energy trying to bring some measure of quality entertainment to the public. In all of his attempts, I do not believe he ever broke even. He would be so disappointed and tried not to let it show. He was a persistent man, always looking for the hook or an angle to achieve his goals. Instead of trying to book the more well known artists, he aligned himself with a second rate blues singer.

Lee "Shot" was his stage name. Not that I was an expert on blues singers, but in my opinion I heard cats and dogs howling in pain who sounded better than this guy. Big Frank put so much blind faith in this man's lack of ability, so much so that he chose to take the "Lee Shot" blues review show on the road. Big Frank would book him in various holes in the wall nightclubs and lounges around the country. Big Frank had no experience promoting or managing club acts, but his skills as a hustler came in handy. He would convince the club owners that Lee Shot was about to blow up, and they should hop on the bandwagon before his asking price would rise beyond their reach.

The two of them would become good friends over the years, which later would pose problems for Big Frank. During one of their trips in the south, Big Frank came across another scheme to make money. He decided to try his hand at becoming a nightclub owner. While on one of their concert stops, Big Frank came upon Andalusia, a small town located in southern Alabama.

A run down bar he discovered was available for lease. I had just started my sophomore year in high school and I was beginning to get into the flow of the environment there. With little advanced noticed we packed up our belongings and left Mansfield like thieves of the night. The trip was long and tiring, and with every mile we rode, I became increasingly depressed. Listening to the same blues eight-track tapes, I have heard a million times before, made the trip more unbearable for me. We had no place to live when we first arrived, but Big Frank convinced some guy he met while on a previous visit to allow us to stay in his house trailer. Frankie was his name, a short dark balding man who was born and raised in the town we now called home.

In many ways, Andalusia was a town where time stood still. The houses many of the black families resided lacked running water and central heating. Some had to burn wood both to cook and to heat the shacks they called homes. The town was very segregated and as in most cities, with the lines between those that have and those that have not was separated by the color line and the railroad tracks, which separated the two.

The major employers of the area were a local lumber mill and a Coca-Cola distributing bottling plant. Those who were fortunate enough to be employed by either were of the opinion that they were living the life, even though the wages they were paid were quite low. From all appearances, life in Andalusia was relatively quiet and calm. Being raised in the north, I experienced racism, but it was covert and subtle.

When I was told we were moving to Alabama, I had images of Ku Klux Klansman walking the streets, and every white person uttering racial slurs as naturally as taking a breath. The actual reality was the furthest thing from my perceptions. However, the one thing I did take issue with was the measure of disrespect that some white men displayed toward their black male counterparts. A black man could be 200 years old, but would still be called a boy by some of the local white residents.

Every time I heard the term, the hair on the back of my neck and arms would just bristle. I was more upset that the vast majority of the black men when addressed in such a manner would respond with a smile, skinning and grinning with a "yes sir Mr. So and So" when beckoned. In all of the places I had lived thus far, I must admit that I appreciated the naked honesty displayed by most whites I encountered in the south. I could at least respect a person who was honest in their hatred of me more so than someone who would put on pretenses and wear a phony smile.

It was several weeks before I was enrolled in school, helping my mother and Big Frank clean up and paint the building to prepare for its grand opening. One day, my mother and I went to the local high school to sign me up. There was only one high school in town, housed in a building that appeared to me to have been built during times of the American Revolution.

I met with the vice principle Mr. Bryant, who was the nephew of Coach Bear Bryant of the University of Alabama Crimson Tide college football team. His office walls were covered with UA paraphernalia, and an autographed picture of himself and his famous uncle. After reviewing my transcript, I was taken on a tour of the school. The school was painted in a dull blood red color with the trim painted a glossy white. To me, the school looked more like a mental hospital or detention center. The one thing I must admit I was quite shocked how well the black and white student body seemed to get along.

Upon returning to his office, he and the high school counselor proceeded to discuss what type of classes I should take. I was unaware at the time, but I had taken advanced courses in history and literature while attending my previous high school, Malabar. I also was taking advanced Spanish, but Andalusia High did not offer a foreign language program at the time. I was placed in senior's level history, and junior level English literature. One of the teachers Mr. Paramour, a black man, taught Spanish at the school before the program was discontinued.

He agreed to instruct me so I could receive my foreign language credit. Mr. Bryant suggested that I take sophomore level classes in algebra and biology. Mrs. Crawford taught biology, and I was fortunate to have been assigned to her class. She had taken an instant liking towards me. Upon arrival to her class, most of the students did not appear to express an interest in biology. When Mrs. Crawford assigned homework, a few other students and I were the few whom regularly completed the assignments. When she posed questions to the class, I would wait for someone to respond but more oft than not, anyone would. She and I would go back and forth during the class engaging one another.

The kids would look at me as though I was an oddity, with their heads motioning back and forth between Mrs. Crawford and myself as though they were watching a tennis match. Perhaps she appreciated having someone showing any measure of interest in what she was trying to impart. I had a free period after her class, which happened to coincide with her lunch break. We would sit and talk to each other about anything under the sun.

For a while, I was somewhat of a minor novelty at the school, treated almost like an alien from another planet. Perhaps it was because I was the only kid in school from the north. My manor of speech was different and since I pretty much kept to myself, I unknowingly created an air of mystery. I had a rather interesting time in the history and English classes as well. I was a fourteen-year-old boy amongst a class of students ranging from seventeen to nineteen. Actually, there were a few freshmen students attending the school who were pushing twenty years of age.

Assuming because of my age I could not possibly know or keep up with the senior members of the class, both the students and the teachers underestimated my abilities. English was never one of my strong suites, but this particular instructor just rubbed me the wrong way. He would call on me non-stop attempting to catch me slipping by if I did not complete the homework assignments.

I made sure that I came prepared, and we too engaged in a volley. To some students I am sure that I appeared to be showing off, but I was not going to let this man make a fool of me. I had gotten into an altercation with this particular instructor over a grade he placed on one of my assignments that I believed was unjustified.

I never became comfortable with my writing skills, so I always printed my assignments. He stated that in his class, his students would turn in all assignments in script form. Because I had printed my assignment, he reduced my grade by one-letter. I stated aloud that the grade was bogus (not the actual choice of words I used), and he called out my name. I responded by saying "yes", but did not call him by his surname.

He insisted that I did so, but I refused. He made a comment about my lack of respect, and that apparently my parents were negligent in teaching me proper respect. I calmly stated that I gave no one respect just because someone was older than I was, or held a different title or occupation. One must earn my respect, for it is never freely given. The kids in class gasped at my remark, and made various other sounds of surprise and approval. He was livid, and proceeded to take me to the vice-principal's office. This incident happened during the third week of my enrollment at the school.

As the English teacher proceeded to tell the story, he changed the context and the sequence of events. When the vice principal question me, I essentially stated that the teacher was lying and stated I would not address him as Mr. until he gave me the respect he expected to get from me. My mother was called to the school, and at first, she was ready to leap all over me. As I began to tell the story, she calmed down. I was always the poorest of liars; anytime I attempted to tell one my mother could see it written all over my face. She knew I was telling the truth, and agreed with the statement I made. The teacher was red and steaming like a lobster.

The vice principal rocked back in his chair and paused for a moment, not sure what he should do at that moment. I requested that I be placed in a different class, because I was of the opinion that I would never get a fair chance as long as I stayed in his class. After the incident, I was moved to a different class. I felt damn good about myself at that moment and was quite proud too.

The nightclub, which Big Frank named the Hideaway, was going to have its grand opening. It was a Friday night and in Alabama, Friday nights meant high school football. Football has always been king there, and the Andalusia team was one of the best in the state at the time. The games typically kicked off at 8:00pm normally to a sold out crowd. The club opened around 9:00pm.

Because we were new to the area, Big Frank had no clue about the ritualistic following of the high school football team. As I recall, five or six people arrived for the opening night. I could tell Big Frank was nervous and disappointed at the low turn out. His spirits would soon pick up as more patrons began to arrive at the club. As soon as the game was over and the adults went home to change, the crowds started to show up.

The opening night turned out well for him and my mother. She pretty much managed the club, because she had the experience gained from running several of the bars back home. The first few months after the club opened, a steady stream of clientele would come through and Big Frank would bring in his protégé Lee Shot to sing on the weekends. It appeared that things were finally looking up for us, and the business was prospering quite well.

The cramped living arrangements at the house trailer were about to change also. The man we were living with was an alcoholic and was of the opinion that because we were living there he was entitled to free drinks at the bar. He was a nasty and belligerent drunk too. When he would get drunk, he would play an album he owned by Bobby Womack an R&B singer. I can still hear the song "Harry Hippie" ringing in my head to this day. He would play the album repeatedly; I believe in part to torture and antagonize us into leaving. It ultimately worked.

Big Frank and my mother found a house on the outskirts of town for rent. It sat out in the country on a red dirt road in the middle of a wooden area. The house was made of cinder-block, with a wooden back porch, which were supported on stilts. The stove and heating system was fueled with propane gas and because we were outside the city limits, we could not get access to cable TV.

We were literally living in the wilderness, there were wild pigs and chickens abound. Poisonous snakes, spiders and red fire ants were everywhere. My sister and I the second day we moved in went on a hike through the woods. We came upon an area that had several ant mounds that stood five or six feet tall. We did not know what they were at the time, but I found out real quick. I had taken a stick and hit one of the mounds, and red fire ants were everywhere. My sister and I took off running towards the house like bats out of hell. We did not venture back into the woods after that.

There was a pack of dogs that lived in the woods nearby. We adopted them as pets, providing scrap food and water. We would put water and table scraps into bowls on the back porch for them to eat. The leader of the pack was a big black dog we nicknamed Blacky, but my sisters liked this little white dog, which was the smallest of the group. I would sometimes chase some of the larger dogs off the porch in order for the little one to get something to eat.

On the weekends when Big Frank and my mother worked at the club, we were bored. Living that far away from civilization with only two or three TV channels we could pick up almost drove me insane. Since the kids who lived in the shack next door were considerably younger than I, further limited social interaction was non-existent.

A short time after we moved, Big Frank came to know a few of the locals who patronized the club. There was one individual I remembered who went by the name of Little Mike. Little Mike was in his early 30's, physically deformed at birth whereby his growth was underdeveloped. He was a dwarf with a large hump on his back and both his arms and legs were of dissimilar length. He was highly intelligent, and could shoot a mean game of pool.

Big Frank befriended him, and brought him to our home for a short visit. I liked Little Mike a lot, as he would play with my younger sisters, and helped me with my algebra homework. There were a few occasions on the weekend Little Mike and I would stay up all night talking. We would discuss issues such as race, life on other planets and we talked about God. He lived with his mother at the time, and I can only assume that she as most people raised in the south were of the Christian faith. Little Mike believed in God, but he questioned whether Jesus and God were one in the same. He also did not believe that God was capable of causing harm to His children if we did not follow the teachings as stated in the bible. I was somewhat puzzled and amazed that he would have such an opinion of God.

I asked Little Mike about his deformity. Whether or not he believed that somehow God was punishing him. He smiled at me and said that he considered himself blessed to be alive. During the time of his birth, there were several times he almost died. He told me he received good grades in school and graduated at the top of his class. His mother was afraid to allow him to leave home to go to college. All of the intelligence and brainpower he had packed into his small frame essentially had gone to waste. He smoked weed and drank occasionally, I suppose as a means of dulling his pain to escape from his predicament.

Little Mike had a very sharp wit and a wicked tongue, as well as a great command of the English language. Sometimes it got him into trouble, with both his mother and others. There was more than a few occasions' that Big Frank or my mother would have to come to his rescue at the club. After a few drinks, Little Mike would engage in a battle of words with some of the other patrons.

I admired Little Mike for his courage, as most people if faced with a similar situation would wallow in self-pity and loathing. He took it all in stride, keeping a big smile on his face and enjoyed his life. He would not allow anyone to feel sorry for him, and he had a way of making people laugh so hard that tears would fall from their eyes. Little Mike taught me to laugh at myself and not to take life so seriously.

As time went by, I was slowly adapting to our new environment but it would not last for long. Being a fat kid, buying and finding clothes that fit were always difficult. The clothes were more expensive, and the places which sold them were few and far in between. I had four pair of school pants, and seven or eight shirts that I wore on rotation.

One day while attending gym class, two of the girls in class decided to make fun of my sense of fashion. One of them was a skinny, bugged-eyed girl and the other was actually taller and fatter than I was. The gym teacher was lining up teams for softball and it was my turn at bat. The two girls, who I considered a Black Country version of Laurel and Hardy, began to shout out the colors of the pants I would wear. No one else was aware of the meaning behind her little chant, but the more she sang the angrier I became.

I suddenly lost it, as I ran carrying the bat in hand towards the other side of the field where the girls stood. It had taken several of the boys and the gym teacher to hold me back from attacking them. We were all sent to the office, and once again, I had to face vice Principal

Bryant. The gym teacher told the story, but because I attempted to attack them, I was sent home for the remainder of the day. I walked from the school to the club, and I was still fuming with anger. During the bulk of my childhood and teenage years, I bent over backwards in my attempts of trying to be nice to people.

I made many allowances, and deferred against my better judgment not to retaliate in many cases in order to keep the peace. In doing so, I buried my feelings deep within to get along. As time would pass, the pressure within me would build like a volcano or a time bomb ready to go off. When my volcano blew its top, the lava of my anger would spew in verbal or physical form at those I felt caused me either pain or harm. This was a learned pattern; one that I would carry well into my adulthood.

Upon my arrival at the club, my mother had asked why I was released so early from school. After I told her of the situation, she saw how angry and upset I was. I understood what our financial situation was and I never asked for much. I told her I was tired of the ridicule and of wearing the same thing day in and day out. She went out a day or so later and bought me a few additional changes of clothing. To this day, she does not know how much that meant to me.

When I arrived at school the following day, I noticed a marked change in attitude of the few students I had come to know. They were a little more kind towards me, perhaps feeling somewhat understanding of my situation. Because the two loud mouth girls were not very well like, I gained a few additional brownie points from my misguided actions. My becoming the subject of ridicule was no different from those experienced by school children since the beginning of time.

It does not negate the short and long term effects that such abuse can have on the psyche of a child well into their adulthood. Those who choose to have kids should provide the type of guidance and instruction to teach children to respect the feelings of others different from themselves. The pressures heaped upon children at very early ages to conform to the so-called social norms in dress and appearance can have disastrous consequences.

The very teaching methods used within most western cultures are based on the philosophy of collective thought. Most people today are not familiar with the subject of collectivism. Collectivism is a based on the premise that conformity to the desires of the group takes precedence over the need of the individual. Leonard Peikoff, the author of "THE OMINOUS PARALLELS" defines collectivism as the following:

"Collectivism is the theory that the group (the collective) has primacy over the individual. Collectivism holds that, in human affairs, the collective-society, the community, the nation, the proletariat, the race, etc., -- is the unit of reality and the standard of value. A totalitarian state is founded upon the denial of individual rights. On this view, the individual has reality only as part of the group. The individual only has value insofar as the extent to which he serves it; on his own he has no political rights; he is to be sacrificed for the group whenever it—or its representative, the state—deems this desirable."

The ultimate goal of those who espouse its philosophy is to mold the person into an obedient, subservient individual. To create a person who will go along with the crowd and accept orders without questioning either the intent or purpose. Upon taking our first breath as newborns, we are immediately exposed and indoctrinated to the collectivist philosophy. Children receive these teachings from their parents, who are the primary informational source.

The secondary source of reinforcement is provided by the educational system the children at the hands of their teachers. Children are taught to follow a chosen leader, and in order to get along with the group they must submit themselves to the collective will of the group. The games "Follow the Leader" and "Simon Says" is prime examples of how the philosophy of collectivism is disseminated to children at the early stages of development.

The foundation of collectivism goes back millions of years. Many species including man discovered that it would be far more efficient to form alliances to enhance the chances of survival. Many mammals formed hunting parties to forge and hunt for food. Primitive cultures then formed tribal communities establishing ruling bodies comprised of group elders.

The elders would create the rules deemed necessary for the survival of the tribe. Through the millennia, these communal tribal practices evolved and brought forth the monarchial and feudalistic forms of government practiced in Europe, Asia and Africa. As a by-product, disunity and chaos spread throughout the lands and many wars were fought to gain control of precious mineral resources.

The Greek and Roman Empires created a system of governance into a forum whereby the group collective selected a body of men to represent them. Initially these groups were comprised of intellectual men of good will and conscience. The senators were chosen by the citizens to become the collective voice of the people. This gave rise to the Republic that brought forth order to a chaotic world. This system concentrated and centralized the power base, which was shared by the Senators and the chosen emperor given the title of Caesar.

Through their many conquests, the Greeks and Romans ruled much of the known world under this system of representative government. Corruption, decadence, and greed permeated the body politic of the Roman Empire, which ultimately, caused the demise of the Republic. The emergence of Christianity came into existence and emerged as a powerful liberating force of freedom of both body and spirit to an enslaved people weary of tyranny.

The very causes of the murder of Jesus were rooted in collectivist philosophy. There were those of both monolithic and multi dietetic beliefs that felt threatened by the potential loss of their material wealth and base of power. Because of His actions, the leaders handed Jesus over to the Romans charged with treason, blasphemy, and sedition for spreading the true word of God.

Collectivism gave way to the many systems of government practiced around the world today. Whether democratic, parliamentary or socialist based, each has at its roots some element of the tenants of collectivist thought. Philosophers throughout the ages have debated whether the dictates of the majority populous take precedence over the importance of the personal freedoms of the individual.

Each of the aforementioned systems of government has given rise to atrocities committed by those who chose to follow the ebb and flow of the societal group dynamic. There are examples throughout history whereby the collective will of the majority caused massive destruction at the expense of the lives of individuals.

The laws of the Democratic Republic of the United States permitted the enslavement of people of color. During the period between the late 19th and 20th centuries, it was a common practice of the era by vigilantes to form lynches mobs. The events of Rosewood, Florida and Tulsa Oklahoma, which occurred in the 1920's, were examples whereby white mob justice sanctioned the killing and lynching of blacks.

During World War II, the United States placed American born citizens of Japanese decent into internment camps. The Bill of Rights and the Constitution was hit by the tidal wave of xenophobia that existed in the country. The rises of Fascism and Nazism are other examples of collectivist forms of government created by fear and fueled by hate. The very creation of the tenants of socialism by Karl Marx came into being via the principles of cause and effect.

Karl Marx's cynical perspective and negative viewpoint regarding capitalism was based upon the realities that existed during the time. Great Britain, France and the United States were reaping great financial rewards from the power generated by the engine of the great industrial revolution run on the backs of cheap labor. The resources exploited from the continents of Africa, Asia and Persian Gulf created great wealth for the monarchies of Europe. Karl Marx saw the inequities of the capitalist system and saw socialism as the antithesis solution to combat poverty. His vision was to create a utopian society whereby the production and distribution of goods would come under the control of a centralized government.

From each according to his ability, to each according to their need as wealth would be equally distributed amongst the populous. The peasant workers led by Lenin in their fight against the Russian monarchy gave birth to what became known as Communist Revolution. Joseph Stalin's regime under communism massacred millions and forced millions more to a life of misery and poverty for the so-called good of the collective. Adolph Hitler came into power and took control of a nation by the support of those who followed his collectivist-based philosophy.

Many held the belief that the so-called Aryan race was superior above all others. Without the overwhelming support and following of the vast majority of German people, there was no way that Hitler could have orchestrated and carried out the mass murder of millions of Jews.

Although the system of government differed from case to case, the collectivist mindset was at the root cause of the conflict and atrocities that subsequently arose. The causes were different but the effectual outcomes were very much the same. The catalyst of each conflict started out as a noble cause rising from despair, fear, and hopelessness. The dream ultimately turned into a nightmare for the participants involved. Individuals that go along with the flow and follow the crowd without giving thought as to the consequences can find themselves in too deep to turn back.

The crowd can be quite fickle; those who follow the dictates of the crowd can find that doing so can be detrimental to one's health or someone else's. Doing what is popular is not necessarily, what is proper or righteous for the individual involved. The value systems of the group can become misguided and misdirected.

For if the individual is unwilling to stand up for what is right better prepare to be knocked down by the brutal force of those who benefit from maintaining the status quo. The current social norm idolizes athletes or entertainers over those more intellectual career pursuits are an example of a misguided group. The adoring public is willing to spend hundreds of millions of dollars to support the salary of a sports figure.

In the same token, society is unwilling to raise the base salary of those charted to guide and instruct the youth. Watching your favorite movie star may provide a means of escaping reality, but it comes at too great a price. Whatever the individual is attempting to escape from will be waiting for them as soon as the credits disappear from the movie screen.

There are so many public schools systems lacking the necessary funds to maintain operations. When levies are proposed, many voters refuse to pay additional taxes to improve the quality of education and increase in teacher's salaries. However, if a professional sports franchise is looking to relocate, the same people will vote to spend hundreds of millions of dollars to build a new stadium.

Today it is considered unpopular and not cool to display one's intellect in a group setting. In order to gain acceptance, one must "dumb down" what they know in the presence of others, or adopt the uniform style of dress. Some will fake their way and display dysfunctional patterns of behavior to gain popularity with the clique one attempts to belong. If who and what you are does not fit into the dynamic of the group of your interest, find another group.

No one individual or group has the right to dictate or force a lifestyle upon another as a means to control or gain favor. When the behaviors of the collective promote exclusion instead of inclusion, a group of social outcasts and misfits are created. Being ignored or cast aside may cause the outcasts to seek attention by less than desirable means. Any individual placed under such pressure has the capacity to emotionally snap or break under the weight placed upon them by their peers.

Prime examples of such behavior are the school shootings that took place in Columbine CO and Paducah, KY. These acts of violence were perpetrated by teens that were considered as social outcasts by the group collective. Such incidences are in part a by-product of teenage group peer pressure applied by dysfunctional conformists. There are those who use tactics such as bullying and intimidation in order to force the individual into submission.

Other means used to apply peer pressure are to minimize and ostracize those deemed as misfits by the so-called leaders of the pack. Parents who dismiss such behavior and make statements such as "kids will be kids" or "It happened to me therefore its okay" can find the consequences to be quite grave.

It is the inherent nature of the human spirit to be free, to be happy and live a joyous life with minimal restrictions. Therefore, anything that goes against the natural essence of the human spirit will be resisted. The individual must be taught to think logically and act rationally. Parents should give children the tools required to make conscience choices to become independent thinkers.

By doing so, the chances of another totalitarian form of government or dictatorship regime coming to power are substantially reduced. Society and the individual must strive to strike the balance between doing what promotes the common good of both parties. To do what will cause no harms nor foul; nor infringe upon the rights and freedoms of another. This is a necessary requirement in order for the true spirit of freedom to exist and flourish.

My self-esteem would take another serious blow. One of the seniors in the world history class was bragging out how well he performed on his ACT examination. He scored 31 of possible 36 points and stated that his I.Q. was 140. I always wondered what my I.Q. was, and decided to find out. I walked down to the school counselor's office and asked to see the transcripts that contained my I.Q. score.

She handed me the page that contained the results of the test I had taken in the second grade. The score was 85. I sat there and stared at it for about two or three minutes. I never thought of myself as a genius by any means, but now I saw the score I felt so stupid and ashamed. The counselor then proceeded to tell me that I should perhaps consider a vocational trade in lieu of pursuing a college education.

When I left her office, I was emotionally devastated. What measure of self-respect I had was destroyed the moment I saw the score. The entire weekend I stayed in my room and said next to nothing to anyone. The following Monday I struggled to get ready for school. I felt like a zombie, a member of the walking dead.

When I arrived in Mrs. Crawford's biology class, she knew something was wrong. I did not bother doing the weekend homework assignment and did not participate with our daily routine of question and answer. After class was over, she asked me to stay and talk to her. I told her what had occurred, and although I tried to fight them back, tears began to fall from my face. She looked at me smiling and said that I was stupid. I looked up at her, and did not know how to react. She started laughing and at first, I felt angry. She immediately put her arms around me and said that I placed too much value in a test that was far from an accurate measure of one's ability to learn.

She pointed out the fact that I was a fourteen-year old student with above average intelligence. She also noted that I was taking advanced level courses, and was one of the brightest students she had in her many years of teaching. Mrs. Crawford told me that there is a difference in the ability of one to take a test, and one who could apply the knowledge that they were taught. Anyone with a good memory could perform well on tests, but doing well in life takes more than scoring well on a standard test.

She spoke of some teachers at the high school who held master degrees in education but did not have the common sense to come in out of the rain. Many of their students were performing very badly, but some lacked the ability or desire to reach them. Perhaps some did not care whether the students grasp the lessons, to the benefit of no one.

She told me she almost fell into that trap, until I came along. She was considering retiring at the time because she was of the opinion that she had outlived her usefulness. When I came to her class, with an enthusiasm to learn, I gave her a renewed sense of purpose. Some of the students who rarely participated in class before I arrived began to become more involved.

I had no idea or clue that I made such an impact on anyone, let alone her. She told me I had a bright future, and I would do great things with my life. She told me that I am worth far more than a score on a test I had taken years ago. Do not allow a number to stop me from achieving my goals in life. After that conversation with Mrs. Crawford, I felt as though I had been awakened from the dead.

She gave me a hug and from that point forward, I looked at myself in a very different light. Until that time, I placed so much value and concern about the opinions and perceptions of others about me. The opinions about my clothes, being fat, or the attempts of some to challenge my level of intelligence that I decided I would not give as much credence to the minions of opinions. For probably the first time in my life, I became comfortable and loved the skin I was born in.

CHAPTER SIX

Business at the nightclub began to falter. Big Frank and my mother spent a considerable amount of money to remodel the place before its grand opening. Red owned the only other bar in town that blacks frequented. His place was on the other side of town, a run down establishment that in all honesty was not fit to slop hogs let alone human beings. I can only surmise that the vast majority of the black population of Andalusia had grown accustomed to the type of atmosphere Red's place provided.

The Hideaway was far too upscale for their tastes. Some people viewed Big Frank and my mother with scorn and envy. Being northerners, the proverbial "Crabs in the Bucket" syndrome came into play, which afflicts so many in the world today. When some of the patrons would become loud and disruptive, my mother and Big Frank did not hesitate to ask them to leave.

As time progressed, they began to notice that the upholstery and tables were cut up, and some folks would purposefully urinate all over the restroom floors and walls. I do not know if it was in retaliation by some of those who previously were asked to leave; or if Red sent people to the club with the intent to cause damage.

The number of patrons that previously frequented the club began to fall off dramatically. Big Frank began to hit the road again to hustle up money to keep the club afloat. Red even pulled a page out of Big Frank's playbook and began to book live blues bands. Before, the only entertainment he provided came from an old beat up jukebox with records released five years previous.

As the club struggled to stay alive, there were only a few months left before the school year ended. I really worked hard to keep my grades up during this period. The words of the counselor kept ringing in my ear "perhaps you should consider a vocational trade in lieu of pursuing a college education".

The more I thought about what she said, the more unsettled I became. I sometimes wondered how many students, especially black students she gave similar advice. How many students had their lives misdirected due to her expectations and limited scope of their potential? Many of the student's parents did not obtain a high school diploma, nor pursued higher educational opportunities beyond high school.

If there is no one in a child's circle of influence whom places or instills the value of obtaining an education, its value more oft than not shall be diminished. If no one is willing to guide and direct the child into believing that the options in life are limitless and boundless, they can be easily mislead and fall into the trap of apathy and hopelessness as so many do.

I am sure that many students blindly accepted the advice given by the high school counselor without questioning the motive or intent. I being only fourteen years of age at the time was not consciously aware of the subtle nuances behind her statement. It appears to me that if she were truly looking after my best interests, all options for my future should have been placed on the table, including attending college. For her to make such a quick assessment upon a cursory review of my I.Q. test score, I question her sincerity.

She totally disregarded my academic records to date and never asked me what course of study I was interested in before rendering such an opinion. Again, an individual in a position of authority presented me with an issue, which brought forth my feelings of distrust. Through my experience's taking wood and metal shop, lawn work, painting houses, and working on a garbage truck, I knew within myself that I had no desire to pursue those fields as career options. I felt no pleasure, gained no joy from engaging in those activities whatsoever.

To be content with one's lot in life is no crime if what you choose to do for a living brings you joy and fulfillment. One would hope that as parents and teachers, exposing children to as many options and choices as possible would be one of the primary goals one would seek to achieve. It was a less than a week before year-end finals and by this time, our family was back on the ropes again. The club closed and the creditors were requesting payment. Big Frank had just came back from one of his road trips and brought another of his associates back with him. The man was also a hustler, and his woman was a prostitute.

As I recall, she was quite an attractive woman and the two of them had a son together. Big Frank brought them along in order that they could hustle up on a few dollars and at the same time use them to help move our belongings. It was hectic; I was trying to study for my finals at the same time we were packing our belongings up in a hurry to move. It was the Friday before exam week and the heat miserable with the mosquitoes out in full force. Big Frank placed some rags in a metal tar bucket and set them on fire on the front porch. The wind was blowing the smoke into the house, and he asks me to move the bucket away from the house.

The bucket had a plastic handle, I proceeded to grab the handle and move the bucket to the middle of the front yard. The moment I released the handle, I realized that the handle melted in my hands. I screamed bloody murder, and ran into the house. I damn near passed out from the pain, but leaned up against the kitchen sink as cold water was poured onto my hands.

Between the pain and agony, I was enraged. I did not know whether to be mad at myself for being so stupid for not realizing the handle would be hot, or for listening to Big Frank in the first place. I just happened to finish a term paper I had to turn in for world history class. I began to worry as to how I would be able to take my written exams with both of my hands swollen from being burned. My left hand was burned worse than my right and by the time, Monday morning came; I was barely able to hold a pencil.

I was able to take both my English literature and Spanish exam orally. My final exam was the biology class taught by Mrs. Crawford. After I finished the exam, I stayed and spoke with her for two hours. She asked me if I would be taking the senior's biology class she taught the following school term. Somehow, she knew that she may never see me again, and I did not have the heart to tell her that I would not be returning.

I gave her the biggest hug and thanked her all she had done for me. She started to cry, and it was all I could do not to follow suit. I believe God places certain people in our lives, but if only for a short time to give to us just what we need to continue on our path of evolution. Mrs. Crawford restored my faith and confidence. God only knows where I would have ended up in life had we not crossed paths.

Later that same night, our family packed up what belongings we could pack into our car and the rental trailer and took off from Andalusia in the same manner we arrived…with little money and under the cover of darkness. We traveled to Louisville Kentucky, where we left the majority of our belongings with Big Frank's associate Willie and his wife.

We would never retrieve our belonging because Willie was a junkie, who sold most of the items to support his habit. Joliet, Illinois was our next destination. Big Frank had two older sisters who lived there and being that Lee Shot resided in nearby Chicago, made the decision to relocate to Joliet all the more logical in Big Franks mind.

Before our actual relocation to Joliet, my sister Monya and I were left with one of Big Franks nephews who lived in Harvey, Illinois. Harvey is a suburb of Chicago with a high concentration of poor and lower middle class blacks. As with most areas, Harvey had a reputation for being a tough and dangerous place, with a high crime rate.

Big Babe and Strut (I never knew their real names) had four daughters, three of which were teenagers. Having that many teenagers under one roof was bad enough in and of itself. For a while, I somewhat liked the arrangement. The two eldest daughters would take turns competing for my attention by offering to braid my hair into cornrows, etc.

The street they lived on had many teenagers who resided there, and in the evenings, it seemed as though half the neighborhood would congregate on Strut's front porch and hold court. Some of the teenage girls in the hood were quite bold in expressing their desires to drink, smoke and of course, have sex. Some were as young as twelve, and most cursed like a fifty-year-old around the way woman.

I recall one evening while sitting on the front porch; I was summoned across the street by one of the local teen girls. She was a friend of Struts oldest daughter Debbie, and apparently, I was a subject of conversation. She was very attractive as I recall, and as I proceeded to walk across the street, she stood up.

She was fourteen years of age, but her body was that of a girl four or five years her senior. I was nervous as all hell, trying to keep my cool. I sat down next to her as she proceeded to give me the third degree about which I was, where I came from, etc. She then invited me inside her home taking me by the hand. I did not know what she had planned, as I was shaking like a quake 10.4 on the Richter scale. She led me to the laundry room area and laid a kiss on me, such that had I not been leaning against the wall, I would have probably fainted. She then reached over and pulled a laundry bag from the back of the dryer. Inside the bag was more weed than I have ever seen in my life. She went into the kitchen, grabbed a sandwich bag stuffing it full and gave it to me.

I looked at her and this bag full of weed and asked her what was I to do with this? She said it was a gift, for me to do with what I chose to do. She then told me that she had a boyfriend, who was seventeen and that I should keep quiet about the kiss. We went back outside, and just so happened that several of the kids in the neighborhood saw me coming out of the house. So of course, they started chiming in about what they perceived we were doing inside, but I said nothing.

She told me to leave, because her parents would be coming home soon. I left but from that point forward, she never outwardly expressed any further interest or extended invitations to me again. The boy she was going with as I later came to discover had been in and out of the juvenile court system with the reputation for hitting girls.

I went across the street back to the house, and showed Debbie this bag full of weed I had. She called up her cousins who lived around the block to come over. Tyrone was 16; Alma was 17 and Junior 13, lived with their father. Their mother had passed away and since their father worked a lot, they pretty much fended for themselves. They all marched upstairs into Debbie's room, and Tyrone had two brown paper bags. One contained a bottle of wine; the other was a bottle of Sloe gin. Debbie showed Tyrone the bag of weed, and asked me where I got it.

When I told him, he gave me some advice not to hang too tough with the girl across the street due to her involvement with her boyfriend. Tyrone knew the boy, warning me that he had a reputation of wielding a knife with the willingness to use it. Tyrone then proceeded to roll a joint, light it up and passed it around.

This encounter was my first time both engaging in the use of drugs and alcohol. Until this moment, I had been around adults throughout most of my life that indulged in the use of alcohol. I saw first hand the effects of alcohol on several of my own family members, but I gave no conscience thought or consideration of either when the bottle and the joint were passed to me. When I took the first hit from the joint, I coughed and hacked as though my left lung would collapse. They all just laughed so hard, and Tyrone instructed me on the proper method of inhale and hold. My head felt as if it was detached from my body and everything in my surrounding appeared to me to be moving in slow motion.

I was sitting between Debbie's legs as she braiding my hair, and everyone seemed to be moving in slow motion. Tyrone came up with the idea of selling some of the weed I had, that way we could buy more alcohol and some pizza and have a party at his house. I handed the bag of weed to him to sell as immediately grabbed it and took off. Between drinking and smoking, time appeared to have stood still. The one thing I do remember is that my sense of hearing and vision was more acute. At times, I felt as though I could hear my own heart beating through my chest. Big Babe and Strut also drank quite heavily, and both were very belligerent and loud when they had too much to drink.

They would curse at the girls quite often and argue amongst themselves. They knew that their daughters smoked cigarettes & weed, and consumed alcohol. As long as the girls did not do it directly in front of them, I suppose they operated on the "out of sight, I don't mind" principle. A few hours had passed, and Tyrone called the house informing us to come over. He had sold half of the bag for $80 dollars and bought an array of alcoholic beverages, snacks and ordered pizza which was coming shortly. I was still buzzing from the earlier session, but we all put on our shoes and proceeded to walk over to the house.

Once we got there, the party was on and popping. The house was an absolute mess, with clothes, magazines and a multitude of other stuff just thrown about. Tyrone motioned us to go upstairs while he and his sister Alma brought the goods with them. When we got upstairs everyone found a spot to get comfortable. In the background, Tyrone was playing the song "What's a Telephone Bill?" by Bootsie Collins. As I sat back getting into the flow of the moment, Tyrone had tossed me a beer.

We drank, ate, smoked, danced, and played cards all night long. Everyone had pretty much passed out from drinking the night before. I woke up with the most awful headache, and it seemed that every cell in my body ached. My stomach started to churn, and I got up and ran to the bathroom. I was sicker than ten dogs.

One by one, everyone else was waking up, slow moving moaning and groaning. We laid there until shortly after noon, at which time Debbie and her sister finally got up and went back to their house. I told them to go on and I would be there later. Tyrone's sister Alma woke up coming out of her room.

Tyrone and his brother Junior had went into their father's room and crashed out. Alma was a homely girl, but she had a nice body. I was lying next to the stereo directly across from where the TV was located. She positioned herself with her legs open, within my line of sight and began to stare at me. I being naïve had no clue that she was attempting to seduce me. She began to start rubbing and touching herself.

Between being hung over and in a state of shock, I just laid on the floor frozen like a statue. She looked at me smiling with her teeth more jagged than a picket fence. She eventually stopped when she heard her brother stirring around in the room, and that was my cue to get up and get gone. From that point forward, I made sure I was never left alone in a room with her.

The time I spent there was much the same routine involving drinking and smoking. There was one night that I hung out with Tyrone and several of his friends. We had walked up to one of the corner stores and while in route, a worker of one of the restaurants was in the back smoking. One of the guys made some crack about him being Mexican, and the man began to call us a pack of wild niggers.

When we proceeded to walk towards him, he ran inside the restaurant. Tyrone picked up a broken brick and threw it, breaking a window. We all took off running. After we ran about a block or so, we stopped running and proceeded to laugh and joke about what just occurred. All of a sudden, we heard several police sirens and we all broke out running again. There were six or seven of us, and we decided to break off in pairs running in different directions. I was struggling to keep up with Tyrone and his friend, but we made it back to his house. The other boys ran to their respective homes, and called Tyrone to let him know they made it. I was scared to death, with all sorts of thoughts running through my head about what could have happened to me.

The thought of getting shot or being locked behind bars being told when to eat, when to sleep gave me reason to pause. This was the second time in my life where I experienced and felt guilt and anxiety involving criminal activity. The first time is when I shoplifted years earlier. After that incident, I started to back away from Tyrone.

I also began to hang with one of his friends, who also questioned the nature of his relationship with Tyrone after that night. As it became more apparent to Tyrone that I was distancing myself, he became upset and angry with me. It was about this time that my sister and I began to wear out our welcome with the teenage daughters of Big Babe and Strut. Both of them liked my sister and I right out the gate, and showed some measure of favoritism towards us. We were always respectful towards them, whereby their daughters would talk back and curse at them if they became upset. This situation led them to become jealous and resentful towards us.

After about a week of bickering and feuding, Big Frank and my mother had finally returned to retrieve us. They came just in time too. They had found a house for rent that required some work before our moving in. Although I was happy and relieved to be leaving, that feeling would be short lived once we arrived in Joliet.

We left Harvey late on a Friday afternoon and arrived in Joliet. When we pulled up in front of that house, my heart sank and my jaw hit the ground. In all actuality, the house should have been torn down. The house sat across the street from a housing project, and one of Big Franks sisters lived in a house next door. The house was unoccupied for months and the back yard area looked like a jungle.

We all got out of the car and proceeded to walk inside. The exterior of the house made the interior look like paradise in comparison. It had two bedrooms, a very small kitchen area, living and dining room. The walls had tattered and worn wallpaper and paint, the floor was uneven tilting off to the right. When we walked into the kitchen area, it had the most awful smell and when the property owner peeled a section of some tile back; the wall appeared to move. This place was infested with roaches.

I jumped back, and immediately went outside feeling as though I was about to throw up. As part of the move in arrangement, the property owner would pay for all materials if we performed the labor. Again, I was tasked to perform a great portion of the labor. I was upset to say the least that once again I had to participate in such a massive undertaking with no voice in the decision. We slept at Big Franks sister's house, whereby the reconstruction project would commence the following morning.

Strut worked at a chemical processing plant, and Big Frank asked him to bring a load of yellow sulfur with him. They planned to burn the yellow sulfur to bomb the house of roaches. Sulfur when burned, emits a poisonous gas quite deadly if inhaled. When Big Babe and Strut arrived Saturday morning, we began to drop aluminum pans full of sulfur in every room. I went downstairs to the basement, placed six pans down, and ignited them. As I ran upstairs to escape the plums of smoke, Strut had already ignited the pans upstairs. I tried to leave from a locked door that led outside from the basement area. The entire house was full of burning sulfur, and I began to cough and gasp for air.

My eyes were burning and tearing up so badly I could not see. To this day, I do not know how I did not end up dying in that house. Once I got upstairs, I could barely see daylight through the thick smoke as I moved toward it. I made it to the front door and once outside, leaned up against one of the banisters. Everyone was just standing around as though nothing was wrong. When some of the smoke cleared from my lungs, I could barely speak. I damn near lost my life due to ignorance and carelessness, and the fact that no one seemed to care made it all the worse. As the old saying goes that God looks out for children, old folks and fools as He most certainly saved my young foolish life that day.

Later that day, we started the job of ripping up the old linoleum and wallpaper. We installed door and window trim, painting the entire interior and exterior of the house, replaced floorboards, and laying new vinyl linoleum. We worked on that house almost two full weeks before we could move in to it. As I stated earlier, the back yard had been unkempt for months. There were weeds taller than I and after all the work I had already performed around the house, I was the sole one designated for yard detail. I was livid as Big Frank handed me a dull sickle blade threatening to whip my ass if I did not clear the backyard to his satisfaction.

He would periodically peer out of the kitchen window shouting out orders. Here I was cutting down brush, sweating with calluses forming on my palms while he was in the house in front of a fan. With every swipe of the blade, I cursed him as my blood boiled. I had cleared the tall brush and weeds in two days low enough to use a lawn mower. After doing all that work, Big Frank said nothing. He always had plenty to say in regards to being dissatisfied with the method and manner of my work. Why would I think it would be any different? No matter what I did, it was never good enough or fast enough. Little by little, as my hate for him grew, I became less and less fearful of him and his threats.

With only a few weeks left before the start of school, I had yet to make my way around the neighborhood to familiarize myself. My sister Monya, who was always such the social butterfly, met a family who lived across the street in one of the project housing units. Big John and Dot had a large family, with eight children ranging in ages from twenty-two to four. My sister became friendly with one of the older daughters Carolyn who had just turned eighteen. I went over to the house one day with my sister, and she introduced me to the family.

With five girls and three boys residing in one apartment, it was most always a ball of confusion. Upon entering the apartment, I heard several different arguments going on amongst the brood. Their mother Dot hollered upstairs was ordering them to cease their bickering. Two of the younger boys Kelvin and Delbert came running down first. Kelvin was a year younger than I was and Delbert was slightly over two years younger. They both slapped hands with me and were eager to show me around the hood. Before we stepped out the door, their sister Niece came down stairs. I just froze like a Popsicle as she proceeded to flash the prettiest smile I had ever seen. She was the same age as I, with smooth dark skin wearing blue shorts with a white blouse.

When she said hi to me, I do not know what came out of my mouth if anything. Niece was a junior varsity cheerleader for Joliet Central High School, the same school I would be attending. Her brothers grabbed me by the arm, and pulled me out of the house. I was totally taken with her, and was so grateful that my sister brought me to their apartment. Kelvin and his brother decided to show me where all the local hangouts were in the area. We walked over to another set of project housing units where the boys would go to shoot basketball.

Once we arrived, a few of their friends were there shooting around and with our numbers, we had enough to run a game of three on three. I was far from the greatest shooter in the world, but I made up for my lack of offense with my defense. Being I was larger than most of the boys, I would pretty much stay in the low post area riding the baseline to block shots if anyone attempted to drive the lane to the basket.

After we lost the game by a basket, one of the boys Khazai introduced himself. Khazai attended the same middle school as Kelvin and was a very well spoken young brother. He lived in one of the units where we played ball, and he decided to hang with us as the boys gave me the grand tour of the neighborhood. Khazai loved to talk; speaking on any and every subject, he thought he knew something about.

We walked around for a good three hours, and Khazai's mouth was running for at least two and half-hours. As we were returning towards home, I noticed several people hanging around the fence area in front of the unit Kelvin lived in. One of the boys had a large Afro, as he was holding a young woman in his arms. Kelvin immediately began to chime in on him making smart comments about how nappy his Afro was, and told the girl she had better watch out before she was cut by one of the naps. I did not realize that it was his older brother at the time, as I am trying to get him to stop snapping before he became angry.

The young girl just laughed, and we all just sat on the fence talking. Before long, there must have been more than twenty people on the fence, with music coming out of one of the bedroom windows occupied by Kelvin's sisters. There would be many such nights throughout the remainder of the summer on the fence line. I thought to myself how good a time I was having with my newfound friends and that life at that moment could not be any better.

CHAPTER SEVEN

The new school year was about to begin, and my mother and I went to the school for my enrollment. Joliet Central was one of four high schools in the city. The student population of J.C.H.S was over 2,600, comprising quite a mix of racial and ethnic groups. The vast majority of the students came from either poor or working middle class families. Of all the high schools I attended, it provided the best array and variety of classes available. Upon speaking to the junior class counselor, I had discovered that due to the types of courses I had taken previously, I essentially had enough credits to qualify for early graduation after I completed the first semester.

After hearing that news, I was on cloud nine! From the start of kindergarten, I had the consummate love/hate relationship when it came to the subject of school. I dreamed of the day I would walk down the aisle in my cap and gown, looking at the school from the rear view mirror of my life. I was now confronted with a new situation…what would I do with the rest of my life after high school?

Until that moment, I never really gave it much thought. As a kid, I never spent much time daydreaming about being an astronaut or President of the United States. I have always been pragmatic, looking at the more practical aspects of my life and my surroundings. The one thing I always dreamed of was having a family of my own that I could love and would love me in return. I loved my mother and my sisters without a doubt, but I felt somehow incomplete less than whole.

At the time, I did not love Big Frank or viewed him as a father figure. All I came to respect about him was his physical size and power over me. I vowed to myself that when I had a family of my own, things would be different. In my vision of what I desired for my future family, a house of chaos and discord would be left at the front door. In time I would find that the fantasies I fostered in my mind would be far different from the reality I would face.

The first day of school finally approached and I was a nervous wreck. The school was about nine or ten blocks away from the house. I left early to gauge how long it would take to walk the distance. The high school counselor placed me in a mixture of junior and senior courses. I had taken a combined physics and chemistry course where I met three boys who would later become friends of mine.

Jeff was a tall handsome brother who was the first I would meet. He wore his hair processed, combed back "Pretty Tony" style as we called it back in the day. Jeff was cool, and was popular amongst the junior class especially the girls. At the time, I wore my hair Afro style; I and one other brother in the senior class vied for having the largest Afro in school. He sat next to me and broke the ice by commenting on the size of my Fro. We then started to rank the girls in class classifying them as being ugly or cute. Greg and Larry sat in the row in front of us, and jumped in on the rating of the females as they entered the class.

Greg also wore an Afro, with black glasses and had a slight squeaking tone to his voice. He rather reminded me of the character Dwayne on the TV series "What's Happening". Larry was the number one class clown amongst us. He always wore a cap of some sort, and with a money back guarantee that at least once a week, Larry ended up being sent to the office for making wisecracks to one of his teachers. Jeff and I became lab partners, and we began to hang tight.

He lived about two blocks from me, so he and a few of the boys from around the way would walk to and from school every morning. Not one morning would go by without someone starting in by playing "the dozens". The rules of engagement in playing "the dozens" involved finding some character flaw about the person or their family member. Anything was fair game, as long as you kept it all in fun and sought not to disrespect anyone.

Because I played the dozens during my junior high school years, I was quite good at it. One of the strategies was that you did not provide any fuel or ammunition that could be used against you. I kept my family members names secret, decreasing the chances that one of the crew would find out and use the information against me. Jeff's mother was named Gloria, so as we would get close to school I would say, "Well, I guess I will be "glowing" to first period class".

The boys would start cracking up, but being I never told Jeff my mother's name, he did not have anything to snap back on me. One day, Jeff came over to the house to see me. My youngest sister Shay was only five but she was crazy about Jeff. When I went inside, he had Shay whisper my mother's name into his ear. The following morning on the way to school, a slight wind blew.

Jeff hollered out "Damn, it's mighty Brendy outside" and I just about lost it. The guys were just rolling in laughter because up until that time, no one had a means of getting at me. Jeff just laughed his ass off, grabbing me around my neck shaking my head. It felt good to have met a group of guys I could cut loose and be comfortable being myself.

I had taken an U.S. history class as one of my electives. Since history was one of my favorite subjects, I had no problem mustering up the motivation to do the homework assignments. Much of the material I was exposed to in previous history classes, so the class was easy for me. I scored high on almost every quiz and test, and just as I did with Mrs. Crawford's biology class, the teacher and I engaged in the volley of question and answer.

The students in the class gave me the nickname of "The Brain", and they would just sit there in awe, as I would correctly answer the questions the teacher posed. I eventually started tutoring some of the girls in class during my free period in the library. As my reputation began to spread, other students in different periods would come to me to check their homework assignments before turning them in.

The teacher began to notice that the overall averages of quiz and test scores among all of his students were rising. I was in the first history class he taught, so I would record the answers to every quiz and test. I would then modify a few of the answers and make two different sets of answers to pass on to the following classes. My ego was boosted somewhat that so many people would come to depend on me and I thought I was actually helping them to pass. I thought about how I felt when I saw my I.Q. score, and that many of the students I was helping to cheat on exams may have felt the same shame by bringing home poor grades to their parents.

I guess this was my way of self-justifying my actions. The history teacher had given us a test covering the Illinois State constitution and U.S. constitution. In order to qualify for graduation and receive their diplomas, all students must pass both sections before the end of their senior year. I knew the material cold, and sat ready to receive the test. Upon receiving the test that was a combination of multiple choices, true and false with a few essay questions, I completed both sections within a half-hour. After rechecking my test, I proceeded to jot down the answers to pass around to the members of the class. I would write the answers on a small piece of paper and being I sat right in the middle of the students, I was able to pass one set of answers to the right and left of me.

The rule was that each student would change at least one answer on his or her test. This would further reduce the possibility of the teacher catching on. The last two students who held the crib notes were responsible for passing them on to the next set of kids coming after our class ended. I noticed that the teacher periodically peered in my direction. One girl apparently could not make out one of the answers. She began to whisper to me, but the teacher was watching. I attempted to ignore her as I saw him rise from his desk. I pretended to review my test when he walked up behind me and said, "She wants to know the answer for question no. 8".

It was so quiet at that moment you could hear an ant cough. The teacher told the entire class that the previous test scores were invalid, and a retest would be given later. When the bell rang, every one left except for me. The teacher had asked me to stay, and questioned if I had been providing the cheat notes to other classes.

As he waited on a reply, he graded my exam. I had scored a 98%, he saw by the look on my face that I was guilty. He looked up at me, shaking his head. He said in all of his years teaching history, he had met some bright students. He truly marveled at my level of comprehension on the subject matter. He asked me what my punishment should be. I shrugged my shoulders and apologized for what I had done.

He dropped my test score by one letter grade and reassigned me to the advanced senior's history class for the following semester. I was grateful on one hand, because he could have rendered a far worse punishment, but I was afraid of being just an average student in the advanced class. I would no longer be "The Brain", just one of many brains.

The word had gotten around both the student body and some of the teachers about what I had done. I was a hero in the minds of the struggling students who I had helped, and at the same time scorned by those who considered themselves smarter than I was. I was just happy that I did not get into more serious trouble, and that my mother did not find out what I had done.

Being in classes with juniors and seniors, I did not have the opportunity to see Niece much. She had my heart in her hands, and I had a Jones for her in a major way. I used any and every excuse I could come up with to go over to her house. However, she had no interest in me at all. She was going with a teenaged boy who by today's standard considered as a thug or a roughneck. My first teenage love interest experience was getting ready to take an unexpected turn.

Jeff had just started going with one of the girls in our science class by the name of Stephanie. So one chilly afternoon on a recess break, the boys were hanging about talking trash as usual. Stephanie saw us, and proceeded to walk towards us with one of her friends. She introduced her friend around, and upon our introduction, I was frozen like a popsicle at the vision of beauty before my eyes. Anita was her name, a very attractive young girl with the pretty smile and the most gorgeous brown eyes. She was also a member of the junior class, and was quite active in both choir and theatre. I did not realize it at the time, but she told me she had kept an eye on me for quite some time. Her sister Bonita was in the same English literature class as mine.

Being she was already aware of my presence, I assume that I was a topic of conversation between herself and Bonita. We hit it right off, smiling and laughing at one another the entire time. My last class normally ended at 2:45pm, but I hung out at the library until she finished her drama class at 5:00pm. After she finished practice, she met me at the library and I walked her to her locker. She was seventeen years old, and I being the shy introverted fifteen-year-old boy, I was nervous as a turkey come Thanksgiving. This was the first time that I had been the true object of anyone's affection, and the fact that she was so pretty made it all the more better.

Just before arriving at her locker, she sat me down on a nearby window ledge to thank me for waiting after school for her. She wrapped her arms around my neck and proceeded to kiss me, and I just melted in her arms. Time stood still at that moment, and let's just says that I could not stand up for awhile due to my being aroused by Anita.

Anita and her sister lived across town with their grandmother in an area called the Hill, which was on the Far East side of town. The area was similar in makeup to the area we lived, comprised of a series of project housing and single-family homes where poor and lower middle-income blacks resided.

The people who lived on the Hill had a reputation for being tough and criminal minded. Her grandmother attended the church down the street from my house, and Anita would periodically come down to see me for a hot minute after Sunday service or bible study through the week.

Since we did not have a phone and I was too young to drive, the only time Anita and I spent together was during school. I had no clue about the power of female sensuality, but every time she came within 100 feet of me, I would shake like a leaf in a windstorm. I could not hear or see anything or anyone but her when we were together. I daydreamed about what life would be like with her, and the topic of sex developed during the course of one evening's conversation.

Anita left bible study a little early and drove down to my house to see me. I hopped in the van, and we drove back up the street to the church. We kissed as we always did, and began to caress one another. We stopped for a moment to come up for air, and Anita asked me if I loved her. I said yes, whereby she then asked if I wanted her. My naïveté caused me to pause for a second, but when I looked into her eyes, I knew then what she meant. I told of course I wanted her, and she gave me the biggest hug and the longest kiss.

She told me that she loved me, which was the first time we both declared our love. Being in the church parking lot, I felt a little uncomfortable talking about sex. I told her that I would not pressure her to have sex or to think that I was going with her for the expressed purpose. Most boys at the age of fifteen have had multiple sex partners, but I wanted it to be special with her.

She heard the sincerity in my statement, and at that moment, tears began to form in her eyes. I never could stand to see a woman cry. We just sat in the van hugging one another until her sister and grandmother came out. We kissed each other goodbye, and I walked back home. My stomach was flipping upside down the entire way home. The following day at school, we saw one another, and it was as though we met each all over again for the first time. Living so far apart from one another was a good thing. For I knew that with the feelings we had for each other, any sexual encounter would be both frequent and explosive.

The emotion of love and my ability to express it has been an issue I have had difficulty dealing with most of my life. I viewed love as being like a priceless gem, something I could not afford to have in my life. I saw love from a perspective of weakness or a weapon one could use to control or over power. In my opinion, love was like kryptonite; I was reluctant to give someone such power to control this superman. When I looked around at those I had come to love in my life such as my first stepfather Calvin, Grandpa Will and my uncle Skip, each of whom betrayed my trust; love was no friend of mine.

When Anita asked me if I loved her, extreme anxiety came upon me. I nervously replied with a yes as we proceeded to kiss again. At that moment, I thought back to the love I had and lost when my Grandma Suzy passed away. I linked my ability to love anyone to my ability to trust and by nature, I am very cautious, gaining my trust never came easy. Trust comes in many forms, whether shaped in the form of spoken words, or in the shape of person actions. Many have lied to me both male and female alike, but the lies from the lips of a female would be the ones that affected me the most.

Winter was coming upon us, and the cold winds of hard times always seemed to blow in about the same time every year. Big Frank began to travel again in search of another payday and we ended up on the welfare roll once again. The winter winds also blew in a blast from our past that would stop for a lengthy visit.

Early one Saturday morning, I was awakened to knocking on the front door. As I rose up to answer it, I peered out the window and could not recognize who it was. I called out to my mother and Big Frank and both came to the door. When they opened it, my Uncle Skip rose up his head with a weak grin and staggered into the door. Big Frank had to hold him up, and both he and my mother walked Skip over to the sofa I was sleeping on. Until that moment, I had seen Big Frank come close to crying one time before. He had tears forming up in his eyes, as well as my mother. Skip looked terrible, his face was sullen and he would periodically wince in pain.

His clothes were filthy, and his skin was two shades darker than normal from the dirt covering him. Big Frank went into the kitchen to make him some coffee and something to eat, while my mother helped him to the bathroom to be cleaned up. He was serving time in a Michigan minimum-security prison having injured himself during his escape. As he had done years earlier when he had gotten himself into trouble, he turned to my mother for help. At that moment, I unconsciously wiped my ill feelings and memories clean that I had harbored against my Uncle Skip.

I considered him as part of the family again, with the love and trust that I had within to give. The wound on his leg was badly infected whereby he was immediately driven to the hospital. He was kept several weeks and my mother and Big Frank would go and check up on him daily. During that time, my uncle met a nurse there by the name of Bonnie. I am quite sure that he used his usual nickel slick smooth rap to bring her into his confidence. Upon his being released from the hospital, she brought him home. Although he looked 100% better than he did upon his first arrival, he was still thinner than normal.

Over the next few months, he began to regain his strength and increase his weight. It had been over three years since we last saw Skip, and it felt good to have him around. I had introduced him to my man Jeff, and my sister Monya was showing him off to her friend Carolyn across the street. Slowly but surely Skip was getting back into the mix of things. He started spending more and more time with his new girlfriend Bonnie. The one thing I did notice is that he did not mention his wife Gloria or his kids.

My uncle did have very many clothes, so he would wear some of my shirts. In time, his new girlfriend would buy him new outfits and he would drive over to the house in her car while she was at work. Uncle Skip was working the same tired game from his playbook again. Deep down, I knew he did not really care about Bonnie and I somewhat felt sad for her.

Besides Granny, I truly doubt that he loved anyone beside himself. All his life he spent his time and energy trying to run game or hustle on someone for what he could have gotten for himself, by himself. He never seemed to learn the lesson of life and retribution…that what goes around comes around.

Skip continued to repeat the same bad scene from the same sad play of his life's story repeatedly. He could not understand that every attempt he made to trick someone out of his or her possessions, he only ended up losing out himself. Nothing attained through ill-gotten gain will be retained for long. I too had to deal with a few chickens that were coming home to roost. As part of the agreement regarding my involvement with helping the students from the history class, I was transferred to the advanced level class.

The teacher Mr. Black was one of the most intelligent men I ever met. He took great pride in his profession who taught history with a very logical and objective point of view. No one dared come to his class unprepared, and he only dealt with historical facts not opinions. He welcomed me to his class and proceeded with his lecture. After class, he gave me the rundown on what he expected from me. My previous history teacher informed him about the incident that brought me to his class.

Mr. Black stated under no circumstances would he tolerate cheating or assisting students during exams. Mr. Black also informed me that as part of the overall grade, I would have to write a term paper. The term paper constituted 40% of the total grade. The rest of the class already had a head start, having provided an outline and weekly evidence of performing research by the way of turning in note cards. He also told me that he would be giving a comprehensive final, and suggested that I obtain class notes from his previous lectures from one of the other students.

As I listened to him, I truly underestimated how tough his class could be. I also knew that I had no alternative but to dance to the music I paid for through my actions. From that moment forward, I spent every free minute I had during the day at school library and at the public library on weekends. I had homework assignments to do in all of my other classes, and after I arrived home from school the bulk of my evenings were at the kitchen table.

I spent many a night having fallen asleep at the kitchen table with books all over the place. I did not realize it at the time, but the rigors of my predicament were going to prepare me for what I would later face in college. I decided on a topic comparing the democratic capitalist form of government practiced by the United States versus the communist socialist form of government practiced by the USSR. Why I chose that topic, to this day I have no clue. Nevertheless, this term paper was as difficult an undertaking I faced before entering college.

I was carrying two book bags the last two semester of high school. One contained my class textbooks; the other contained the books for my research paper. I had to leave earlier in the mornings and stayed after school until the library closed so I could not hang with the boys as much. My time with Anita was cut short, but we would spend some time at the library after her theatre practice. What measure of fun I had ceased to exist and I received an early lesson in life about paying the price for my actions.

I did not really have serious thoughts about going to college until one of the guys in my English literature class brought up the subject. Eric was in the senior class and lived across the Des Plaines River that separated the West Side of Joliet from the East Side. His parents were of Slavic descent, and he was a member of both the wrestling and football teams. He had already received a letter of intent from Southern Illinois at Carbondale. We would talk about his plans to go, what he should declare as his major, and he would try to convince me to apply for admission. He was always nice to me, telling me stories of how his Grandparents came to America and worked in the local steel and paper mills to provide a better life for their families.

His father and mother were so very proud of him, and he would be the first of their family to attend college. It was so important to him not to let his family down. When Eric brought up the subject of college, it was the first time I really gave any serious thought about it. I figured with my love for science, especially biology I would study cryogenics or biochemistry.

Joliet Central was a true reflection of America in that the student body was comprised of individuals from almost every economic, ethnic, racial, and religious class. With such a large and diversity student population, one would think there would have been conflicts abound.

Outside of the normal teenage scuffles, I do not recall one incident that was racially moti-vated. As an adult, I always wondered and marveled how well the administrative and teach-ing staff was able to maintain the peaceful environment at the school. Many students came to school from single parent run households; poverty and plight, bringing the same type of behaviors and situations many school systems continue to face today. The atmosphere at the high school was very calm and harmonious, in many ways reminiscent of life on a small col-lege campus. There were a few times the peace was disrupted, but all and all Joliet Central provided a great educational environment for learning.

As with most high schools, drugs and alcohol was a part of the experience students would meet at some point in time. There was a period where students would bring oranges injected with vodka or gin into class. I guess when the janitorial staff took notice of all the oranges tossed into trashcans reeking of alcohol; the principle banned citrus fruits from the campus. Angel Dust was the popular drug of choice, and I saw first hand the effects of it.

After my stint smoking weed while in Harvey, I chose not to smoke but I would periodically drink beer or some cheap wine. One teen in the neighborhood, Tyrone had a reputation for having the best weed around. During the occasional meetings with Tyrone, I do not recall one instance where he was not high. When Tyrone would come to class, he just sat in the back of the room with his eyes glazed over like a dozen Dunkin Donuts. He always walked around in a daze, with a smile not having a care in the world. Tyrone would sometimes break out laughing for no apparent reason, or began to converse with himself.

When he would get a little out of hand, some of the guys from around the way would talk him down and convince him to chill out or to go home. One morning in physics class, we all noticed that Tyrone was not sitting in his usual seat. We began to wonder where he was, Jeff had come into class and proceeded to tell us the tale. Tyrone had tripped out after smoking a joint laced with Angel Dust. The paramedics had come to his mother's home to take him away in a straightjacket.

From that point, no one heard about Tyrone ever again. I became worried for my man Jeff, because I knew he smoked weed on a regular basis. I would go over to Jeff's house and we would sit around drinking beer and listening to music. There was very few times, where Jeff did not fire up a joint, and we would engage in discussion to solve all the worlds' problems. After Tyrone's incident, I ask Jeff if he was afraid that he might get hold of some altered weed.

Jeff was in full confidence that he would never get caught up like that; because he knew the man, he bought his supply. I just asked him to be careful, because I wanted him to be around to become the high priced attorney he dreamed of becoming. The end of the school year was coming close, and I was beginning to savor the sweet smell of success. I was working hard to raise my grade point average before graduating from high school. The many late night sessions at the kitchen table were taking a toll on me, and I began to lose my appetite. I started to lose weight and since I was not trying, I viewed the stress and the pressure as a great way to drop the excess fat I was carrying.

A couple of months before graduation, an incident occurred between my Uncle and I that once again destroyed the relationship, love and trust I had with him. My relationship with Big Frank was already tenuous, and I would avoid speaking to him to prevent any opportunity for drama. At the time, I can say that I hated him. I hated him for putting us in the financial situation we lived under for years. I hated him for always having something demeaning to say in my regard. I hated him for continually uprooting us in search of his dream that always ended up being a living nightmare for us. I voiced my opinions and displeasure's about Big Frank to my Uncle Skip one day in what I thought was a private conversation.

While I was at school, Skip had come over to get some of his things and to tell my mother that Bonnie was pregnant with his child. I was unaware as to how I came up in the discussion, but he told Big Frank how much I hated and despised him. I had a great day before coming home, but when I stepped in the door, all hell broke loose.

As I stepped in the door, Big Frank asked me if I made the statements. I was stunned at first; for I knew Skip had run his mouth yet again. When I replied yes, Big Frank unloaded with a barrage of angry statements about my being fat, lazy and ungrateful. He also went on to run down a list of all the things he had done on my behalf. At that point, I do not recall what else came from his mouth, for it did not matter to me.

I began shouting back at him and said that the foundation of my hate was rooted in the very same behaviors towards me he was now displaying. I said that he was my mother's choice, not mine. I also said that just because he would buy food or some clothes that he was not entitled to treat me in any manner he so chose. I was sick and tired of the name-calling, tired of being put down, and tired of being the one who had to be understanding, forgoing my desires for material items.

At that moment, he stood up from his chair ready to hit me. In the past, I would have attempted to run away in fear of being hurt. There would be no more running for me that day. I stood right in the middle of the floor looking him dead in his eye. My eyes were filled with tears of anger streaming down my face. I was ready to die that day, but I would be damned if I backed down from him. As he approached, his entire facial expression changed, from either one of surprise or disbelief that I stood unmoved.

I did not know what to make of the change of his expression. It could have been the result that what I said had the ring of truth to it. On the other hand, perhaps he saw the look in my eyes of someone who no longer was afraid. Almost simultaneously, my mother jumped between us crying. I left the house and went across the street, as Kelvin was outside and heard all of the shouting. I was so angry I could not see or think straight. Kelvin told me to come with him and we walked until almost 11:00pm that night.

On the way, back we stopped by Jeff's house, and I told him and his mother what had happened. I did not know if I would be allowed back into the house, so I had asked if I could stay there that night. His mother Gloria gave me a hug and said it was okay, so I headed home to get my clothes. When I arrived back home to gather some of my things, he was away from the house. My mother was waiting for my return; I told her what I had planned to do. I really felt bad for her, and although I calmed down considerably, I still had no plans on staying in the same house with Big Frank. I redirected my anger towards my Uncle Skip, telling my mother that I never wanted to see him again.

He could lie dying in the middle of the street, and I would not lift one finger or expel one breath to help him. For the second time in my life, this man betrayed my trust in him. For the second time, I had to contend with another traumatic situation caused by his hand. For the second time he pushed the button on the drama bomb, I was the one left catch the shrapnel when he was nowhere to be found.

My mother always had the means of calming the monster within me; a voice of reason when the seas became choppy. She and Big Frank apparently had a long talk while I was away. I was unaware of the intimate details regarding the conversation they had about me. When he returned home, Big Frank just stared at me and walked into the bedroom. A few days had passed before we spoke to one another, but nothing else was said in regards to the incident.

Since childhood, I had always been a strong willed individual but I tended to bury my feelings and acquiesce to avoid conflict. As I grew older, instead of burying what I felt, I began to react immediately with anger if slighted or disrespected in any way. My silence had continued to be mistaken for timidity or weakness, and no longer was I willing to be either. Graduation was rapidly approaching, and both the pressure and excitement of finally getting out of high school was beginning to build. I finally put the final changes on the term paper I had been working on for history and studying for final exams.

I never really gave it much thought at the time, but I was on the verge of something great. To be a high school graduate at the ripe old age of fifteen was no small feat, and I would be the youngest member of the graduating class of 1978. My classmates were preparing for the high school senior prom and graduation ceremonies, but due to our lack of finances, I was unable to attend the prom. I did not let my disappointment show, but I really wanted to be there with Anita and dance my ass off.

I ended up making up some story to explain away my absence, but I was depressed about missing the celebration. The following Monday at school after the prom, my friends told me of the fun they had wishing I had been there with them. It was all I could do to contain my disappointment, but I managed to feign my excitement for them and the good times had by all.

It was a week before graduation, and a series of incidents were about to occur to disrupt the occasion. I had borrowed several books from the school library to write my term paper, and returned all but one of them. As I was placing the final touches on my paper, I inadvertently placed the book into my book bag with the rest of my class books. The librarian saw what I had done, and accused me of attempting to steal the book. I was taken to the vice-principal's office and my mother was called in.

Upon her arrival, I told her what the deal was. She went ballistic, telling the vice-principal and librarian that I was not a thief, and nothing was going to prevent me from walking down the aisle. After hearing the complete account, the vice-principal decided to squash the incident and allow me to graduate. I had labored long and hard, but I finally completed and turned in my term paper for history class.

The history teacher called me into his classroom, and stated that of all the term papers he had read that year, mine was far and above the best. Because I was a week late turning it in, he dropped my grade to a B+ from an A+. I did not care though, his opinion of the quality of my work counted far more than the actually grade I received from him. I thanked him for being patient with me, and for being so kind towards me under the circumstances by which I entered his classroom.

It was the weekend before my graduation; I had walked to the local barbershop in the neighborhood. My friend Jeff told me not to go there, because the barber was old and known to "jack up" heads. He said the moment the barber and his friends started to talk about baseball and coon dogs (beagles used to hunt raccoons) anyone sitting in the chair would be in trouble. As I stated before, I had the largest Afro in school. The graduation cap was too small to fit on my head, even after having my hair braided in cornrows. Therefore, I had to get it cut. As I sat down in the chair, I was very reluctant and told the barber not to mess my hair up. There was a baseball game on his black and white TV and his friends were playing checkers.

I closed my eyes and the clippers were going full bore, I did not want to see my hair hitting the floor. My ears began to perk up when the barber and his friends started to comment on the game and just like Jeff said, the conversation moved to coon dogs. By then, it was too late. The barber spun me around to the front to look in the mirror, and I went nuts. As I looked and stared, this fool transformed me into the character Larry from the Three Stooges!

My hair was cut low in the middle, with two larger tuffs of hair on the left and right. I was ready to kill him! I ranted and raved like a mad dog, and stomped out of the shop without paying him. As soon as I arrived home, my mom and my sisters just busted out laughing. There I was looking like a circus clown days before my graduation. I ended up having my haircut low close to the scalp. When I stepped into school the following Monday, it was as though the earth stood still. So many were accustomed to seeing me with my afro bouncing that I thought my friends were about to have a series of heart attacks. I hated that I had to abdicate my crown, but it did not matter for I was about to graduate.

I did not have a large selection of clothes in my closet, my mother embarked on trying to find a suit for me to wear. In the 1970s, polyester was king; and oh boy did my mother find a suit for me. It was a multi-plaid blue three-piece suit flare legged. If you were to have told me that I was not so fresh and so clean, you would have had a fight on your hands. The day I had been waiting for since kindergarten had finally arrived. Graduation day was on a Friday evening, and it was miserably hot. The senior class had to arrive two hours earlier in order to get the graduates arranged by alphabetical order. Oh boy was that comical!

Many of the students had consumed alcohol before coming to the school, and provided much in the way of comic relief from the searing heat of the afternoon sun. The school rented heavy wool graduation gowns. That someone did not pass out from heat exhaustion was a sheer wonder.

The graduation class of 1978 at Joliet Central High was in excess of seven hundred students; well over one hundred and twenty was ineligible to graduate. I felt more relief than excitement that finally after all of the years of struggle, ridicule, and angst I experienced attending school was over. I was somewhat disappointed that because of our frequent movement, I was ineligible to become a National Honors Student. However, the disappointment was short lived.

The graduation procession was finally starting to move into the auditorium. I had my own small cheering section that included my family, my friends from the junior class and my girlfriend Anita. Anyone who has graduated knows the pains of having to endure the many long-winded and boring speeches. The graduation ceremony started at 6:00pm, but the actual handing out of the diplomas did not happen until almost 8:00pm.

You can imagine how anxious a packed auditorium full of people sweating from the heat could be. When the superintendent finally spoke my name to rise to the stage, you would have thought I got there on wings. As he passed the diploma to my hands, I threw up my hands up as though I had won the heavyweight championship of the world and hollered out

"Mom, I did it"! My small cheerleading section was hollering from the upper balcony, and I skipped my happy self back down to my seat. After the ceremony, I went into the hallways milling around trying to find my family and friends.

My girlfriend Anita found me first, and laid a kiss on me that nearly caused me to pass out! There were many parties going on that evening but due to my age and lack of a driver's license, I spent my graduation night at home. About a week at went by, and one of my friends told me about a summer job work program sponsored by the local junior college. I signed up for the program, and had attended for a few weeks. The program was designed to align the worker in a field of interest to them, while attaining some job related experience.

At the time, I was interested in the field of biochemistry, so I was assigned to the biology department as a lab assistant. I was so excited and really looked forward to getting on the bus and making the long trip across town to the college. My excitement would soon turn to disappointment and disillusionment.

CHAPTER EIGHT

I had arrived at the college and proceeded to the biology lab to perform my duties feeding the various animals and reptiles in the supply room. After completing my work, one of the associate professors engaged in a conversation with me about my plans. I told him that I planned to attend college and study either biochemistry or cryogenics. He raised an eyebrow in astonishment.

I am still not sure whether he was shocked that I knew anything about either field. On the other hand, perhaps it was an expression of doubt about my ability to excel in either field of study. He then asked why I chose those particular fields, and I responded quite quickly "because I can make a lot of money". At that moment, he became somewhat more solemn and stated that if money was my motivation, and then I should be aware and face the realities of what I was about to embark upon.

The instructor told me that it would take at least eight years of college in order to obtain my Ph.D. More oft than not, I would be relegated to performing research for corporations under grant sponsorship, or the government. During the pursuit of my undergraduate and graduate degree programs, I would more or less become a flunky performing work assisting someone else achieve their own fame and notoriety. Regarding the aspect of money, I was told that based on the amount of the research grant supporting the project and after the expenses and salary of the lead researchers were paid, I might bring home $15-20K a year. After his comments, I was completely stunned and speechless. I had formed so many grandiose dreams about making millions of dollars discovering a way of using cryogenics to place humans in a state of suspended animation.

The breakthrough research of mine as I envisioned could one day enable humanity to reach the outer reaches of space. Alternatively, my research could possibly place a person with an incurable disease in cryogenic suspension until a cure was developed. I began to ponder the amount of time I spend to attain the degrees, and calculated the associated costs to obtain them. I viewed the long return on my investment of time and money as a deterrent.

I wanted to make as much money as fast and as quick as I possibly could. The idea of becoming a professor's flunky or gopher was not appealing to me either. I felt both dejected and disappointed as I pondered the professor's words on the bus trip home that afternoon. The courses I selected my last year of high school I chose to prepare me for my first year in college. I had not applied to any universities at the time, because I did not know where we would be living. So there I sat, with no direction, no idea or clue as to what I was now going to do with my life.

The excitement and luster of graduating high school quickly wore off. I began to worry about my future as to whether or not I was destined to live a life of poverty. I looked around the neighborhood in which we lived; saw first hand on a daily basis what despair and hopelessness could do to a person. The project-housing complex across the street contained several generations of families who were on public assistance. Some who lived there had jobs, but the wages made barely paid the rent. For so many people life was a never-ending struggle to survive.

I hated being poor, not having money to do simple things most teenagers were able to do. Due to the lack of money, I could not attend the senior prom. Due to the lack of money and my age, I missed all of the post graduation ceremonies. I could not even afford to take Anita out on a date because I did not have a job and we only had one vehicle, which Big Frank kept on the road trying to make ends meet. I was not totally unprepared for what I was told by the professor nor had a clue as to what I should do. In my mind, I was already living in a mansion with four cars with a wife and kids living the life of Riley.

With my dreams now smashed, I was at a complete loss as to what occupation I should now pursue. I never spoke of my plans to anyone. After the discussion with the professor, I was even more reluctant to speak about my feelings. I never took what I considered bad news very well, and was quick to internalize and personalize whatever came my way. When I think back to those times, I know now that I was depressed. To those on the outside looking in, I appeared happy and joyful. I was an emotional wreck inside, and I began to panic about a future that had yet to materialize.

About a month or so had passed since I graduated, and we prepared once again to move. When I found out where we were moving too, my heart sank. I became afraid and more depressed because we were moving across town to the area known as The Hill. My girlfriend Anita resided this same area with her sister and Grandmother. From the time we first moved to Joliet, I had heard so many stories about the Hill. I recalled my first impression about the area from a previous visit that we had taken to the area previously and it made the area we were currently living look like Shangri La.

Like so many impoverished areas, the area was full of houses that either was condemned or should have been. There were several project-housing complexes, and the neighborhood was replete with liquor stores or mom and pop establishments. As in most situations, these stores charged the people exorbitantly high prices for goods. The crime rate in the area was high, and the reputation of those who lived there was far from stellar.

Although I would be physically closer to Anita, that added benefit provided little comfort to my already troubled mind. I began to envision myself engaged in never ending series of mortal combat, having to fight every day for my very life. I began to start fashioning my game face, trying to look as hard, emotionless and fearless as I possibly could. Having lived on Joliet Street for a year was no picnic or paradise, but it was very different from where we were about to embark. We packed our belonging and made our move across town. As we began to unload, I recall how some of the neighbors in the adjacent units looked and stared.

I believed they were planning to rob or assault us so I put on an act for them. I picked up a large box, which had items that were light in weight, and placed the box on top of my shoulder to give the appearance of strength. I noticed a few young brothers sitting on a fence post directly across the street, and tossed my hand up at them. One of them, a teen by the nickname of Pookie, hollered, "What's up"? I stopped unloading for a moment, and proceeded to display my coolest "pimp" walk as I headed toward the group. To the casual observer, I must appear as though I had broken my leg but in my mind had to put on an act of cool and aloofness.

The age ranges of the teens ran from seventeen to twenty and goodness gracious were they comical! They liked me right out of the gate, and after my brief encounter, I made quite an impression. I went back to finish unloading, but I returned later that evening to continue with my conversation with the boys. I noticed that Pookie appeared to be the brunt of many jokes. He tried not to let it show, but I could see that the jokes truly bothered him. Pookie lived with his older sister and his niece because of their mother's death years earlier. His sister appeared to be overly protective, I later would understand why.

Although we lived on the Hill for only a few months, I was beginning to become increasingly apathetic and pessimistic about my future. I was becoming acclimated to the environment with the thought of participating in the so-called "fast" life that so many young black males are attracted. Growing up, I had been exposed to the trappings of what the "fast" life could provide by watching Big Frank and his associates plying their chosen professions.

After the conversation with the professor at the junior college, I could not envision myself spending eight or more years in college. All that I began to focus on was how I was going to make quick buck. The impatience of my youth was beginning to overtake my better judgment. As I began to get to know some of the brothers in the neighborhood, it was amazing how similar the story of their lives were. Most came from households ran by single females who were receiving public assistance. Many of their biological fathers abandoned them at birth. Most had little or no positive male influence in their lives outside of the occasions when their mothers had live in boyfriends.

Money was in short supply in many of these households. The lack of dividends played a major role by which some of these women decided to allow these males into their homes. I use the term male instead of men because in too many instances, the influences some of these males had on the children of the family were far from positive or manly.

Drugs, alcohol, physical and emotional abuse came into the household with some of the boyfriends as well. The number of boyfriends many of these women had produced additional children that were ultimately abandoned by the males who fathered them. Many of the mothers became apathetic and passive in providing the quality of parenting and guidance their children required. On too many occasions during my life have I heard people say, "I am grown, this is my life and I will do what I choose to do". The statement is correct and very true. Many exercise their freedom to choose without taking into consideration the short and long-term impact of their choices. How those choices may affect themselves or those within their circle of influence.

This cavalier type of attitude becomes the catalyst for much of the societal dysfunction that children bring into their adult lives. As with most species, the human female provides the nurturing and is the first teacher of a child. There is a direct connection between the quality of the parenting a child receives and the emotional stability of the child. The quality of guidance, instruction and rearing provided to a child during the early formative stages will affect the child's social development.

If the child receives love, nurturing and is taught to think logically and lives their life in a respectable manner, the chance for that child to grow into a well-adjusted stable minded adult is greatly enhanced. Such an adult will be capable of living and adapting to life in a civilized society. For the last two generations, there has been an increase in the number of children born to single females across all race and economic strata. The statistics bear out that in most circumstances, many of these mothers have not completed high school or in pursuit of higher education.

The children born are more than likely exposed to impoverished conditions, receive poor educational opportunities. The children are more prone to become involved with drugs, alcohol, and criminal activities. One cannot negate the value and importance of a child receiving the positive influence of having a father in their life.

It is very important, especially in providing the physical attributes and examples of true manhood whether the child is male or female. It is a given that you can only impart or share what you have come to know, thus you cannot give what you do not have. A female cannot teach a boy to become a man and in the converse, a male cannot teach a girl to become a woman. For those females who state they do not need a man, that may be true but if you have children, they most certainly do.

Having the ability to procreate does not equate to being a responsible parent. Far too many people engage in casual sexual encounters whether unprotected or not, without giving great thought and consideration to the possibility of creating a life. For no method of birth control is 100% fool proof it only reduces the chances of one becoming pregnant. Every instance whereby one engages in sexual activity increases the element of chance no matter how small, that a female can become pregnant. Not intending to become pregnant will not negate the potential to become pregnant. Biologically speaking, the female of the species was the gender chosen by the Creator to become the vessel for the creation of life.

The responsibility falls upon the female of the species to provide nourishment to both the body and mind of the child. This situation, as unfair or inequitable as some believe it to be nevertheless exists. Out of their resentment in being placed in such a position, some females choose to abdicate their parental responsibilities.

When there is a vacuum or absence of substance in the presence of need, it is the nature of man to seek a means of filling the void. You cannot count on nor miss what you never had to begin with. Some females may chose to harbor resentment towards their sexual partner who elects not to maintain a personal relationship with them. Being vile and verbally abusive will not force a male to step up to his responsibility as a father to care for the needs of the child. The fact that the relationship has ended does not exempt you as a mother from your responsibility to protect and raise your child.

Children who receive little or no moral guidance shall become misdirected adult menaces of society. Like a car without a driver, the child's life spins out of control into a downward spiral of hopelessness and despair. This contributes to the exponential growth in the level of social dysfunction, which breeds and plants the seeds of discontent both here in America and across the globe.

Children born to immature and irresponsible parents are more at risk in becoming such menaces. Some single females, out of guilt will attempt to compensate for the absence of a positive male role model for their children in a variety of ways. Some will use material items as a means of appeasing their guilt. No amount of toys, video games, clothes and shoes in the world are a substitute for the discipline, love and guidance every child needs in their life.

Out of this same guilt, others will abdicate their parental responsibilities and attempt to become their child's best friend. They place their child on an equivalent peer level of respect reserved for adults only. I have witnessed on too many occasions whereby five and six-year-old children dictate the terms and conditions of their behavior to their parent.

Some vowed to themselves in their youth that if they had children, they would not subject their kids to the same parental methods experienced during their youth. In the 1960's, many parents flocked towards the advice given by so called experts such as Dr. Spock, who advocated a more passive approach. The baby of the tried and true methods of parenting such as rewarding positive behavior or enacting consequences for negative behavior literally were thrown out of the window.

Some mothers choose to acquiesce to the pressure of parenthood by becoming their child's best friend. Therefore, some children can draw no distinction in the relationship with their parent versus those of their adolescent peer group. In time fostering such a belief, the child will lose respect for the parent. Viewing themselves as equals, some children elect to disobey and disregard the instructions given to them by other adults. They will become disrespectful of adults in general including those who occupy positions of authority.

When there are few or no boundaries of behavior established, the child is less capable in adjusting to external forces in their environment. Especially those experiences encountered whereby self control become necessary. In time, the same attitudes of "anything goes" displayed by their parents will be adopted by their offspring. Thus, the group opinion formed is disrespect towards others in public, which therefore becomes socially acceptable.

The discipline problems experienced within so many school systems on a daily basis stems from this mindset. This is because parents allow their children to conduct themselves in an unruly and disrespectful manner at home. Disrespect is a learned trait, not one that we are inherently born with. It is human nature to desire affection, attention, and love.

If you elect to have children, be prepared to be a parent for life. A child will have friends come and go during the course of their life, but each are only given one set of parent(s). Parents are responsible for teaching self respect and the respect of others to their offspring. This is one of the minimum basic requirements needed in order for an individual to become a productive member of a civilized society.

It is natural to attach to situations that are familiar to your own experience. To change your circumstance requires that the individual uses their conscience mind and expends the time and energy it takes to assess their condition. Due to the lack of emotional maturity and understanding inherent with being young, most of what a child can impart to another child is quite limited. It takes time to acquire knowledge, and wisdom is knowledge applied. Knowledge is power in any society. If you lack knowledge of self in addition to lacking in critical thinking skills, your ability to make quality decisions and choices becomes severely limited.

The woman who chooses to keep company with an abusive mate and becomes pregnant does not take into account the impact of her choice upon her own psyche and physical well being. More oft than not, the woman does not consider the present or future consequences of raising a child in such an unstable environment.

The same is true for men who through reckless or careless behavior engage in unprotected sexual activity with multiple sex partners. They do not consider the short or long-term impact of their actions upon the women they sleep with, or the children left behind. A man, who chooses to impregnate a woman addicted to drugs or alcohol, does not take into account the impact of her addiction upon their unborn child.

The ability for an individual to assess their situation and make determinations is important. To decide whether different choices are necessary to change their life's condition is key. The individual must be honest and true to self in order to determine if the unpleasant drama in their life is to be continued. To consider whether one should continue to practice that which no longer serves their ultimate purpose in life.

You cannot change what you do not acknowledge exists. I use a phrase quite frequently that if you want something different, choose something different. It is a very simple concept, but many choose not to place it into practice. It is because most human beings are resistant to change. When presented with issues or situations, which bring forth pain or discomfort, some individuals still may be reluctant to make the changes necessary to have a more positive outcome. To face the truth, review the facts and make the choices necessary to change their current life experience.

After a few limited conversations, I had begun to notice something about Pookie's behavior. I believe that he had some level of mental retardation or impeded emotional development as a child. I noticed how his sister's behavior towards him being very overprotective. She was very concerned about the company he kept, and I later understood why. I later found out that when Pookie was younger, a female in her 30s seduced him. His sexual involvement with the woman became common knowledge in the neighborhood, whereby some of their activities caused Pookie to become the brunt of many jokes.

I could tell that every time someone cracked a joke, it upset him no matter how hard he tried to hide it. If confronted with the same situation, very few teen-aged males would not take advantage in being the object of sexual affection from a woman. The fact that she was an adult who chose to take advantage of someone who lacked mental maturity spoke to the quality and caliber of the woman she was. She was already involved in a relationship with a man, but when he was away, she allowed Pookie to perform odd jobs for her. In lieu of paying him for his labor, she gave him sex.

In dealing with adults, a fair exchange is no robbery. To rob a child of its innocence, dignity and self-respect is a crime. Her actions were more than a statutory crime against the body, but of the mind and the soul. The years of ridicule, which Pookie experienced was a very high price to pay for his youthful indiscretion. I am sure that the situation would have been handled differently had his mother or father had been around.

Sometimes in the game of life, you must play the game with the cards you are dealt. Due to circumstances beyond her control, the cards his sister turned up in life placed the burden and responsibility for the care of her brother upon her shoulders. Lacking knowledge in regards to Pookie's extracurricular activities and her lack of parental skills limited her ability to prevent the incident.

I paid a visit to Pookie and his sister one Saturday afternoon to use their telephone to call Anita to let her know where I was. Her grandmother picked up the telephone and told me she was in the shower and she would have her call me back. I never received the telephone call and thus never spoke to Anita again. She was very talented in many ways I sometimes wonder what became of her and how her life turned out.

The same afternoon, Big Frank returned from one of his moneymaking ventures and informed us that we were moving back to Ohio. We were all overjoyed at the news, but none was more joyous than I was. To come back to familiar surrounding provided some measure of comfort to me. So on a late Thursday afternoon, we loaded up our belongings and headed back to Mansfield.

Upon our arrival, one of things my sister Monya and I did was track down her father. It had been over two years since we had seen him, and both of us were anxious to see him. My sister and I proceeded to walk over to his apartment for a visit, and he was very surprised to see us. Calvin almost started to cry when he came to the door. He had changed a lot since we last saw him. He stopped drinking heavily and lost several teeth, in addition to losing some weight. We did not have a place to stay when we arrived back in town, so we ended up staying with him for a few weeks.

We spent the time getting to know one another again and it felt great. My sister and I also started getting around finding old friends of ours that we had not seen for years. We ran into one of her old boyfriends from middle school, and started to hang out with him. He would get his older brother to buy us some cheap wine or beer, and we would drive to one of the local parks and shoot ball, play cards, or just shoot the breeze.

My mother and Big Frank had found a duplex for rent. For the first time, we were able to move into a house without having to perform any major remodeling or painting. The fall season was upon us, and I still had no clue as to what I was going to do with my life. Calvin had a friend whose daughter worked at the local J.C. Penney's store, and was able to get me a part time job.

Christmas was just around the corner, I wanted to earn money to buy presents for my family. I started out working both as a janitor and stock boy in the men's clothing department. I remember on the first day I reported to work and my goodness, the stockroom looked as though a major explosion occurred. I worked ten hours straight for two consecutive days restocking the shelves and returning the stockroom to order. I also performed an inventory for the department manager. To make some extra money, I also came in early to clean the store and buff the floors.

One of the first things I purchased was a stereo for my room. I was so proud of myself; it was the first major purchase I ever made. Although it was of cheap quality, it was a precious as solid gold as far as I was concerned. I also used the money I earned to buy Christmas presents for my family, and I used a portion of it to take driving lessons. I failed to get my drivers license while I was in high school, and was tired of having to walk or take the bus to get where I wanted to go. Upon receiving my license, Big Frank bought me a used car as part of a late graduation gift and peace offering. It was a 1969 Buick Electra 225, known on the street as a deuce and a quarter. The car was so big; it could seat fifty people and got about ten gallons to the mile.

I was so happy and proud of my car, and almost of the money I had earned went towards maintaining and paying the insurance on it. After the holiday shopping season was over; I was later transferred to the auto center. I really enjoyed working there. The mechanics and the sales representatives were great guys to work with. Little did I know how labor intensive the requirements of the job would involve.

I had to keep the garage area clean, clean the show room floor, stock shelves, assist with the inventory, and pump gas. I recall coming in one morning to mop and buff the floors and in my haste, I did not pay attention to a display sign behind me. I back into it, tripped slipped and fell to the floor. During my fall, I lost control of the buffing machine and as it spun out of control, it knocked several rows of items onto the floor.

A few of the mechanics were in the break room and heard the commotion; they ran inside to see my laying on the floor covered with canisters of gas treatment, car wax and a few other items. They stood in the middle of the floor just busting up laughing, and all I could do was laugh to. Rick, who was the manager of the auto center, was a bona fide jackass. He turned beet red and proceeded to start cussing and shouting at me. He would not dare to give the mechanics such grief and beef. He treated the sales representatives and me quite badly at times. I would have lost my job had it not been for the roaring laughter of the guys because of my clumsiness.

There was one fringe benefit to working at a garage, I was able to get my car repaired at a discount and J.C. Penney received quite a bit of my small check. As the cold of winter became bitter, I began to dislike my job. The luster had worn off, and my patience in dealing with Rick and some of the customers I encountered wore just as thin. I recall one cold morning when the temperature dipped far below zero, so cold that my car would not start. I proceeded to walk to work, which was about three miles from where I lived. As soon as I arrived, I became sick to the stomach from a mild case of exposure. Other than the service manager and me, no one else had showed up.

As soon as one of the mechanics came in, the service manager drove me home. I was out for two days and upon my return, Rick had some measure of an attitude because he had to go out into the cold and pump gas. I told him that my life was worth far more than the minimum wage he paid me. He could choose to stay pissed at me or could choose to get a grip upon himself.

Oh boy, the little beet faced wonder became very angry but I did not care. Later that morning I became involved in a verbal altercation with a customer. An elderly man and his wife pulled up to the gas pump wanting a fill up. It was a very cold morning as he passed me his store credit card, which bowed in the middle.

As I ran the press over the card, the cold temperature caused the card to become brittle and it snapped in two. I approached the man to return his card and to offer my apology. I informed him that he could get a replacement card at the customer service office in the main store. Before I could finish my statement, he proceeded to cuss me and called me a dumb black "nigger".

I was in a state of shock and was not sure what my ears were receiving. As he repeated the statement, several more times I had enough. I went into a rage and began to "go off" on him verbally. If it were not for the fact that his wife was present, I would have probably pull him out of the car and beat the old man down. I told him that his wife saved his life, and that he had better drive off before I forget my manners about respecting my elders. He sped off to the main store and about two hours later, here come the general manager and the human resources supervisor.

The general manager came stomping across the parking lot ready to kill, set to fire me on the spot. I was egging for confrontation at this point, still steaming from what the old man said to me. As he began to go into his tirade about treating the customer with respect and the customer is always right speech; I stopped him mid sentence.

I proceeded to tell them about the incident and of the subsequent racial slur spoken by the old man. I told them that they could not pay me enough to take that type of verbal abuse from anyone, let alone at a minimum wage. I stated that if they planned to fire me, then I quit. After I repeated the statements that led to my reaction, everyone was silent. The human resource manager stated that under the circumstances, she understood my reaction. At the time, I was one of only two African Americans who worked at the auto center. This was not the first time I was called a "nigger", but this experience changed my perception regarding respect and race.

As with most children growing up, we are taught to blindly respect our elders and those of authority no matter what color they are. I recalled the incident with the English teacher in Alabama who attempted to abuse his power and authority over me. Self-respect or lack of therein, is a quality of character acquired through learned behavior. Without it, it is impossible to garner respect for anything or anyone.

Respect, as with trust, are virtues not given purely based upon the age, color, economic status, or title of the individual at hand. We all deserve, due to the nature of our shared spiritual lineage and linkage to the divine power and glory of God, humane respect. We as the chosen caretakers of this planet should respect life in all manner of form, to creatures large and small. Anything beyond this, requires that one earn another's respect through the result of one's deeds or actions. There are varying degrees and criterion by which a person can be measured which garner respect.

You can come to respect a person's word, intellect, physical prowess, wisdom, knowledge; etc. This is a show and tell world where the words spoken or actions displayed are not necessarily reflective of the true nature of the person speaking them. In time, the truth will reveal whether or not individual intentions are genuine, worthy and deserving of respect. You can profess being the greatest basketball player on the planet. Saying so does not make it so for one must first step onto the court willing to put their skills to the test. Until then, all that truly exists is an unproven theory based upon empty rhetoric.

Humanity has and continues to base the issuance of respect upon the amount of power or money a person has. In most cases, the respect of a nation rises in direct portion to its willingness to use brute force. To use its military power and supremacy for the express purpose to control or acquire material wealth or precious resources. The human race has wrestled and continues to wrestle with many fear-based issues in regards to race, sex, class, and religion for thousands of years.

Humanity has progressed and has made much in the way of technological advancement and progress. In spite of these advancements, man has yet to attain greater spiritual enlightenment much beyond our current state of existence. We continue in the same downwardly spiral behavioral patterns, which minimize our collective spirit and social development. Through advances in technology, man has created smart bombs, but still miss the target when it comes resolving the many social ills which plague this planet. Technology can send probes to outer space, but humans will not muster the resolve to end world hunger within our own living space.

In this age of information, humanity has collected and stored enough data to fill the library of Congress 10 million times hence. With all of this acquired knowledge at our disposal, not much has truly changed. Billions of people are functionally illiterate and uneducated. Still billions more exist in a state of blissful ignorance, hopelessness and despair. As the saying goes, the most dangerous person in the world is the person who has nothing to lose. There are billions of people on this planet with this self-destructive state of mind. Many believe that the only way they can survive is to kill, steal or wreck havoc and destruction upon another.

It is this state of mind, which perpetuates the bloodshed, and loss of life in the Middle East all in the name of God. The warring factions justify their killing one another over the claims to the so-called holy ground of Jerusalem and West Bank region. Each side touts their religious beliefs as an end to justify the means, which is in my opinion, the greatest of hypocrisies ever spoken. Those who stand up in church on Sunday, the synagogue or the mosques on Friday praising the glory of God on one hand and preaching hate and divisive rhetoric with the other perpetrates the greatest of frauds.

Man has superimposed its own neurosis and psychosis upon the Lord, espousing that God is an angry and vengeful being. Some still teach that the Creator is a narcissistic, vain and jealous God. Some still preach the false message that those who fail to praise Him is destined to fall into the fiery pits of hell. I never have or never will buy into that description or belief about God.

In the heavenly realm where God resides, love is absolute and flows eternally from Him. " He that loveth not knoweth not God; for God is love. There is no fear in love but perfect love casteth out fear because fear has torment. He that feareth is not made "perfect in love" (I Johns 4:8,18).

Everything in this universe came into being at the result of God's Divine nature. God needs nothing from man, for the Creator already has ownership of all that exists. That includes our love or our hate, our worship of Him, burnt offerings or sacrifices.

From the subatomic to the atomic, from the organic to the inorganic, the essence of God is ever present. From the Creationist beliefs contained in Genesis to the hypothesis contained within Darwin's Theory of Evolution are the answers to the origin of man. Is it more important to know from which we came, or is it more important to know where we will end up?

No one religion has exclusive rights to God for the Creator loves all of His children saint and sinner alike. The words of the Torah, Quran and the Bible were created to benefit the lives harvested from the seeds of Abraham. Each belief system contains the common thread of truth that we are to love one another, as we love God and ourselves. The human race has yet to embrace and celebrate our similarities. We are not yet willing to address the needs of those that are less fortunate; to truly place our faith where our mouths are to love and become our brother and sisters keeper.

Our mind, body and spirit contain the same matter found in the universe and science has proven that we share 97% of the same genetic code with the flora and fauna on the planet. With this being the case, it becomes a matter of acknowledging that the human race came from the same cosmic dust, created from the same essence as the Creator. God's essence is contained within us whether in mind, body or spirit. One of the principles of physics is that matter is neither created nor destroyed; it merely changes. Water, no matter if it is in the form of a liquid, a gas or solid in the form of ice, the chemical composition is still H20.

Using the ocean as a metaphoric comparison of God, the ocean is both vast and deep. You cannot tell where it begins, or where it ends. It has the power to create life, sustain life and to take life. If you dip a glass into the sea, does it cease being water? The glass of seawater taken from the ocean is physically separate from it, but still is very much a part of the same whole.

Due to the difference in mass based upon the volume of water in the glass versus that contained by the ocean, one could not expect to pilot a ship in the glass. The properties and capabilities of the ocean can due to the power of the undercurrents, effect great changes in both the weather patterns and life both on land and under the sea. The water in the glass has the same properties as well, but the potential impact upon life is on a much smaller scale.

If man spent as much energy embracing our similarities as we do despising our differences, paradise on earth would be a reality again instead of a lost dream. There is no ground, brick, or mortar on Earth as precious and holy as the life the Creator placed upon this planet. Far too many people would rather sit idly by and ignore and in some cases, condone the senseless violence committed in this world. Society engages in justifiable homicide that is state sponsored or sanctioned by the government.

People attempt to draw a line of distinction between murders committed at the hands of an individual versus that perpetrated by a government agency. Death is death; killing is killing no matter who pulls the trigger. There are those who would rather fuel the flames of discontent or complain about the condition and plight of their lives than to put up a fight to change it. Life is not a fight or war to be waged in the physical sense, but in the intellectual and spiritual sense.

If those who engage in war, terrorism or other acts of violence would put their own selfish interests aside. If people of conscience were willing to lay down their weapons for the sake of their children's future, how much better off would their lives be? The human race could then begin the healing process and live together as civilized human beings.

It had taken me several days after the racial incident to calm down and diffuse my anger. At work, where I typically engaged in jovial conversation with the guys at the auto center, I became quiet and reserved. Although a few of them attempted to break the ice with me, I was unwilling to cast my anger aside.

I ultimately came around, but I still harbored some measure of anger. None of the men at the shop had caused me harm, but I unconsciously took my anger out on them. I later felt guilty at my behavior towards them, and I did apologize for my actions. I started to refocus my attention towards my plight as to what I would do with my life. I remember sitting up in my bedroom early one Saturday morning, staring at my stereo. I thought back to when I was about ten years old. We had an old black and white television set that had a bad picture tube. When the picture would fade out, I would take the back off of the set and jiggle the tube until the picture came back on.

This one particular occasion I had jiggled the picture tube; afterwards I received a jolt and was knocked back three feet. Picture tubes can carry more than 30,000 volts, so I was quite fortunate to have survived. I had also repaired several radios and small appliances with no more than a set of pliers and a screwdriver. The longer I stared at my stereo; it came to be that I should pursue to study electronics.

I spoke to my mother about it, and she thought it was a great idea. I had yet to take the SAT or ACT, so I began to fill out a slew of forms to apply for financial aid. I had taken the ACT on a Saturday, and applied to the electronics-engineering program at the local junior college. I was excited about the choice I had made and I was looking forward to attending the college to start the fall quarter.

Spring had finally made it and no one was happier about it than I was. I had purchased an eight-track player for the car and bought a set of tires for it. I was ready to start hitting the street looking for some action. Most of the people I knew were still in high school, and most of the older kids would hang out at one of the area parks.

I was too shy to approach girls and my being fat did not help my self-esteem. I would sometimes head up to one of the parks and play ball to work off some frustration and burn off some nervous energy. One day after I got off work, I went straight home instead of heading to the park. My mother told me that I had received a telephone call from the admissions office from the junior college; the message was that I was accepted.

I jumped for joy, but I also received an added bonus. The college had a job placement office, and inquired as to whether or not I would be interested in working for a telephone equipment refurbishing company in town. I was quite interested, and after a brief conversation over the phone, I was immediately hired.

I gave my two-week notice, the people at the garage pitched in, and had lunch catered in to send me off. Everyone pitched in; with the exception of the red faced wonder. I had come to gain respect from the men for my hard work, and I thanked them all for befriending me.

Although I would miss them, I did not miss dealing with the poor level of management and attitudes displayed by my superiors.

I had to attend a plant tour with several other students hired through the job placement the Friday before we were to report in for a first day of work. There were a total of eight of us hired, and for the next two years, we would become like family. The company refurbished various types of telephone equipment for several independent telecommunications companies.

The bulk of the employee workforce was comprised of middle-aged women, who performed much of the fine detailed work required to repair the defective products. Some of these women were real characters too. The shop opened at 5:00am and as soon as the doors opened, the factory sounded like a hen house with the chattering of the women in the shop. I was initially was placed as an apprentice lab technician repairing coin telephones and audible sound devices such as horns, chimes, etc. Jerry, who was the only other African American beside me in the entire factory, had taken me under his wing. Another great individual I had come to like and respect a great deal was Dave.

Dave was the technical director responsible for all of the technicians, and the few engineers employed by the company. In fact, the entire technical department had either already graduated or were attending the junior college. He was a funny guy, and so knowledgeable and intelligent in the field of electronics. Dave drove a beat up TR-7 convertible and his two favorite musical groups were the Bee Gees and the Village People. He played the soundtrack to "Saturday Night Fever" non-stop. We would sometimes tease him about his choice of music, and would imitate the sounds of the Bee Gees and spoof the dance routines as well.

He would turn red from laughing so hard and took our teasing all in stride. Of all of the individuals I had come to know at the factory, I was closest to three young men. Rick, Mike, Scott and I were partners in crime the entire two years we attended the junior college. Rick and Scott grew up in small rural areas located outside of my hometown, and Mike grew up in suburban Columbus Ohio.

Although there were a few black kids who attended the school system Mike went to, Rick and Scott exposure to the black experience was rather limited. I remember the first day on the job, and Rick started cracking jokes about some of the women on the line. Rick was of American and German ancestry, his father grew up in Kentucky and met Rick's mother while stationed in Germany. Rick's perspective lacked color and contrast when it came to issues of race resulting from the influence of his parental upbringing.

He was a great person, and was very willing to take the time to get to know me. Rick was dating Mike's sister, who was still in high school. Mike and Rick were looking for an apartment to avoid commuting the distance. We had a few months before college started, so we spent quite a bit of time together getting to know one another. The NBA draft of 1979 provided the backdrop for our first discussion on the issue of race. The two most prominent players of the 1979 draft were Larry Bird and Magic Johnston, selected by the Boston Celtics and Los Angeles Lakers respectively.

Those two teams were polar opposites and their respective fan base was reflective of the American society of the time. Most of white America was fans of the Celtics, and blacks supported the Lakers. The media hype at the time constantly compared the two players and the two NBA franchises they played for. Both would later make NBA history through their display of amazing talent. During a lunch break one of the men at the table posed a question as to which of the two were the best players.

Jerry and I were the lone supporters of Magic Johnston, and the rest chose Larry Bird. I asked them by what measure did they based their decision upon, being the consummate "devils advocate" that I am. A few touted his collegiate achievements on the court, and spoke about the rich championship history of the Boston franchise. I said I can agree with his measure of talent, but the number of championship banners, which were already hanging in the rafters of the Boston Garden, had nothing to do with the question I posed. I ask them that being Michigan State did win the national championship, if I was to use their logic and rational that by their standards Magic was the better player. Rick then stated, "You are only saying that because he is black".

I looked at Jerry who rolled his eyes up towards the ceiling and started to rub his forehead. I then continued with my argument. I asked Rick to name a few players from the Celtic roster of the time and some previous players. He began to rack off names such as Kevin McHale, Bob Cousy, and John Havlicek and then he paused trying to think of a few others.

As he pondered, I knew I had Rick hooked like a trout. I asked Rick why he could not readily think of any other great Celtics basketball players. I said what about Bill Russell, KC Jones or JoJo White? Could it be he had trouble coming up with names of non white players and thought that Larry Bird was the better player because he was white? Everyone sat silent as Rick immediately went on the defensive. "Oh no, no I don't like him just because he's white" Rick said as he turned red and tried to back peddle his way out of his previous statement. Jerry and I just busted out laughing and I said that I believed his statement as much as I do in the tooth fairy and Santa Claus.

Jerry made an observation as to how the media characterized Larry Bird as a floor general a thinking man's type of ball player. Magic Johnston portrayal by the media at the time as a player with great speed and athletic skills. I did not know exactly what he meant at first or where he was heading in his comment. Jerry provided a clear example of how race colors the perspective of those belonging to the majority population in this nation. He posed the question to Rick as to what he thought of the press statements.

"So, does that mean that Magic Johnston lacks the ability to think? If so, how could a non-thinking man only equipped with physical skills and quick feet win the NCAA national championship? Rick was silent. Jerry got up from the table, saying "Think about it", and went back to work. For probably the first time in his life, Rick was face to face with his own prejudicial opinions about race.

I could tell that Rick was somewhat embarrassed about the situation. As with so many things, the game of life will provide you a different game plan to assist you in your personal growth. Sometimes the light of a person's knowledge is dim or burned out. A more enlightened external source is sometimes required to bring one out of the darkness of ignorance into the light of awareness. After that incident, I noticed that Rick and some of the other folks began to ask my opinion on many questions relating to race. At times, I would become a reluctant spokesperson for the entire African American race. But I did not mind, because I saw that they truly want to know more about my culture to gain a greater understanding that they otherwise would not receive.

CHAPTER NINE

Summer was ending and we were becoming anxious about starting college the following week. Big Tony was one of the engineers who previously graduated from junior college the year prior was preparing us for what we would face. He would sit down with us during our lunch or breaks and tell us about some of the courses we would take and clue us into the personalities of the instructors who taught the courses.

We all would come to depend on Big Tony to help us with our homework and lab assignments, and he was always willing to lend a helping hand. Monday had finally rolled around, and we all had to go to the auditorium for orientation. We then proceeded to our first class, which was a basic course on electricity.

Mr. Grass was a tall middle-aged man from Georgia, and spoke with a thick southern accent. He and two other men, Mr. Francil and Mr. Smincek comprised the electronics-engineering department. I would come to enjoy and respect these men a great deal, and much of the knowledge and wisdom I have today came through their patient efforts on my behalf.

The total number of students who enrolled in the day program was a little over forty students. By the end of the two-year session, only twenty students would survive the rigors of the engineering program. The junior college shared some of the building facilities with a satellite campus of one of the major state universities in Ohio. As the week progressed, we all were overwhelmed with the amount of homework we had to complete.

Rick, Mike, Scott and I would walk over to the library between classes and get a head start on our assignments. I noticed that in transit to the library, the bulk of the students who attended the satellite campus were hanging out either at the student lounge, or outside engaging in various activities.

There was an unspoken measure of rivalry and animosity between the two college campuses. Those who attended the satellite campus looked down upon the junior college student body. At times, they would make wise cracks about the junior college being a glorified vocational school for wayward youths that could not cut it at a major university.

Those who attended the junior college viewed the satellite campus as a glorified daycare center for teens. This was because some parents did not trust their ability to handle the unsupervised atmosphere present at the main campus. Mike and Scott commented about the load of homework we had. They wondered how those who attended the satellite campus had the time to play and hang out at the student lounge.

Rick hollered aloud, "It must be all of those tough courses they take, such as underwater basket weaving and archery". We all just broke out in laughter. After a few weeks, we had several students drop out. I stated that the electronics program would separate the mice from the men. I also said that if anyone of us were to think about quitting, that everyone else was to make a cheese sandwich and give the person the sandwich as well as a measure of hell about quitting.

I was really struggling early on; my study habits were non-existent after taking a year off from school before enrolling. My old nemesis, mathematics posed problems for me. This also affected my performance in some of the other courses I enrolled in involving math. Mr. Hoffman taught the math class, and shared duties as well teaching physics with another instructor, Mr. Noser. Mr. Hoffman had a daughter who also attended the junior college enrolled in the same engineering program as I. She was a tall attractive young blond woman very bright and well educated, whom was hired by the same company I worked for part time.

She lacked a measure of common sense and the ability to see things from an abstract point of view. As part of the core curriculum, most of the electronics courses included components of both in class and hands on learning in a lab environment. Where I struggled with the bookwork, I excelled in performing most of the lab project assignments. I teamed up with her sometimes in the lab, whereby I could lend a hand to her and she could help me with my math. The lab assignments were my redeeming qualities in addition my performance in the non-core curriculum such as technical writing, psychology, etc.

I had a passion for coming up with nicknames, so one by one I came up with nicknames for all of our instructors. We had T. Grass; Mr. Goetz a.k.a. "Mr. Jingle Ling", who taught psychology, Joe No, Andy Ho, Sminey, and Mr. Francil's nickname, was Bugging Out. When Mr. Francil became excited or upset, his eyes would bulge out and sometimes he would pull at his hair, hence his nickname.

I was amazed at how quickly the nicknames caught on with our class and they stuck like glue. Bugging Out was a real cool instructor and the love for jazz music I came to enjoy was a result of taking his classes. He was very much a product of the sixties, his hair was long, and he usually kept it tied back with a rubber band and sported a long beard. During his labs, he would play either jazz or reggae music on this beat up tape recorder he had repaired years prior. Most of the students did not care for the brand of music much, being fans of either rock and roll or country western.

He would play Miles Davis, Charlie Parker, Thelonius Monk, Dizzy Gillespie, but he was a big fan of Bob Marley. I really got lost into the smooth flow and grooves of the music, and time appeared to past by so quickly during his lab classes. Sminey was a laid back individual as well with a very pragmatic view to his approach at life and in his teaching methods.

Although we used textbooks, Sminey stressed the importance of being able to look at problems from many angles, and to think "outside of the box".

One method he used to assist us in this area was to take an electronic circuit board or device and either remove or insert a few defective parts. As part of our lab assignment projects, we had to repair the defective item using a methodical and logical systematic approach by first looking for and removing the obvious possibilities.

Through the process of elimination, the root cause of the problem could therefore be determined. I am not a detective, but I am sure that Sherlock Holmes used a similar approach to solve crimes. I recall during a course I had taken during the second year of the program, which we had to build a circuit board from scratch. The class had used the same circuit design layout, but the depiction of the drawing was flawed.

Consequently, when the class attempted to construct the circuit as depicted, the type of transistor used to power the OP Amp chip produced too much current causing the chip to burn up. We burned up every chip in the supply room, and then went out and bought up every chip in the surrounding area and ended up smoking them as well.

Sminey went ballistic, not because we burned up the chips but because we did not use our abilities to think and look for a different resolution. It became obvious after the second occurrence, common sense dictates that if the design we used is causing continued failure, one should try another approach. He then posed the question as to what other options we had at our disposal. One of the guys suggested that the class use a different type of transistor that operated within the design limits of the OP Amp.

At that moment, everyone else in the class felt dumber than a box of rocks. The suggestion worked, and taught me the life lesson that just because information is contained within a book, does not make it accurate or true. Moreover, if what you have done in the past does not work try something different. It is incumbent upon the individual to seek out information from different sources, verify the validity of the information presented, and when in doubt, check it out.

It was a very taxing and stressful time for me, going to school fulltime as I worked minimum of thirty hours a week. For the entire two year period, I saw very little of my family. I would leave the house at 5:30am work for two hours then drive to college for an 8:00am class. Depending on the day, class did not end until 5:00, whereby I would leave heading back to work until 9:00 or 10:00pm.

I would then drive over to Rick and Mikes place, where we all would do our homework or study for a test until 1:00 or 2:00am. I would then head home; get two hours of sleep, and start the party all over again. On the weekends, we had to put in a minimum of eight hours but typically worked ten to twelve depending on how many orders we had to fulfill. In spite of the very grueling schedule I kept, I really enjoyed and was proud of myself for the choice I made in going to college.

Finals were coming up and the pressure was affecting us all. The Christmas break was approaching and the telephone refurbishing company we worked for was feverishly trying to fulfill its commitments to its customers before the two-week shutdown period. Trying to study and prepare for the exams in the midst of this situation caused tempers to flare, mine included. I had not taken a break from the action since the fall quarter started, and an opportunity to have some fun presented itself to me.

My sister's boyfriend Jerry told me about a Parliament Funkadelic concert held in Columbus and I gave him money to buy tickets for us. On the day of the concert, a big snowstorm hit the area and it snowed all day long. I went to work that morning all pumped up about attending the concert. The building I worked in did not have windows, so I was unaware as to how much snow had fallen. Earlier that morning, I noticed that my car was running hot and I had planned to drive to the concert. After I had gotten home from work, I ran inside to shower and change clothes.

I made some mention to Big Frank about the car running hot, and I told him that I had checked the radiator for coolant. My mother overheard my conversation and as I prepared to leave the house, she said that I would not be attending the concert. I went berserk, shouting that I had already spent my money on the tickets and was going. She said if I was to leave the house, not to come back. I threw my coat on the floor and stomped upstairs to my room fuming. She entered my room and said that since I displayed such an attitude, that she was taking the car away from me.

I then threw the car keys to her and angrily said that I did not give a damn and since she was going to take the car, I might as well quit school. When Monday morning arrived, I called the admissions office and informed them that I was dropping out. Big Frank dropped me off at work earlier that morning. When my friends came in, they asked why I did not attend class. I told them about the incident, and my decision to drop out of school. When the evening break approached, Scott, Rick and Mike had driven to a local grocery store.

They called me into the break room and each one of them handed me a cheese sandwich and proceeded to start squeaking like a mouse. They squeaked at me almost the entire time we were on the plant floor and no one knew but us what the real deal concerned. After we completed our shift, we all went back to the break room before they headed home to study for the finals. They each told me that I was making a mistake and to come back to college. Mike and Rick told me not to worry about getting back and forth, as they would take turns picking me up and taking me home.

So Rick said, "what excuse do you have now Mighty Mouse?" all I could do is laugh. They used my own words against me and removed any excuses from the table in order to convince me to go back to college. I decided to return and enrolled the following morning but dropped the Physics course to avoid getting a D. Once again, I had allowed my rage and anger to overcome my better judgment and common sense.

Out of my anger, I was ready and willing to throw my entire future away, without giving any thought as to what my future would consist of without receiving the education. For as much as I hated being impoverished, out of my angry reaction I was setting myself up for a dismal future living a life of more poverty. Through the grace of God, a previous statement I had made in jest to my friends was the very statement that placed me back on my life's path. Had it not been for Rick, Mike, and Scott teasing me in their comedic way, more than likely, my life would have ended up as so many young African American males. I probably would have gotten myself caught up in the system as another statistic or worse, dead.

Because of their care and concern about me, they prevented me from making the worse decision I could have ever made. I have often thought what my life would be like if my friends had not intervened and convinced me to have a change of mind. Since the deuce and a quarter was over ten years old and had excess of 100K miles; Big Frank decided to sell my car. I had said little to either my mother or Big Frank after the incident about the concert. After a few months went by, the situation diffused and things at home began to calm down.

Early one Saturday morning before I left for work, Big Frank called me into the kitchen to talk to me. As he typically would do, he was staring at the floor smoking a cigarette deep in thought. He then looked up at me and began to speak. He knew I did not like him much and he apologized for the way he treated me over the years. I sat down at the table next to him and continued to listen. He proceeded to say that the reason he was so tough and hard in my regard was that he was preparing me for what I would face in life.

Big Frank spoke about things he observed out in the world while trying to get some pay. He saw an increase in the number of cold hearted and scandalous people in the street he came across on a daily basis. He said that times were becoming harder and harsher on the boulevard than during the times he came up. The street game had changed, and that in the years to come people would face two choices. Individuals can choose to become either the lion or the lamb the hunter or the hunted. He spoke about how people appeared dead behind the eyes speaking bold face lies to get or to gain something they wanted and warned me to be aware of them.

He said place your trust in no one, unless proof is given that a person can be trusted. If someone proclaims to be Superman, then we should see evidence and traits similar to the man of steel. The person making the claim should be able to fly, bounce bullets off their chest, and leap tall buildings in a single bound. Whatever you claim you can do, you had better be prepared to do it when called upon. From the first instance that you choose to sell "wolf" tickets, someone may be there to buy them. In other words, do not let your mouth write a check that your body can't cash with payment in full.

The law of the jungle was coming back in full effect, where only the strongest will survive. In this type of environment only those who have the skills to recognize the game and its rules with the desire to be in it to win it, shall survive. He then began to talk about some of his associates and the hardships they were going through. He spoke of the men that proclaimed to be his friends; of the many times he gave them money or other assistance without question in their time of need.

When Big Frank was in need of help, some of these very same men turned their backs on him. These were the same men I saw growing up driving the fancy cars, flashing the big bankrolls and pretty women wearing the flashy clothes. Big Frank said that when trouble strikes and the shit gets thick; you come to find out who is down for you real quick. In other words, those who stand with you during the sunny days and good times do not measure true friendship; but those left standing by you when trouble comes raining down upon you.

All of his friends were catching major hell; many of them lost their girlfriends, homes, cars and some strung out on drugs living from piddle to post. If you look for friendship, companionship or relationships in a pile of garbage expect to find trash. That after all the time, money and effort they spent keeping up appearances running game and hustling, they had nothing to show for it. For many of them their lives had come full circle. He said take a close look at the way in which we were living.

Back in the day before he came into our lives, money was easy to come by for him. Now it was becoming harder to come by and he had come to realize that in the long and short of it, which the game of hustling was bullshit. It was less fulfilling, and the bitter aftertaste was far from great. "Do allow your self to get caught up in the game; don't be me, be better" he said with a tone of sincerity I had never heard. Up until that moment, I could literally count on one hand how many times Big Frank had even spoken to me. He spoke at me, but rarely to me.

His was mostly a monologue, rarely a dialogue where he spent the bulk of his conversation berating or riding me to perform in a better manner. I sat there in the chair, taking in every word he spoke to me. He also said that he would do what he could to help me, and in return asked that I would always look after my mom and my youngest sister Shay. I looked at him in a puzzled way, for he was speaking with a tone of finality as though he was going to leave and not come back.

From that moment on, I looked at him and myself in a very different way. I heard the horn blow out front, and headed out the door on my way to work. I was speechless. I thought about what he said the entire day and the sounds of his words sank deeper and deeper into my mind. I arrived home later that evening; Big Frank was sitting in his recliner smoking a pipe. Our eyes had linked up, and he just nodded his head.

I acknowledged through my glance that I had heard what he said, and would heed the advice he had given me. I had never spoken of his conversation with me to anyone until now, and we never spoke of it afterwards. I had a renewed sense of purpose and for me; failure was not an option I could entertain. From my life's perspective up to that point, I had the opportunity to see life from basement as well as the first floor.

I knew the taste of rotten fruit that fell from the tree of poverty; the bittersweet taste of fruit picked from the tree of opportunity of the middle class. I could only imagine the sweetness of the nectar of the fruit from the top of the tree of those fortunate enough to live the lifestyle of the rich and famous. I equated money with happiness and I thought that by having pockets full of money would be the cure all to my perceived shortcomings. That money would provide comfort away from the feeling of unhappiness I perceived was coming from the pocket full of lint I was accustomed to carrying.

I remembered a very profound statement Sminey made to me one day while working on a lab project. The class had begun a discussion about what their plans would be after graduation. Some of the students planned to attend a four-year university to obtain a bachelor's degree, others such as I was anxious to start a career. Sminey had told us about several companies he worked for earlier in his career. He spoke of becoming unhappy and disenchanted with the lack of upward mobility and gained no joy from his work. Once fed up, he chose to leave his employer to teach at the junior college. With his salary cut in half, Sminey had no regrets with the choice he made.

I shook my head in disapproval, saying that there was no way I would be willing to cut my pay in half. "For the right amount of money, I could put up with most anything just brings it on" I said in retort. Sminey said that the day would come where I would find out that money could not buy happiness or a peace of mind. I laughed. Little did I know that years later his words would be prophetic and mine would come back to haunt me.

I had struggled through the first year to maintain a C overall grade point average, and going into the second year, I decided to pick up my effort to raise it up. My friend Scott came to my aid to help me with my math and one of the core elective courses within our major. When one of the students in the program was getting down, the others would pick them up. It was as though we were part of a battalion struggling to get through the jungle and we would not leave anyone behind. However, we had many casualties, as we lost over half of the initial number of students who enrolled in the program.

The company I was working for began to financially struggle as well and the work atmosphere was far more dark and the tone and tenor more serious. Most of the workforce had been with the company since its inception. Many held the opinion that since the company's revenues had grown substantially they should get a greater piece of the action. There was a covert movement to unionize the plant with one of the local steelworkers unions. As the result of a petition, a vast majority of the workers voted to have union represent them in the bargaining process.

The owners balked and after a few weeks, the workers went on strike. The strike was in full effect and many of the picketers who were once friendly co-workers became hostile enemies. Being we were only part time workers, we were not part of the bargaining process. However, some of the picketers did not view it as such. The strikers had flatten the tires on several of the vehicles, so Dave arranged for a van to pick us up from the college and drop us off for the duration on the strike. The strike lasted about a month after which the company came to an agreement with the union and the strike ended.

The remnants and ill will that came because of the strike lasted far longer than the actual strike. The quality and the level of productivity by the workers began to drop, and the tensions in the plant remained strained as well. The company began to lose several major accounts due to the poor quality of workmanship. The company suffered a major blow when Dave resigned his position with the company.

We were all surprised and devastated. Dave treated us like family and provided a positive and supportive work environment. Under Dave's direction and vision, the company began to diversify its offerings to include designing telephone products specifically to customer order to compliment the repair operations. His wife had received a promotion requiring them to transfer and due to the aftermath of the strike, he decided to resign. He tried to put a positive spin to it, telling us his decision to leave was strictly personal. I saw on his face how the strike affected him personally.

People whom he had worked with for years now hated him, because of his managerial status. On his last day, a potluck luncheon was held in his honor but the mood was far from joyous. I had come to respect Dave for being genuine, kind and for providing me with the opportunity to gain work experience I otherwise would have never received. I kept my distance, eating my lunch at the workstation instead of the break room for fear of losing my composure. Dave was packing up his things, and some of the guys helped to load up his truck. One by one, the engineers and the lab technicians went into Dave office to say goodbye.

I was the second to the last one and as I stepped into his office, I could tell Dave had already been crying. It was all I could do to keep the tears from falling; I gave Dave a hug and thanked him sincerely for giving me the chance and for sharing his wisdom and knowledge with me. He told me that he knew that there was something special about me just by hearing the sound of my voice on the telephone. He said that once he met me he knew he made a good choice. He repeated a similar statement that Sminey had said to me that no matter what I chose to do, do something that I would enjoy.

He said life is too short, be happy with what you choose to do in life. Just before leaving, Rick, Scott, Mike and two other guys started singing "Staying Alive and started dancing down the hallway. We all just busted out laughing again; the guys had no sense of rhythm at all. They were gyrating as though they were part of a handicapped dance troupe. After Dave finished loading his truck, he came back into the plant and walked the floor one last time. We all said our last good byes and followed Dave out to the parking lot. He flashed his smile, and started his truck turning up the volume on his stereo blasting the very same song the guys tried to sing earlier.

When he drove off, the atmosphere felt as though someone had died. We all went back inside, but no one felt much like working afterwards for the mood was very somber. For all intents and purposes, this was the beginning of the end and subsequent demise of the company. The spring quarter had finally come upon us, and we were all getting excited about graduation. Due to my dropping the physics class the year prior, I had to carry 21 credit hours in order to graduate with my class. I practically lived at the college but the sweet smell of success was the fuel that kept me going. One of the core courses we had to take was business economics taught by Mr. Grogoza who I gave the nickname of Willie G.

He taught the major core elective classes under the mechanical engineering program. He spoke with a low monotone voice and his mannerisms were definitely from the old school. With the other instructors, we were very informal calling them by their first name. When he called upon us for questioning, he used our surnames. During the entire two-year period, I attended the junior college, for the exception of two elective courses; I was the only African American in the class. The economy at the time was in recession, which was the topic of discussion. During that discussion, the topic of affirmative action had come up.

Several of the guys in class thought that no one should receive special treatment or consideration just because of the color of the skin. One guy in particular became quite vehement about his beliefs, saying that the person most qualified should get the job. At first, I just sat back listening to the comments and opinions and I began to bristle. My emotions must have been showing on my face, but before I could open, my mouth Willie G. offered his opinion on the subject. He told the class to look around the room, and asked them how many people of color they saw. He then asked them how many people of color they knew, and how many had people of color as close friends.

Outside of those who worked at the plant with me, no one else's hands were raised. He then posed the question as to what they perceived the reasons where so few people of color attended the junior college. No one spoke up, so he offered his rational and hypothesis as to the cause of the circumstance. He said that we all come into this world in the same manner, but by no means do we all have the same opportunities.

Opportunity comes in many ways and many forms, such as being born to loving and caring parents, or being born into privilege. In our society, being born with white skin also provides some measure of opportunity and privilege as well. White America had a head start of over two hundred years, and stacked the deck against people of color for almost another 100 years through the advantages afforded by the Jim Crow laws. He pointed out that the Civil Rights act of 1965 was created to help equalize the playing field, but in and of itself was not the cure all to make up for past injustices.

"To whom much is given, much is expected" he said, and much of the wealth this nation accumulated came as the result of free slave labor and a massive loss of life. Those of good conscience should do everything possible to strengthen the weakest links among us. We the people, who represent the majority of this nation, should expect our government to do no less to help those willing to help themselves.

He pointed to me and said here sits one young man trying to help himself. Shawn chose to take advantage of the educational opportunity offered to him. Willie G. stated he was willing to help in my efforts to succeed. I was prepared to once again play the lone defender of the black race. After his eloquent speech, there was nothing more for me to say. The issue of affirmative action would come up again sooner than I anticipated. The college had invited a few companies from around the state for a job fair. We were all excited about the prospects of potentially being hired, after all of the hard work, trials and tribulations our efforts would finally pay off.

Several utility companies and electronics manufacturers had interviewed me. I was quite reserved about the possibility of getting hired, being the consummate pragmatic man that I was. Several students had higher grade point averages than I did. One of the interviews I had was with an independent telecommunications company, which is now one of the major incumbent local exchange service providers in the country. I met with a man by the name of Bill, who worked for the company as both a manager in the outside plant-engineering department and recruited for all of the engineering disciplines within the company.

I hit it off with him right out of the gate; he was a middle-aged man with a quiet air of wisdom. I was a little nervous, and he immediately set my mind at ease telling a few corny jokes. He had interviewed about half of our class, and stated he was quite impressed with those he had met thus far. By virtue of his making that comment, I assumed that he had already selected several candidates so I just went through the motions of appearing interested.

Bill told me he had been with the company for over thirty years, and spoke highly of the company. However, he also acknowledged that the company had very few minorities, and even fewer in the engineering department. Out of four groups that comprised the engineering department, there were only two African Americans. He stated that the company was attempting to make a concerted effort to increase the number of minorities within the workforce. I asked him about promotional opportunities, and from a realistic perspective how far could I go in the company. He gave me the proverbial corporate line that if I worked hard and played by the rules, the sky was the limit.

He asked me what I thought about what I had just heard, and I stated that it sounded great. He began to ask me of my opinion about the college and a few of my fellow students. I was somewhat puzzled at first, but I spoke highly of all that he mentioned for I truly liked them. We ended the session and shook hands, and as I left the room, I thought for sure that I would never hear from him again.

The following week I received a phone call from Bill, asking me to come to the company for a formal interview. I was in a state of shock to say the least. When I arrived to school the following day, I told the class of my pending interview. Everyone appeared to be happy and excited for me, especially those who worked at the telephone refurbishing company with me.

I had taken the Saturday off from work to ride with Big Frank, who drove me to Cleveland to buy me a suit for the interview. Capitol clothing was the store he shopped frequently for years, where he bought his own suits and those he sold on the street to clients when hustling to make money. He bought me a dark brown suit and a pair of dark brown Stacey Adams dress shoes. I was suited down and dressed to kill and he told me that he knew the job was mine. The following Friday I drove to the state operations headquarters which was located about an hour away. Bill met me again, and he proceeded to show me around the building.

I met with the director of the engineering department, as well as the four men who managed the traffic, switching, transmission, and outside plant disciplines. After the meetings, we went to lunch. The managers were impressed and essentially offered the job to me on spot. I had the added option of selecting the department where I would receive my training. I kept a calm cool and collected expression on my face, and told Bill I accepted the offer and would call him next week informing him of my choice of department.

I left the restaurant entered the car and hollered to the top of my lungs. I drove home and as I stepped into the door, my face told the tale. My mom started crying my sisters were jumping up and down and Big Frank started laughing so hard until he made himself cough. They were excited and overjoyed, but I had come to find out later that I had a few detractors that were not happy in the least. When I told Rick, Mike and Scott I had gotten the job, they were just as excited for me as though they received the job themselves.

Several members of our class became upset that I received an interview, let alone considered for employment. At that moment, I was livid, as I felt both angry and betrayed. The prevailing opinion of my detractors was they were more deserving, because they had a higher grade point average than I did. I asked them who made the statements, but they refused to tell me who because they knew I would confront them. I told them to carry my statement back for all to hear, because those who held the opinion were too cowardly to share their feelings about me face to face. I had undergone and put forth the effort to attain my degree just as they did. I also worked part time in the field of telecommunications, which provided me the work experience.

Although I acknowledged the fact that part of the reason I was hired was due to my skin color, it was not the sole determining factor in the decision making process. I still had to interview with five different people, who unanimously came to the decision that I was qualified.

During the entire two-year period, I had treated everyone in the class with the utmost of respect. When they were going through personal problems, I was there to listen and lend assistance. Now that an opportunity was presented to me, a few individuals had come to show their true colors. I stated, "You can tell them to kiss my a@*". If anyone has anything to say, be man enough to step up and say what is on their mind. Rick, Mike and Scott were a little taken aback, but they understood my anger. Together we all rocked in the same boat and persevered through the experience. As they were from the moment of our first encounter, they were in my corner.

I had come to find out later that the three of them came to my defense. It was of no surprise to me for they were true blue friends. I was later told that one of the guys in class was going to throw an after graduation party. After the conversation we had, I said that I doubt that I would attend it, for I did not want to be in the company of back stabbers. I never had a tolerance for those types of individuals whom were quick to skin and grin, and then stab you from the back.

My words had gotten back to the group, and I could tell a marked difference in the behavior and attitudes of some of my classmates. The guys told them that I would not attend the after graduation party, and the host of the party called me aside to talk. He let me know that he was not one of the detractors and asked me to reconsider my decision. I saw in his face how sincere he was, and I told him that I would think about it. The graduation ceremony was on a Friday afternoon, which was in conflict with my new job assignment.

As part of my training, it required that I travel to the eastern district on the other side of the state. Besides, after the ordeal of dealing with school and my newfound detractors, I lost my enthusiasm. I ultimately decided not to attend the graduation ceremonies. I did attend the graduation party hosted by one of my classmates, for it would be the last time we would all be together before we went our separate ways.

I had to study for my final exams, and reduced the amount of hours I worked at the refurbishing company. The financial situation at the company was in dire straight, and one of the founders had taken on a new partner to gain needed funding. As a condition, several employees were laid off to cut costs. Since I had accepted a new job, I was let go before the end of my two-week notification period. I went to the plant to pick up my tools and other personal effects, as a few of the women who worked on the assembly line were upset that I was let go.

I told them not to worry about me and I appreciated their concern. I had mixed emotions about leaving, because I knew that for many of them especially the single mothers the factory work was their sole means of income. For two years the company was my home away from home. I had come to know so many good people. It was a bittersweet departure, for I knew that for them more hardships and bad news was coming their way.

Just as Dave did before me, I walked the entire plant from the warehouse to the assembly line and said my last good byes. I was surprised at the outpour of emotions on my behalf, and again, I failed to realize that I had such an impact upon anyone. I reflected back to the day I started; at the enormity and speed of all that had taken place in such a short time. Had it not been for Rick, Mike and Scott, I too could have faced the same dilemma as those whom I would leave behind.

Armed with just a high school education and living in a small town, the opportunities are few. My options would have been limited to working at some fast food joint or low-level service oriented occupation. I silently thanked God for once again saving me from myself, and for placing those crazy friends of mine into my life. I was looking forward to starting a new CHAPTER in my life, and as I have always done in my life, I never dwell on what was but looked forward to what the future would bring.

CHAPTER TEN

The last week of college had finally arrived, and no one was more joyous about it than I was. I had taken my last finals and made my rounds to say my good byes to the instructors who had been so much a part of my life during the two-year period. My disdain for higher education was well known, but for the first time in my life, I was truly happy with the decision I made to attend college.

Through the entire struggle and strife working through the rain and the pain, I had survived the educational gauntlet. Through the instruction I received at the junior college, it afforded me the means to take a small leap forward. Our engineering program was one of the first recipients of two personal computers in the entire county.

If my memory serves me, the college in 1980 paid $7,000 for an APPLE II and $8,000 for an IBM PC that had essentially the processing power of a high-end calculator. Those who came into the high tech workforce during that period witnessed the transition from electromechanical and vacuum tube based technology to digital computer technology using integrated circuitry.

The early 80's were a very exciting period within the high tech industry for that was the period of the creation of many great new technological innovations. Companies such as IBM, Apple, and a new entrant into the industry, Microsoft brought the power of computing to the mass population forever changing the way we live and work. The education and on the job training I received enabled me to become a participant of the great wave of change which overtook the world by storm.

I went to the engineering building to say my farewells to Sminey and Bugging Out. One of our instructors, T. Grass had left months earlier to accept a teaching position at his alma mater. I would not miss the homework and lab assignments, but I would miss those instructors very much. When I think back over the years, I had come to know very few people who truly loved their work. Although we periodically stressed them out, overall they kept a smile on their face and kept the class time fun and lighthearted.

As I proceeded to bid my good-byes to Andy Ho and Joe No, I thought about the time both expended on my behalf. They each spent many hours trying to drum the concepts of math and physics into my brain. I always struggled with math throughout the course of my scholastic endeavors. I asked myself what value math or science could add to my life. I did not comprehend or perceive the intrinsic value at the time, but I have come to understand and know the relevance of them now.

Geometry and Trigonometry is the study of relations, properties, and measurement of solids surfaces, lines, and angles. Physics is the science of the relational interactions between matter and energy. The many principles, postulates and theorems that govern each discipline, also apply to our existence. The game of billiards is an example of the application of both physics and geometry to every day living. Billiards is a game of vectors, angles, and kinetic motion.

I shall use the analogy of a cue ball to depict as a thought, word, decision, or action. When the player strikes the cue ball, a series of mathematical and physical laws comes into play. The laws of kinetics govern the velocity, speed, and energy of motion applied to the cue ball. Trigonometric functions will dictate the angle and trajectory of impact. Once the cue ball strikes its designated target, another series of chain reactions occur which cause the balls to scatter across the table.

The player faces a series of choices that entail studying the placement of each ball on the table. One must take into account the many variables before making the next shot. For the player to be successful, it is required that some measure of cognitive forethought be undertaken before attempting to sink the next shot.

One variable to consider is the relative proximity of the cue ball to the other balls on the table. The player considers how much force to apply with the cue stick before striking the ball. Other variables under observation include the angle of trajectory to the open pocket. Whether the cue ball should directly strike its target or contact it via banking off the side rails. These are just a few of the considerations taken into account before making a final decision.

Every shot has an associated cause and effect element; both an offensive and defensive component associated to it. If the player has the knowledge and understands the relationships of mathematics and physics to the game of billiards, the chances of winning the match are increased.

These very same principles apply when an individual faces a situation that requires a decision or some course of action. The very first step in using the power of conscience thought is to observe the various angles and external forces weighing upon the object of consideration. Through keen observation and methodical analysis, one can identify the potential sources or root causes of a given problem.

After determining the cause of the problem and the associated outcomes, one can better prepare, anticipate, and develop possible solutions. The individual can choose to use the process in a proactive manner to hedge or ward off potential problems. On the other hand, the process could be used in a reactive manner to deal with situations or dilemma as they arise.

This process can be quite time consuming and sometimes emotionally very painful for the individual to undergo. In order to improve the quality of ones life experience requires that one be willing to expend the necessary energy and effort to change the condition one faces. One should first think before uttering a syllable to engage the power of the mind to direct and focus upon the desired effect the individual desires to experience or cause another to experience.

Simplicity is fine for the relaxation of the body and the mind. In order to strengthen the synapses of the brain requires that one exercise its great capacity through engaging in cerebral activities. A body in motion stays in motion, a mind at rest stays at rest. It sometimes becomes necessary that a person engage in activities that will tax and stretch the cognitive thinking abilities of the mind. Just like the perfect state of being of a rubber band without stress or strain placed upon it. Such do we strive to find balance in both mind body and spirit.

As we begin to grow and evolve, the stresses and strains of the choices and decisions we face sometimes pull our spirit in one direction and mind in another. A person can engage in activities such as working crossword puzzles or studying complex theories in logic and philosophy. Through training, the brain increases both the capacity and capability to solve life's problems or stave them off before they arise. By doing so, this will assist the individual to avoid potential consequences before engaging in some act. One will greatly reduce the possibility of receiving negative feedback from the external environment.

In this manner, the individual can better anticipate the resultant reaction they will receive. Make your intentions clear; is to hurt or to harm; to heal or to remove from harms way? Be clear as to what the purpose and intent of your words or actions are to serve. The return to the stakeholder is enormous, providing an immediate payback on the time and effort invested in the process.

 The spiritual market indicators for the individual will rise in direct portion to the time and energy invested in the continued use of the process. The power contained within the mind is limitless and knows no bounds. By making choices that are more informed and decisions, it is possible to improve the quality of ones life. The returns on investment in inner peace, happiness, serenity, and soundness of mind with increased emotional stability are the dividends one can expect to receive.

Monday had finally arrived and I drove in to report for my first day on the job. Before my arrival, I had informed Bill that I was interested in the switch-engineering department. Approximately a year before my hiring, the Ohio State operations merged with the Pennsylvania State operations. This merger was the beginning of a multitude of reorganizations the company would undergo, as well as I in the years to come. I had taken my picture for a photo id badge, and filled out a myriad of new hire paperwork.

I walked to the second floor, to meet my new boss and fellow coworkers. Harry was the manager of the engineering department. He rose through the ranks with a demeanor was somewhat brash. Harry spoke with a tone and curtness that would intimidate most people.

He was a very matter of fact type of individual, but I must admit that particular trait is quite common to those who work in the field of engineering. The qualities inherent of those who choose the engineering profession require that an individual take a pragmatic, practical and organized approach to performing their job.

Engineering requires that one be efficient, logical, rational and have the ability to see abstracts outside of the norm to resolve problems. However, when it comes to interpersonal affairs, many with the engineering mindset view life from a black and white perspective not cast in the contrast of gray. The values are based on the principles of logic; you do or you don't, you will or you won't.

Using the mindset of an accountant, life tends to follow an arithmetic progression whereby person's actions should add up if one does their math. I could tell from the moment I met Harry, that he had very little patience for dealing with people he viewed as living life in the gray zone. Many within the engineering department had this point of view of the rest of the company. Those who occupied other non-engineering related positions added little intrinsic value. The other departments were necessary evils so to speak; tasked more with getting in the way than getting the job done.

The guys who transferred over from Pennsylvania were a highly trained and intelligent group of individuals, but many lacked tact and diplomacy in the area of corporate politics. In time, I would come to adopt the some of the same mannerisms as my coworkers. In time, this would pose problems for me further down the road in my career.

I felt an undercurrent of tension and hostility in the air between the Ohio and Pennsylvania contingent, due to animosities regarding the selection of some from Pennsylvania to key managerial positions throughout the company. I became exposed to the world of corporate politics and bureaucracy very early on in my experience. For the first few months, I kept silent and observed my surrounding with a keen eye.

I met a man named Richard, who was one of the few African Americans who held a managerial position anywhere in the entire company. I would come to rely upon his wisdom and guidance as a mentor and role model. Richard attended a historically black university in the south. The company later hired him eight years before my arrival. He was a mild mannered brother, but when the occasion called for it, he could be quite forceful in voicing his opinion.

One common trait that I saw with the Pennsylvania clique was that for the most part, that they commanded a great deal of respect and were fairly objective and fair in their approach to dealing with situations. I sat down and spoke to Richard for at least a half-hour, whereby he was clueing me in to several of the office dynamics that were in play. Although I did not initially interview with him, he was aware of my pending arrival.

Richard told me that there were very few blacks employed by the company, and even less in management positions. He let me know right away that people who would resent the fact that I was hired. The resentment related to the company's attempts to bring qualified minority candidates into the fold. Richard made sure that I received assistance and treated fairly by members of the department.

I reported to the eastern district of New Philadelphia to work with the state installation crew to gain some on the job training. I gathered up my belongings, and traveled the three plus hours arriving at my new destination. I would spend the next five months working side by side with the technicians on the state installation crew. Actually, the concept was novel and quite sound.

I was hired as an associate engineer tasked with generating equipment design, layout, and ordering specifications for various network telecom projects. The technicians on the state installation crew were responsible for installing the projects in accordance to the design and engineering specifications provided by my department.

They also were to perform system testing, activate, and subsequently turn over the finished product to the operations department. The concept behind sending associate engineers to work with the technicians was to gain experience with the different types of network equipment, and to obtain a perspective relating to the importance of providing the technicians with the necessary information.

Mark was the district manager for the area to whom I reported during my on the job training period. He was a man of high caliber and strong work ethic, and had a sincere focus in providing the customers within his district with the best service possible. I had worked with during my training period several different installation crews. I truly enjoyed working with two people in particular. One of them was Bernie who was an elderly man who had been a technician for over thirty years.

He was a very kind soul, and was willing to show me the ropes right out of the gate. The state installation crews were members represented by one of two unions the IBEW or CWA. The relationship between the union members and management personnel were quite tenuous. The installer's were a suspicious lot, believing management sent individuals out on fact-finding missions. In their mind's eye, I could have been a possible infiltrator or spy for the company. I worked with Bernie for the first two months and he spent a great deal of time telling me the history of the company.

Bernie taught me the basics from wire color-coding, proper wrapping and soldering techniques. He shared some additional information with me regarding the various personalities of some of the engineers located back at state headquarters. He gave his personal assessment as to the quality of their work, strengths and perceived interpersonal shortcomings. He did not have the same level of distrust and disdain for management as some of the younger guys. I attribute that to his age and wisdom.

During our travels throughout eastern Ohio, I was in amazement at the beauty and scenery of the surrounding area. I had resided in Ohio most of my life, and had never visited that part of the state. The winding roads and rolling hills covered with trees, and the area's population included both Amish and Mennonite. We would travel in the early mornings and sometimes come upon an Amish horse drawn carriage.

That was the first time I encountered the lifestyles of the Amish culture. They lived a simple, back to basics lifestyle similar to those practiced by Quakers. They considered the use of technology as sinful, although some of their young would buy cars and store them at remote locations. I was definitely an odd sight in their eyes, as I would receive major stare downs when we would stop by local eating establishments.

Bernie's wife had passed away several years prior, and he spoke of her often. As he spoke of her, I could see the pain, as he would sometimes force back his tears. He loved and missed her very much and kept working to avoid being lonely. Some of the younger guys would poke fun at Bernie, who moved quite slow and appeared to be in suffering in pain from arthritis. The years of hard, work and traveling on the road had taken its toll on him. Bernie would rather be in pain working than to be at home alone.

He was very patient man who took great pride in the quality of his workmanship. He was of the opinion that by taking the time to show me the proper techniques of performing a given task would prevent future troubles for some technician down the road. Another technician I would come to respect was Clyde. His brother was one of the senior engineers back at the state headquarters building. Arnie's father and mother came from Germany, with him and his brother Clyde being the first generation born in American.

He shared some of the stories of their growing up that his brother would later confirm. His father was a stern man with a strong work ethic who demanded no less from his sons. Both had graduated high school and attended a local junior college in their hometown. Clyde was very opinionated, especially when it came down to racial issues. I never met his father, but you could hear his father's voice resonate through him when he spoke.

In the same manner that I engaged in similar conversations many times before, Clyde and I, one day had a discussion involving the subjects of racism and affirmative action. Clyde said that his father did not own slaves or a plantation, and could not understand why he should pay reparations or taxes to aid someone of color.

He was of the opinion that if his father who came to this country with little money, with only his skills and his family in tow and makes a living, anyone else could. I responded that he was entitled to his opinion and although overly simplistic, the premise of his statement did not hold much water with me.

His father came to America of his own free will, and could trace the lineage of his ancestors back to some common point of origin. Clyde's father arrived to this country with the full knowledge of his culture intact. During the 1700's and through the early 1900's, there was a great influx of European immigrants to the United States. Many who left their nations of origin came to America to make a better life for their families.

The United States is a nation of immigrants and those arriving endured great economic and financial hardship as well. However, at the same token, those immigrants were able to sit down at the gambling table of America. People who came to the shores of America staked a claim without having to risk their skins in the game, so to speak. Under the mantra of the Manifest Destiny, those who fought to be free from tyranny began to enact its own form of terror upon those natives born in America.

Flying the flag of the union jack, the leadership of the newly formed republic sought out to conquer the untamed wilderness. Entire Indian tribes were systematically killed in order to gain control of mineral resources and claimed property under rights of eminent domain. Those who fled religious persecution in Europe used the same tactics to convert the so-called "heathens" towards Judeo-Christian based beliefs.

Many people of color came in shackles against their free will to America long before the arrival of Clyde's father. Men like Crispus Attucks and women alike who lost their lives for the freedoms his father came to this country to enjoy. The ocean bottoms of the world hold the remains of those of African descent, which were taken from their homelands, families, and all that was familiar to them. Those who held the knowledge of mathematics, science and their native languages were killed as well as those who exhibited leadership ability. Slaves were starved, beaten, diseased, and crammed into the hulls of wooden ships traveling thousands of miles across the ocean.

Once arriving in America, the slaves were subjected to a series of brainwashing and spirit destroying techniques guided by the blueprint provided by Willie Lynch. Under this blueprint, slave owners would indiscriminately rape black women producing biracial offspring. These children received "special treatment" given positions of authority over people of darker shades. The slaves were segregated, whereby the darker skinned blacks would live in dilapidated shacks and the lighter skinned would reside in the plantation house.

The practice of divide and conquer were used pitting those who had the same maternal blood ties against one another. These actions fractionalized members of the same family, thus producing disunity and fostering what is now known as the "Crabs in a Barrel" mentality. As one crab would attempt to climb up and out of the barrel, the rest would pull it down all jockeying for position. These slaves were denied the opportunity to read or write and those caught doing so were immediately executed.

Knowledge is power and wisdom is knowledge applied. In order to harness the power of knowledge and wisdom, one must be able to see truth where it exists. To know the truth sometimes requires that one be able to read between the lines in order to recognize the lies intertwined within the story line. A fool can justify in their mind anything they so choose; for what a fool believes is just that…what a fool believes. A foolish person does not have the capacity or the desire within to question the validity of the information presented to them. If you cannot read or comprehend, your ability to discern the truth from the lies within is limited. The individual is thus kept in a state of blissful ignorance and docility.

In such a state the individual is tricked into believing that what is portrayed as truth is in actuality a lie in disguise. The continued use of these brainwashing techniques over a period of a few centuries gave rise to the creation of a nation of apathetic people. People of Asian, Latin and Hispanic origins have played a pivotal role in the creation of America's economic success.

The many inventions, cities, roads, products, goods and services that we all have come to enjoy and rely upon came as a result of free or cheap labor by people of color. Those that tilled and toiled the soil that made the ground fertile gave rise to the most vibrant and robust economy on the planet. People of color have placed a great deal of skin in the game in the building of this nation. Those of African decent deserve to reap the benefits from the harvest so many gave their lives to sow.

I told Clyde that his father could lose his accent tomorrow, but never the color of his skin. That provided him with a measure of protection and comfort that people of color have never known anywhere on this planet. I said to him that his father held a very high-minded opinion and self righteous attitude regarding the issue of race.

The one great thing about living in America is that he is entitled to have such an opinion. Clyde stated that his father owned his own business, which afforded him the means to take care of his family. I ask him how prosperous would his fathers business be if he had no overhead expenses?

He looked at me with a puzzled stare, and replied no business could exist without overhead. For the period in which slavery existed, many plantations and factories were fueled by the availability of free or cheap labor. The overhead expenses associated with paying workers living wages can be quite high. The cash flow of any corporation could benefit greatly if they did not have to bear the expense of paying a living wage.

He thought about it, and his eyes lit up as though it was the fourth of July. He finally understood where I was coming from. Many white Americans have yet to come to grips with one of the greatest crimes ever committed on the face of the earth. When the mind and body are traumatized, mental blockages are constructed as a defense mechanism, which lead into a state of denial. This country has tens of millions of people who still live in a state of plausible deniability of the harm caused by slavery.

Many continue to seek comfort in the blanket of plausible deniability. Some continue to deny the historical facts of America's involvement in the trading of human life. Many seek refuge through personal internalization. Some believe that since they did not directly commit the act, they can deny any culpability for the outcome. Some still believe that slavery never existed; that it was just a fairy tale myth told by blacks to gain sympathy or favor.

Let us use the example of an adult who suffered a great physical and emotional abuse growing up as a child. There have been many studies on human behavior and psychology over the years. Studies, which show that many of the dysfunction's that come into the human experience is directly attributable to the lack of nurturing or mistreatment, received as a child. The effects of neglect and abuse that occurred in one's youth can manifest itself into traumatic social disorders well into a person's adulthood.

Imagine the effects of such an impact on the psyche of a mass of people if the abuses occurred over a period of 300 or 400 years? These abuses were never addressed or psychiatric treatment administered for neither the perpetrator who committed the acts of abuse, or those victimized by it. Any illness left untreated continues to cause damage to the host in all areas of mind, body and spirit years after the initial impact.

In the same token, the type of self righteous indignation displayed by people such as Clyde's father is far more common than not. To foster the belief that the effects of slavery have no bearing on the present conditions that exists in this country. In my opinion, this is the ultimate of fairy tale myths. For all that, we do in life; there is a supreme price to pay. The bill of lading regarding this issue is long overdue with interest continuing to be compounded daily.

In this case, the interest accrued for this debt comes in the form of high school dropouts, crime, substance abuse, and teen pregnancies that lead to the creation of millions of unwanted babies. Some are born with various physical and mental disabilities, which affect both the ability and capacity to learn and function within a civilized society.

These ingredients when combined create the toxic cycle of social dysfunction that gives rise to the birth of many menaces to society. The effects of this dysfunction are just as dangerous and deadly as dumping chemicals and toxins into the environment. The actions committed by this menace increase the level of crime and substance abuse. Society pays a high price by way of spending funds used to build prisons instead of schools. The world governments spend far more in order to purchase machine guns and bullets instead of textbooks.

What you fail to deal with today, you will pay a premium price for tomorrow. Most times in life, you pay for what you get, but you do not always get what you pay for. The returns on the continued investment in failed parental practices and social policies are running into negative territory. It has become painfully clear that the current measures used by both individuals and the society are not reaping positive results.

The free labor and productivity provided through the slave trade created wealth. The wealth provided an opulent lifestyle for a select few and a stable quality of life for millions more. The accumulation of wealth by the use of such labor provided for the education, the purchase of land, and the creation of businesses that benefited the majority to the detriment of the minority class.

That wealth was passed down as an inheritance for the benefit of future generations to come. To whom much is given (and in some cases taken), much is expected. Few recipients chose to refuse delivery of the inheritance and took full advantage of the fruits picked from the tree that slave labor produced. As for the millions of white Americans, many who are opposed to affirmative action and equal opportunity for people of color, I say this. Very few refused to take advantage of the myriad of opportunities attained through nepotism or cronyism.

How many white Americans have received loans, jobs, and admissions to universities, associations by a wink and a nod? Cloaked under the guise of "networking" how many individuals gained memberships to country clubs or other organization using the connections of friends or family members? How many businesses take advantage of the "corporate welfare" system contained within the tax, financial and accounting laws to avoid paying their fare share into the state and federal coffers?

Most school systems in America are funded using property taxes. The more valuable and affluent the homes are in a particular area, the greater the pool of educational funds available. The inequity of school funding from district to district produces inequality within the educational system throughout this country. Instead of increasing the amount of funds within these at risk districts to purchase new textbooks, pay higher teacher salaries, some offer the solution of providing school vouchers instead. These vouchers would supposedly be used to send students to private schools, schools who do not adhere to open admissions. These schools can selectively accept the best academically inclined children, and reject those with marginal abilities.

Most private schools do not have programs for children with special needs or disabilities. School vouchers are but another panacea offering false hopes, which treats the symptoms but does not provide a cure for what ails many school systems. Another so-called solution is to administer state or nation wide standardized testing. These tests were created from syllabuses taught in the more affluent school districts. When children from poorer school districts are given "standardized" tests, the outcomes are quite predictable. Until educational resources are made equal, the inequality that exist across economic, class and color lines will continue to grow.

As partial payment for services past rendered, a portion of reparations can be allocated towards programs that support the educational, social and psychological aspects of the disenfranchised. To those with the desire, free college tuition or post secondary vocational training towards the attainment of a Bachelors degree made available to all, irrespective of color or ethnicity. In order to make this possible, it will dictate major changes in the spending priorities by the various local, state and federal government agencies. Current levels of military spending must be reduced. This in turn will free up funding for primary, secondary and collegiate education. In addition, the formula and means used to allocate funds for state and local education requires changes as well.

Children who live in urban or rural areas should receive the same quality of educational opportunity as those who attend schools in affluent suburban districts. Equalized educational access will in time, provide equal opportunity and that is an action that should definitely be affirmed. What form the repayment of this debt takes maybe up for debate, but it is without question that a debt is owed. At the end of the day if a change in the heart of this nation does not occur, this country will continue to be a nation divided along the color line. When the citizens become ready to exercise the demons of racism from its past, only then will the hate be buried in its final resting place once and for all.

The one thing I respected about Clyde, and that I would also come to respect about his brother Arnie was their level of honesty. You could take their words to the bank, and if either committed a wrong would not hesitate in acknowledging it. Clyde did not wholeheartedly agree with me, but he was at least willing to listen and open his mind. He at least considered the possibilities that what I was saying contained an element of truth.

I had been driving Big Frank's car since starting my new job. I decided it was time to purchase a car of my own. I had driven home one weekend and asked Big Frank to assist me in finding a new car. He said that I should not buy a new one, but a used one that was maintained. I took his statement as dictating to me what I should do, and I got angry. Because of my own ignorance and immaturity, would cost me in a major way. I wanted a new car, and I wanted it right now. I was making $16K at the time and I had no clue as to the many considerations that one should take when purchasing a car.

I stomped out of the house, and proceeded to drive down to one of the local car dealerships. I must have had the word sucker glowing on my forehead as I stepped into the show room area. I hopped into this 1981 Dodge Charger, which was a small car with a 4-cylinder engine. Since I was six foot one, weighing 240lbs, let's say that buying a car of that size was not one of the wisest decisions I ever made.

One of the salespersons approached me and asked if I was interested and proceeded to give me the pitch on the vehicle. I did not ask him one question, did not attempt to negotiate on the price my entire focus was to purchase a car to spite Big Frank. Since I had no established credit, I needed a cosigner so I approached my Uncle Thomas. Uncle Thomas was actually my great uncle who was the eldest child of my Great Grandma Susie. He became the leader of the family when she passed away. He and my Aunt Dorothy would host the family get together dinner for Thanksgiving.

Uncle Thomas was a funny guy, always laughing and smiling. However, behind that smile was a man who was very wise and serious and never was to be mistaken for a fool. He was an honest man, who kept it real at all times never pulling any punches with the advice he had to give. He could see that I was somewhat upset and asked me what was wrong. I gave him my slanted version of the incident with Big Frank, and asked him if he would cosign the loan for me. He looked me in the eye and told me that he would cosign the loan. If I missed one payment, I could expect to receive a major ass whipping from him. I knew he was dead serious, and I reassured him that I would not betray his trust in me.

I thanked him, gave my uncle a hug, and proceeded back to the house. I thought to myself "I'll show him that he can't tell me what to do" referring to Big Frank. I stepped into the front door like the conquering fool that I was and told my mother what I had done. I had to return the following day to sign all of the paper work. My mother said that I should have taken his advice and allowed him to help me find a car. Big Frank just looked at me and shook his head. He did end up following me to the dealership to see what I selected. Because of my stubbornness and ignorance, I ended up a car too small for me with a high payment and interest rate of 21%.

I ignored the knowledge, wisdom and life experience he had in dealing with such matters. I chose to harbor resentment for his past treatment of me; I made a decision to purchase a car without giving prior thought and consideration for the possible consequences to my actions. I made an uninformed illogical and irrational decision not rooted in a state of consciousness. As you sow, so shall you reap and I would reap a bumper crop of problems because of the choice I made. As I drove the car off the lot, a series of misfortunes with the vehicle would befall me. The very same day while driving back to New Philadelphia during a slight rain shower, I nearly was run off the road by a semi-truck striking a guardrail.

After the first year, the car required some major repair work and a new set of tires. I never believed much in witchcraft, but it sure appeared to me as though someone placed a voodoo curse upon me. In all actuality, I was paying the price for being irrational, ignorant and immature in my reaction to the truth spoken by Big Frank. It was November, and the time had ended for my on the job training assignment. Some of the technicians and I had went out to dinner to spend some final moments together. I had come to like and respect the guys who had taken me under their wing. I gained an invaluable experience working with those men and I had a great deal of respect for what they were tasked to do.

The work required a great deal of physical effort as well as intelligence. The seriousness and dedication each of them put forth was a virtue that I had come to adopt into my own life. I appreciated the honest and direct approach each had in dealing with me on a personal level and without realizing it; they helped me become a more responsible man. As I said my good-byes to Bernie, it was all we could do to keep from crying. He treated me like a son, and we spent a considerable amount of time on and off the job. God created a great man when he made Bernie, and I am so grateful that he placed him into my life.

I was somewhat worried and concerned that Bernie would go back to being a recluse and made him promise that he would get out of the house and enjoy life. He said that he really enjoyed the time we spent together, and thanked me for all the laughter and good times I gave to him. As I approached Clyde, we just shook hands and he gave me a quick hug. He told me to remember what we had discussed and to keep my eyes and ears open for there were many wolves in the woods in sheep's clothing. To be aware that those who proclaim to be your friend, may be the very ones who will stab you in the back.

At the time, I somewhat had taken his words with a grain of salt because he was of a suspicious nature when it came to management. In the years following, his words were become more prophetic than I could ever imagine.

CHAPTER ELEVEN

Five o'clock rolled around, and I awakened to prepare myself for the forty five-minute drives I would make every morning. I was an early riser and headed into the office by 7:00am, which allowed me the time to prepare myself mentally to deal with the events of the day. For the first several weeks, I reported to the state headquarters building. I worked with two men within the equipment reuse and inventory control department. Steve and Francis were responsible for the inventory tracking, control and assignment of network equipment throughout the state of Ohio.

Francis was a very eccentric individual; a tall lanky middle-aged man with black horn rimed glasses that were the style back in the 1960's. When he laughed, he had a very high-pitched squeaky tone that was so odd sounding that to hear it would start a chain reaction of laughter. Francis was married man with children who he loved dearly. Francis at one time was an installer himself and worked his way up through the ranks into the engineering department. Francis also had a great gift of photographic memorization to the extent I had never seen before.

There were three stacks of computerized printouts containing thousands of equipment inventory items, each stack measuring about eight inches thick. In addition, there were several drawers of microfiche containing schematics of embedded based network equipment used by the company. Francis could recite page and verse almost every piece part contained within those documents. He could give you the history, issue and revision numbers of the items as well. Accounting ledger paper was used to record and track the items and Francis could tell you which warehouse or central office a particular item was stored.

The one thing about Francis you had to contend with was that if you asked him a question, be prepared for a lengthy explanation and a corny joke as well. Francis was well liked throughout the company and was almost a living legend. Steve was in charge of the department, and was responsible for maintaining the equipment inventory stored on the company's mainframe computer. Steve was very quiet and introverted and kept to himself but he took his job very seriously. Both Francis and Steve was patient with me, and provided me with a great deal of equipment knowledge.

I was very busy for the next month or so assisting Steve and Francis with the inventory updates. One by one, I was introduced to the engineers within the department. There was a cast of characters in the department, very akin to a mixed bag of nuts. The stereotypical view of the engineer as being a pocket protector slide rule carrying geek was far from the reality I had come to experience with these guys.

The dynamic characteristics within the group were very diverse. Many of the engineers were retired military men receiving their degrees through the GI bill. The level of discipline and focus to do the best job possible were definitely shaped and molded through the training they received in the military. Most of the engineers took their jobs seriously, but off the clock; some of these guys were some mighty live wires. There were the comedians, the philosophers, geeks and smooth operators. Each provided a different element of experience I would come to know, which served as a necessary component to my personal growth. Clyde's brother Arnie had the type of personality you either loved or hated him.

There was no middle ground in dealing with him on any issues. He spoke with a frankness and honesty that most would take offense. I was attracted to those of like character as myself. I could tell that they were sizing me up; to see which category they perceived me to belong. I just continued to lay low and keep my cool and followed the ebbs and flows of what was presented to me.

The following week I would come to meet two guys who would become great friends of mine over the years. Roger was another brother hired into the department and was coming into the department from his field training stint. He graduated from a junior college located in Columbus, and was hired along with several other individuals from the same college into the engineering department. We became close friends right from the start. Roger came from a big family and he was the eldest of six children. He too came up from the school of bumps and hard knocks. In many ways our lives mirrored one another and I guess that was one of the reasons, we hit it off so quickly.

The other individual who made a great impression and impact upon my life was Ralph. He was one of the transmission engineers I was introduced to by Francis. Ralph grew up poor living on a small farm in the country. He was one of the hardest working individuals I would come to know, and he was one of the kindest men I ever met. Ralph was a devout Christian and family man. I have met many so-called Christians, who have crossed my life's path. I can honestly say that up until that moment, I had yet to meet one who practiced the tenets of the religion as fervently as Ralph did.

He had a peace about himself and serenity that in all of my year's l have rarely witnessed in a person. He was a very soft-spoken man, and never walked around pushing his religious beliefs upon anyone. He was in my opinion the epitome of a true Christian, who did not talk about being a Christian he was a living example. Ralph was the type of man who would literally give the shirt off his back, and helped anyone in need friend or stranger alike. His wife Emma and his children were his life and a blind man could see the love he had for his family and the love they had for him. In the years to come, Ralph would play a very important and crucial role in my life that to this very day brings great sadness whenever I think about it.

Roger began to carpool from Columbus with a few other brothers by the names of Commodore, Bob and Dick, the brother who had met the first day I started with the company. Commodore also worked in the transmission-engineering department, and Bob worked in the sales and marketing group. Both had been with the company for several years and would become associates of mine during my career.

Commodore was a lighthearted fun loving man and because of his nature, was rarely taken serious by his peers. He loved to have his fun, but it sometimes came at the expense of dealing with other priorities in his life whether it relates to personal or business matters. Bob was a handsome man, very cool suave smooth talking kind of brother, and he and Roger were definitely the consummate lady's men.

A few of the sister's who worked for the company would fall victim to their charms, but I must admit that both were quite honest and up front when it came to dating. Bob was divorced, and made it quite clear that he had no desire to marry again anytime soon. Roger loved the freedom of being a bachelor and neither of them was willing at the time to be tied down to any one female. I looked forward to Monday mornings, when I would receive a debriefing about the exploits of their weekend. We would engage in rather lengthy conversations about relationships, marriage and other pressing issues that would arise.

I was the baby of the bunch, but I had some very strong opinions about some of the subject matter of our discussions. Because of his experience, Bob had a pretty strong point of view about black women. Let us say that his opinions about them were less than positive. Commodore was in a so-called committed relationship at the time, but a good-looking woman in a skirt could easily turn his eye. One day at lunch, Commodore began to discuss some drama he was experiencing in his relationship. He had been dating a woman whom he was living with for several years. She had asked him when they were going to get married, and he replied that he was not ready to be married.

From the gist of the conversation, this was not the first time the question was posed to him. They argued quite frequently from subjects ranging from discipline problems with her children and his unwillingness to commit, to his close ties to his mother. It appeared to be quite clear to me that his girlfriend received the answer to her questions a multitude of times. As is the case with so many people, she could not accept his reply for it was not what she wanted to hear.

In the movie "A Few Good Men", Jack Nicholson used a phrase about people not being able to handle the truth. This situation was a classic case, which typifies and drives home the poignancy of the phrase. Commodore made it clear on too many occasions that he was not interested in marrying her. She elected to stay in the relationship knowing that the likelihood of Commodore changing his mind was slim and none.

People are who they are long before they cross your path in life. They come with their strengths, weaknesses, shortcomings, failings and character flaws. Some may be honest when it comes to divulging these shortcomings, but most will attempt to mask their faults out of fear of being rejected. When someone is being honest, the onus falls upon the other involved party to hear the words spoken and accept them for what they are.

In dealing with people, not all is what it appears to be. Just like a trick mirror at the carnival; very rarely is the reflection displayed reflective of the true nature of the individual who stands before it. Many have become quite masterful at disguising their true inner selves, some whose facades have shiny and glossy veneer. The veneer can come in the shape of the clothes, jewelry they wear, the cars they drive, or the house they live in.

Just as the props used on a Hollywood set, once you go behind the façade you soon discover that there is no substance to support the structure. In order to determine if the reflection of a person's character is genuine requires that one take the time to discover the true nature of their essence. Whenever someone is putting on an act or perpetrating a fraud, to do so requires a great deal of energy to maintain the illusion.

It requires that one remember the lies told, and to whom the lies were told. No one can keep up such a ruse for any extended period. The nature of the universe is such that lies tend to cast a shadow or hide under the cover of darkness. People spend far more time and effort selecting their clothing or purchasing a car than they do in sizing up a potential mate. The first question many people ask of someone with whom they are interested is "What Do You Do for a Living"? The question posed is rather "How Are You Living" for this is the question, which truly begs the answer. The answer received will reveal volumes about the mindset, spirit and quality of character of the person giving the response.

In time, what is hidden in the dark will be brought into the shining light of truth. As my great Grandma Annie would say, the dirt will come out in the wash. The truth shall be revealed in time, but not necessarily when the individual wants it to be. The truth will come when the individual is ready to receive and recognize the truth for what it is. When one enters any relationship, enter it with your eyes wide open. You are more apt to recognize the patterns of inconsistencies when you view things in a more objective manner. Truth is at least consistent but not always constant; but a lie is always in a state of flux constantly transforming.

Those who have mastered the game of life do not live their lives in the shadows of falsehoods. They do not exist in this life with their eyes shut and their minds closed. They exist in a state of full awareness of their surroundings being in full control of their emotions, thoughts and actions. For they recognize that, the truth is like a newborn baby, pure and naked with no clothing. The difference between the wise man and the fool is the one who can recognize the truth for what it is. Not try to color or shape it into what it is not. If something looks like a duck walks like a duck, swims like a duck, quacks like a duck then in all likelihood it is a duck.

People enter personal relationships for a variety of reasons not necessarily involving the desire to love and be loved. Some seek to use or manipulate the other to obtain what they lack whether it is sex, money, material wealth or in some cases, to avoid being lonely. As was previously stated, what you lack within you go without. Whenever ulterior motives other than to share the love you have with another exists, built in stress fractures affect the stability of the structure of the relationship. This is typically how so many of them end up tossed over the cliffs of despair and ruin. Because one or both parties were not honest about the reasons, they elected to engage into a union from the start. Honesty is the best policy when shared with the object of one's affections.

Being honest will reduce the possibility for a dysfunctional unhappy relationship down the road. Put your hands where the other's eyes can see, and turn your cards face up. If after viewing objectively what is placed before them they can then choose to play or walk away. The individual does so with the full body of knowledge whereby no one can claim to have been taken advantage of. This applies to the individual who is a recovering addict that desires to start a new relationship.

This also applies to the individual who has had scores of previous sexual partners now willing to settle down. If there was neither shame nor guilt in your game when making the choice to be sexually promiscuous, why be ashamed to let it be known now? As a youngster, an old man posed a series of questions to me relating to this subject that I still speak of today. The old man created a scenario whereby I was to imagine that I was carrying a dinner plate full of food.

To imagine that I would walk through a crowded room and allow each person I passed by to put their unclean hands in the plate and take a portion. He then asked me if after scores of people placed their hands into the plate, I would then choose to eat my dinner from that plate. I of course responded with a resounding no, and he asked me why not? I looked at him puzzled, and responded that because I did not know if the people cleaned their hands or not.

He looked at me with a grin, and said to me "remember this lesson when it comes to choosing your girlfriend or wife". He told me to be the type of person who can offer a "clean plate" to another for no one wants to eat their dinner from a dirty or soiled one. The most precious gift you can give to another is yourself, whether it is your body, your heart or your life. Be selective and be very careful as to whom you share it with. We each reserve the right to choose the caliber and quality of the company we keep. What may not be a great choice for one person will be an excellent choice for another? Rejoice in the choices that you make in this life. For it is, you that chooses to make each one. By pulling your so-called skeletons of your past out of the closet, the chains that bind you emotionally or spiritually are broken.

The power from what was done is taken away, and the guilt associated to one's past actions is removed. God's love is unconditional no matter what infractions or misdeeds we have committed. God has full awareness and knowledge of all that was, which is, and will be making it possible for the Creator to love us regardless of the indiscretion. The same is required by each of us in dealing with others. What we do or have done has the potential to come back to us from the principle of "what comes around goes around". The consequences of those actions may very well affect the lives of those involved in your life today and tomorrow. This is an issue of fairness and conscience to allow the other to choose whether or not they will accept, share and support you no matter what the conditions past or present may be.

Spending so much time and effort over the years going to school and working did not leave much time for extracurricular activities. While I worked at the telephone refurbishing company, I had participated on the company's bowling team with Rick, Big Tony and a few of the other guys. My great Uncle Thomas and a few of my other uncles were involved in two weekend leagues at the local bowling alley. My sister Monya and I would hang out there on the weekends, and after some coaxing, was convinced to join.

The two leagues were primarily composed of African Americans, and one could imagine the types of characters and situations that could come as a result. I could barely breath most times from the billowing amounts of cigarette smoke abound. The other times my shortness of breath would come as the result of the many jokes and antics performed by the clowns and jokesters abound. When it comes to having pure unadulterated fun and mayhem, few can compare to a gathering of African Americans. Up and down the bowling alley, you could here the combination of pins falling and people falling out from laughter as the result of some antics performed.

Some of the teams were quite serious about winning and would sometimes become so upset if their individual performances were not up to pro bowling quality standards. However, do not let one of the bowling alley clowns bear witnesses to it. Some of these guys were quite masterful at playing head games with their opponents, and if they saw a weakness or kink in the armor, they would attack it like a piranha.

One Saturday night, my sister introduced me to a guy who would also become a great friend of mine. My sister always had a passion for taking chances, and she was betting on who would strike. Monya made out quite well at this particular event. She had come to know a few of the men she was gambling just as well.

This particular evening she had introduced me to Donnie, who bowled on one of the best teams in the league. I had met a few of his teammates earlier, but had to make his acquaintance. We began to talk that night and later hung out afterwards. I had found out that he was the half brother of one of Big Franks running partners Hank, who I had known since I was ten years old.

He lived with his mother at the time, and I remembered her as a child when she used to sell penny candy and ice cream from her home. I thought how strange it was that I knew his mother and brother, but had never known of him. Donnie worked for the city, fairly well known by his peers. We began to hang out together more and more over the coming weeks, and he introduced me to several of his friends that would later become friends of mine as well. Christmas time was approaching and for the first time in many years, I was getting excited about the holiday.

Not having the means to do much for my family, I saved some money to buy presents. I remember coming home from work one evening and Monya's boyfriend Jerry was waiting for my arrival. He wanted me to go with him to pick out a present for her, and I decided that would be a great time for me to do my shopping as well. Big Frank called me into the kitchen and began to get quite loud with me. He opened up the refrigerator and asked me what I saw, and there was next to nothing there. He started into a tirade about my being selfish and that I should not come into the house empty handed. I was home no more than four to five hours during any given day since I enrolled in college.

So, I shouted back as to what the empty refrigerator had to do with me, when I did not eat meals there. We continued to shout back and forth until I literally became horse. I told him I did not owe him a damn thing, and if it was rent money he wanted, then to let me know how much. I stomped out of the house and grabbed Jerry and left. I thought back to all the times my sister and I would go out and hustle up money to take home. I thought about the times I had saved up my lunch money to buy something I wanted, but gave it up to my mother to buy food or gas for the car. I remembered the many times I sacrificed my own desires so that my sisters could have.

For him to have made that statement to me in light of all I had done over the years to help take up the slack to the extent a child could set me into a blind rage. I was so angry I could not see straight, and had to allow Jerry to drive my car. I told him to drive to the grocery store, and I spent my entire savings on groceries. Jerry helped me carry them into the house as we stacked them on the kitchen counter. I hollered upstairs to Big Frank "Merry Christmas". I told him to make sure he explains to my mother and sisters that this was their Christmas gift from me. Before he could come down stairs, I had left, for I did not want to hear anything else he had to say.

I had not come back home until late that Sunday night, having hung out over to Donnie's house the entire weekend. When I woke up the following morning to head to work, Big Frank was sitting at the kitchen table as he normally would. He called me into the kitchen, and I said that I was not going to argue with him about anything. Before I could complete my statement, he handed me the money back I had spent plus a few extra dollars. I just stood there looking at him and for the second time in my life, he apologized to me.

I was speechless to say the least, for I was prepared to engage in an all out battle if need be. I did not know what to say and in all honesty, all I remembered from that point is taking the money and heading off to work. I remembered while driving to work asking myself was this some trick or head-trip he could possibly be playing upon me? As with so many of the encounters I had with him over the years, for all of the blaze and thunder which had taken place, the battlefield would remain silent afterwards never to be spoken of again. The time had finally come where I would receive my permanent assignment within the engineering department.

Harry had informed me that due to the lack of direct experience with some of the newer switch technologies, he assigned me to work with the analog-switching group to gain additional experience. Steve and Francis reported to Harry, and told him of how great a job I had done with handling the equipment inventory. Harry said that he liked me, that I had a very sharp and quick mind and would one day welcome me back into his department. He would keep his promise years later, but in ways that I could never imagine possible.

I was assigned under the supervision of a man who would be my boss for the next three years. Dick was his name; a stern faced man with a crew cut and tough demeanor to suit. He as many of the other men in the department was an ex Marine. He was shorter and smaller in stature than I, but he spoke with a loud voice and tenor that you could not ignore. I had noticed him on several occasions getting into verbal altercations with Arnie and several others of the engineers on the floor.

When I think back, I believe that he purposefully would attempt to intimidate those around him to see if the person would cower to his will. If so, he would use their fear of him as a tool to manipulate them to further his own agenda. Growing up in the house with Big Frank, who was of far larger stature than Dick, prepared me well in my dealings with him on the job. I called me into his office for a one on one discussion.

I sat back and listened quite intently, as he gave me the run down as to the quality of work he expected this and so. He stated that he was a very demanding individual, and if I had tender feelings or thin skin that I had better be prepared to toughen up. He also stated that he would not tolerate insubordination, at that; moment is when I made my sentiments known. I told Dick straight out of the gate that I would do as instructed, but I would not be led blindly. I said that as far as respect went, I respected those who respected me.

As I have stated previously, respect and trust are virtues that are to be earned, not freely or blindly given. If one cannot respect the character of or trust in a person's judgment, they are not then fit nor qualified to lead anyone. These are the basic principles I live by, and there is no leeway or yield given in upholding to this standard of living. I went on to say that I was not a military man and chose not to become one because I was unwilling to take orders. I said I will accept requests, but I do not follow orders or demands. If I did not accept them from my own mother, I certainly was not accepting them from the mouth of anyone else. Dick looked at me over his glasses and reared back into his chair. He was silent for a moment, then stood up and shook my hand welcoming me into his group.

The in-your-face-tell-it-like-it-is approach is one that I always valued and appreciated in those who conducted their life in such a manner. Many are half-hearted in the use of the approach, being quick to tell it like it is but not be very receptive to receiving the truth in the same manner.

Although some individuals did not care for Dick's level of candor, he was at least consistent to those whom he respected. He made decisions based on the facts presented, and he backed his people whenever it became necessary to do so. God be with you if you were perceived as someone he could intimidate or lacked respect of therein. Dick noticed how low my starting base salary was and without my asking, petitioned the human resources department to give me a raise. I showed my appreciation for the gesture by taking on as many assignments as I could handle.

The performance objectives the engineering department was measured by were based on the number of projects completed on time, on or below the budgeted amount of capital and expense dollars allocated to a given project. During my entire career with the company, I worked a great deal of overtime putting in no less than ten-hour days. On some occasions, I would even come in on Saturday and put in the work.

For the first five years of my career with the company, I would come to thoroughly enjoy my job, and few cheered louder or worked harder than I for the home team. Whereas the Bell operating companies would have more specialized positions, one group responsible for switching, another for power design, yet another to design cable and wiring layouts, we were task to do it all from soup to nuts. The tasks also included the timely ordering, scheduling and budget for a given project assigned to the department. The work was very challenging and demanding but I was thoroughly enjoying myself. The requirements of the job made it necessary to gain the skills and the ability to work with a myriad of people and departments.

Each group operated with diverging goals and objectives not necessarily in alignment with one another. My skills of persuasion became honed to a razor edge and as a byproduct; I was slowly coming out of my shy introversive ways. One Friday after work, I had followed the guys down to Columbus to attend a happy hour function. I was still only 19 and not of legal drinking age, but due to my mature looks was I very rarely prevented from entering bars or clubs. I finally got a chance to see my boys in action, working and weaving their magical charms on the ladies at the lounge. I was so shy in those days, and both distrustful and afraid of being rejected I just stood back at watched as the game unfolded.

Bob had seen a very attractive woman that caught his eye and he motioned to the bartender to send her a drink. Once it arrived, she acknowledged Bob and motioned him to sit with her. We all gave him a pound as he proceeded to walk over to the young lady. The music has just started playing and Roger was ready to strike next, as he noticed a few ladies gathered around the dance floor area.

He pushed me on the shoulder and pointed over to them and said let us go asked them to dance. I was as nervous as a man on execution day, as I followed Roger through the crowd. He asked one if she wanted to dance and she immediately accepted. Her girlfriend, who was not the most attractive woman in the world, had asked me to dance before I had a chance to ask one of the others in the group.

The other women coaxed her on for being so bold, and I did not want to embarrass her so I accepted. As we proceeded to the dance floor, I had noticed that we were the only ones heading to the dance floor; so all eyes were on us. Oh man, I was really starting to get nervous but I kept my cool.

We started getting into the flow and it was though the whole world was watching. Up until that moment, I could count the number of parties I had attended and my dancing skills were far from the greatest. But when the DJ started spinning the cut "Pull Fancy Dancer" by the group One Way, it was as though I was having an out of body experience. I started getting into the flow and I do not know what I was doing, but the crowd appeared to love it.

I was making up freestyle moves as they came to me, and as the crowd became more involved, so did I. Before long the entire dance floor was packed. We had danced for at least an hour before we sat down, and on the way back to the table, I was getting looks and comments about how well I could work it out on the floor.

I was the man of the hour, and I was soaking up the attention like gravy to a biscuit. My ego received such a rush; it was a wonder that my head did remain connected to my shoulders. Roger and Bob collected telephone numbers from the women they had met, and I could tell that the woman I had danced with was waiting for me to ask for hers. The rest of the night went great, but I did not strike up the nerve to approach the one young woman I initially was interested in dancing with. In order to get a chance to ask her out I would have hurt her girlfriend's feelings, so I just danced the rest of the night away.

I ended up heading home without receiving my dance from her or a phone number. Of all the places on the planet where a person is less likely to let their true selves show is a nightclub, lounge or a bar. This would be one of the few occasions in my life where I would even consider the idea of dating someone I met within the venue of a club setting. Early the next morning, I had received a telephone call from Donnie asking me to drop by his house to hang out. I brought my bowling attire and proceeded to head to his crib. I told him of the night I had before and the great time that I had. That perhaps we should hit the same spot sometimes. He then told me that he occasionally spins records with a few of his other partners, whose names were Eric and Bobby.

These two men would become very close friends of mine and are two of five individuals who are the closest thing to blood brothers I have. Before we headed to the bowling alley, Eric and Bobby stopped by to pay Donnie a visit to pickup the subwoofer cabinets he had stored. The two of them were going to DJ a cabaret function that was held at one of the local union halls. They told us what time it would start, and wanted to make sure that we would stop by and hang out with them after we finished bowling.

From the first moment, I met these two; I knew that they were unlike anyone I had ever met. There was an immediate kinship right from the start, which to this day strikes a certain measure of wonder in my mind. Their characters were the antithesis of my own, both being very carefree extroverted and unabashedly uninhibited personalities to my more introverted and reserved demeanor. As promised, Donnie and I attended the cabaret and as we entered into the room, Eric was at the DJ booth announcing our arrival as though we were some foreign dignitaries. Bobby was spinning the records at the time, but very few people were on the dance floor.

As Donnie and I approached the booth, I stood along side of Bobby and watch as he masterfully mixed his way into the next selection attempting to move the crowd. The hall was about half capacity at the time, mostly filled with women. Eric spoke on the microphone attempting to coax some of the people to get up and dance. Due to the ratio of women to men, I think most of the women were shy about being the first to hit the floor.

I asked Bobby to play "Rapper Dapper Snapper" by Edwin Birdsong and I promised him that I would get the crowd motivated. As he began to play the record, I hopped off the platform and just started dancing by myself in front of the DJ booth.

As I began to get into the flow of the music just as happened the night before, a woman walked up and began to dance with me. I noticed Donnie walk over and ask a young woman to dance as they proceeded to move in our direction. After about ten minutes, the floor was packed and the party was moving in full swing. We danced for well over an hour straight as Bobby was mixing and transitioning a myriad of some of my favorite cuts with flawless perfection.

As Bobby began to slow the set down, I had walked the woman I was dancing with back to her table and headed to the bar to get something to drink. As I went back to the booth to catch my breath, Eric motioned me to stand next to him. Eric was a very exciting person, with a wildly high energetic personality that the women appeared to be quite attracted to. He was going on about how well I could dance that he never saw anyone just get up and start dancing without a partner.

I did not tell him that until recently, I had never done that before, and to this day, I do not know what prompted me to do so. I was the man of the hour in less than twenty-four hours. I had asked him how long that he and Bobby been DJ's and of the equipment that they used. I was intrigued by the two of them and wanted to know more about the lifestyle they appeared to have a great deal of fun in doing. I had come to find out that I had went to school with one of his brothers, and knew another brother of his who I frequently met while playing basketball at one of the local parks over the summer.

Eric lived with his grandparents, and worked fulltime at one of the local factories, which manufactured washers and dryers. Bobby had taken off his headphones and joined in the conversation. Bobby worked fulltime at a metal plating company nearby his mother's home. As I began to speak to him, I was amazed to know that we had so much in common in our lives on many fronts.

My sister's boyfriend Jerry was his first cousin; his family attended the same church I attended as a child. He was also the first cousin to the son of one of Big Frank's nieces, and I had attended middle school with one of his sisters. His father had passed away several years prior, and his mother worked as a nurse at one of the local hospitals. Bobby and Eric had been good friends for several years, traveling around seeking fun and adventure wherever they could find it. Both of them were excellent roller skaters, and were introduced to disc jockeying through their association with several of the local area DJ's around northern Ohio.

I would spend the bulk of my free time with Donnie, Eric and Bobby the next three years. This marked the transition from my being an introverted shy teenaged boy in a cocoon to the bright butterfly of becoming a man. Before I met these guys, I had focused my entire life on getting out of something. Whether it was to get out of school or my attempt to leave poverty in the rear view mirror of my existence, my sole purpose in life was to remove that which I hated from my life.

In my serious state of mind, I did not allow much room for fun and relaxation in my life. I became indifferent and callous in my dealings with people, and I too wore masks to hide my fears of failure or rejection.

I would come to appreciate the comic relief and lighthearted approach to life that Eric, Donnie and Bobby would provide to me. Little did I realize the importance and value of their friendship would become in my life in the months to come.

CHAPTER TWELVE

During the early 80's, canines with temperaments and reputations for viciousness were all the rage. Rottweilers, Doberman Pinchers, and Pit Bulls were the prized possessions of those who would breed the dogs to fight for money, or bought as a reflection of one's persona to display a hardcore image.

At the time, you could rarely find a backyard in the area that you would not find one of these animals barking and snarling. Bobby's family had a German shepherd named Bo who was his father's K9 patrol dog. That was one of the smartest animals I had ever seen, and I liked it because it reminded me of the German shepherd my great grandmother Annie had year's prior.

Donnie had bought a Doberman pincher that he kept in the backyard. One would come to expect Donnie to provide some great comic relief, although it came by unintentionally most of the time. Any life form whether it was plant or animal did not stand much of a chance under Donnie's care. Since Donnie was on the move a lot, things that required care and attention tended to fall by the wayside very quickly.

We used to tease Donnie about his dog, and some of the facial expressions the animal would make when we visited his home were too funny. The dog was so skinny and scrawny it looked as though it was too tired to bark, I sometimes made fun of the dog. One time when I walked through the backyard, I joked that the dog whispered to me saying, "Hey if you hook me up with some food, I will bite anyone you want me too for free". However, one too many cold winter moments had taken its toll on the poor animal. The temperature had fallen well below zero one night and the poor dog froze to death.

Donnie knew he was in trouble with us as soon as we found out his dog had died. I started spinning a story telling of the last moments of the dog's life. There were a few of the guys who came over to Donnie's place who were part of his bowling team, as well as Eric and Bobby. As we started drinking and cracking jokes on one another, I began to speak of how Donnie's dog in an act of desperation, broke free from the chains of bondage.

I proceeded to paint a picture of the dog trying desperately to scratch through the deep coating of ice on his dog dish to get to the few morsels of food frozen at the bottom to no avail. The dog then dragged itself through the deep snow climbing its way up the back porch stairs pounding its paws on the back door to come in from the cold. With its last dying breath, the dog drew a note in the snow, which said "Donnie, how could you leave me out in the cold and treat me like a dirty dog? Payback is a mother brother, and with my last breath, I swear that I will get you for this". I was crawling on the floor on my hands and knees as I raised my fist frozen in mid air pretending that I had died.

The guys began to fallout on the floor from laughter, tears streaming from their face coughing and hacking as though they had a chronic case of tuberculosis. Donnie had to laugh himself, and over the years, the incident became known as the Great Dog Caper of 1982. There were countless moments we would snap and crack on one another with reckless abandon no matter the time or place. Few of us had much in the way of disposable income. However, what we lacked in funds we made up for in having fun. On the weekends, we would have card parties, barbecues, and on some evenings when we were not clubbing, would buy food and drinks and watch kung fu movies on TV.

One of my favorite kung fu actors was the late Bruce Lee, who was also a very wise and philosophical man. I remember as a child watching the "Green Hornet" being awestruck at the speed and skill that Bruce Lee used on the show. I have seen his movies countless times, but little did I realize the depth of Bruce's spiritual and philosophical nature. Bruce believed that the mind body and spirit of man was unlimited in its capability to perform superhuman feats. In the book "Striking Thoughts: Bruce Lee's Wisdom for Daily Living", he discussed his belief in the following concepts about the mind:

"An intelligent mind is constantly learning. Styles and patterns come to conclusion therefore they [have] ceased to be intelligent. An intelligent mind is an inquiring mind. It is not satisfied with explanations or conclusions; nor is it a mind that believes, because belief is again another form of conclusion.

To be one thing and not to change is the climax of STILLNESS. To have nothing in one that resists is the climax of EMPTINESS. To remain detached from all outside things is the climax of FINENESS. To have in oneself no contraries is the climax of PURITY".

"You are the commander of your mind and the captain of your vessel". Bruce recognized that man would always confront circumstances caused by external influences. He realized that man has the power from within himself to command and change his condition. By tapping into the power of the conscious mind from which circumstances grow, allows us to evolve beyond our current state of being.

In order that the mind may function naturally and harmoniously, the individual must free itself from all attachment to opposing notions. To let the mind take its course unhindered by self imposed physical limitations. Not the cultivated innocence of a clever mind that wants to be innocent; but that state of innocence in which there is no denial or acceptance, and in which the mind just sees what is.

These lessons and concepts are ones best taught early on in the educational process of a child. To teach them not to be narrow minded and short sighted. Not limit themselves to the finite, but to the infinite number of possibilities that are available in life. Just as in teaching a child to ride a bike, parents should use a guiding hand to discover their natural abilities and stretch them to the limits. To cast aside the fear of failure and self-doubt, being of the belief that if the mind can conceive it; the heart can believe it for there is nothing that is impossible to accomplish.

I spent a minimum of twelve hours a day to meet the demands of my job. I came to look forward and appreciate the weekends when they would finally arrive. I began to spend more and more time with them, and before long I ended up mimicking the same time compression lifestyle, I had while attending junior college. There were days that I operated on less that three hours of sleep and I was living like a pat of butter barely staying on the roll.

I never cared much for sleep even as a child, for I felt as though I was missing something. As I became older, I had overheard someone say that we slept a third of our life away. I have always had a measure of discomfort knowing that we spend so much time sleeping. I unconsciously made sure that I would compress much activity as I could within a twenty-four hour period, not allowing my life to pass by while I slept.

I was starting to get into the flow on both the job front and my life outside of work, squeezing as much as I could from every minute of the day. I was pushing myself, as hard as I could and there were many days on my way home from work that I nearly nodded out from sheer exhaustion. My sister Monya and I were always close, and since I did not have, a girlfriend would take her with me when I desired to go to a concert.

I was uncomfortable being alone in a public setting at the time so she and her boyfriend Jerry would roll with me periodically. When I think back to those times, other than when I slept I was rarely alone. I always felt the need to be in the company of people, perhaps to avoid being alone in my thoughts. Several months had passed by since I received my new job assignment, and soon thereafter, I traveled out of town on my first business trip. One of the central offices in the northwestern portion of the state was experiencing repeated outages. I traveled with one of senior engineers to assist him in investigating the cause of the problem, and to also to evaluate a new piece of testing equipment.

Dave was an experienced switching systems test engineer who traveled extensively assisting the state installation crews in their efforts to successfully test and commission into service various network systems. I was so excited to receive the opportunity in order to gain experience on the latest technology of the era. Dave was a short dark haired man of Italian descent who grew up in Pennsylvania, and came to Ohio as part of the two-state merger and operations consolidations effort.

We drove the distance to Sylvania, Ohio and first checked into the motel. We then drove to the central office where we would be working for the week. I was as excited as I walked around the central office gazing at the switching equipment. When I was a kid, I thought that the ability to speak on a telephone was the result of magic. As I gazed across the rows of equipment with lights, flashing on and off which cost several millions of dollars to purchase gave me an appreciation for the efforts taken to place a phone call.

We left the central office to get something to eat and headed back to the motel to get some sleep. All testing and maintenance activity took place at night, as not to potentially disrupt communication service. Dave gave me a wake up call around 10:00pm that night and I showered up and got dressed ready for our assignment. Upon our arrival, the supervisor handed Dave a stack of computer printouts that logged the number of alarm conditions and types of troubles encountered.

I went to the car and began to carry in the various manuals and testing equipment, as Dave was organizing the items on one of the benches nearby the computer maintenance terminal. The office visit served a two-fold purpose one being to repair the defect in the telephone system and to evaluate a new piece of test equipment. Dave began to open the box containing the testing equipment, and glanced over the manually quickly. He then walked over to the area where the test panel was located and placed the equipment on a shelf. He called me over, and handed the testing manual to me to read.

For the next two hours, I read the manual and began to perform the various test procedures. I took notes indicating the location of the control buttons and setting. Dave then proceeded to investigate the causes of the switch outage. What an ego boost I received, as I began to familiarize myself with the equipment as I though back to a similar encounter I had while attending junior college. Several test equipment vendors requested that our class participate in an evaluation of some of their products. I was quite familiar as to the processes necessary to perform an objective evaluation.

I had taken a break and walked over to where Dave was sitting to find out if he had any success in discovering the cause of the switch outages. I sat and marveled as I watched Dave sitting at the maintenance terminal keying a variety of software commands. He opened a capture log file to assist him in tracking and tracing alarms and software glitches, as they would occur.

This went on for the next two nights as Dave continued to flip through the log reports and waiting for the problem to reoccur. During the afternoon on the third day, the problem reoccurred and the switch went down. The central office supervisor immediately called the hotel, and told Dave of the situation. We quickly showered, dressed, and hurriedly drove back to the central office. Dave sat down at the terminal and reviewed the event log report. I watched him move with the precision of a doctor as he began typing various software commands.

He glanced at the trouble reports, and he immediately saw the cause of the problem. A defective power supply was leaking excess current to one of the common control cards. This caused one of the components to burn out, and corrupted some of the software files that caused a cascading effect which ultimately shut the switch down. Dave went to the maintenance spares cabinet and both the spare power supply and circuit card. After he deactivated the affected shelf and card slot, then replaced the defective units and reactivated the system.

It took several hours to reload the complete system generic software via magnetic tape. After the generic had reloaded, the system was up and working in no time.

The district manager came in shortly thereafter, and congratulated Dave on his efforts in resolving the problem. He had received much opposition from the various businesses in his serving area that lost revenues as the result of the outages. I was proud of Dave as I also hopped on the congratulatory bandwagon. He finished his work, and started working on writing the incident report. We later finished the evaluation on the test equipment. After completing the evaluation, we began to gather up our belongings and head back to the hotel for some much needed rest.

 We woke up around 10:00am, checked out of the hotel, and headed to a restaurant to get something to eat. Since Dave was still tired, I drove back to the office while he caught a nap. We arrived back at the office building around 3:00pm that afternoon, and as soon as I stepped into the office, I noticed several people staring at me. I began to wonder what in the world was going on when both my boss and the group secretary came over to me. I headed home immediately because of a family emergency.

I got on the telephone and called my mother to ask what was wrong, and I could tell that she had been crying. She would not tell me what was going on, but asked that I hurry home. I had no idea what happened, but when I arrived, I noticed several cars in front of the house. It was March 15 , my youngest sister's birthday and as I stepped through the door I could hear people crying. I looked around and saw my sister Monya and my mother on the couch with their arms around Shay. Big Frank had died of a massive heart attack earlier that morning.

He and one of his friends had been out in the streets attempting to hustle up some money to buy Shay a present for her birthday. After stopping by a junkyard to buy a part for his vehicle, he keeled over and died on his way to the hospital. I was in a state of shock as I sat down on the stairwell staring at the floor in disbelief. The word of his death had traveled very quickly, as many of his friends and associates came by the house to offer their condolences.

As the stream of people began to file into the house, I looked over at my little sister. I thought back to the time that she was born recalling the day my mother went into labor. My mother had begun to have labor pains and around 5:30am, Big Frank had taken her to the hospital. Later that morning, Shay had been born with a full set of hair and little squinty eyes Monya had taken to her right out from the start, and you would very rarely see one without the other.

Shay was far from the typical baby and did some of the funniest things. I remember when my mom would put her in the baby walker and she would run with a full head of steam, lifting up her little legs and laughed as the walker spun into a circle. As most babies would learn to walk by first crawling, she never did. She would get around by scooting around on her ass, then grabbing onto a chair or table to pull her self up.

She learned to speak at a very early age and was very smart too. I saw how Big Frank interacted with his adult sons, being very terse and standoffish. Shay had him wrapped around her finger and he doted over her every chance he got. She would lay in the bed with my mom and Big Frank drinking her bottle. When she drank all the milk, she would climb out of the bed holler out either my name or Monya's and toss the bottle over the stairwell rail, as it would hit the floor.

We would fill it up, while she waited for one of us to hand a full bottle back to her, as she would head back to the room. She was crazy about the TV show "Starsky and Hutch" that she pronounced as "tusky and husky". I remembered when she started her first day of kindergarten and Big Frank was at first reluctant to even allow her to go to school. He had taken her to school and walked her inside to begin her first day. Mom said he looked like a lost puppy dog that entire day until he picked her up.

She and Big Frank were very close, and most times when he would come home from one of his moneymaking excursions, he brought her a small gift. She was very fond of Twinkies, and he would buy her a pack of them every time he came home with snacks. For a while, we gave her the nickname of the "Big Twink". Shay was always larger than most girls her age, and had to contend with some measure of ridicule. She had a short temper, and in time grew weary of the teasing and taunting.

She would sometimes come home upset, and after telling Big Frank of the cause behind her angst, he was set and ready to take care of the problem himself. Shay most always could put a smile on Big Frank's face with little effort. Everyone's life had changed in the blinking instant of an eye, for now Big Frank was gone. Big Frank had been a part of our lives for over ten years, the majority of which he spent chasing the proverbial pot of gold at the end of the rainbow.

He was the consummate dreamer; whereby he spent the bulk of his life attempting to make the one big score he hoped would put him on easy street. I began to remember the many places we had been together as a family. I thought about the hard times and the struggles we endured trying to make it from day to day. He would try anything at least once to achieve his desire to have the good life. If there was fear within him, he never revealed it to us. He pursued his dreams with reckless abandon, and was willing to bet the farm to achieve his objectives. Big Frank took many risks in pursuit of achieving his dream, and I am sure that in some cases he even risked his own life.

Through the many occupations he held as a laborer, street hustler, gambler, would be businessman and entertainment manager. He was willing to roll the dice on the game table of life and take his chances as they came. However, in most cases when he threw the dice, they rolled up snake eyes. Although Big Frank was willing to assume risks, he tended to cast his bets on the long shot not concerning himself that he could come up the loser.

Big Frank stacked the chips on the table and let it ride for it was all or nothing with no in between. He was willing to set sail to catch the winds of opportunity, without first checking the prevailing conditions. Sometimes life situations create conditions that result in bringing forth the perfect storm. Those who choose to ignore the current weather conditions of life can find themselves caught in the eye of the storm, and their ship capsized. The storms of life can create great tidal waves and hurricane winds that can topple the mightiest of ships. Big Frank was the captain of our ship and we were the passengers on that vessel.

As a family we all rocked in the same boat, and felt every wave and ripple during the years he piloted his ship through treacherous waters. The one thing I admired about the man is that in all of his attempts and subsequent failures, he never stopped pursuing his dream. Being a hustler requires the ability to adapt to the ever-changing environment and to expect the unexpected. He was quite capable of adapting to the varying conditions that would arise in the street environment. Like a fish out of water, he was out of his element unable to adapt to life outside of that environment.

Big Frank had a great deal of common sense and his level of street knowledge was unrivaled. All that occurs in life is not strictly relegated to what occurs on the street. He lacked the necessary skills, education, and experience in the world of business. Because of his ignorance, he had taken risks he could ill afford to make. He could have refocused his efforts into other avenues where the element of risk was lower but produced higher returns. Big Frank spent tens of thousands of dollars playing the numbers and other gambling activities. He could have invested his money into property, a college fund for his daughter, stocks anything that would have produced a dividend and increased in value over time.

The choices he made in his youth limited the opportunities he had available to him as an adult. He was unwilling to redirect his efforts towards those pursuits, and chose to gain his education through the university of the school of bumps and hard knocks. A few individuals in history have amassed great wealth without the benefit of a formal education.

The education received from the school of bumps and hard knocks can be quite harsh, few forget the painful lessons taught. Having a college degree or certification is much like having an emergency survival kit in the wilderness. It is always best to prepare against the worst-case scenario, to have the kit and not need it than to need it and not have it. Those who choose to conduct business in the underground economy do not make a living; it is more akin to an existence.

An existence based on the exploitation of someone else's misery, ignorance misfortune, or weakness. Whether the role chosen involves theft, pimping, prostitution, drugs, loan sharking, or hustling each requires both a host and a parasite to set the wheels of the game into motion. The hopelessness of those who choose to exploit or be exploited becomes the catalyst that fuels the engine of the underground economy. Nothing from nothing leaves anything and seldom do we get something for nothing in this life. More oft than not, the activities engaged in making the fast buck ends up costing the individuals involved far more than the effort was worth.

To live a life whereby you constantly look over your shoulders, to sleep with one eye open is no way in which to live. To risk one's honor, freedom, self-respect, and possibly your life for a dollar is far from a wise investment. The picture painted on the canvass of the mind of those who make their living on the street has no color or contrast. The color of that canvass is black because most do not foresee a future with themselves painted on it.

As a result, some individuals are willing to risk their life and the lives of others to have what they want in the here and now. Some parents provide for the material wants of their children but become derelict in providing for their educational or emotional needs. Too many parents are willing to spend hundreds of dollars for toys and video games, but are unwilling to put money aside for their child's education. Some parents are willing to spend their last money to ensure their child wears the latest designer clothes. But some are not willing to spend the time or money to assist their child in improving their study habits. Many children believe that every whim and wish is to be granted without putting forth the effort to work for what they desire in return. This fosters the belief that they will be rewarded for giving less than their best.

Some children harbor the belief that the world owes them something by virtue of their existence on this earth. Many kids and teens lack the will, the skills and desire to work for what they want. As a result, great expectations form in the mind that ultimately will create a false sense of reality when the child goes out into the insecure world of free enterprise. The free enterprise system of capitalism operates on the premise of exchanging goods and services at a fair market price.

The deregulation of the free marketplace and the security of it depend upon the underpinnings on which it stands. It is a necessary requirement that those who operate within the marketplace are individuals whom are honest and above board in their business dealings. The laws of supply and demand dictate the price for these goods and services. We all to a great degree depend on the wants of others and needs of the marketplace to make a living.

It is the inherent nature of man to adapt to its environment in order to survive. When basic needs are not satisfied and life is threatened, man will adapt and resort to extreme measures in order to survival. The underground economy of any nation exists because of those without means tend to move towards those avenues that will immediately satisfy and provide for their basic needs. Crime exists in part because at some basic level, the needs of the poor go unfulfilled.

The situation worsens when advertising and marketing firms attempt to sell products or services through creating "artificial needs". Those within a population without self worth, self-image and self-esteem will look outside themselves to fill the void and emptiness inside. As in the days of old, there are many snake oil peddlers selling false hopes and dreams in a bottle.

The companies who produce items such as clothes, cars, alcohol and drugs use advertising as the primary meanings of selling their products to the public. Marketing advertisers manipulate the minds of the masses by push many placebos and an array of other products touted as a means to improve the quality of ones life. Those of weak mind and spirit will believe that the clothes will make the man; the shoes will make them jump higher. The makeup will make the woman more attractive; or the pill will cure what ails their troubled mind.

The manner by which a corporation conducts its business or the manner by which a government operates depends upon the quality of skills and character of those in positions of leadership. Many CEO's and politicians alike are hustlers and hucksters in their own right as they too peddle in snake oil. Just like a snake, they speak with forked tongues and talk out of both sides of their necks. The only difference between them and the street hustler is the amount of money involved is far greater, and the impact of their actions far more reaching.

For what affects the one of us, affects the soul of us for we are a global nation under God indivisible. To the extent, we as a race continue to ignore this basic premise; we can expect the underground economy and those whom participates in criminal activities to continue to flourish. Big Frank expended a great deal of effort to scratch out an existence to the extent possible from hustling on the street, instead of looking elsewhere at ways to dine from the counter of opportunity. In spite of his shortcomings, he was faithful and loyal to the few men he considered as his friends, even to his own detriment.

He spent a considerable amount of time and money on promoting his friend Lee Shot who attempted to make it big in the music industry. A deaf man would cringe upon hearing him sing but he continued to support him out of blind loyalty. I had come to find out many years later that on many occasions, he spent funds needed to maintain our own household. He spent thousands of dollars in order to buy recording time or to promote concert events.

I remembered the times when one of his friends would stop by the house how he would have their sides splitting from laughter. On other occasions, he would piss these same friends off when he would spit the truth at them in regards to dealing with a particular situation. Those who came into his presence would come to expect nothing but the real deal from him no matter if the person was friend or foe.

As I sat there and stared, my thoughts turned to my baby sister. How she would no longer receive the big hugs from him, or hop in his car riding around town. No longer would she be able to lie next to him in the bed watching TV and teasing him. She would not look forward to receiving any more presents, gifts or tokens of love from him. More important, how his death on her birthday would leave a lasting impression upon her memory for the rest of her life.

For the next two days, the house overflowed with a barrage of visitor's and phone calls from people all across the country. In a way, it was a good thing, because with the number of people coming in and out helped to keep our minds off the reality of the situation. It was a cold and sunny morning the day of the funeral as we entered the car that led the procession. As we approached the funeral home, the mood became very heavy and somber between my sister's and mother.

Cars lined up and down the street for as far as the eye could see, and upon entering the funeral home, it was standing room only. You would have thought by the turnout that some dignitary had passed away. Several friends of mine from the company attended to provide moral support including my man Roger. There were countless numbers of flowers, plants, and wreaths sent as tribute to Big Frank.

As I approached the casket with my family to view his body for the last time, time appeared to stand still at that moment. I did not know what to feel on one hand; I felt sadness for my mother and sister's for the grief they were going through. I felt a measure of relief that the days of what seemed constant badgering and conflict between Big Frank and I were now over. I felt guilty about the feelings I was having as the guilt began to turn to fear. The relationship I had with him was far different and strained than what he apparently had with others. For once again, we were all alone, and I wondered how we would survive without Big Frank around.

As several people stood up to eulogize Big Frank, I had no idea how many people whose lives he had touched. People of all colors, economic status attended from across the country. As each person spoke, it was as though the individuals were referring to a total stranger. As we drove to the cemetery, I looked back at the long line of cars in the funeral procession. Upon entering the gates of the cemetery, the emotions of grief began to overtake my family.

As the pall bearers removed Big Franks casket from the hearse, the sounds of people crying and wailing began to grow. Many of his family members were grief stricken, many of whom he had little contact with in years. I looked around at the mass of people, the many friends and associates and relatives and the tears streaming from their faces. I was standing by my mother as I attempted to console her, but I could not shed a tear. My heart had become too callous and cold over the years in my dealing with Big Frank. For me, over ten years would pass before I was able to come to grips with my feelings about him. It would take many years before I could comprehend and appreciate the magnitude of what he attempted to prepare me for as I approached manhood.

The pastor spoke the last rights as a cold wind began to blow through the crowd. I looked around the crowd and saw some of Big Franks running buddies standing with tears falling from their eyes. The tough veneer that I was accustomed to seeing from these men was far from the emotions they were displaying.

It was time to leave as the mass of people began to head towards their vehicles. We went back home and there were so many people at the house, we could barely get through the crowd. The mood was more upbeat as people were reminiscing telling their stories or jokes about Big Frank. I had been to several funerals, but I had never seen so many people and so much food in my life. I stood against the wall sipping on a drink as I panned the room looking at the number of people standing about. I began to question the sincerity of some of the attendees and their true motives.

Big Frank was somewhat of an enigma as he had traits similar to mercury being very elusive and hard to grasp exactly what he thought about a given situation. The cross section of those who attended the funeral provided a prime example of the many facets of his persona. He had a very magnetic personality, and a charm that could make a shark willing to give up its fin to him.

He had a style and an innate ability to communicate with people and made them feel comfortable to be around him. Using his quick computer like mind, he was able to find out what made a person tick by finding out what interests them. Once he discovered a person interests or perceived weakness he could then find ways to manipulate their emotions and bring himself into their confidence. Big Frank was a confidence man in every sense of the word that walked with his head held high and kept his eye on the prize. He died trying to provide for his daughter who was his pride, his prize and his joy. He lived his life in accordance to his own rules, and lived his life in his own way.

You either loved him or hated him, but you could not ignore him. He had a presence that commanded attention, and his flamboyant lifestyle was a reflection of the dream he died attempting to achieve. I sometimes wondered how different our lives would have been had he not crossed our path, or how different our lives would have been had he lived. He never spoke the words, but in his way, I think he loved me to the extent that he could. In my youth, I denied the need within me to hear the words come from his mouth.

To a great degree, the anger and animosity I displayed toward him came because of my needs to hear the words "I love you". In the years since his death, many of his words and opinions about the world have come to pass. The world has become a colder, crueler and harsher place in which to live. In the years following his death, I would come to know and experience first hand, some of the very things he forewarned me about in my youth.

I would come to know many individuals who spoke with forked tongues. Individuals that in time, I would come to trust betrayed or deceived me. In his way, he attempted to prepare me to face head on those who had less than my best interest at heart. The greatest lesson he taught was to recognize the truth for what it is and to face my trouble head on.

I have long since forgiven him for my perceived mistreatment and slight and I now have come to appreciate what he had done for me. In his absence traveling around the country trying to make a dollar, he inadvertently taught us to be self reliant and independent. To create our own opportunity, not sit around waiting for opportunity to come knocking on your front door. To be willing pursue our dreams but not the expense or to the detriment of anyone else.

For as much as I disliked the methods and approaches he used in my regard, I would later come to emulate and repeat many of the same behavior patterns displayed by Big Frank. My life was about to going to undergo some drastic changes over the next several years to degrees unimaginable. I would come to know first hand the meaning of the term "the more things change, the more they stay the same".

CHAPTER THIRTEEN

Several months had passed since Big Frank's death as I started to undergo my transformation. I had stayed close to home for the first few months after his passing to ensure that my mother and sister's were adjusting to our new life without him. I slowly began to get back into the mix of things and started to hang out with Donnie, Bobby, and Eric. In my absence, Donnie had informed me that he had recently purchased a used motorcycle from one of his bowling associates.

He had been learning to ride the bike by practicing in the alley adjacent to his home. One of his friends, Milton was an experienced rider spent time after work showing Donnie how to operate the bike. Eric was in the process of buying one as well. Not wanting to miss the fun, I began to visit several of the local motorcycle dealerships in the area looking for a bike. Several years prior, I had asked my mother to borrow some money to purchase a bike from one of the people at the telephone refurbishing company. She balked at the idea, fearing for my life and flatly denied my request.

I had not discussed my thoughts about purchasing one with her, for I knew what her opinion would be. One of my coworkers, Chuck owned a Honda Gold wing motorcycle that was a large bike with an engine about 1100 cubic inches in size. I had told him that I was looking for a bike and he gave me a few suggestions as to what features I should look for. So one Thursday after I returned home from work, I stopped by a local Honda dealership.

When I walked through the show room door, I gazed upon a Honda 750cc custom motorcycle. I had straddled the seat and it felt as comfortable as I formed a picture in my mind of me cruising down the highway. At that moment, I knew I found the bike for me, so I filled out the application for the loan and made the purchase immediately on the spot. I also purchased a blue open-faced helmet with a dark smoked plastic face shield.

I arranged to pick up Milton at his home the following day after I had gotten back to town to ride my new motorcycle to Donnie's house. Our home did not have a garage, and I did not want my mother to discover that I purchased a bike. I was so excited I could barely contain myself as I followed Milton watching as he rode the bike with such ease.

Upon our arrival, I had asked Milton to teach me how to ride. Riding a motorcycle requires both timing and skill in order to shift the gears and operate the hand clutch. I had difficulties timing the sequence of shifting the gears and working the clutch. Milton suggested that

I learn to handle his first, which was smaller in both size and weight. The gears on his bike were not as sensitive as those equipped on my bike, and after a few days, I was riding his motorcycle with ease.

When I went to work the following Monday, I had informed Chuck that I had finally gotten the hang of riding the bike. He slapped my hand in approval and suggested that I immediately go to the department of motor vehicles to obtain my learner's permit. I drove to the DMV that afternoon and picked up the test booklet to study before taking the written exam. I continued to practice my skills after work with Donnie as we rode up and down the street in front of his house. The following Monday I had taken the written exam and passed with flying colors.

I would come home from work to shower and change clothes and drive over to Donnie's house where he would be waiting for me in order that we could hit the streets rolling. We would then ride across town to Eric's house to pick him up. We would ride to the various parks around town showing off our new toys. Eric had been receiving an automobile and motorcycle parts magazine, as we would flip through the pages looking at the various accessories we wanted to adorn our newfound toys. I saw leather riding jacket and gloves to add to my riding attire that would complete the desired effect.

One Saturday day afternoon, we had ridden over to Bobby's house to pay him a visit. His mother Annie greeted us at the door as she smiled with the biggest grin. She was a very sweet woman, who had worked hard struggling as a single mother to take care of her family. In time, she and I would become very close, as I would seek out her advice on many subjects. She had recently started to date a man by the name of Narvie, who was from the small town of Andalusia Alabama we had once lived. He was an associate of Big Frank and knew of our family through his dealings with him.

Narvie belonged to one of the local motorcycle clubs in town, and was an experienced rider and mechanic. He would periodically enter various drag races held at motorcycle track meets around the tri-state area. Narvie and Annie were truly the odd couple in that they came from two very different backgrounds and lived their lives in exact opposites. She was a hard working church going woman and although he worked as well, Narvie was more streetwise and wild in his approach to living life.

One day I had rode over to Bobby's house on my motorcycle. I had not completely engaged the kickstand, and the bike fell over scratching up the gas tank. I was so upset with myself, and Narvie came outside after hearing me cursing like a storm trooper and offered to paint the tank for me.

Narvie proceeded to inspect the damage I incurred as he gave me instructions as to the type of paint I should buy, in addition to the proper way to park a bike. In our discussions, I had come to find out that he was the uncle of one of my old running partners David, who was one of the local DJs in town. We had lived in the same duplex rental our parents occupied growing up as little kids.

As we entered the house, Bobby's sister Lana came downstairs and I froze like an ice statue. I had been to Bobby's house several times and met the rest of his sisters, but this was the first time I had met her. I was hooked like a catfish as she smiled and proceeded to the kitchen. She was tall and slender with smooth brown skin and deep dark brown eyes. At the time she was in an on again, off again relationship with one of the local pooh butt brothers in town. Over the course of the next two years, I would attempt to pursue her as a love interest to no avail. Bobby was in the kitchen with his girlfriend eating a late breakfast. Annie's kitchen was the meeting place where anything meaningful took place, from eating to discussing serious issues.

We would play cards or talk major trash from the confines of the small kitchen area. Bobby had informed me that Donnie arranged for Eric and himself to DJ the bowling league banquet and requested that I join them as an official member. The name of our group was "The Knights of the Sound Table", taken from a song titled by the funk group Cameo. After Bobby finished eating, we went into the family room where he proceeded to give me my first mixing lessons. I knelt down as I watched Bobby work the switches on the mixer and varying the speed and pitch of the turntables. I noticed the series and sequences of the steps he used as he began to mix the song "Jewels Groove" by Jewel.

Bobby began to explain the process of selecting music with similar beat counts and tempo patterns. He also had a rule of thumb that over the course of an hour, he would play up-tempo music for the first fifty minutes and slow it down the last ten. This would allow the crowd to rest and catch their breath. Slowing down the tempo also gave us the time to segue from one DJ to the next one up on rotation would occur.

He had an excellent ear for music that came because of his mother enrolling both he and his sisters in the church choir. After watching Bobby mix for about twenty minutes or so, he got up so that I could try my hand. Oh boy, my first mixing lesson was terrible! In my effort to impress both Bobby and his sister Lana, I lost focus on what I was attempting to do. The mix was way off tempo as I had difficulty matching the speed of both turntables to synchronize the beat count. It sounded as though musicians were stumbling and falling on their instruments.

Bobby started cracking up laughing and told me to calm down and take my time. I tried mixing Michael Jackson's "Billy Jean" which had a much easier beat count to follow. I was still quite shaky at mixing, but I was getting the hang and the feel for it. One of Bobby's neighbors Eddie, nicknamed "Hoss" from the same name as the character portrayed in the TV series "Bonanza", came into the house with two forty ounces in hand.

The Harriston's were also a very musically inclined family. The family of eight children could sing, and a few of them could play a variety of instruments as well. One of the boys, Vernon was an excellent keyboard player who had the talent of music by ear. Vernon could listen to a song and repeat the chord patterns flawlessly. Vernon was a great fan of jazz music and he rekindled my interest in the genre.

Eddie was home on his summer break from college and came to pay Bobby and his family a visit. I had not seen him since I had transferred from Appleseed junior high to Malabar. He had become a phenomenal high school running back, and had received a football scholarship to a small university in Kentucky. He was big muscular brother, but was big fun to hang around. He had heard my sloppy attempt at mixing coming through the door acting as though he threw his back out in the process of trying to keep up with the beat of the music.

We started cracking up laughing; as I got up from the floor and Bobby proceeded to take control of the turntables bring order back to the music flow I had wrecked. Eric had pulled up on his loud Kawasaki motorcycle, and began shouting out his arrival, which was about as loud as his bike. Bobby had informed Eric that I was now a member of the crew and to celebrate, he had taken my car around the corner to the carry out beer dock.

When he returned, my hatchback was full of beer, cheap wine, and snacks. Within about an hour, there must have been at least a dozen or so people on the front porch as Bobby was spinning the music as everyone began to twist the caps on their bottles of brew. The party was in full swing as some of the people played spades and the other dominoes. I noticed that Eric was staring at me, and I asked him what the deal was.

He started laughing and said that they had to come up with a DJ nickname for me and he was looking at me to get an idea. The initials in his name contained E&J, so he was nicknamed "EJ the DJ". Bobby nickname was "Baby Ray" the DJ, being junior to his father. Eddie Hoss, who by this time polished off at least two 40-ounce bottles of beer, popped up and said my nickname would be "M.C. McDuff". It was a take off my last name and as I thought about it, I added "I promise not to bite rhymes and I will serve no rhythm or rhymes before their time".

The crowd on the front porch voted unanimously, and I was thus crowned. Eric had five brothers and a sister, and Bobby had four sisters and a slew of relatives. Between the cadre of friends and associates they both knew, we had an instant party crowd. We played for a multitude of functions both in and out of town. It was common to have a caravan of partygoers follow us wherever we were playing.

Bobby and Eric were very popular with the ladies as well. At the time, both had their main entrees at home, but both had a few tasty side orders in different area codes as well. By definition, they were the consummate atomic dogs in every sense of the word. However, Eric was by far the worse of the two. I would watch in total amazement at how he would approach women he was interested in. He was very brash and up front about what he wanted from them. Eight out of ten times, he ended up with them at the end of the night.

Bobby was smoother and laid back in his approach, using a blend of comedy and a smooth rap to gain a woman's affection. He was more of a comedic Casanova Brown, but he treated the women with far more respect than Eric did. To put it bluntly, Eric plain just did not give a damn about anyone's feelings and was going to do whatever he chose to do.

Eric was a wild and carefree spirit willing to try anything once and take chances most would not dare consider. His life was much a kin to a light switch; when he was on, it was on no matter the person or circumstance. He loved having his fun going full tilt, but when he was tired or weary he would go into a lightweight coma and sleep for 12 or 16 hours. He was the only person I ever met who could sleep standing up. If you were to compare the personalities of the three of us, Eric would be blazing hot; Bobby would be lukewarm and I the cool breeze.

The weekend had finally come for my debut as a DJ and I was so excited. Since I was attending the banquet as well, I was nervous and somewhat concerned as to how I would perform. My uncles, aunts and several other people I knew would attend and I did not want to look like a fool in their eyes. We had gotten up early Saturday morning to pick up the subwoofer cabinets from Donnie's house.

We headed to the hall earlier that afternoon to set up the equipment, and met with the president and treasurer of the bowling league to square the deal. I had showered and changed clothes at Bobby's house and drove over to Eric's to help him load up the albums into his van. We nicknamed his van "The Green Hornet", because of the multitude of sexual encounters he had in the backseat of the van.

The van had many battle scars, dents, scratches, and dings. It looked as though it participated in military combat operations. In order to start it, you had to pound on the dash, jiggle the ignition switch and pump the accelerator peddle. You could not help but laugh sometimes, but the van was Eric's pride and joy. We drove over the banquet hall and later met up with Donnie as the participants began to come in. We stood around jaw jacking and making cracks at some to the clothes the folks were wearing. Now no one would ever mistake Eric for being a runway model. He wore his hair in a wild Afro and wore blue jeans and gym shoes the bulk of the time.

Occasionally he would wear some dress pants if we were going to a club, but Eric wore them under protest. I picked up a thing or two from Big Frank when it came to style, and learned that just because you are large, doesn't mean you have to dress and look like a bum. The banquet ceremony started as the president began to hand out trophies and prize money to the best bowlers. I was going back and forth from my table to the DJ booth, nervous as all get out. Bobby was playing some jazz and mellow R&B music while the people were dining. After dinner was over, it was time to get the party started as Bobby started out the first set.

He had played about three songs and no one got up to dance, so I had to get the crowd moving. I walked up to the booth and asked Bobby to play "You're The One for me" by D-Train. I walked over to one of the adjacent tables and essentially snatched up one of the single females and proceeded to the dance floor. One of my uncles shouted out "go ahead son" and folks started laughing as I was doing my version of "The Gigolo", which was one of the popular dances at the time. People started getting up from the table dancing and prancing their way to the center of the floor. The nervousness and butterflies I had experienced earlier had gone away as Bobby was mixing different selections and Eric was on the microphone egging the crowd on.

I had danced through Bobby's set, and had walked the woman I was dancing with back to her table with her friends. Bobby's girlfriend had entered the banquet hall and he proceeded to head in her direction. It was Eric's time to keep the party going as he played a slow cut after Bobby had everyone sweating up a storm. I stayed at the booth overlooking the crowd as I watched Bobby slow dancing with his girlfriend. I heard someone call out my name in the crowd, as I saw my uncles slow dancing with their wives. I was really enjoying myself and having a great time.

It felt good to just be able to cut loose and not be concerned with the troubles and concerns of life. I went to the counter to get Eric and myself something to drink, as I proceeded back to the DJ booth I noticed a woman staring at me. She came as a date of some other guy attending the banquet. It was very dark inside of the banquet hall, and the only lights available were the spot and strobe lights we had positioned near the booth. She and her date came out onto the dance floor, but I noticed she kept staring in my direction.

I had asked Eric if he knew who that woman was, as he shook his head not having any idea as to her identity. I had picked up the microphone and started to pick on a few of the guys from my bowling team, some of whom were dancing as though they had nails in their shoes. As Donnie danced, he pointed towards us in approval of the music. I started to pick on him, shouting out his next dance steps before he performed them. Eric's skills at mixing were not that much better than mine were at the time. As he began to attempt to mix from one song to the next, he decided he wanted to dance with some woman he spotted out in the crowd.

It was now my time to shine as he passed me the headset and headed towards the direction of the woman of his interest. I looked through the crates of albums we had trying to figure out what I would play. The dance floor was about half full, as I selected "Mr. Groove" by the group One Way to play. Once I put that record on, it was as though we were at a church revival. A few folks hollered out "hey" and damn near tripped over each other heading towards the dance floor.

I was proud of myself, as I was looking out towards the crowd and saw all three of my boys dancing. Eric could not dance a lick, and he had about as much rhythm as a leaf shaking on a tree. He had a patent dance step, as he would wave his arms around as though he was about to take off in flight, as he jerked from one leg to the next. Tears were welling up in my eyes from watching Eric dancing and Bobby and Donnie laughing at him at the same time.

The time had come for me to attempt my first mix, and I was nervous as all hell. At the last minute I had came up with an idea to help cover my lack of mixing skills. I selected the next record and had it cued up on the turntable. As I started into my mix, I grabbed the microphone and started talking to provide cover as I hurriedly slid the fade switch over. Bobby and Eric looked up noticing the slop in my mix, but the crowd kept dancing. I was so relieved that I had pulled it off, as I would later repeat this technique throughout my stint as a DJ.

The crowd was in full swing and after that climatic event; I was in need of another drink. I motioned Bobby over to relieve me and as I headed back towards the counter, the woman who was staring at me earlier in the evening motioned me with her finger.

I was both surprised and nervous as I walked over to the table she was occupying. It was still very dark in the hall, and I could not really see what she looked like in the face. She was wearing a long white dress that accentuated her body. I sat down next to her as she proceeded to congratulate me on how well I dressed, and how well she enjoyed the selection of music I was playing. She began to ask me where my girlfriend was, and I told her that I did not have one. Bobby was slowing the set down as she asked me if I wanted to dance with her.

I was shocked and flattered at the same time, and I asked her if her date would have any problems with me dancing with her. She told me that they were only friends, and he was already married but his wife was out of town. We proceeded to the dance floor as Bobby selected "Send for me" by Atlantic Star. I normally do not slow dance with just anyone, but I obliged her request. Bobby and Eric were on the microphone saying "Go McDuff" as we were slowly swaying and dipping to the beat of the music.

After the song was over, I thanked her for the dance and walked her back to her table. The guy she came to the banquet walked over to the table, as I thought something was about to break out. She went into her purse, gave me her phone number, and handed it to me right in front of this cat. He just looked, and said that everything was cool and he was just came over to make sure everything was okay. She stood up and gave me a hug, and they proceeded to leave the hall.

I would later call this woman, and we went out on one date. Once I saw her in broad daylight and had conversation with her, I found nothing attractive about her. I found inconsistencies in statements she had made and I questioned the so-called "friendship" she had with the married man at the banquet. I was not about to get myself caught up in any drama, so I opted out of the scene all together. As I was making my way back to the booth, several people were commenting on how well we played and the great time they were having. I was in the zone at that moment, for my debut as a DJ went off like flying colors.

Some patrons asked me for our telephone numbers in order to book future engagements. I finally made it back to the booth and told the guys what happened, as we slapped hands in approval of our performance that evening. Being a DJ was so far from anything I had ever done up until that point in my life. It was as though I had an alter ego being the quiet shy mild mannered engineer by day; then transforming into a dancing hype man at night. Before then, I would only speak when spoken to. At the time, I very rarely initiate any conversation, being the soft-spoken type of person. I was the antithesis to Bobby and Eric's character and persona but the differences provided a powerful and undeniable dynamic.

Our group was electrifying, and many would question and wonder how we could be so different but manage to get along so well. We accepted each other for whom and what we were not seeking to change one another. Through my association with them, my personality slowly began to change. I was not as shy and fearful of allowing the lighter side of my personality to shine through. I became able to bringing some measure of balance to my life, and as a result was able to laugh at myself.

No matter where we went, we became the center of attraction. Eric was the wild man; Donnie was the unintentional jester, Bobby was the joker and I, the perfect gentleman. People could say many things about us, but no one could deny that anywhere we went or any venue we played that each person left having a great time. The time had come for me to attempt to pass my rider's test to gain my motorcycle license. I had ridden my bike in that morning and scheduled the test during my lunch break. A month had passed since I purchased the bike and I was riding it almost every day. The riding course simulated conditions one would face on the street. There were a series of left and right turns, and at the end of the course, I had to accelerate the bike to 30mph and bring it to an immediate stop.

At no point could your feet touch the ground to maintain balance. As I was attempting to make a left turn, the weight of the bike and speed I was traveling caused me to lose balance. I placed my foot on the ground into the turn and failed my first attempt. I was upset with myself, and rescheduled to take the test in ten days. On the next attempt, I used Milton's motorcycle that was smaller and lighter. My friend Chuck had rode his Gold Wing in that day, and followed me to the DMV for emotional support. I proceeded to navigate the course and made the turn I had failed to pass before.

This time around, I passed the course with flying colors. Chuck gave me a high five and we headed back to the office. I was beaming like a headlight, and I was the first of our crew to obtain the endorsement. June had finally come and my sister Monya was preparing to graduate from high school. It was a melancholy celebration for her for though she was very happy to be graduating she was still somewhat sad that Big Frank was not there to see it. The original plan of holding the graduation ceremony at the high school football stadium changed to the auditorium due to heavy rains. The air was hot and muggy as we waited and waded through a sea of people competing for seats in the stands.

It was a mini reunion for me, as I met a few teachers as well as old classmates who I had not seen since my departure during my sophomore year. It was great to see and speak to some old friends, as I marveled at how little time changed their appearance and character. Monya's boyfriend Jerry had spotted a place for us to sit, as we made a beeline to stake our claim. Monya was very well known and popular at the school and had many friends and associates in attendance as well as our immediate family.

Jerry and I were looking around to see if there was anyone else, we knew. I saw Eric with one of his brother's walk into the auditorium. I stood up, whistled, and motioned my arms to gain his attention. He looked up and hollered out "Hey McDuff" so loudly that his voice carried over the noise of the crowd. He made his way over to us as we started laughing and joking about some of the outfits the parents were wearing. I normally hated attending such large functions, but with Jerry and Eric present, made it bearable for me.

The ceremony finally was about to begin, as the multitude of long-winded and boring speeches almost lulled me to sleep. The time to pass out the diplomas finally arrived and no one was happier than I was to see the students marching to receive their hard-earned sheepskin. We were sitting on the edge of our seats when they called out Monya's name, as we stood up hollering and whistling in approval. Monya had a very big cheerleading section spread throughout the auditorium, as she grabbed her diploma as though it was a track baton and quickly skated off the stage.

We just laughed, and I was so very proud of her because I knew how much effort she put forth in order to graduate. She was very much like me in the aspect of not liking school, and had her struggles just as well. She was the woman of the hour, and soaked up the much-deserved congratulations. The following Saturday we decided to ride our bikes on our first out of town trip. Once again, Donnie would provide some greatly needed comic relief from a stressful workweek. The night before, we agreed to meet at Donnie's house around 11:30am. One by one, the guys were pulling up and waiting out front of his house.

There were about dozen or so riders with bikes of all makes and models. With the amount of noise we were making laughing and joking, several of the neighbors had walked onto their front porch. Donnie had finally come out of the house from the rear, riding his bike in the alley adjacent to his house. Donnie was somewhat cheap, and had purchased a used helmet that looked like a large yellow fishbowl on top of his head. He purchased his riding boots from one of the local department stores.

They were brown with a large hard yellow rubber sole. Upon making his grand entrance into the opening that led onto the street, he came to a full stop. It was as though the event occurred in slow motion, as he and the bike fell over to the right. The street just roared with laughter as the kids and adults looked over in our direction and began to bust out laughing as well. Eric and one of the other riders had gotten off their bikes to help lift the bike off Donnie as he flapped around like a flounder. Afterwards, he stood up and dusted himself off as the laughter continued.

I was sitting on the curb laughing hysterically as Donnie stood there; probably wishing he could disappear. When his mother poked her head outside of the front door to see what all the commotion was all about, the laughter started all over again. After about fifteen minutes of cracking up in laughter, we had finally wiped away the tears from our eyes and proceeded on our way.

In time, each one of us would ultimately end up "biting the dust" while riding our bikes. Consequently, we came up with the street moniker affectionately known as the "Crash Crew". We rode to provide moral support to one of the riders participating in a softball tournament. When we arrived at the ballpark, the spectators turned away from the game to gaze in our direction. We were still cracking up over the incident with Donnie as we were trying to find somewhere in the bleachers to sit.

One of the softball players had brought along a cooler of beer, so we made a mad dash to his van. Since we were on motorcycles, we drank only one beer as we were cheering and jeering with the ebb and flow of the game. I was thoroughly enjoying myself in the company of this crazy and wild bunch of guys. After the game, some of the guys were trying to holler at a few of the female spectators to invite them down to the annual Soul Brothers softball tournament held in Mansfield.

We finally left town heading back home, and we decided to stop by a local drive up restaurant to get something to eat. As we proceeded to get off our bikes, Eric started screaming out in laughter as he was pointing to Donnie's feet. One of the heels on his riding boot had partially melted from the heat of the exhaust pipe. You could see smoke flying from the exhaust pipe that smelled as if he hit a skunk. We started howling in laughter as Donnie looked down and started cursing at his foot.

One of the guys started hopping up and down as though his feet were on fire and began to imitate James Brown singing "Hot Foot" instead of the original lyrics of hot pants. It was a good thing Donnie paid no more than ten dollars for those boots. He gave us far more in value with the comic relief that was provided, and he took our clowning all in stride. Purchasing that motorcycle was one of the best investments I ever made. It was as though I received a set of wings and had learned to fly. The excitement and feeling of freedom I had when riding provided a great deal of therapeutic medicine for my emotional and spiritual well being. Riding a motorcycle requires the ability to balance several tasks simultaneously.

The rider must be very aware of the road and traffic conditions, as well as the environment around him. I came to appreciate the view of life sitting atop my motorcycle versus the driver's seat of the car. Most motorcycle riders appear to be more friendly and outgoing towards their fellow man. As I would occasionally pass a rider most always, would they wave or flash their headlamps as a means of acknowledging our shared love of riding.

My life as a part time DJ provided me with a needed emotional outlet outside of the workplace. My ability to cut loose in a party atmosphere enabled me to become comfortable in speaking in a public setting. This would become of great value to me in my later years as my career on the work front began to change as well. I always loved music, but gained a greater appreciation for the skill and talent required of an artist to create great music.

I admired the talent that Eddie's younger brother Vernon had in his ability to play by ear. He allowed me to borrow several of his jazz albums, and told me to listen to them. In my becoming involved in disc jockeying, I had trained my ears to focus on the many facets of a song. I could make distinctions between the various types of instruments, the quality of the lyrics and vocal range of the singer. Becoming a DJ improved my ability to tune in and focus. I would listen for the nuances and subtle changes in the chords, melodies and rhythm patterns.

To notice if there were messages contained within the lyrical content of the song or rap that I could make use of in life. I would use these techniques on the job front to deal with issues and situations I would face. Jazz and Hip-hop would become my Ying and yang as they emerged as my two favorite forms of music. Jazz helped to calm the noises in my mind and to sooth my spirit. Hip-hop would pump me up emotionally, and depending upon the artist would energize my mind and nourish my soul.

Through Hip-hop, I came to listen intently to the words of others, to not be so hasty to speak. One of my favorite rap tunes of the time was "The Message" by Grandmaster Flash and the Furious 5. The song spoke to the pain and plight of urban life in cities across America, and served as a warning sign that drugs and crime were on the rise as well. Many individuals of the older generations complain about the violence in the lyrics or that some artists promote drug use and sexual promiscuity. Music like any art form is a reflection of the social conditions, which exists as art imitates life.

In their effort to "Keep it Real", many artists are unabashed and unashamed to speak about the many social ills they have experienced. I say to those who do not care for the manner the tone or the tenor of what the rappers speak about, take the necessary actions towards changing the social conditions of which they speak of. Give them something else to rap about or sing about that will create a different dynamic and reality than what is currently experienced.

Change the condition; change the reality whereby a new verse and chorus flows through the ears and minds of the masses. In doing so, the lyrics, rhythm, and rhyme are in synchronous harmony with both the messenger and those willing to listen. To speak positively to the mind, body and soul resonates the message that God is with us and loves us all. Each of us has the capacity to change our lives and our surroundings for the better. It requires that we each place a new spin on life as the reel to real of our existence turns. We can then become a people whom are living their lives uplifted and enlightened.

I enjoyed this period in my life that I experienced and remembered for the rest of my life. We were inseparable and you would rarely find one of us without the other. As in all things in life, we can not escape the reality that all good things come to an end. The only inevitable guarantee in life is that change will happen with or without your consent. The nature of our relationship would begin to undergo a transformation as we began to mature and grow in our outlook on life. Life is for the living and we are to savor every moment. This period in my life was the first time that I could honestly say that I truly enjoyed my life. By no means had I come completely into my own, but I was well on my way.

CHAPTER FOURTEEN

A new club in Elyria, a suburb of Cleveland opened called Studio 93, named after one of the popular radio stations in the area. Because Mansfield was so small, meant that if we wanted to enjoy the club atmosphere we had to travel out of town to enjoy the experience. One of Eric's friends Henry G. had an associate who went by the nickname of The Pleasure Man. He was a tall, light skinned brother of Puerto Rican descent who had serious mixing skills on the "ones and two's" (turntables).

Henry G. actually gave Eric his start into becoming a mobile DJ. He was a short man, with a wildly styled Afro and big black plastic rimmed glasses. You would picture him as a DJ by any means, but he definitely had the persona and was one of the best masters of ceremonies (M.C.) I had met. Pleasure Man's real name was Guy, who was a soft-spoken brother who was very unassuming at first glance. However, when he got behind those turntables, he brought a heat and an energy that could power all of Northeastern Ohio.

At the time, he was one of the premier DJ's in the Cleveland area and the women just loved him. He would have a string of women lined around the DJ booth every time he played. It was the opening night of the club, and of course, there was no way that we were not going to attend the grand opening. I was still underage at the time, and gave no thought that I could not gain entry. The security that night was heavy, to deal with the massive crowd that came to participate in the event.

Because of the sheer amount of people, we could not gain entry into the club and were greatly disappointed. We ended up going to some hole in the wall joint across town, as well as many other patrons who attempted to attend the opening night gala. Although our initial plans were changed, we still ended up having a great time. The following weekend we made the trip again with about ten guys.

We were dressed to kill, wearing our John Wayne shirts, pleated pants and bow ties that were the fashion style at the time. The Gheri curls were in full effect and my hair had more waves flowing than the Pacific ocean. We arrived at the club early as it first opened, making sure we did not miss the party again. It had been raining most of the night, and it was a sight to see people trying to duck and dodge their way through the rain. Upon our entrance, we saw Pleasure Man setting up his equipment and walked over to the booth to speak to him.

He was very happy to see us, for he knew that with our presence the club would be jumping for sure. The booth stood right in front of the entrance to the club, which provided a perfect view to see all the pretty women come in and out. We walked over to the bar to buy some drinks, and proceeded to walk back towards the DJ booth. About an hour had passed as the crowd began to grow in size in spite of the current downpour of rain.

Some of the guys were walking around the club looking for females to dance with before the music started. Eric, Donnie, Bobby, and I stood by the entrance. One of the local clowns from our hometown we nicknamed Simple Sonny came stepping through the door. I had worked with his older brother at the telephone refurbishing company, but never met him personally. The first time I ever saw this guy was at a local high school football game. It was a cross-town rivalry and we all decided to go to the game after we had gotten off work.

The game was about to start and we had just sat down when Simple Sonny walked into the stadium. Someone was sitting in the upper level hollered out his name in order to get his attention. As he turned around to respond, he opened his arms up wide and said "hello everybody" as though the entire crowd shouted out his name. We just busted out laughing as he tried to cool step his way up the stairs.

The cheerleaders were going through their routines when one of them fainted. The paramedics immediately ran over to the young girl trying to revive her. All of a sudden, Simple Sonny comes trotting down the stairs, jumps over the banister onto the football field. He walked over to the paramedics looking over their shoulders. Cupping my hands over my mouth, I shouted out "Sonny, paging Doctor Sonny" as the crowd just roared with laughter. He looked up as though the crowd was cheering his efforts, and we just cracked up all the more.

It amazed me how this guy, whose IQ didn't match his shoe size could attract the attention of what appeared to be some rather intelligent females. The moment he opened his mouth, it was plain to see that he was the furthest thing from a Rhodes Scholar. I guess women have the same opinions about some men who have girlfriends dumber than a mop handle. As we were standing around watching the parade of females coming into the club, I was in awe of some of the outlandish outfits these women would wear.

Some of the women did not wear undergarments; when combined with sheer clothing meant nothing was left to the imagination. Many of the females who paraded themselves at the club were some of the most gorgeous women I had ever seen. But I learned a long time ago that what may look great in appearance or taste good to you may not be the best or the right thing for you.

We attended the club frequently, and of course, you would come to recognize familiar faces and bodies. I would see some of the same women come in with a different man, or leave with a different one than the one from the previous encounter. As these women would pass by, some of the men would make comments and in some cases reach out to touch someone. I know that you should not judge a book by its cover. Nevertheless, I wondered what some of these females were thinking as they dressed, and the manner in which they conducted themselves in public. Women take great offense when men make derogatory remarks such as "bitch, whore or slut" and direct the comments towards them.

Now I do not condone any man putting their hands on anyone without their permission or promote the use of such language. How you present yourself will have an impact on the quality of treatment and respect you ultimately receive. We all choose the labels we decide to wear, and the image we choose to portray. If you desire to be treated with respect, then one should conduct them selves in a respectable manner.

There are very few females on the planet that does not look into a mirror at least twice before leaving their home. This being the case, the opportunity to perform a "self-check" of one's appearance reduces the chance of being the subject of ridicule. Perception is a form of reality and the way one's conducts themselves in public will definitely affect the type of responses received.

It is said that the clothes one chooses to wear, speaks volumes about an individual's character and personality. The individual has total control over the image they project to the outside world. If you choose to wear outlandish multicolored hairstyles, 10-inch long nails, clothes three sizes too small, and too much makeup don't be surprised when people stop to look and stare. Give thought and consideration as to the image and statement the individual intends to reflect upon the mirror of the world at large.

My suspicious nature was ever present, especially when it came to females in a nightclub setting. I can literally count on one hand the number of times I approached females in order to pass them my telephone number. I was not willing to expend the effort or take a chance to find out if the image of a particular female I thought attractive was a lady of substance.

Dave Chappell, a well-known stand up comedian expressed my opinion on the subject better than I could have myself. He gave an example of a man dressed up in either a policeman's or firemen's uniform who in actuality was neither. If the casual observer saw such a man on the street and an emergency arose, one would assume that the person in the uniform was whom they purported themselves as being. Females that wear very revealing clothing out in public do seek to gain attention by virtue of their willingness to "let it all hang out". There are those who become upset when they garner negative attention or comments based on the attire chosen.

As Dave said, "If women choose to put on a hooker's uniform then why be surprised when men perceive you and treat you as such?" The clothes were purchased, worn with the intention of gaining a man's attention. A female cannot possibly be seeking to appeal to the mind of a man by wearing revealing clothes. Nor can they be seeking to gain respect for their keen intellect. The choice is to place the focus on their physical assets, whereby some females cast their bets on the quick hit. The rewards received are short lived and the chances for winning the grand prize of a long term loving relationship quite slim. One should expect such a man to move on if a better-looking package deal comes along.

Within a span of about fifteen minutes, most men categorize women into one of several types. The first type of female is the freak; the promiscuous type of woman a man only desires to have sex. Another type is the gift giver, the type of woman who caters to the materialistic desires of a man. The last type is the potential "wifely" woman who appeals to all aspects of a man's needs to connect on a physical, intellectual and spiritual level.

The first two types of women will never be considered as potential long term relationship prospects for they only satisfy one or two of the needs of the man. If a man perceives a woman as being sexually free and loose, she is identified as such and will be treated accordingly. The male will assume that if the female was so quick and willing to give herself to him, then surely she has done so many times before.

If a woman attempts to buy the affections of a man, he will accept the gifts given freely given. However, he will continue to look for the wifely type of woman elsewhere. The criterion used is based upon the type of reflection given by the female. Females by virtue of how they present themselves dictate the degree to which they are respected. In every instance, the behavior and manner by which the female conducts her will dictate how well she is treated and the level of respect she receives. No man, either the good guy or the dog desires to have as his future wife a woman considered as being "community property". If the female has no self respect or honor with no "shame in her game", she should expect to be treated with disrespect.

Eric's treatment of women is a prime example of my statement. He slept with countless women and was the epitome of what women describe as a dog. He initially lied to some women in order to sleep with them, but he also told the truth to some as well. Once the truth was known that he slept around or just wanted sex from them, many of these women chose to stay with him. I would sometimes bristle in the manner in which he spoke to some of them.

As with so many women the 98.6 rule comes into effect; all that matters is having a warm body to lie next to. In the minds of many women, sharing a man is far better than not having one at all. His main girlfriend knew the truth about his inability to be faithful but continued to stay in a relationship with him. I was the eyewitness to many a bad public scene whereby some of his female friends would confront one another on the street. No one forced these women to continue to have sex or to continue to buy the gifts Eric was so willing to accept.

Once the truth about his character was known, the opportunity to move on was an option that few females chose to exercise. Most believed that they could change him, make him somehow love them exclusively.

He seized the opportunity given to him, so in no way could these women consider themselves as being used for they gave their bodies and gifts to him of their own free will. There is a saying which goes "a fair exchange, there can be no robbery", such was the case with Eric.

Simple Sonny was about to provide us with some more of his comical antics. He was wearing a cream colored suit with matching hat, and a long tibbar (rabbit spelled backward) fur coat and walking cane. He stepped into the club as though he owned it and thought that he was the sharpest man alive. As he entered the club, he stopped to strike a pose to make sure he was in plain view.

What he failed to notice, due to the raindrops on his sunglasses, were the two steps that led to the dance floor area. He proceeded to walk; missing the steps and tumbled head over heels with his hat, glasses, and cane flying in every direction. His long trench coat flew over his head as he hit the floor and slid about a foot. We all hollered in unison as Eric ran into the rest room after almost pissing on himself in laughter. Donnie and Bobby were screaming and I was dry heaving as tears were falling down my face

Simple Sonny's date was still standing at the top of the stairs looking down at him as the crowd continued to fall out in laughter. The facial expression on the Pleasure Man was priceless, as he did not even bust a smile just shook his head and continued to play. Simple Sonny finally picked himself up off the floor, as another woman walked up and handed him his glasses and hat. I lost it again as she was trying to contain herself in the process of returning his belongings.

When the so-called pretty boys such as Simple Sonny would make a fool of themselves in public, I cherished every opportunity to laugh at them. Guys like him who thought they were so cool most always ended up looking like a damn fool.

Growing up I had to contend with the ridicule of those like Simple Sonny, but as a man, I cherished every opportunity to crack right back. In his attempt to have the spotlight of attention thrown his way by dressing like a circus clown, he as so many others seeking the spotlight fail to recognize one thing.

When standing on stage before the crowd in front of the spotlight, a shadow is cast behind the individual. Whatever is done good or bad as the individual stands before the spotlight is on Front Street for the entire world to see. Frank Sinatra is a prime example of such an individual. In the eye of the public, he was considered one of the coolest and hippest men of his time.

When he stepped on stage, he held the crowd in the palm of his hand as he gave them the performance of his life every time. However, his manic personality and short fuse temper caused him problems in his personal life that the press brought into the spotlight of the public. Standing in the spotlight places you at the center of attention, but it also places you at risk of being the center of ridicule or scorn. If the quality of one's performance is in any way lacking, the light of truth will always shine through to show the true essence of the individual.

The situation on the job front began to take some interesting twists and turns. There were rumors abound of another pending merger of state operations in the air. The rumors to merge the Ohio and Pennsylvania operations with those of the state of Indiana were beginning to emerge. The company had already lain off several thousand employees at the time. The rumors made an already paranoid employee population all the more nervous.

The company had solicited an outside consulting firm to evaluate the myriad of job descriptions and responsibilities among the state operations. Each employee was handed a lengthy form to describe every task and function performed supposedly to ascertain if individuals with like job titles were treated equitably.

The "fix" was in the mix from the very beginning. A meeting was being planned to discuss the metrics involved with merging the various departments and organizations of the combined tri-state operations tentatively planned. The managers and supervisors had gotten together amongst themselves to define the various job descriptions.

They gave us a template that matched the current job title we occupied, as we were instructed to sign our names at the bottom line. Those unwilling to comply were coerced into believing that they could potentially be laid off pending the next forced reduction.

Part of the plan was to separate the switch engineering functions whereby the new digital technology group transferred to Ft. Wayne, Indiana. The engineering for the legacy enterprise analog switching systems was retained by the local state entities.

During this period, many of the regional telecommunications companies were in the midst of modernizing their switching networks. The electromechanical and analog electronic based switching and transmissions systems equipment were replaced with high-speed digital and fiber optics gear. The skills required to design and install these systems were similar, but required specific training.

The issues regarding promotions, training and corporate politics was one that I struggled with during my entire career with the company. The method by which promotions and merit increases were given was the process of management by objective (MBO). This process was supposedly to establish goals and objectives of the company that were to increase shareholder wealth. The objectives were broken down by department and assigned to individual contributors.

Executive bonuses and pay raises were to be determined by qualitatively measuring the achievement of those predetermined goals on a quarterly basis. This would determine the amount of money allocated towards salary expense and subsequent increases in pay.

I learned early on that the MBO process was the furthest thing from fair or objective. The process was more akin to "management by subjective". Some would receive pay raises based upon who was the designated winner of the popularity contest within the department. Merit increases were used as a means to control behavior, not reward ones contributions to the company.

Many corporations such as the one I worked for expended much energy to restrict and control the thoughts and actions of its workforce. The use of fear and intimidation as tools to increase productivity were quite common. Corporate conformity was the norm of the time, whereby maintaining the status quo was done at any price. Original thought or any efforts to change the status quo were unwelcome. Those who exhibited any measure of individuality outside of the norm were dealt with swiftly and unmercifully.

On one hand, the corporate leadership sought to change the company by constantly transitioning from centralized to decentralized management control. These changes were nothing but an illusion and did little to foster or promote the innovation or exchange of ideas among the employees. Nor did this consternation bring forth new products or services to the customer. The primary reason for restructuring or reducing the size of the workforce is to reduce operating expenses, thus boosting the balance sheets and profit margins of a given company.

From the moment, I was hired and long since my departure, the company had undergone countless reengineering and restructuring efforts over the years. Very few understand the importance of adapting to the ever-changing climate of business. Those businesses that do not embrace change in time shall become extinct. It is one thing to change one's business practices to improve the quality of the product, or to become more competitive. Many of the so-called changes undertaken by corporate America are little more than window dressing to appease the Wall Street analysts or investment community.

A few corporations use change as a means of fostering the free exchange of thoughts and ideas among its workforce to create new products and services for the consumer. The overuse of the phrase by politicians and corporations over the years has cheapened and lessened the impact of its meaning. One may as well cry wolf as if the masses are to believe that those who tout change are honest about truly changing the system of corruption within the institutions of both business and government.

For the more things change, the more they remain the same. Billions of dollars are blown like so much fairy dust into the eyes of the employees and shareholders alike in the guise of transforming the company to become more mean and lean. The finance and accounting departments of some corporations use smoke and mirror tactics in the keeping of financial records and transactions giving the illusion of profitability.

In most cases, these cloak and dagger measures of "cooking the books" are a means of covering up the inept management decisions of the CEO and board of directors. Alternatively, in some cases many will stretch the limits of accounting rules to color the financial statements. In order to ensure the receipt of bonuses and executive stock options tied to the rise in stock value.

Therefore, when their plans go awry, they announce the next round of layoffs or spin and sell off major assets of the business. The markets rewards those same individuals whose decisions caused the necessity of such drastic measures in the first place by making recommendations to buy the companies stock. So, the cycle continues, as those whom create and perpetuate these inept management decisions receive compensation nonetheless. There are no ramifications enacted as the executives and their duplicitous boards of directors continue to collect hefty salaries and stock options. CEO pay has spiraled to astronomical levels, whereby the average pay exceeds 200-1000% percent of that of the lowest paid worker. Those left holding the bag are the employees and shareholders.

If any employee dares voice their concerns with the decisions made by their superiors, they would face being fired or demoted. This was the situation within my company. The atmosphere within the walls of most corporations is similar to those of the three monkeys; see nothing, hear nothing, and say nothing. I participated in many conversations with coworkers who would voice their concerns about some business decision in private outside of the earshot of theirs superiors. If given the opportunity to say what were truly on their mind most would remain silent in the presence of their superiors. There were a few guys in my department who had no fear to speak their minds. Arnie, Chuck and Rex were the designated radicals of the department.

Keeping it real and telling it like it is came at a great price, financially speaking. All three were denied promotions because they would not cow tow to their superior's wishes. All three of them were highly skilled and were among the top performers in the department. As I stated, performance had nothing to do with being given a raise or promotion. I highly respected them for their candor and willingness to maintain their individuality.

The relationship among the members of the engineering department were already tenuous, but became even more so now that the possibility for the potential transfer of functions loomed overhead. The Indiana State operations were somewhat further along with their network modernization program. Their engineering department had several individuals trained on the latest equipment provided by several of the major switch vendors

The atmosphere was similar to a blue light special at Kmart, as managers and supervisors were jockeying for position to cherry pick the engineers they deemed as "franchise players". The performance of the department was still measured based up the amount of capital and expense in ones budget. None of the managers or supervisors was willing to give up their prime time experienced engineer's to the newly formed group.

One afternoon several of us began to discuss the situation and our feelings about the manner the process worked. We were treated more like livestock, being poked and prodded before being selected for breeding stock or designated for slaughter. Although it would be almost a year before the transition was to take place, the atmosphere within the department was more corrosive and divisive than it ever was before.

Most of the senior level engineers had received formal training both as installers and as engineers on the various switches deployed into the network. I had already been with the company for well over a year, and had yet to receive any formal training. What I had come to learn about systems engineering came at the result of on the job training and trial and error.

I ramped up the learning curve quite quickly during my tenure within the department. In doing so, the level of complexity in the types of projects assigned to me increased. The switch engineers had responsibilities for the allocation of floor space for other non switch related equipment that required that we communicate and interact with the outside plant and transmission systems groups on a regular basis. Ralph and Commodore would provide me with a crash level course in basic transmission engineering.

This increased my understanding of the interrelationships between the switch and transmission network components necessary to complete a call. In my own way, I was taking the initiative to train myself in order to increase my knowledge and value to the company. I was still very naïve and blind to what was going on around me in the aspects of both the culture and politics of the company. It was a very strange period for me as I think back, for I saw with my own eyes the dynamics of what was happening. I felt immune, almost bulletproof in foolishly thinking that I was somehow exempt from the same forces, which affected the rest of my coworkers.

I remember one late afternoon having a discussion with my mentor Richard, the brother who had taken me under his wing. I asked him how long it had taken him to receive his first promotion after he was initially hired. It had taken him almost four years to receive his first promotion, and then he received two more during the next four years. He spoke of facing several individuals who harbored prejudice and resentment towards him.

He was fortunate to have had a boss who was fair and objective in the treatment of his employees. Richard was an avid golfer and used his love of the game as an opportunity to network and gain favor with other members within the company. He was respected for both his game, and his knowledge and capability to get the job done. Richard was not the confrontational type by any means. Richard would not back down if he were of the opinion that he was in the right on a certain issue. He was of the opinion that a more passive conciliatory approach to dealing with the issues of race was more effective, especially being a black man.

Of course, I disagreed with some of his philosophical ideas about race. I used the manner by which Roger and I was hired as prime examples to drive home my point. The fact that the Civil Rights Act and Affirmative Action legislation was enacted to redress past inequities in the treatment of people of color speaks to the inherent nature of mankind. The very fact that the company had to take extraordinary efforts to bring people of color into the fold speaks to the important aspect of our discussion.

Time and time again when given the opportunity to "Do the right thing" from the onset, the onus upon the majority seems to select the exact opposite. If left to its own avarice, those in the majority choose the path that causes harm or exploits over that which serves the common good. To make choices that benefits the wants of the few over the needs of the many. Like a moth to the flame burned by the fire is the road down the path of least resistance the one most often traveled.

One of the negative aspects of the free enterprise system is the practice by some of the theory of the zero sum game. The belief that wealth or opportunity can be attained only as a result of another's equivalent loss. To have a slice of the American pie of opportunity is grossly insufficient for some. That in order to be deemed a success requires that one owns the pie or better yet the entire bakery. This philosophy negates the needs of others, whereby profit is the sole motivator. To achieve the bottom-line at all costs, even if it means to attain profit at the expense of someone else's pain, misery, or personal well being.

This process was the norm during the early decades of the industrial revolution. Many companies exploited child labor to work in the many factories, mills and coal mines around the world. Muckrakers of the era such as social activists and newspaper reporters were willing to risk their lives and careers to shine the spotlight on the abuses of children. It had taken a concerted effort to make the public aware of these practices before laws were enacted to bring the situation to a halt. The onus within the business community to do the right thing was not the primary concern. Increased profit through the utilization of cheap child labor was. After all, it was the free press that brought the issue to the public arena that pressure was applied to the corporations to change their business practices.

The company I worked for was formed through the acquisition and merging of smaller, rural telephone companies. The company hired many of the employees from the very same rural communities that it served. In many instances, some people grew up lacking the exposure and opportunity to interact with people of color. Coupled with the racist views taught to them by many of their parents, it was to no surprise that the company lacked diversity. This mix of dysfunction fostered the prejudicial state of mind that permeated the workplace. Where prejudice exists, bigotry is sure to follow. Therefore, these practices became quite common place throughout pockets of the company.

The chances that one would even consider hiring someone whom their parents taught to hate let alone respect is as unlikely as finding a snowball in the Sahara desert. The goal was not to hire the best person for the job, but to maintain the status quo. The status quo was maintained through hiring a steady stream of friends and family members willing to perpetuate the cycle of exclusivity.

This ensured that those within the circle of influence would have the economic and financial means to take care of those who took care of them. The practice of "one hand washing the other" or to scratch the back and satisfy the itch of another to gain favor was commonplace. Therefore, it is no wonder that the company found itself in a position whereby affirmative action became the vehicle to address the lack of diversity.

Richard and I engaged in many heated discussions about issues of race, corporate politics and the current situation that existed at the company during my tenure. I respected his opinion very much and although we disagreed on many occasions, I appreciated the wisdom and straightforward discussions we had. I had been with the company for a little over a year and was already becoming bored and restless with the role I was given to play.

The company owned a telecommunications equipment-manufacturing subsidiary. Several of the engineers in our department were involved in field trials to beta test a new digital switch the company had heavily invested in at the time. I watched with great envy the manner by which they were free to travel, and had the opportunity to place such an important role.

Early one morning I had asked my boss what it would take in order for me to become more involved with the new technology. In short, there was a pecking order based upon seniority and that I would have to wait my turn. Senior members of the engineering department were given first consideration. He stated that there was still much for me to learn. As my skills improved, he stated that I would receive more challenging work assignments.

I had been task to update the power consumption charts for the entire southern district of Ohio. Two other associate engineers', who were hired about the same time as me, were task to perform the tasks for the remaining districts with the state. Due to the pressing issues of other higher profile projects, the other engineers did not keep the charts up to date. This was not exactly what I had in mind at the time. I was of the opinion that this was a menial task and at first took offense.

However, as a measure to show how much of a team player I was, I accepted the task given me. The charts depicted the power consumption based on the current drain of the equipment installed within a specific location. Once the demand exceeded the design capacity of the power plant, this would trigger the necessity to expand the size by installing larger batteries and rectifiers. It had taken me a little over a month, but I was able to complete the assignment given to me.

Dick was pleased with my performance and as promised, he gave me projects that were more challenging. One late afternoon a bulletin posted to announce the annual company picnic. I attended the eastern district's company picnic the year before and had great fun. As I started making inquiries into the types of activities involved, I immediately lost interest. The picnic area was located in a small town about twenty five miles away from the office. Some of the employees had a rag tag band that would be playing country and western and 60's rock and roll.

There was no way I was going to travel over 100 miles round trip to listen to country western and eat hot dogs. At the time, I had some reservations about being one of a hand full of blacks attending company functions. Ralph had tried to convince me to attend in order to meet his family, but I skirted the offer by telling him I had a DJ function to perform. As stated before, the attitudes towards the departments outside of engineering was less than cordial.

Many of my coworkers held the view that to attend any company sponsored function was an act of treason by fraternizing with the enemy. There existed a seething dislike for the sales and marketing department of the company. I had attended a few meetings with members of the sales department, and the manner in which they spoke irritated me. The vocal tone and the reflections used when they spoke were so disingenuous, fake and phony. You could bet that if you posed a question, not to expect a straight answer. Just like a crooked politician, those within the sales department spoke with forked tongues and out of both sides of their necks.

The fact that the sales force had a tendency to speak with such a condescending attitude only added fuel to the fire of discontent. Speaking to us as though we were savant idiots only served to widen the gap between the engineering and sales department. Those within the sales and marketing department would concoct some hair-brained schemes that were either not technically or economically feasible. If an idea or customer requirement were not feasible, they would feign being concerned that the engineering department could not serve the needs of their potential client. The only concern most of the sales people or marketers had been to line their pockets. To obtain their bonuses and meet sales quotas at all costs.

In order to meet the goals and objectives of the state executives, the engineering department was tasked to attempt to bring some of the pipe dreams into reality. If we were successful, then the glory and accolades went to those in the sales and marketing department. I never had much respect for those who were willing to lie or trick their way up the corporate ladder. This practice was far too common then and still too commonly practiced now.

The straightforward approach was the best way for one to gain my confidence or respect, for this was the manner in which I conducted myself. When I observed anyone who attempted to pull the wool over my eyes, I would become highly upset. To those challenging my intelligence I would show no mercy or provide no assistance too. If one viewed the organizational chart, most of those occupying senior executive level positions came from the sales, marketing, revenues or finance departments. Very rarely would one find an executive above the title of director who came from the engineering ranks. It was this inequity, which bred the level of mistrust and cynicism within the department towards the company as a whole.

For the first few years of my career with the company it was though I was sleep walking. It was surreal; viewing and experiencing all that was going on around me, but felt detached. I heard with my own ears the jabs and saw with my own eyes the personal attacks made towards some of my coworkers. I did not pay attention to the signals and signs around me for I was viewing my life through rose colored glasses. The advice given to me by both Big Frank and Clyde to be leery and aware of those around me went unheeded.

I was oblivious to the fact that so many of the engineers had been in the same job, in the same department for twenty years or more. The career path for those in the engineering department provided limited growth opportunities. The salary bands were lower in comparison with those of other departments as well. The executive management of the company tended to type cast and pigeon hole those within the department. In spite all of what was going on around me, I held on tightly to the belief in the statement made by Bill the college recruiter.

I believed that the sky was the limit, that I had the chance to move up the ranks if I performed my job well. I respected the wisdom and experience of those who worked for the company far longer than I did. I was not truly aware of the relationship of the group's dynamic to the company as a whole. I did not pay attention to the ebb and flows of negative perceptions towards the engineering department by other groups. I did not recognize nor correlate the potential impacts of those perceptions upon my career.

In my naïve state of mind, I bought the hook, line and sinker believing that I would be treated with fairness and provided the equal opportunity to move up the ranks. I thought that as long as I played by the rules and paid my dues the world was my oyster. As time progressed, I would find out the hard way that the rules of the game were forever changing. To discover in time the quality of my work did not matter in the great scheme of things. My performance ultimately was judged based upon criteria that had nothing to do with the manner of the work I completed.

The game was rigged long before I sat down at the table as the deck was stacked and the cards I was dealt were marked. That in order for me to move up the ladder I would have to be willing to use the same tactics as those who held the positions of power and authority. I would have to become self-serving, be willing to lie on demand and mistreat people.

I would have to be willing to compromise my self-respect and personal code of ethics. This would be the criterion others gauged before receiving my gate pass into the ranks of executive management. I unknowingly at the time would be in for some might rude awakenings on many fronts in the months and years to come. My entire world would soon turn upside down, and I would come to see my life in an entirely different light.

CHAPTER FIFTEEN

One afternoon I had stopped by Bobby's house for a visit as he had yet to arrive home from work. His mother was there and as we would often do, started to have one of our many sincere discussions. Bobby's girlfriend asked her whether Bobby was cheating on her, but she refused to get herself involved into his affairs. Bobby's relationship ran hot and cold like a faucet, and both he and his girlfriend had very bad tempers to match.

His sense of chivalry was strange in that he was very protective of his sisters and would be quick to come to their defense if necessary. However, when it came to his personal affairs, it was a far different matter. This was the case with most of my homeboys at the time. They each had girlfriends as their main entrees, but they also had many side dishes as well. When we had our cookouts or other gatherings, I sometimes felt left out because I did not have a girlfriend.

All of their girlfriends liked me though, wishing that their men were more like me. At times, they would confide in me with some of the troubles they were having. I would sometimes attempt to mediate the conflicts when they would arise. I felt very uncomfortable in the positions my boys would place me in at times. They would use me as an alibi while they crept on their girlfriends, but I would not give up the ghost no matter what. It was very hard for me to relate and understand why their girlfriends would be so willing to stay in a relationship. Especially when so much distrust and unhappiness existed within their relationships.

There is a song called "A Thin Line between Love and Hate" and my boys crossed the line many times with their girlfriends. The arguments at times became quite heated, and in all honesty, I wondered why my boys were upset. They knew all too well that the accusations leveled against them were 100% true. If the script was flipped and their ladies cheated on them, they would be ready to commit mass murder. The belief and opinion that some males have that what their partner does not know cannot hurt them is another relationship fairytale that does not hold water.

To be so willing to deceive and betray the trust of someone you supposedly love in my opinion is one of the most hurtful and harmful acts one could do to another person. Cheating within the bounds of a committed relationship is probably the number one cause for the breakup of marriages and families in America. The statistics bear out that today just as many women as men are prone to engage in extramarital affairs or infidelities. To seek outside the bounds of their relationship what they perceive lacks within it. The attraction, danger and allure of infidelity can be as addictive as any drug. With the U.S., divorce rate exceeding sixty percent indicates how destructive the impact of such behavior can be to the foundation of the structure within the family unit.

The continued swing of the pendulum as it relates to the ever-changing definition and relative importance of commitment that is at the core of the problem. How over time its value has become increasing diminished within the context of personal relationship cuts to the heart of the matter. The restrictive social mores of the 40's and 50's created a backlash of sentiment of the first born of the baby boom generation. With the advent of the beatnik and hippie counterculture, young men and women began to rebel against the monolithic social structures and foundations of "the establishment". The Civil Rights movement also caused many to question the status quo of the times. The youth rebuffed the "us versus them" conformist attitudes of their parents that led to the permissive carefree attitudes of the "Free Love" movement of the 60's and 70's.

The creation of the anti establishment counters culture, free love and feminist movement planted the seeds of discontent and destruction of commitment. The movement sought to liberate those who felt restricted by the attitudes and actions of those whom occupied positions of power within the society. In any revolution, there are casualties and in this case, truth, commitment, and respect were some of the soldiers left dead on the battlefield of change within the social order.

It is no longer a secret that many have come to find out that the so-called "good old days" were not always as good as they seemed. As information became more widely available, new revelations came into the forefront of the American public. With the advent of talk shows, the stories of multitudes of people victimized in their youth were being uncovered and spread by the news media. Most of the abuses kept in the closet have been brought into the light of public eye.

Many of the parents and grandparents of the baby boom generation inflicted many harmful acts upon their children. Acts of physical and emotional abuse were committed, many times as the result of alcohol or drug use. These abusive acts damaged the psyche of those so affected. Some chose to bury the pain they felt deep within. Others as a defensive mechanism lashed out, choosing to rebel against those who caused them harm. These abuses took place within the home, the schools, and the churches attended by these children.

Since the social norms of the times did not facilitate the discussion of such personal matters, no one spoke of them. As a result of their fear and shame, those victimized would not seek legal recourse or protection. Because many times the abuses were caused within the home, those victimized were reluctant to trust their other family members. So many people were left to suffer their fate in silence and under the cover of darkness.

The trusses within the framework of both family and religion were left irreparably damaged. The trust that many people placed within these institutions became broken and frayed. Consequently, many people sought refuge in the various counter culture movements that were prevalent at the time. Some members of the feminist movement viewed marriage and motherhood as stifling and restrictive to their cause for so called personal freedom.

Many became involved in the experimentation of drugs as part of the counter culture to escape the pain and anguish caused by the mistreatment they suffered. Those who chose to use these mind-altering drugs lost all inhibitions and a measure of self-control with each occurrence. Some people, experiencing the false sense of freedom induced by the drugs also helped foster the hedonistic sexual practices of those involved as well. The "Do Your Own Thing" attitude gave rise to the birth of many children whose parents would become far too permissive and derelict in raising them. The central focus being towards satisfying ones urges and desires took precedence above all else.

In an effort to slow the decay within the social fabric, the attitudes and practices of some began to change. This in turn swung the pendulum back towards the far right during the decades of the 80's and 90's. The residual effects from the previous decades of the hedonistic behaviors and societal attitudes of self-gratification still existed. The desire to find the next high or to seek the next sexual conquest provided little time for family concerns. The necessity to provide a stable home environment for children also became of little concern. This was especially true for those who were addicted to drugs, alcohol and the allure of the fast life. The need to satisfy ones urges took precedence over the need to provide guidance and nurturing to the children born.

These are the same children that were created as the result of exercising ones so called freedom of sexual expression. One of the popular phrases of the time was to live fast, die young, and make a good-looking corpse. Individuals became more willing to place themselves and their families in compromising situations. In time what was once, considered unacceptable social behavior became acceptable. Many individuals substituted the personal virtues of family, truth, trust, and respect for less than desirable traits. Lying, cheating and stealing became more socially acceptable as a means of satisfying personal desires. The willingness to commit to anything or anyone beyond the individuals owns selfish interest became the new social norm.

The apple does not fall far from the tree or the berry from the bush, so it should be of little surprise that many of the youth of today lack the willingness to commit to anything. In a land where ones word means nothing and "no fault" divorce is as common and plentiful as blades of grass on a football field. For many of those individuals who gave birth to them lack the virtue as well. It is no wonder the institution of marriage has fallen down, with the legs of the family structure wobbling waiting for the ten count. The willingness for people to commit to ones marriage vows has become almost nonexistent. The vows spoken have become as cheap and worthless as the paper printed on.

As for me, the risks of deception far outweighed the rewards of being involved in a relationship. That as it is in any game, there is a price to pay and for me I was unwilling to pay the price. Subconsciously I must have feared the potential of karmic retribution, not desiring to get back what I put out. In the years to come, I too on several occasions would have my mettle tested. I too would face circumstances and temptations to cheat in my relationships.

During my conversation with Bobby's mother Annie, I expressed to her my interest in her daughter Lana. It was no secret that I was crazy about her and any time she would walk into the room, my feelings for her was written all over my face. At the time, she was in one of her breakup periods with the guy she was dating at the time. I had asked Annie her opinion as to why she thought Lana continued to stay with this clown. He too was cheating on her, drank heavily and had a reputation for being a substance abuser.

She told me that love makes you put up with some mighty crazy things from the object of your affection that otherwise would not be tolerated. She spoke of her experiences as a young woman who married early in life. How she too had dealt with infidelity in her marriage and the pain she endured all the while knowing her husband was unfaithful. She placed the needs of her children and maintaining the stability of her family before herself.

She said that it is very easy to give advice to others in regards to how they should handle a relationship issue. Sometimes following your own advice can be quite difficult to do. Looking at a situation from the outsider's perspective, you can be more objective about the dynamics and issues taking place. When it comes down to addressing your own situation and shortcomings, most people tend not to see and deal with the underlying issues presented before them. For that requires that one be able to be honest with them and for most people that is the most difficult thing to do. People are quick to point out what the other should or should not be doing. Most people are not so willing to address the changes they need to make in their own life.

She knew how much I liked Lana, and wished that Lana would drop the zero she was dating for a young man such as me. She had spoken on my behalf to Lana that she should quit wasting her time on someone that did not love or respect her. Unbeknownst to me at the time, she suggested to Lana that she should consider giving me a chance to get to know her. However, for reasons unknown or unspoken, Lana kept me at arm length from her.

I remember one occasion seeing her looking so sad, and I could tell that she was upset behind something relating to her boyfriend. Sweetest Day was approaching that weekend, so I ordered a dozen roses and had they sent to her home. When she arrived home from her weekend duty at the army reserve station, they had just been delivered. She at first thought they came from him, but when she read the card attached, she came over and gave me the biggest hug. I would periodically do such things for her, but I grew both impatient and disappointed that time after time she would go back to her boyfriend. I purposely did not actively pursue a relationship during this period; holding out the hopes that she would see the light and come to her senses.

Perhaps she was of the opinion that because she knew how both Bobby and Eric were when it came to cheating, that I would treat her the same way. It was not the first time such an opinion was held about my character. Not knowing me personally, many females around town made the same assumption that I too was a dog. Because of my friendship with Bobby and Eric, I was made an unknowing victim of the "guilt by association" syndrome. I did not display any dog like tendencies and most often treated women who were respectful with respect.

The cloud and mystique being a DJ created a persona they did not help matters much either. When information is lacking, the mind begins to create images in the vacuum whether it remotely resembles the truth or not. In the same token, I too was also very fearful of letting anyone get too close to my heart as well. I had a blazing inferno in my heart that definitely burned for Lana. If I took the chance to get to know someone else and Lana came around, I would have dropped the woman like a bad habit. I chose not to place myself in jeopardy in the event that she changed her mind. In time I only ended up having my heart broken by waiting on a dream that would never become real.

In speaking to Annie, I subconsciously found myself attracted to the qualities of older more mature women. I perceived that older women due to their age were more aware, mature and sure about what they wanted. My man Roger dated a few older women and told me of his preference over females his age. When he first told me of his preference, I could not understand the appeal but in time, I would. I perceived females my own age as being flighty, childish, insecure, and over emotional about things of insignificance.

In my opinion, their mannerisms were cartoon like and behavior very infantile. Older women appeared to be more grounded in their outlook on life. My perception regarding this matter too would change in time. Age in and of itself does not guarantee that one shall attain wisdom, knowledge or maturity. As we would often due over the weekends, my crew and I hung out all afternoon. Later on that evening, we had heard of a cabaret that was taking place in a small town called Wooster that was about 30 miles east of Mansfield. We were bored out of our minds and decided to make the trek to bring some measure of excitement into our lives.

We had been playing cards and drinking all day, so we broke camp to clean ourselves up. We synchronized our watches and decided to rendezvous back to Bobby's house. Since there were seven of us, we decided to all pile into my sister's boyfriend Jerry's Ford LTD. Eric had stopped by the local drive through and bought a case of beer and some other alcoholic beverages.

Once we all arrived back at Bobby's, we drank for at least two hours before we decided to leave. Most of us were not in any shape to drive, so Bobby drove the car. We had stopped by a local gas station to fill the tank on the behemoth vehicle. We bought a few more beers for the trip, and proceeded to head out. One of the guys fired up a joint and began to pass it around. My head was already swimming, as it had been almost five years since I last smoke weed. I at first declined, but after Eric persistent cajoling I had taken the joint and began to draw on it. The joint had gone out, and Eric passed me his lighter to fire it up again.

Bobby, who did not smoke was flapping his hands like a dolphin waving the smoke away and I began to laugh at him. I was so high I could not see straight and in my attempts to light up the joint, I almost burned my lip. The guys just started cracking up in laughter, as I passed the joint and the lighter back to Eric. We arrived at the exit and as Bobby made a right turn, all of a sudden the strobe lights of a county sheriff's automobile began to flash.

We were all in such a panic, and luckily had thrown out the cans and bottles from the vehicle miles back. Donnie had some breath spray as we all began to take several hits and Eric even sprayed some inside the vehicle. As the officer approached the driver's side window and took Bobby's license, I began to panic. I was scared, fearing that the officer would some how discover that we had been drinking and smoking weed. The officer went to his vehicle to call in the license, then came back to the car and asked Bobby to get out of the car.

He kept his cool as he got out of the car. All of a sudden, Eric had turned around to look out of the rear window and just started laughing. I had gotten nervous and a little upset because Eric was laughing so loudly and I saw nothing funny about what was going down. The officer had asked Bobby to go through a series of sobriety tests. We all watched as Bobby was tilting his head backwards touching his nose.

He then was made to walk a straight line, then we all busted out laughing as he was stepping wide legged. Bobby was bowlegged and with every step he took, it appeared as though he was about to mount a horse. The officer was finding amusement with him as well, as he bent over to observe how straight Bobby was walking the line. The tests ceased and he issued Bobby a warning ticket for not using his turn signal. I had become very suspicious at that point, and I knew that was not the real reason why we were stopped.

Bobby did use the turn signal and little did we know that later that evening, we would once again be faced with a similar situation. We had dogged a serious bullet at that moment, and I came down off my high quite quickly because of the incident.

We had finally arrived at the hall where the cabaret was held as we each reached into our pockets to pull out a five spot for the cover charge. I noticed how everyone was just staring at us when we walked in, but did not pay it much attention. The ratio of females to males was about two to one in our favor as we began to scan the room to find available females with which to dance. Donnie and I were leaning up against the wall looking out over the small dance floor while the rest of the crew began to walk through the crowd.

I noticed again that both the males and females present at the function were checking us out. It appeared to me that some of the men were upset that we were there drawing attention from the females. The females were staring as well, attempting to both recognize and size us up. I started to get a little nervous thinking something was going to break out. I pointed the situation out to Donnie as he too began to notice the looks being shot in our direction.

Bobby and Eric had found two females willing to dance as they hit the floor. I finally grew tired of holding up the wall and asked an older female to dance. We worked our way in the direction of where Bobby and Eric were dancing. I really could not enjoy myself thinking about the situation with the county sheriff deputy and the atmosphere in the dance hall. The

DJ was slowing the set down and the guys went to get something else to drink. After that escapade, I did not want anything else so I just bought some ginger ale.

The cabaret was closing down at 1:00am as the crowd started to leave the building. The two females that Bobby and Eric were dancing with needed a ride home, so they hopped in the already packed vehicle we drove and left. This time I was the designated driver because the rest of the crew was either too tired or too high to get behind the wheel. We had to find a gas station that was open, as one of the females proceeded to give me directions.

The tank was damn near empty as we were riding on fumes trying to make it to the gas station before the fuel ran out. We finally arrived at the station and Eric went inside to pay for the gas. I asked Eric to buy me a bag of barbecue potato chips and another ginger ale. We left the gas station having to drive clear across town to where the females lived.

Eric and I were the only ones awake as we finally pulled up in front of the house. After exchanging telephone numbers, we pulled out of their driveway to head back home. Eric rode shotgun with me in the front seat as we drove down the road to the exit leading to the highway. I noticed a car heading in the opposite direction flashing its headlights at me.

I did not know what was going on, so I attempted to flash my back. Being the car I was driving was an older vehicle; the switch was located on the floor and not on the turn signal lever as with my vehicle. By the time I felt around on the floor to locate and hit the switch, we neared the exit. At the very same moment, I looked back and saw the strobe lights of a highway state patrol car come on. He drove up behind me and signaled to pull over. He got out of his car with his hands on his pistol and motioned me to exit the vehicle. Eric saw what was going on as some of the guys began to wake up.

I got out of the car and was instructed to pull out my license slowly and hand it to the officer. I felt a combination of both anger and fear as I preceded to hand him my license staring him dead in his eyes. He glanced inside of the vehicle and asked where we came from and where we were going. I told him we just left the cabaret and were heading back home. I then asked him why I was stopped as he snapped back that he was asking the questions here.

That really set my blood boiling and it took all I could muster not to get flip in return. The officer then instructed me to follow him to his vehicle and to get into the front seat. My frustration level continued to increase, but I knew that I had done nothing wrong. The patrolman asked if we had been drinking, and I said that my boys had some drinks at the cabaret. He then asked what was that he smelled on my breath, and I responded "Snyder barbecue potato chips and ginger ale sir" as though I was speaking to a drill sergeant.

He looked up at me and smirked with a grin trying not to laugh. I calmed down at that moment as he handed my license back to me and told me that he pulled us over for failing to shut off the high beams. Now I knew that was a bogus excuse, but I said nothing. He handed me a warning citation and told me "next time, you better be careful so head home". His statement at first puzzled me as I proceeded to walk back to the car.

Memoirs of an imperfect man seeking inner peace through the life and light of Jesus Christ

At that moment, the light bulb turned on inside my head as to the meaning behind the patrolman statement. The more I thought about it, the more angry I became. In little over two hours, we were accused twice of moving traffic violations. It finally dawned on what he meant; if we chose to return to the area we would be arrested. The circumstances were too obvious and far too similar to be coincidental. I do not condone the behavior that we engaged in earlier that evening. We were dead wrong in choosing to drink and drive and for being in possession of an illegal substance.

I accept full responsibility and accountability for making such a poor choice because I knew better. It was fortunate that I chose not to drink anything else while at the cabaret, for only the Lord knows what may have happened. In the same token, to have been stopped twice was far from coincidental. Being pulled over for driving while black was just as wrong. When both of the officers saw a car load full of black men, that was reason enough to pull us over. This situation is far too common an occurrence and it has gone on for far too long in this country.

Police departments were created to protect and serve the public, and the use of racial profiling ends up doing a disservice to people of color. Many officers when outside of the eye of public scrutiny abuse the power and authority gave to them by the citizens of their respective communities. Racial profiling is unjustifiable, unconstitutional and disproportionately effects people of color.

Due the frequency in which people of color are targeted, the chances for instances that people of color will fall prey to the whims of the police are enhanced. People of color are citizens of this country and are obligated to pay taxes just as their white counterparts. Therefore, they are entitled to the same protection under the law just as those of their white counterparts. One takes for granted that those who have taken a sworn oath to protect and serve the public interests are of sound moral character. The ranks of the law enforcement are but a small microcosm and reflection of the larger society.

The true morality and character of an individual is not measured by ones willingness to do the right thing in the presence of others. It is determined as to whether or not the right thing occurs when no one is around to bear witness. If justice and respect is measured only by who posses a firearm or wears a uniform, expect the respect to be a fleeting thing.

Many officers speak in condescending tones and a display a disrespectful demeanor by the mere fact they wear a badge and brandish a gun. How could they then realistically expect those on the receiving end to be respectful of their derisive behavior? Therefore, mothers and fathers of African Americans and Hispanic/Latino young men have to be on constant vigil and on guard every time their sons leave home. As part of their lessons in life, those teenage boys of color must be taught to act in a certain manner if pulled over by the police.

The manners of ones dress the style of haircut and attitude displayed can be cause enough to be stopped by police officers. If a person's actions fall within the parameters of the police profile, one can become subjected to questioning without due cause. In the decades since the riots in Watts during the sixties sparked by police brutality, little has changed. Since then, there has been a multitude of riots in cities across the country and most recently Los Angeles that stemmed from the same misguided behaviors. There are countless stories across this country in both urban and rural communities alike. There are numerous document reports of people of color being beaten or shot through the use of deadly force by law enforcement officers.

When the average citizen is accused of killing or committing an act of murder, it is treated far differently then when the police commit a similar crime. Because society gives those agencies the license to kill, the act of killing it therefore justified. If thou shall not kill, there is no line of distinctions drawn in religious text based upon whether or not one has a badge or uniform.

When police brutality occurs, those officers involved invoke the code of silence to protect the wrong doers. When these cases go to trial, in most cases the jury finds these very same officers not guilty of committing the acts charged against them. The community condones their actions and thus becomes accessories to their unjust behavior. In the minds of the jury members, the ends justify the means. The opinion being that there is now one less nigger on the street, or one less wetback for society in which to contend.

According to some religious beliefs, it is considered immoral and unjust for the state to commit murder. One would think that the shooting of unarmed citizens or killing individuals by lethal injection would apply. It appears that many of the more humane beliefs espoused in religion are the very ones most prone to be discarded by its followers. Individuals that follow religious doctrine tend to readily accept the passages that advocate the violent treatment of their fellow man. Many are quick to forgo the passages that speak to the heart and the soul. To be all too willing seek vengeance through the adage of "an eye for an eye". To be so quick to dismiss the more peaceful and loving words contained within the text.

This is the same state of mind taken when it comes to adhering to the written word of the law. As with many things in life, individuals are prone to push the envelope of the laws that will infringe upon the rights of others. Some readily engage in unlawful practices and do not hesitate to abuse the power given them by the community they took an oath to protect. A few good cops choose to err on the side of exercising great discretion and attempt to do the right thing. As stated before, the lines that distinguish the cop from the robber have become distorted beyond recognition.

Ultimately, the citizens of a nation must take responsibility for rooting out police corruption where it is found. Far too many are willing to sit in the darkness of denial than to flip the light switch to uncover the truth and see it for what it is. Decades ago white America turned a blind eye and chose to ignore the warning signs that drugs were affecting the lives of those in the black community.

When the flow of drugs began to creep into the black community, the concerns went unheeded. The lives of people of color were seen as being of lesser value to the society at large.

Therefore, the price for drug intervention and interdiction was deemed too costly to pay for. In time, the drug problem reached epidemic proportions within the households of the white community. Only then was the white community willing to acknowledge that a drug problem existed.

When a person is physically ill, the medication given is administered either intravenously or orally. The medication performs the healing process from the inside out. The same goes for the healing of the spirit, for the truth more oft than not is a bitter pill to swallow but necessary in order for the person to redress what ails them.

For as long as the public are willing to condone the mistreatment of some of its citizens. For as long as there are those who are willing to turn a blind eye to the injustices committed by the officer's in blue. Until justice is truly blind, we can expect more bloodshed, distrust and unrest in the streets to occur. Those chartered to protect and serve the public interest should do just that.

If not, the statement will continue to be no more than just another empty catch phrase. Justice will not be served by allowing those who chose to wear the uniform to become the self-appointed judge, jury and executioner. For as long as nothing changes, nothing will and the majority risks the chance of falling prey to the same types of abuses and injustices experienced by the minority.

The laws and statutes written apply to all members of society, but the scales of justice are far from equal or balanced. For as long as the philosophy of "He who has the gun makes the rule" continues to be the law of this land, all are at risk.

Following the incident, we were able to laugh about it, but not forgotten. I would not be as careless and reckless again as to place myself in a similar situation. I saw first hand how easy it could be to get yourself caught up into more trouble than you can handle by not thinking before acting. I saw the incident as a wake up call, and took full advantage of it. I would continue to drink, but I would become more responsible in doing so.

Until that moment, I never realized how much drinking had become a part of our social activity and how much it has affected my life. Growing up, alcohol played a major role in the social dysfunction of our family. I had started drinking at an early age as well, to fit in with the crowd. Alcohol is as much of Americana as mom's apple pie and I as so many others swallowed more than my fair share. Drinking had become so ingrained as part of my extracurricular activities taking on almost ritualistic proportions. Whether it involved attending a "happy-hour" function after work, cookouts, clubbing or spinning records a drink was almost always present.

I equated fun and relaxation with drinking and as I grew older my consumption increased as well. I did not classify myself as being an alcoholic by any means for there were many occasions when I would go months without having a drink. I never missed a day of work or an appointment because of drinking. Therefore, in the classic definition, it did not apply to me.

However, I would keep a watchful eye over myself to ensure that I would not slip over the edge and lose my self-control. I would not to fall into the abyss that lay at the bottom of the bottle that swallowed a few members of my family. They found out the hard way that the message in the bottle provides no solaces, quick fixes, nor easy answers to their problems.

CHAPTER SIXTEEN

The club scene would once again provide a vehicle to help me break out of my introversive shell. We returned to the scene of the crime of where we watched simple Sonny take a fall. We entered club Studio 93 one Saturday evening after a long absence. The crowd had changed whereby a much younger audience had begun to frequent the establishment more so than the mature crowd before. Instead of taking full advantage of the serious mixing talent of the DJ Pleasure Man, the majority of the crowd was just standing around styling and profiling.

After watching the spectacle for about an hour, I got tired of standing around waiting for someone to get enough nerve to hit the floor. I told Eric to walk over to the booth and ask the DJ to play "Trans Europe Express" by the group KraftWerk to get the party jumping. As soon as I heard the cut, I went to the floor and started performing the line dance of the time called the "Smurf Monorail" which was similar to the current dance the "Electric Slide".

I went to the center of the dance floor and proceeded to start working the combinations of footsteps slowly at first in front of a table full of females. Eric came out to join me as he attempted to step in time with me. Now Eric could not dance a lick if his life depended on it, but he provided some comic relief to the women as he struggled to catch the groove. As Eric and I began to finally get in synch with one another, some women rose up from the table and started to get into the flow with us. In less than ten minutes, we had the entire dance floor packed as the crowd moved in unison to the beat of the song.

We danced for at least a half an hour as the Pleasure man continued to slice up the turntables like cold cuts. He switched up and began to mix in the song "Knee Deep" by Parliament Funkadelic and the crowd went wild. I was sweating like a pig at a black family picnic but was having the time of my life.

We returned home that evening dropped off Eric and proceeded to Bobby's house. I was so tired that I chose to sleep there instead of heading home. The following afternoon Bobby and I were lying around watching football when we heard the sounds of what appeared to be a chainsaw buzzing in the front of the house. It was Eric pulling up in front of the house on his motorcycle, and he had a female passenger riding with him. They both entered the front door as Eric in his usually loud manner introduced us to Jill. He had apparently been riding down the street one afternoon as she sat on her front porch with some of her family members. He just pulled up and struck a conversation with her that began the start of another one of his many clandestine relationships.

Bobby already knew her, having attended middle and high school with one of her older brothers. I was leaning up against the couch as she and Eric sat down as we spoke of the time we had at the club the night before. At the time I did not say much to her, but in time we would become intimately involved. The following day at the office, the shoe had finally dropped. The news of the tri-state merger was final, and a tentative date announced that would start the relocation process for some members of the engineering department. The mood was somewhat solemn and pensive for the weeks to come, as some of the people who had worked together for many years and formed strong friendships would soon part.

Roger and I were discussing the matter with Richard, whom we both had come to rely on for his wisdom and mentoring. He tried to put a positive spin on the situation as he would often do, but I could tell he had his reservations about moving as well. Those of us left behind felt like rats on a sinking ship as we watched some of our coworkers getting on life rafts heading to safety. One of the negative aspects of seeing things in the black and white perspective is that it sometimes clouds ones vision. It is rather difficult to "see the big picture" when you do not know where the theatre is located.

The company was formulating long range plans to spend hundreds of millions of dollars to modernize the network. The existing equipment had to be maintained, so Richard reassured us that the need for our skills still was a business necessity. I felt somewhat better about it, knowing that Richard would not pull punches or pull the wool over our eyes. He told both Roger and me to stay focused and to do the best jobs we could until the dust on the merger settled down.

Roger's supervisor was selected to lead a group in one of the newly formed departments, and his staff was transferred under the supervision of my boss. His previous boss was a more mild mannered, outgoing and friendly type of individual with a more hands off approach management style. This was the exact opposite to Dick, who micro managed our activities every step of the way. Almost immediately, there was an instant friction created between Dick and some members of Roger's group.

They did not care much for his micromanaging hands on style of management. Dick would pick apart their projects and frequently reject them for approval. As a test to the fact, Roger had asked me to give him one of my projects that were similar in scope. He used the same budget justification statement and format that I previously submitted that received approval.

However, when he turned his project in, Dick immediately rejected it. Once his opinion was formed, it was next to impossible to change it. Once Dick penciled a person's name on his "hit" list it was next to impossible to be removed from it. Roger and I most always had taken our coffee breaks together and occasionally Dick and some of the other engineers would join us. I would attempt to keep the conversation light by sidestepping work-related issues.

Roger and Arnie were both very knowledgeable when it came to sports related subjects. So most often, our break conversations would revolve around the subject. Very few could hold a candle to either of them when it came to statistics and historical sports facts. I noticed a change in the level of confidence Roger displayed when the conversations involved work-related issues. He seemed to have difficulty in articulating his thoughts and ideas, especially if Dick was present. If Dick sensed that he could intimidate an individual, he would take full advantage of the situation. His demeanor was similar to that of a piranha smelling the blood of prey in the water.

The tone and tenor of the working relationship with Dick was established during the first encounter. With the exception of one person, Dick perceived the members of Rogers's group as somehow less than worthy of his respect. The odd thing about him was that he was very protective of his people. He would be quick to come to the defense of members of his group when called for.

As Dick continued to apply pressure, stress fractures began to crack both the attitude and quality of work throughout the department. People dealt with pressure in a multitude of ways, which manifests itself in some outward manner. The continued restructuring of the company did not help matters much either, as it began to take its toll upon the employees. The pressure to perform and continually face the position of justifying one's existence can be very stressful. Individuals with the strongest of character will begin to doubt their own abilities and self worth if subjected to constant pressure. The management style of the company during the time when Dick was hired was very Draconian.

As with the biblical saying, employees were to be seen but not heard. Most of the employees were middle-aged males, of which a high percentage came from a military background. They also brought many of the military like management practices into the workplace. Planning, organizational and self-motivation skills are necessary for any successful business endeavor. Leadership is a skillful art; one is born with not a science that can be taught in a classroom environment. The individual either has the leadership qualities within them or they do not, and there is no way to fake it. Those who lack the inherent skills will find other means to command respect, and more oft than not fear and intimidation are the ones typically adopted.

These methods may work perfectly for running a military operation. In a society that claims to promote freethinking, independent thought and self-expression, friction is sure to occur. As with parenting, people tend to use the same practices familiar to their own life experience. The militaristic, micromanaging style of management became a common method used to run the company. Those who came from military backgrounds felt most comfortable with the methods used to manage their activities. The incumbent occupying a leadership position must have qualities that will command respect. It is a given that a person is more likely to follow the lead of those whom they can readily identify with.

That people are more willing to follow the advice given by those who have attained a greater body of knowledge and wisdom. If there is no core intrinsic quality a person has other than the title of the position one occupies, a scarecrow like image is then created. A scarecrow occupies space, but lacks substance; whose limbs only flow when the wind blows. For its sole purpose is to intimidate crows and nothing else.

Millions of individuals occupy positions of authority that lack the qualities inherent of true leadership. Many times these individuals lack the skills and knowledge pertaining to their chosen field or occupation. Knowledge is power; those who acquire it will more often than not command respect. Leadership requires that a person have the vision and foresight to anticipate the needs of those under their supervision. Leaders have great intestinal fortitude and pursue their goals with bold determination.

True leaders are willing to sacrifice their own personal desires for the greater good of the team. So again, when a vacuum void of leadership exists, some matter or substance will seek to fill it whether it is physical or spiritual. Those who lack the aforementioned qualities will fill that void by abusing the power of their position by the use of threats, coercion, or intimidation. The Peter Principle, whereby a person is promoted to their level of incompetence is the principle most often practiced in corporate America.

For example, a financial accountant, who excels at analyzing the financial conditions of the company, maybe an excellent bookkeeper. However, being proficient in one's job in and of itself does not qualify one to lead nor manage a group of people. This was a classic case and a common occurrence practiced by people such as my boss and his contemporaries of the time. His technical knowledge and competence were great, but his supervisory skills were very questionable. His managerial skills were out of step with the changing times and in many cases, his behavior was out of line as well.

The goals, statements, and objectives expressed by upper management spoke to the importance and necessity to change the business. The rhetoric clashed with the style of management in place and mindset of the corporate culture that existed at the time. For any meaningful change to take place requires that those impacted have an active role in bringing forth the desired changes.

As spoken before, change for the sake of change ultimately changes nothing. Actions must be in alignment with intent by enacting new processes and procedures to facilitate a more smooth transition from the old to the new. When the rules of the game have changed, one must be quick to recognize and adapt to those changes into their game plan. The rules of engagement changed for my friend Roger and his fellow co-workers the moment they came under Dick's supervision.

You cannot win the Indianapolis 500 by entering the event with a tricycle. Roger and members of his group were at a disadvantage and in a no-win scenario. They chose to either ignore or resist the change in leadership, and failed to adapt to their new environment. However unfair and dictatorial Dick's style and approach was, the corporate culture that existed at the time supported and backed his chosen methods.

The company saw its profits continually rise because of the use of fear and intimidation. If what you do brings forth profit, you will continue to use and enact the same measures used to perpetuate the condition. Since the company legally operated as a monopoly, there were no outside competitive pressures. There existed no external forces to cause the leadership to enact different approaches to lead the workforce.

It did not matter if the methods used to direct the herd by the shepherds of the company caused harm to the individual or the group. If one sheep among the flock of employees moved in a direction opposite the rest of the herd, the sheep could expect the sheepdog to bark and if necessary, bite. If the sheep was not careful, it could become the main dinner entrée for the wolves that lurk in the dark. I would face a similar situation a few years later when I too failed to adapt to the changes occurring around me.

As time progressed, I began to become restless with what I perceived was a lack of progress in the direction my life was heading. As some of my friends and coworkers moved on, my desire to stay and remain content with my current lot in life diminished. I also was unsatisfied and unhappy with the lack in progress in my desire to be romantically involved with Lana. I wanted to have her in my life so badly at the time and although I outwardly displayed a demeanor of aloofness; I was torn up inside. I considered myself honorable man; this was the only virtue I truly had at my disposal. I was ill equipped and ill prepared to be involved in a loving relationship that would stand the test of time.

One evening while hanging out with Bobby, he received a telephone call from one of his ex-girlfriends. We stopped by to pay a visit earlier in the week so he could visit with his children. She had a female cousin visiting for the summer that she wanted me to meet. As we approached the house, I began to get a little nervous. Bobby told me that this woman had a young child fathered by his cousin, and that she might trip on him about the situation.

We got out of the car and proceeded to walk up the stairway, when the front door swung open. His ex girlfriend was ready and waiting for us, and Bobby's son ran out the door to give him a hug. As we entered the house, her cousin was leaning up against the wall just staring and smiling at me. She was a short slender woman who spoke with a thick southern accent. Her face was far from the most attractive I had seen, but she was not a complete mud duck either.

Bobby's ex girlfriend offered us something to eat as we all proceeded to the dining room area. Her cousin just stared at me the entire time smiling, as I cut a glance towards Bobby as he started to chuckle. After eating our dinner, the girls wanted to play cards. As we began to clear the table, this woman proceeded to reach over me brushing her body against me. She leaned over and whispered in my ear saying that she wanted me, and that I would not be going home tonight. She then licked my ear lobe and took the dishes into the kitchen.

We proceeded to play cards, and during the course of the game, she was touching and caressing me. We had been drinking beer, and Bobby started to get sleepy, having worked a twelve-hour shift earlier. Her cousin had taken my hand and led me into the bedroom she slept in. She sat me down on the edge of the bed and proceeded to kiss me. We spent the entire night having sex and intermittent pillow talk.

She told me that she liked me, and that she was falling in love with me. I immediately bristled upon hearing the words, as though I was a porcupine raising its quills bracing for attack. She then asked me if I loved her; I was taken aback by her question. I told her that I thought she was a nice person, but I did not love her. She proceeded to start crying, asking me what was wrong with her that I could not love her.

I felt so bad and awkward at that moment I did not know what to do, I just held her. I tried to explain that love takes time to develop. She repeatedly asked me if I could come to love her, and said that I do not use the term if the feelings are not real.

If I had the opportunity to run away, I probably would have. She as so many females view having sex in the same vain as making love; the first is a pure physical act the later a pure spiritual one. At the time, I did not a have a clue as to what true love was, but I knew I felt nothing of the sort for her. As I think back to those days, I know now that I truly did not have a clue as to what constituted real love. At that point in time in my life, I did not truly know myself nor did I truly love the person that I was. I was unaware of the ingredients of a true loving relationship that consists of respect, trust, truth and honor.

I lacked the ability to trust anyone 100% other than my family members. I also had a measure of self-loathing and doubt, which prevented me from truly loving and respecting the person that I was. I lived my life by a very strict moral code and ethical standards, and was very judgmental of those who did not live accordingly. I was self-disciplined, goal oriented and a self-motivated individual. Being a very pragmatic and practical individual, I could not relate to those who did not live their lives in a similar manner. I was very impatient with those who talked too much, whined or complained and offered a litany of excuses for their shortcomings in life.

The morning sun had come up as Bobby had awakened me to get up. I slipped out of the bed as not to awaken her, put on my clothes and left. I dropped Bobby off at his house and went home to shower and change clothes. As I returned and walked through the front door, Annie and her boyfriend Narvie were sitting in the living room. They both began to stare and smile at me, as I could smell the aroma of food.

Bobby was in the kitchen cooking breakfast when Narvie commented on how my night was and proceeded to start laughing. I was both shocked and very embarrassed, not quite sure of what to say at that moment. It became obvious that my sexual exploits from the previous evening were a topic of discussion. Bobby told me that his ex girlfriend had called, passing on a message from her cousin that she wanted me to come back over. I sat on the couch staring at the floor and said without thinking that I did not want to see her again. Narvie made some wisecrack about what did I do to her to have her calling out for me, when Lana came downstairs. My heart just sank, because I knew she had overheard the discussion.

I looked up at her as she gave me a very weak smile as I thought to myself "what have I done". Annie asked me why I would not go back to the house as I quickly replied "I got what I wanted". I made the statement without thinking trying to portray how macho I was in front of Bobby and Narvie while at the same time, indirectly making Lana aware that the girl meant nothing to me. At that moment, I experienced a series of mixed emotions ranging from shame to a false sense of pride. Sorrow that in my rebuking the advances of the female I slept with, that I caused her more hurt and pain. Sorrow in that whatever chances I had to one-day make Lana mine, I threw away as the result of my actions.

At that moment, I could feel the change within as I became more withdrawn and distant from my feelings. I was of the opinion that due to the incident Lana thought less of me. Because of actions, others viewed in the same light as Bobby and Eric. A few months had passed by since the incident. A situation occurred which finally driven the stake into my heart of any hopes that I had of being with Lana.

Eric had gone out to one of the local hole in the wall lounges the night before and saw Lana's boyfriend out with his other girlfriend. The following day he told Bobby and I of his encounter and made the comment within earshot of Lana. I could not tell whether she was upset or not but she tried not to let it show. I overheard her making a comment to Bobby's girlfriend that she was through with him, and inside I was jumping for joy.

The following weekend Bobby and his girlfriend hosted a barbecue to celebrate the new home they bought. I had been riding my motorcycle with Eric all day and rode to buy some beer and rum. I had ridden my bike back to the garage to pick up my car and proceed to get ready for the event. Once we arrived at Bobby's house and I stepped through the door, I saw Lana sitting on her boyfriend's lap. At that moment, it was as though I had been stabbed in the heart. I looked at him with his eyes glazed over from the weed and beer he had consumed with such contempt. Then I looked at her and just shook my head in disbelief. I proceeded to mix Eric and myself rum and coke and chased it with beer. The more I drank, the more upset I became.

I finally had enough, and told Eric that I wanted to leave and hang out downtown. We left the house and went to the same hole in the wall lounge Eric witnessed the scene of the crime. We walked upstairs high as hell from drinking and I just walked over, took some woman by the hand, and proceeded to the dance floor. I danced the entire night with my body soaking in sweat. Eric ran into one of his women, told me he would was about to leave, and would catch me later.

I closed the club down and went home afterwards feeling numb mad and sad all at the same time. I had finally come to the realization that I was living a fantasy and hanging onto a dream that would never become real. I could not understand how she could be in love with someone who treated her so badly. I had placed myself into a holding pattern for almost two years hoping that she would have a change of heart to no avail.

This situation signaled the beginning of a war that raged within the deep recesses of my heart and soul. Just as with the story of Dr. Jekyll and Mr. Hyde, I engaged in a bitter battle with myself. I thought back to the feelings I held after sleeping with the cousin of Bobby's ex girlfriend. The power I felt knowing I could manipulate the feelings of another was both exhilarating and intoxicating.

I began to detach myself from my emotions, as I began to view females as mere objects. Outside of the love I had for my mother and sisters, my ability to feel compassion towards women began to erode. My outlook towards females was becoming more jaded and callous. My heart grew numb, anesthetized as though injected with Novocain. My thoughts began to focus on satisfying my sexual urges no matter the consequence. I remembered a conversation that Bob; Roger and I were having about the age-old phrase female's use about there not being "any good black men".

We discussed some of the past encounters we had with females going back to high school. Many of the females had the tendency to go for the bad boy, the pretty boy or the jock athlete. These boys had the pick of the litter and more oft than not, treated these females very badly. These females use the same pattern of selection in their adult years; continuing to be lied to used and abused. They could have just as well chosen the good or nice guy early on in their relationship experience. However, being loved and treated with respect is not high on list of priorities of many women.

When the nice guy or good man finally does come along, he becomes the recipient of the drama caused by men from a woman's previous relationships. The nice guy is the one left holding the bag, facing at least a decade's worth of pain, hurt and drama perpetrated by the hands of other men. These women assume that the good guy will treat them in the same manner as the men who abused them before. To paint the next man using the same brush and canvas; casting a suspicious eye towards the next man who had yet done a thing to warrant such treatment.

The next man becomes subjected to the bitterness and venom of women who as the result of their choices inflict their pain onto the new partner. After a time, many men decide it is worth neither the time nor effort to seek relationships with such women. If the good man is going to be treated in the same manner as the men who dog women, some may begin to take on the persona. Others may decide to look outside of their race or culture, where they perceive they may receive better treatment.

I began to question myself as to why I expended so much time waiting for Lana to come around. I questioned why I should continue to waste my efforts by being nice and showing respect towards women. I often witnessed the benefits received by some men who treated women with such contempt and disdain. My decision to live my life as the consummate understanding nice guy did not reap many benefits or dividends for me.

I tried to resent her in my hopes to erase what I felt in my heart for her, but I could not no matter how hard I tried. In my limited capacity, I loved her, but as the song states…"It Takes a Fool to Learn that Love Don't Love Nobody", and I no longer desired to play the part of the fool. It was as though icy cold fingers were racing across my heart and mind as the urge to wild out began to grow stronger. I began to view women as nothing more that a collection of body parts. Should I wear the dog collar and become the image and persona that so many presumed me to be? To go on a rampage breaking hearts every step of the way, or to continue to be the nice guy next door?

This inner struggle was more than just a battle. This was a full-fledged war I would fight for many years to come. When these feelings came over me, it was as though a switch was flipped inside. I went from being the shy introvert to an unabashed extroverted tornado like personality. The tone and tenor of my speech became cold and callous. I felt hell-bent on satisfying my hedonistic desires and was willing to cause havoc and destruction to any woman in my path. If I allowed the dark side of my personality to overcome me, in all likelihood I would have ventured down a path of no return. To prevent myself from acting on my desires, I would place myself in a self-imposed exile.

I stayed away from clubs, bars or any other venue that may have a high concentration of females. Although there were several attractive women on the job, my code against dating women in the same company acted as a retaining barrier. It had taken me about two weeks to really get a grip on my emotions before I could go back to Annie's house and be within the same space Lana breathed. Things never were the same and I do not know if it was a matter of coincidence or not, but the relationships that everyone had at the time would undergo drastic change. I do not know if it was something in the air or water at the time, but almost in unison, the personal relationships of those closest to me began to unravel. My sister broke off her long-term relationship with her boyfriend Jerry. Eric, Donnie, Bobby and his mother also had their respective relationships end with their primary love interests.

Since Eric was now free to roam, he began to spend more time with some of his other girlfriends. He started to hang out with Jill, the young woman he introduced me to previously at Bobby's house. We would sometimes ride our motorcycles over to her parent's house to pay her a visit. Her parents moved to Mansfield from the south, to work and start a family. She came from a large family of nine children consisting of four boys and five girls, she being the third eldest daughter.

Through our conversations, I can come to discover that she was born with a congenital birth defect. Consequently, her legs did not fully develop whereby she learned to walk with prosthetics. I was astounded at how well she could walk, for until she spoke of it I had no idea. I was even more amazed with her bright outlook on life as well how she appeared to cope with her predicament. She was very pleasant and unassuming and lived her life like anyone else.

She worked as a cashier at one of the local department stores, and she had a little boy. He was a smart little boy, who had big brown eyes and curly hair. When we would stop by, her son and his little cousins would walk over and begin to start picking wanting me to play with them. At the time, I was not crazy about babies or small children. I do not know what it was about me, but kids were always attracted to me. But it never failed that he come to me as he would sit on my lap and attempt to read a book or show me one of his toys.

Her family was very close, and when they would have their family gatherings at the house, I was always felt welcomed. Her father was an excellent cook, as he would often hover over the barbecue grill working his magic. The one person I truly enjoyed was her brother in law Sam. He was a fun loving, hardworking and straightforward type of guy who did not pull any punches.

I did not realize at the time, but her eldest brother LA was an associate of Big Frank's. I vaguely remembered him from the few times he stopped by our house when I was younger. He too was caught up in the game of pimping and hustling. Like so many of his peers, he too was paying the price for his past indiscretions. He was on lock down at the time, and it would be a few years before we would cross paths.

I was unconscious of it at the time, but I began to spend less and less time with Bobby and his family and more time with Eric. Subconsciously I was distancing myself as a means of healing the pain I felt in my heart for Lana. I needed the wild fun loving side of Eric's personality to sooth the hurt feelings and to help tame the raging beast within me as well. As time progressed, each of us appeared to be losing our desire to perform as DJ's. Unless someone sought us out, we did not actively pursue engagements as heavily as we did before. Eric was the only one of our trio who still had the flame within to continue.

He reminded me so much of Peter Pan, the story of the boy who never wanted to grow up. I sometimes wished I could be as carefree as he was, not giving a damn about much outside of what was next on the party agenda. I asked him one day why he was hanging out with Jill, for I knew he was not serious about her. He could not readily identify any particular reason; other than, he was intrigued by her physical circumstance. I felt bad for her, for I knew in time she would be discarded like so many other girls who crossed Eric's path.

Although Eric's main squeeze of many years dumped him, they still periodically maintained a sexual relationship. No matter how hard she tried, no one woman could have made Eric be a one woman's man. I believe that he had attention deficit disorder, and it transcended every aspect of his life. He was easily bored, and went from one woman to the next to seek what measure of excitement he could find. His personality was very similar to that of a pinball machine; most always on full tilt mode.

The one thing I could say was that Eric was a loyal friend to both me and to Bobby. We were as close as brothers and always had each other's backs. Ever blue moon, a streak of kindness would come over Eric to do something unselfish. I recall one occasion when he discovered that Jill had never attended a concert. Luther Vandross was touring, and was performing a concert at the Front Row in Cleveland. He told me that he wanted to take her to the show, and wanted me to go as well. She had a younger sister who wanted to attend, so we made a double date of it.

I was very surprised by his gesture, and the level of excitement he had about preparing for the event. We went to Columbus to buy suits for the affair, which is something he would very rarely wear. We went to one of the men's clothing store I frequently shopped, and found two sharp silk blends double-breasted suits. He always liked the Stacey Adams shoes I wore, so he bought a pair for himself. After we tried on our outfits, we looked at one another and slapped hands.

We looked tighter than a suit on an elephant, and could have passed for members of one of our favorite R&B groups "The Time". While we were in Columbus, we drove to the hair salon where one of Bobby's sisters worked to get our Gheri curls refreshed. When we drove to the house to pick up Jill and her sister, the looks on their faces let us, know that our efforts were not wasted. When we arrived and stepped into the concert hall, it was as though we were the featured attraction.

We were sharper than a set of steak knives and the stares and gazes we received affirmed that fact. The concert venue was one of the best I had ever seen; it was circular in design with an acoustical dome over a rotating stage. Luther put on an excellent show, and we all had a great time as well. I was proud of Eric for showing the act of kindness towards Jill. It would not be long after this encounter that their relationship would come to an end.

CHAPTER SEVENTEEN

I had arrived home from work late one evening and received a call from Eric. He asked me to come over to his house, and I noticed that he sounded very nervous. Once I arrived, he jumped in the car with me and we just drove around talking. His many exploits with females had finally backfired on him as he began to tell me of his troubles. He had become involved with the sister of one of his younger brother's girlfriends. She had discovered that he had been sleeping around with other women and an argument ensued.

She struck him, and in a fit of anger, he swung and hit her swelling her eye. She then called the police reporting the incident and out of fear of being arrested, he ran. I knew one day something like this would happen, and until that time I had never saw him so afraid. When individuals are involved in a physically or verbally abusive relationship, nothing good can come of it.

Losing control of one's emotions out of pain is a very common response. As a result of becoming angry with someone who has betrayed your trust or caused you harm in any way, anything can happen. Some tend to lash out in retaliation as a means of inflicting the same pain that one feels within. Love cannot be present in the context of such a relationship. Love does not require the telling of lies or covering up the truth. Love does not seek to control the actions of others through coercion or by playing games with one's emotions.

Because true love seeks to comfort the heart, not to cause it pain. True love lifts up the spirit of the object of one's affection; not seeks to destroy or to tear them down. People who choose to stay in such abusive relationships do so out of ignorance of what true love is. Some stay in abusive relationships out of fear of being alone, insecure within themselves to take care of their own personal needs.

Others stay out of a warped sense of equating the amount of time spent with the abuser as a reason to maintain the relationship. The thought being that because they have a long history with the other that one-day life would change for the better. That somehow it would be better to be in the company of misery and pain than to be at home alone. An enlightened person realizes that if true love existed, the last thing on the mind or in the heart would be to cause hurt or harm. This is the true benchmark by which to gauge the level of love within a given relationship. If one has to entertain the thought of spewing venom from their lips, or physically striking their mate the answer is quite clear…love does not live there anymore.

This is the signal that both parties should separate and seek out professional help before attempting to engage in another relationship. If not, then the chances for carrying the same dysfunctional traits into the next encounter are almost certain. He decided to leave town for a while and hang out with one of his part time girlfriends. He asked me to take him to his grandparent's house to gather some clothing. As we rode across town, I got on my soapbox and started talking to Eric about the direction his life was heading. I was worried about him wondering how serious the situation could get.

I told him that for as long as I have known him that he was playing a very risky and dangerous game. I told him that the train he was conducting was heading on a collision course. With the cadre of women at his disposal, and the fact that he was leading them on, the odds were not in his favor. By continuing to play games with female's emotions, he was placing his life and his health in serious jeopardy.

I foolishly thought this incident should be evidence to convince Eric to slow his roll, and change his playing ways. Eric just sat there staring out of the window and slowly nodded his head in affirmation to what I was saying. He asked me to take him to see Jill to say his good-byes. Once we arrived, he did not reveal the true reasons for his departure. She began to cry inquiring as to why he had to leave as I just stared at the kitchen floor concerned about his fate.

We stayed there for a couple of hours and Eric was ready to leave. I felt bad for her knowing that she cared for him in a manner he was incapable of reciprocating. I returned him back to his grandparent's home and we spoke a few hours more. His grandmother came downstairs and I could tell she had been crying out of concern for him. He was her favorite having raised him since he was a child.

She did all the things most grandparents do when faced with such a responsibility. I am sure she was too permissive with him on many occasions, and was too accommodating to him as well. It did not stop the fact that she loved him and did not want any harm to come his way. She asked me to talk to him, not knowing that we have had a multitude of conversations before this incident.

It was well passed midnight and I had to leave to get some sleep. I hugged Eric and told him to lay low and to stay out of trouble wherever he chose to go. I was fighting back the tears, as I drove home not wanting anything to happen to my friend. Being Mansfield is a very small town, word travels very fast. Word had gotten back to Jill has to the reasons behind Eric's departure that allowed her the means to let go of him emotionally. Eric's grandparents hired an attorney and after a few months had passed by a hearing was held.

I would periodically drop by to pay Jill and her family a visit and we began to talk on the phone. As time passed by, I began to spend more time with her and less and less time with my crew. She invited me over to dinner on Mother's Day, as she was preparing it for her mother. I cannot recall what it was supposed to be, but it tasted something horrible. It was all

I could do to keep a straight face and to choke the food down. When her little boy refused to eat it saying how nasty it was, we all just busted out laughing.

Her mother was slyly attempting to play matchmaker commenting on how cute a couple we would make. She also commented how much her son had taken to me as well. I did not pay too much attention to what she was saying at first but in time, I would fall for her for reasons other than love. Once again, Eric's lucky charms were working in his favor. During the court hearing, evidence was presented by witnesses that she was the initiator of the conflict.

His attorney was able to arrange a plea bargain agreement whereby Eric would pay a fine and receive two years probation. I reminded him how fortunate he was not receiving jail time, and to take advantage of this opportunity to move in the right direction. One Saturday afternoon I stopped by to see Bobby and he dropped a bomb on me. He told me that he was dating one of Eddie's sisters and that she was pregnant. He also informed me that he would be moving to Dallas to find a better job. I was shocked to say the least and I asked him if he was sure of the decision he was making. He was denied a line supervisors position he should have received. With a baby coming on the way, he was unwilling to continue to work for less than his worth.

The spring of 1984 brought forth many changes for us all that would affect the nature of our lives and friendships forever. It seemed that the moment Bobby announced his plans to depart the wheels of motion turned. As they turned, our close friendships began to transform and we each began to go our own separate ways. We would become scattered across the country like dust in the wind over the next few months.

The winds of change began to blow on the work front that would bring me closer to my destined fate. Boredom had long settled in my mind. Little did I realize what was in store for me. I was working to complete several projects that I had on my plate. It was as though some unknown force was compelling me as I thought to myself that I had to quicken my pace. Dick had received a telephone call from the director of the engineering department to create a candidate slate of qualified individuals. Those selected could potentially be transferred to the digital switching systems group located in Ft Wayne. Dick called us all into a meeting to solicit our interest in relocating to Ft. Wayne.

I did not hesitate in letting my desires known that I was very interested in receiving an interview for one of the positions. I was both excited and apprehensive about my chances of being selected. Once I arrived back home that evening I called Jill and informed her about the possibilities that I may move away. We had prior discussions about our desires for the future and she too entertained the thought of moving away.

I was not truly conscience as to what my motivations were at the time but looking back; I can clearly see them now. I began to reflect upon the direction my life was heading. My thoughts at the time were preoccupied with the desire to wild out. To act out with reckless abandon to do whatever I so chose no matter what the consequence. Even after witnessing the trials and tribulations, I desired to imitate and emulate the carefree and sometimes careless attitude and lifestyle of my homeboy Eric.

However, at the same time I had mixed emotions. I began to believe that I was becoming less and less a responsible individual based upon the strong urges I felt growing within. I had yet to act upon these physical impulses but I felt myself slowly losing my self-control. I wrestled with myself on a daily basis as to whether I should succumb to my more carnal desires. If I chose to do so, everything that I had said and done up to that point in my life I would have deemed a lie.

I had spoken to my close friends and even strangers about the pitfalls of living the fast life. I was waging a battle within myself to do the very things that I preached to others to avoid. At the same time, I desired to have a family of my own. To have a safe haven out of the storms of life and have a place where I could have a measure of peace. I looked at my situation and began to subconsciously formulate an idea.

I would plan, organize, and control every facet of my life to create the image and facade of a family. I would get married, work hard, buy a house, have kids and raise them based on the blueprint I had formed in my mind. I looked toward Ralph and his family as an example to the type of family that I desired to have. I have heard from so many men how nervous and apprehensive they became before asking for a woman's hand in marriage. I had no such apprehensions out of my ignorance and arrogance knowing I would not be turned down.

My personality had undergone a massive change from that of my earlier childhood years. Where I once was the shy and introverted fat little boy, I had become an outspoken and extroverted young man. I wore my arrogance like a pair of the finest sunglasses believing that no one would dare deny me what I desired or felt that I deserved.

My newfound attitude permeated every facet of my life and provided me with a shield forged from a false sense of security. When Jill accepted my marriage proposal I viewed it as a piece of a puzzle created by the fuzzy logic formed within my mind. I believed that it was only logical and rational that she accepted my offer. I was relieved that I had found a solution and therefore resolved the conflict within, but it was far from a permanent one.

That dilemma was over so I thought; now I could focus on obtaining the other pieces to my life's puzzle. I told my family and friends of my decision to get married, and my announcement received mixed emotions. Due to the short time, I had been dating her; everyone asked me if I was sure about the decision I had made. I had no doubt in my mind at the time, for I was of the opinion that the solution to my problem was flawless.

I observed that her little boy was in need of a father and I was of the opinion that she needed rescuing from her current living situation. Jill was in a dead end job, and had come to depend heavily upon her family for her own personal welfare. She did not drive, she could not cook and I saw this as an opportunity to mold her into the type of woman I desired her to become. I unconsciously believed that I could transform her as a sculptor with a fresh lump of clay.

By spending the time and energy necessary, I could create the type of home life I always dreamed of.

As I saw it, I could kill many birds with one stone. By vowing to marry her, this would act as a means of keeping my desire to wild out caged within. I knew that I would not renege on my word once I made a promise to someone. At the same time, I could have my dream fulfilled to have a family as well as providing a means of escape for her.

I did not realize that I was trading one set of lies and half-truths for another. I did not have a clue nor understood that in order to have a marriage that would stand the test of time; it must be forged and cast in the mold of true love. The mix I had poured from the very onset lacked the basic ingredients of trust, honesty, and respect. These ingredients are necessary to form a strong, solid and stable foundation for any marriage to grow and flourish.

I drove home that evening from work, having made up my mind that I would ask her to marry me. I did not ask questions of Jill to discover any commonality our personal goals in life were compatible. I did not care if we had common interests or a shared system of values. My focus was to bring forth the image I had created in my mind into reality as to what I perceived family life would be.

The ends would justify the means whereby I attempted to use external measures to treat an internal problem. My inner spirit was disconnected from my mind and physical being. I was not truly honest with myself or with her as to the intent of my marriage proposal. As a result, it was doomed to fail from the very start.

The following week I received the news that five engineers were selected for interviews. I was one of the five candidates chosen. I thought that I would be nervous, but I was not concerned in the least. We all drove up the same day whereby we were interviewed round robin style by the four area supervisors. Since three of the four supervisors were from the old Ohio group, I thought that I was a shoe in. The last interview was with a supervisor named Jerry, a middle aged white man in his forties. He was an easygoing type of fellow and kept a big smile on his face.

I was at first somewhat leery of him, because I did not trust people who smiled too much. I gave him the run down on what I have done in the past, my personality traits, and the like. He then asked why he should hire me. I essentially told him if he wanted the job done right the first time out, there was no other choice to make but to choose me. He cocked up his right eyebrow somewhat taken aback by my statement. He told me that in his area of the state that he had twenty-five central offices scheduled for replacement during the next two years. He then asked me what I required to get the job done.

I replied that all I required was a free hand and the supporting project documentation. I said that as long as there were few obstacles in my path, I could get the job done. He nodded his head in the affirmative and stood up to shake my hand. We were all taken to lunch whereby I paid close attention to the subtle nuances and hand gestures of those talking around the table.

The other engineers interviewed had an advantage in the fact that a few of them were friends with the supervisors from past associations.

With that being the case, I still felt relatively confident that I would be selected. A week or so passed by since the interview and no word as to the decision of which of us made the cut. I received a telephone call from my friend and mentor Richard, who was part of the new engineering organization. He told me to expect a telephone call from him at home later that evening, that he may share some information. I was at first concerned, because it was not typical of him to call after hours let alone to talk about business.

He called me later that evening asking me how the interviews went. I told him I thought they went rather well and I perceived no problems at all. Richard said that the manager and the four supervisors were going to have a meeting to make the final decision. He overheard a discussion whereby all four supervisors initially decided not to hire me into the group. I was stunned at first, as Richard asked me to recall the line of questions directed towards me by each supervisor. I proceeded to repeat by verbatim the exact line of questioning each supervisor posed during the interview, in addition to my responses.

Richard listened intently to the words I had spoken and then made the statement that something just did not jive. He had a great working relationship with the manager and director of the department and requested that he be present at the selection meeting. He told me he would call me back the next day immediately following the meeting. I wondered all day and night as to what I could have said or done to have been unanimously blackballed.

Shortly after lunch, I had received the awaited phone call from Richard and the news was good. He began to run down the events as they occurred in the selection meeting. Richard stated from all outward appearances, most of the supervisors had their minds made up the week prior to the interview as to whom they wanted to hire. Just before they were to vote and make their decisions final, he asked them why I was not qualified.

One supervisor said that I had only been with the company three years. Other than his statement, the rest of the supervisors sat in silence as they struggled to come up with a justifiable reason for not hiring me. Richard got on his soapbox and proceeded to plead my case. He told them of his experience back in Pennsylvania whereby he too was passed over for promotions he was more than qualified for. The criterion by which he was denied the opportunity had nothing to do with his work performance.

He told them that he had spoken to my current supervisor and I received a glowing recommendation from him. The quality of my work was excellent and stated that I consistently put in extra hours to get the job done. He also spoke to several of the senior engineers within my group, as well with members of the planning department. Each had provided him with positive responses and testimony as to the quality of my work. Richard posed the question again, as to what the reasons were as to why I was not qualified to receive the job.

As I sat back and listened to Richard, I felt a combination of both anger and pure bewilderment. I had no idea or clues based on the verbal cues and body language of those I interviewed with that they harbored any reservations towards me. Richard told them that they all are within their right to choose whom they please. Nevertheless, in the process of deciding, be sure of the reasons behind their decision. After Richard spoke his piece, the supervisors sat there in silence for a moment absorbing his words.

Jerry, who was the last supervisor I interviewed reconsidered and decided to hire me. I thanked Richard for what he did on my behalf, and I promised him that I would not let him down. Of course, I could not tell anyone of the events that occurred, and two days later, the official word came down. I believe that Richard was one of my earthbound guardian angels as this would not be the only occasion that he would come to my rescue. I worked for a corporation where the majority of the leadership lacked the moral conviction to do the right thing. I was fortunate to have known a few individuals whose moral compass pointed in the righteous direction. Richard was certainly one of those chosen few individuals of impeccable character.

For the next several weeks, I spent my energies wrapping up projects to their conclusion as I prepared to move. I also was making marriage preparations as well, so my life at the time was quite hectic to say the least. I also spent my remaining time speaking to my friend Roger trying to give him pointers to stay one step ahead of Dick. I was very concerned about him for I knew in time that Dick would increase the heat on the entire group to maintain the level of output performance.

The day had finally come as I prepared to box up my belongings and start on my new journey. My boss Dick had came into the office earlier than normal and called me into his office. We spoke for almost two hours reminiscing over the last three years about all the changes that had taken place. Dick thanked me for all of the hard work and dedication, as well as the many great conversations we shared.

He said that I was a good man, and stated that he truly would miss having me around. This was one of the very few occasions that I saw the kinder side of Dick's personality. I made an attempt on Roger's behalf to smooth over some of the animosities both had toward each other. I said that we each have our own idiosyncrasies and approaches to life's problems. I said there are many ways to skin a cat. For as long as the goals are the same, I said the differences in our approach to address them should not matter.

I told him that I was able to accomplish the things I did because he gave me the freedom to be myself. When I needed support, he was willing to provide it to me without question. I concluded by saying it would take Roger and his group some time to adjust to his way of doing things. To give them some wiggle room to be themselves and to be patient. He said that he would give my words some consideration and ask how I became so wise so young. I jokingly said that I still was dumber than a box of rocks as we just laughed. I rose up and proceeded to walk around to say my good-byes. To give thanks to those who befriended and helped me over the years.

I went over to the transmission-engineering department to say good-bye to Commodore and Ralph. I would miss some of Commodores corny jokes and break room antics. Ralph befriended me and was one of the first people willing to show me the ropes. He was always there for me when I needed his wisdom or advice. He also provided me with the blueprint for the type of family life I desired to have.

Ralph asked me to stop by his cubicle for a moment. He reached into his office drawer and pulled out a bible he kept there. He told me to sit tight as he went to make a copy of one of his favorite passages for me to take with me. I knew Ralph attended church with his family and he very rarely spoke of religion in the office.

He returned with the scripture from the Book of Ecclesiastes Chapter nine verse eleven:

"I returned, and saw under the sun, that the race is not to the swift, Nor the battle to the strong, neither yet bread to the wise, nor yet Riches to men of understanding, nor yet favor to men of skill; But time and chance happens to them all."

I read the passage several times before I came to understand its meaning. Today it is one of the very few passages I can recite verbatim from the bible which holds truth that none can deny. Billions of people on Earth possess great gifts and natural born talent. However, no matter how great one masters their chosen field or craft, none can escape the fact that being in the right place at the right time is a necessary component.

In order to take advantage of opportunity when presented, one must be both prepared to receive it and have the ability to recognize it when it comes. Many successful artists, athletes, and business people who can testify to the truth contained within this passage. So for those who are still struggling to find their opportunity to display their talents to fulfill their dreams, keep the faith for time and chance does happen to us all.

Ralph told me to keep in touch and that if I ever needed him for anything not to hesitate to call. He stood up and gave me a hug and a handshake and I thanked him for being my friend. We kept in contact as promised and within the next two years, our paths would cross again. The circumstances of our next encounter would bring both dramatic and traumatic experiences to our life's experience neither of us was prepared to face.

I went to pay a visit to Arnie's office to say my farewells to him when I ran into both he and the two men named Chuck. These were by far the most outspoken men within the department and I dare say the entire office. The three of them walked me downstairs to the cafeteria to impart some of their wit and wisdom. Each of them asked me if I was sure of the decision I was making both in regards to getting married and accepting the position in Ft. Wayne.

It has been rare in my experience to find men such as these three who were unafraid and willing to speak the truth. Their tone may have sounded brash to some, but I always appreciated the level of honesty they showed towards me. They knew of my desire to move on and were aware of my aspirations to climb up the corporate ladder. I replied that I was as sure as I could possibly be and that I was ready to face whatever I came my way. They advised me to lay low and survey my surroundings before engaging my mouth. They knew how outspoken I could be at times and forewarned me that I was stepping into foreign territory.

Both of the Chuck's had been in the military and spoke to me as though they were preparing me to face combat. They used phrases as keep your head down and be aware of your surrounding for the enemy is everywhere. As I think back, they were preparing me for a series of battles yet to come. They said that I was very smart and had the skills to do the job, but that would get me only so far. If I truly desired to move up the ranks, that I had to adopt the same mannerisms and to hang in the same circles as those who occupied positions of higher authority.

Arnie told me to take advantage of the opportunity given to me, but to be well aware of the prices and sacrifices I must be willing to make as well. He too recognized the warning sign and knew that in time, the engineering operations in Ohio no longer exist. He was entertaining the possibilities of moving, but would wait it out until his eldest son graduated from high school.

His son was a promising baseball player and he wanted to give him the chance to pursue his dream. He told me not to forget him or the many conversations we had over the years. He had complete confidence in me that I would perform my new job, and jokingly told me to stay out of trouble. Arnie was not the overly sentimental type but I could tell that he would miss having me around. He stood up to shake my hand and gave me a hug as well, telling me to take care of myself.

I had planned to drive to Columbus to hang out with the brothers for one last time. Roger, Bob, Commodore and I had decided to go out to hit a happy hour and to go later for dinner. I asked them to help carry my personal belonging to the car at lunchtime, so that we could make a hasty retreat. As we did on so many occasions over the years, we spoke about office politics and relationships. Bob being the elder spokesman of the group gave us all a pep talk regarding the changing times at the company.

He had experienced several reorganizations over the years. He spoke of going through a similar experience while employed at J.C.Penney. He observed that every time the company went through such changes, the opportunities for people of color became harder to come by. Bob knew and foresaw many more reorganizations to come. He expressed concern as to what type of opportunities we would have available to us. We represented less than a handful of black men occupying management positions in the entire company. Now more than ever, we had to perform better than our white counterparts and to continue to prepare ourselves to stay one step ahead of the competition.

Bob was of the opinion that the majority of the executives within the company truly did not want us there. But the fact that the company did business with the state and federal government, that in order to qualify to bid on contracts the company had to hire people of color. To him it was all about the Benjamin's that money was the only reason why we were hired and tolerated in the workplace.

He told us no matter what happens, for us to maintain contact with one another. He forewarned us to be cautious as to whom we associated with, and with whom we trusted. That just because someone wore dark skin that did not mean necessarily the person was down for the cause and willing to lend a helping hand. He said there is strength in numbers; as a means of survival, we should stick together. We all agreed and put our hands one on top of the other and promised each other that we would do just that.

As the evening was ending, we prepared to say our good-byes. I hugged each of the guys and told them how much I appreciated their friendship and good times we shared over the years. I said that no matter what happens to me, I would never forget them. It was all I could do not to cry as I hugged my man Roger. We been through a lot both on the job and in our own personal lives and I would miss him the most. I did not tell him of the conversation that I had earlier with Dick but I told him to try to anticipate the need before being asked. I told Roger to attempt not show fear in his eyes; to be sure and confident when dealing with Dick. We embraced one more time before I got into my car and drove off. Bob must have had some measure of psychic abilities, for much of what he discussed in time came to pass. The company did continue to restructure, reorganize, and transform itself like a chameleon. Although the company would continue to periodically hire people of color, very few made it beyond middle management. We all would experience our own trials by fire, but by keeping the promise to maintain contact helped us to weather the storms as they would arise.

Sunday afternoon had finally come and I was saying my good-byes to both my family and Jill. Until that moment I was completely sure about the decision I had made to relocate. I began to worry about my mom and sisters welfare because this was the first time we would be apart from one another. My mom told me that it was time for me to go and to make my way in life.

She told me not to worry because there was nothing that we as a family have not been through too many times before. She told me how proud she was of me and to not look back on the decision I had made to leave. She knew that opportunities in our hometown were slim and I had to do what I saw fit. That now I was going to become a family man that I had to provide for them the best way possible.

That no matter what, she would help me in any way she could. My mom did not have money but had plenty of love wisdom and advice to give. I gave her the biggest hug and hugged my sisters as well. I finished packing my belongings and said goodbye as I proceeded to Jill's house. Her little boy greeted me at the door and he grabbed me around my legs. She was sitting at the dining room table with tears in her eyes. We sat and spoke about the wedding plans and I gave her a pep talk to keep her spirits up.

I could never stand to see a woman cry as my voice began to crack. I had a long drive to make and wanted to get there before dark so I could get some sleep and be ready for my first day on the job. We said our tearful goodbye and held each other very tight as she walked me to the car. It had just started to rain so I told her to stay inside not to get wet. In all honesty, I did not want her to see me crying. The fear of the unknown and leaving all that was familiar to me had taken control of my emotions. As I drove off the tears were falling from my face as I embarked on a new life.

I had no idea what I was in store for or what would await me upon my arrival. I never considered Mansfield to be my home having always felt as though I was a visitor in a strange land. It was my time to shine now and show the world what I was made of. It was my opening act and I could not turn back for there was nothing truly to come back to. I rode off drying the tears from my eyes and composed myself, focusing my mind on what the future would bring. To prepare myself for what would eventually become an all out assault on my reputation, character and standing as a man.

CHAPTER EIGHTEEN

I had arrived at the motel and settled in for the night and I could barely sleep from the excitement and anticipation I felt. Morning had finally come and it was still raining like cats and dogs outside as I prepared myself to head into the office. I had prearranged to have one of my old partners let me in the front door around 7:00am to get a lay of the land.

In a way it was like coming home week, for there were many individuals I had worked with back in Ohio that were transferred there the year prior. As I walked through the office area, I met a brother who stopped to introduce himself. His name was Aubrey who worked in the transmission-engineering department on the other side of the hall.

We hit it off right away and as we began to interact, I found something familiar about him. He reminded me of my friend Ralph back in Ohio in many ways having a peaceful and joyous spirit about him. I would come to find out that Aubrey, as Ralph was a follower of the Christian faith. Aubrey was hired into the Indiana operations around the same timeframe in which I was hired.

He had qualities very similar to both Roger and Ralph and we rapidly became close friends. He offered to show me around the city to find somewhere suitable to live and to assist me in my efforts to adjust to my new position. Besides Richard, I trusted and respected Aubrey greatly. I would rely upon his wisdom and insight over the years to come. We too engaged in great debates over issues such as religion, race, politics, etc.

I could always count on Aubrey to tell the truth and to keep it real when it came to my concerns. He was a man of great character who had the ability to cut through my tough exterior to get to the heart of whatever troubled me. Aubrey and I finished our introduction and we both headed off to our respective offices. Jerry had just entered the building heading in my direction as he smiled and welcomed me to the group. Of all of the superiors I have had over the years, he was certainly one of my favorites. He had gained much favor in my eyes as the result of having the change of heart to give me a chance.

From the very first moment Richard told me of his decision to hire me, I decided I would repay his kindness through my work efforts. In many ways, Jerry reminded me of Phil Jackson the NBA basketball coach. He had an unassuming and pleasant demeanor with almost a Zen like approach to dealing with people. The engineers within his group were about as wild a bunch as I had left in Ohio. The majority of the guys came from the Michigan operations and they too were a most colorful collection of personalities.

These guys were an outspoken and lively bunch unafraid to speak what was on their minds. Jerry had the ability to motivate and deal with the diverse personalities without being antagonistic or draconian. I sat in Jerry's office for a while as he proceeded to give me a debriefing as to what was going on at the time. Once all of the engineers arrived, he held a short meeting to introduce me to the group. As the introductions were going around two of the guys in the group began to pick on one another. Ron and Chuck on many occasions provided comic relief to the group and greatly relieved the stress that would periodically build up.

I took to them right out of the gate, as I watched them go back and forth cracking and snapping jokes at one another. Jerry did not appear to mind the periodic interruptions, as I believed that was part of his master plan used to motivate the group. Jerry regained control of the meeting as he proceeded to hand out the schedule and reassign projects among the group.

I was given the southeastern district of Indiana as my territory. There were approximately twenty-five central offices scheduled for replacement. Once I received my list, I reviewed the engineering start dates. Six projects were already behind schedule as I proceeded to start formulating a plan of attack in my head. I asked why the projects were behind schedule, as I discovered that the cause was due to the lack of manpower within the network traffic-engineering department. The traffic-engineering group was also behind schedule in providing the support documentation we needed to engineer the projects. I told Jerry that I would get started immediately on the projects assigned to me.

I could perform a multitude of activities without the data included as part of a traffic order. I stressed the importance of receiving the information in order to submit the purchase orders to the associated equipment vendors. As soon as the meeting adjourned, I dived right into my assignments. I asked for a list of telephone numbers to contact my counterparts in other departments to ascertain their specific needs.

I then started to make travel arrangement to perform initial site surveys on the designated central offices. I was scheduled to receive some in house training on the new digital equipment the same week. Upon each break, I made phone calls and proceeded to create the work order documentation. I was really getting into the flow and enjoying my newfound position.

In the midst of all of the action, I had forgotten that I had yet to pay Richard a visit. He overheard my voice coming down the hallway and came out of his office. I was so happy to see him, as we proceeded to walk into his office to talk. He had already heard from Jerry that I was already hitting the street 100-mph and running. I was already receiving positive comments from Jerry as he expressed to Richard how glad he was to have had a change of mind to hire me.

Richard began to clue me in as to some of the other individuals in the building that I should get to know right away. He asked if I had met the engineering manager of my department, to which I responded no. We proceeded to walk in the direction of his office when I overheard a loud chuckle come from the area. Bob came out of his office and introduced himself to me. He was heavyset, with a round jovial face who spoke with a high-pitched southern drawl.

He had apologized for not coming around to me earlier as he had to attend his weekly conference call with his superiors. Richard excused himself as we planned to go out to lunch later that afternoon. Bob ask me to walk down to the cafeteria to get some coffee and to get to know me a little better. Bob was very popular throughout the company, equipped with a quick wit and magnetic personality. He was a very intelligent and knowledgeable individual, having come up through the ranks. He too was very outspoken and straightforward in his approach to dealing with people. Although he had the ability to play the corporate political game, I could tell that he had a measure of disdain for it.

He asked me how I was adjusting to my new position, and I told him all was fine thus far. I mentioned the fact that we were in need of receiving traffic orders and he stated he would speak to the manager of the group to see what he could do. Bob told me that anytime to feel free anytime to come to him to discuss my concerns. I heard this statement before from various individuals who truly did not mean it. I saw the sincerity in his eyes when he made the statement to me. After my brief meeting with Bob, I asked him where Harry's office was located.

Richard told me that Harry had received a promotion and was leading the technical support group for the tri-state area. I walked down the hall and as I turned the corner, I could hear Harry engaged in some heated conversation with someone over his speakerphone. I was first reluctant to approach him, but I decided to stick my head into his office. He placed the phone on mute, and his entire facial expression had changed.

He sprung up from his chair as though someone had stuck him in the ass with a needle so surprised to see me. He asked me to sit down while he returned to his heated conversation. Apparently, some district operations manager had rendered some accusations at one of Harry's support engineers. Harry was arguing in defense of his staff, while at the same time reviewing the outage report.

Harry grew weary of repeating himself, and essentially told the guy to review the particulars contained within the report. He also advised the fellow to essentially use caution and have his facts straight before accusing his people of failing to perform their job. He then turned his attention to me as we both began to laugh, because the last time I saw him, he was engaged in a similar situation. He was happy to see me, and asked me how I was adjusting. I told him that so far, I like the job, but I still had reservations about living in the city.

I asked him how Dave was doing, the guy I worked with a few years back in Ohio. He was on the road at the time, but he had a standing daily teleconference with him and he assured me that he would pass on my regards. Harry also heard how well I was performing stating that when I gained some more experience, he would transfer me into his group. Harry said that he would invite me to his home for dinner some weekend to hash over old times. He had another meeting to attend, so he shook my hand as I headed back to my office. I truly enjoyed seeing Harry again, and a few years later, I would wind up working for him. The circumstances would be far from the ideal situation whereby he would ultimately betray my trust in him.

I was blessed with the ability to perform while under extreme pressure, but little did I know how much pressure my life would endure. In my haste to accept the position, I had not truly considered the costs associated in setting up a household. For the first forty-five days, the company paid for my living expenses. My mind was focused on my new job as well as preparing for the wedding. The wedding would be a small affair of immediate family members and our friends.

We paid for 80% of the costs whereby Jill's parents and older sister and brother in law covered the costs for the banquet hall and food. A good friend of mine would DJ the affair as a favor to me. I was more concerned with the attendants having a good time than of the marriage ceremony itself. I viewed the wedding more as window dressing to put forth the proper image. I would have been just as content to go to the justice of the peace. As a means to appease and satisfy Jill's wishes and desires for the ceremony, I went along. As long as the pieces of my puzzle fit into place, it really did not matter to me one way or the other the particulars of the event.

I would go home every weekend and on one occasion, I decided to bring Jill with me to look for an apartment. As we started looking around for apartments, I was astonished at the cost of renting. I could not afford to buy a house at the time, so renting was the only optional available. As I began to calculate the costs, we would not have much left in the way of disposable income. When the company hired me, I was at the very bottom of the salary range. The incremental increases I received barely kept up with the cost of living.

As I began to listen to some of the other engineers, I had come to find out that I was among the lowest paid staff members. This would pose a problem and become the catalyst for the battle I would later wage. The following weekend finally came around as I proceeded to get prepared for the wedding. I had hung out the night before with Eric and Donnie with a slight hangover from drinking too much. It still had not dawn on me the enormity of the decision I had made. I was so matter of fact about it all so sure of what I decided that there was no shadow of doubt cast in my mind.

I was on a mission and as I saw it, getting married was but a first stroke of the brush on the canvas of the picture I was painting in my mind. Upon arrival at the church, I walked in and started cracking jokes as I waited for the appointed moment. People were walking up shaking my hands congratulating me for getting married as I stood there with my mind focused on the next step on the list. The time had come as I stood before the pastor awaiting Jill's entrance. Her niece was the flower girl and her son Neeko was the ring bearer. I smiled as I watched them walk down the aisle with a gleam and twinkle in their eyes. My friend Vernon began to sing "Always and Forever" by Heatwave as he then began to play the wedding march. Jill began to proceed down the aisle with cameras flashing about.

I looked around and saw her sisters and her mother crying, as I then gazed at my sisters as my mom winked at me. Jill then took my hand and the pastor began to start reciting the vows. She repeated her lines flawlessly, but when it came time for me to recite the lines, my mind went blank. An eerie silence came over the church as I felt that time stood still. It was as though I was in a trance having an out of body experience looking at myself outside myself. I do not recall having a thought at all, as I was standing there like a department store mannequin.

I looked up at the pastor and all of a sudden, the words came rushing from my mouth at 100mph. The crowd in the church just busted out in laughter, I believe more out of relief than anything else. Perhaps that was a high sign I was receiving to indicate that I should do an about face and have a change of heart. As I stated, I did not see any flaws in my plan nor did decision for the ends justify the means. To say that I truly loved her at that particular point in time would not be accurate. It was more a feeling of strong affection, as it would take me almost a year to say that I came to love her in my warped definition of the word.

We danced and all had a great time at the wedding reception, but the good times would be coming to an abrupt end. The following day, I prepared to leave heading back to Ft. Wayne, leaving Jill behind to deal with the movers coming later in the week. Once I returned, I immediately began to search for an apartment. Aubrey had driven me around town looking at various apartments and we finally found one within my price range.

Everything was moving in accordance to plan as my mind was racing thinking about the particulars of the move and issues on the work front. I was working ten to twelve hours a day, and even took work back to the hotel with me. I did not require much sleep because of the DJ lifestyle I led. I was juggling many balls at once whereby I was determined not to drop a single one. My body fed off the adrenaline rush and my ego fed off the misperception that both the company and Jill needed me.

 I was getting into the zone and the flow of the action, as I rapidly moved through the office meeting and greeting new people. My reputation started to grow throughout the company in such a short matter of time. My level of confidence and self-assurance was overflowing, as I felt almost superhuman. The movers had arrived to load up our belongings as I left early to return back to Ohio to pick up Jill. I decided to leave her son there for two weeks to give us time to get the apartment in order. I started the indoctrination and training process with her right away. I showed her how I wanted the apartment kept clean and began to teach her how to cook. I was guiding and instructing her every move like a home economics class teacher.

I knew that the bulk of my time would be spent at the office and there was no way I was going to come home to a dirty house with no food on the table. Order permeated every facet of my life, as everything had to be in its place with no wasted motion. I hate to say it, but for the first several weeks, I treated her as though she was in a boot camp. She was a quick study and had taken my lessons to heart. Everything had to be done with precision both on the work and home front.

The pieces of the puzzle had to fit, and every stroke of the brush had to be made with flawless perfection. Nothing was going to get in the way of the goals and objectives that I set forth for myself so I thought. The first two months on the job, I had spent a great deal of time on gathering information and fact-finding. I wanted to know intimate details as to the process of the paper work flow. I began to foster relationships with people in purchasing, accounting, operations, and installation departments to expedite the handling of my projects.

I developed standardized ways to reduce the engineering interval, such as creating pre data filled equipment-ordering requisitions. I drew up standardized floor plans that I could cut and past onto preliminary drawings to submit to drafting department. I also developed close working relationships with the various vendors I dealt with. I would contact account managers to ascertain shipping intervals, receive firm price quotes, etc. I saw the current process used by the department as inefficient and cumbersome. Therefore, I came up ways to work within the process but get the job done faster.

With my work schedule, Jill was left home alone a great deal of the time. She had finally gotten the apartment into shape, and we were ready to pick up her son Neeko. I had no idea how much of an adjustment it would take on my part in trying to become a father. He was almost three years of age having not yet mastered potty training. During the first several weeks, I observed his behavior with Jill.

He was defiant and tended to ignore her words and attempts to control his behavior. I had grown weary of hearing the same requests made repeatedly. My patience has always been short, and one particular morning his antics worked my last nerve. I shouted out his name and told him to sit down, as he immediately went to the dining room table and sat down sheepishly looking at me. From that moment going forward while in my presence, there was never an instance where he would disobey either Jill or myself.

I was always of the opinion that a child would never dictate the terms and conditions of their behavior in my presence. Disobedience was non-optional, and I certainly was not going to start with him. I gave instructions one time and one time only not to be repeated. I would scoff with scorn at those who would use such tactics as "time out" or play the game of "lets make a deal" to get their children to obey.

I was conscience of the manner in which I treated him, having fresh recollections as to the relationship with my own stepfather. I would be firm but not cruel, and would be as quick to praise him as I would to chastise. He was a very bright child, and I was quite adamant with Jill that she should spend time teaching him the alphabet, counting numbers, etc. I witnessed on too many occasions whereby the mothers of the associates of mine who used the television or VCR as a nanny for their kids. I viewed time as precious as gold that no one could afford to waste. I was never the type of person who took too kindly to apathetic attitudes or lazy behaviors.

Raising children is one of the most difficult and demanding things a person will ever do in life that should never be taken lightly. There is no time for lying around, whining or complaining about how tired one is of dealing with their children. A conscience decision was made to engage in sexual relations as well as the nine month process required to give birth to the child. Once those series of decisions have been made then all excuses and regrets are to be tossed out of the window.

I chose to become involved with a woman who had a child and I saw it has my duty and obligation to give my all to the cause. By virtue of the vows I had spoken, I was committed to give no less than my best irrespective of my unconscious intents. I could not consider myself a man by turning my back on my responsibilities to uphold the promise I made to both Jill and Neeko. Although some may have considered my decision to marry a woman with a child honorable, it was far from noble. The fact that I chose to marry for less than proper reasons turned what should have been a noble gesture into a lost cause.

The vision and image of the future created in my mind, was never communicated nor agreed to by Jill before asking for her hand in marriage. I did not care to know what her vision of the future held, for all I saw was the picture on my screen. Times were tough on us financially for several months, as I was the only one working at the time. I worked countless hours on the job and the salary I was paid left nothing much for groceries or other necessities we required. I was too proud to ask anyone for help and unbeknownst to be at the time, Jill had called my stepfather Calvin for help. I had not spoken to him since the wedding and one Sunday afternoon, received a call out of the blue from him.

He asked me how we were doing and I said we were doing fine. He posed the question again having asked if we needed anything. I at first paused in silence and before I could respond, he said that he would send us some money. I told him that he did not have to do that, as he paid me no mind saying the money would be in the mail the next day. I thanked him and hung up the phone staring down at the table.

As in all things in this life, all happens for a reason. I remember waking up in the middle of the night from tossing and turning from worrying about our financial situation. I decided I had enough, and I would ask Jerry for a raise and what was required of me in order to receive a promotion. I woke up early that morning and headed to the office so that Jerry and I could speak in private. By the look on my face, he could tell I was displeased as he asked me what was wrong. I told him that from the day I first walked through the front door, I chose to commit myself to doing the best job possible.

Although I had been in the position for approximately eight months, I had become one of the top producers. I told him of the number of hours I had worked which reflected in the time sheets that we were required to submit. To cut to the heart of the matter, the salary I was receiving was not enough to provide for the needs of my family. He was somewhat taken aback not expecting to be hit with such a question that early in the morning.

I proceeded to tell him that I needed more money, and that I also wanted information detailing what steps I needed to take in order to be promoted. He rocked back into his chair and put his hands behind his head absorbing the comments I had made. He said that since I occupied the position for less than a year, there was little he could do to get me a raise in salary. He stated that it was against company policy for anyone to receive a two or more level promotion within the same calendar year. He apologized for his inability to assist me with my problem but if I kept up my level of performance, he would lobby for the highest possible increase.

For a moment, I just stared at him not quite knowing how to respond or react to what was stated to me. I had no means to refute what he told me and I also had no reason not to believe what he said. I rose up from my seat, thanked him for his time, and abruptly left. I was not angry but more taken aback in that I had not prepared myself to have my request turned down. He could tell that I was upset as he attempted to engage in small talk during the remainder of the day. Small talk and idle chatter was not going to pay the bills or solve my pressing need created due to a lack of funds.

For the first time in over three years, I worked a straight eight-hour day and went home. My daily ritual was to pour myself a drink, read the newspaper and listen to the evening news. This was my means of depressurizing and relaxing myself after a stressful day. Jill saw on my face that I was disturbed as she sat down next to me asking what had happened. I told her of the conversation that I had with Jerry, that for the here and the now there was nothing he could do. That for now the struggle would continue until the performance review came around. A few days had passed by before she approached me with the idea of her returning to work.

Jill considered returning to work for quite some time but not knowing how I would react, chose to maintain her silence. She had become bored staying at home and since we now needed the money, she was ready to get back to work. I asked her what she wanted to do but at the time, she had not given it much thought. For the next couple of weeks, she would comb through the want ads in the Sunday newspaper searching for a job. She ultimately came across a position working as a data entry clerk for one of the local cytology labs in town.

The position involved entering data from a personal computer, of which she had little experience using one. I decided to take her into the office over the weekends to familiarize her self with using one. She had taken clerical courses in both high school and the junior college I had attended. For the next two weeks, she practiced typing using the extra PC we had in the office. I taught her how to manipulate her way through the word processor software, and in no time, she became proficient in its use. She had scheduled her interview for early that following Monday morning. She was very nervous as I was acting like a coach pumping her up before a big game.

She was one of several individuals who interviewed for the position. I dropped her off at the front door and drove to a local restaurant to get some coffee. She always had a pleasant personality and was very outgoing and friendly. She worked very hard towards any task, so I had little doubt that she would win them over. A little over an hour had passed by before I decided to head back to pick her up. As soon as I pulled up in front, she was just walking out of the door smiling.

She said that the interview went extremely well, and that she would receive word as to their decision by week's end. She was so very proud of herself for she knew she nailed the job. I told her how proud I was of her, and proceeded to drive back to take her home. Just as she hoped, she received a call late that Thursday evening that she was hired and would be starting the following Monday.

We both were very happy for the blessing we received that night that provided much needed additional income. The logistics were perfect in that the daycare center was down the road. One of the lab technicians came in early enough whereby I could drop Jill off and still get to work early. The pressure valve was slowly releasing the anxiety I was feeling at the time.

No one knew of the many sleepless nights that I had worrying about how we were going to survive. As my time on the job progressed, I was given more challenging and high profile projects in which to work with. I led a rapid response team convened to install a new 10K line digital switching center required to provide service to a General Motors assembly plant. I work every angle I could to whittle the typical eighteen-month project installation schedule down to approximately nine months. I approached Bob to receive authorization to switch manufacturing slots to obtain equipment designated for another location.

I walked the purchase requisitions through the approval process, having even driven 240 miles round trip to regional headquarters to obtain executive sign off. The central office was installed two weeks before the scheduled plant opening, and service was provided to the customer's great satisfaction. I also conducted and reported results of beta site field trials of central office power systems, and a modular copper wiring distribution frame. The product cost a third more than the conventional product typically purchased by our department.

This particular project was done under extreme protest on my part. I instinctively knew the product would not perform as touted, as I questioned how much in the way of cost saving could be gained for the higher purchase price paid. I acquiesced, and ordered the distribution frame for I had greater concerns on my mind. I began to refocus my concerns on how to make ends meet, as I still held the opinion that I was not being paid what I was worth.

The contributions I made in addition to the level of effort extended on behalf of the company bore little financial fruit. Rumors began to stir about the company's plan to hire a great number of new college hires. The workforce at the time was aging rapidly with many of the senior level employees closing in on early eligibility for retirement. The company ultimately hired fresh young prospects as soon as possible. The engineering department was the recipient of about fifteen new hires and we received two within our group. One of the new hires Mike was a recent graduate from Memphis State University.

Upon introduction to our group, I was assigned to become a mentor to show him the ropes. I took to Mike right from the start, he reminded me of Jay Leno with a southern accent. He was a very funny guy, but also a very hard working young man eager to learn. We spent a considerable amount of time together for the first several months as I shared some of the methods I used to get the job done. During this time, he introduced me to Little Joe, who in actuality was a very large redheaded fellow.

Mike had spoken to Little Joe regarding my willingness to help him. Some of the other senior level engineers were at first reluctant to help the younger guys, but I did not feel threatened in the least. As long as they were willing to listen and learn, I did not mind helping them in the least bit. We were all in close proximity in age, and on a few occasions, I hug out and partied with them on the weekends. In time, my attitude towards the company began to change, after I became aware of an issue that cut me to the core of my being.

On one occasion after work, we had all went to one of the local bars to have some drinks. After a few hours had passed, I overheard Mike comment to one of his friends the amount of salary offered by the company. I was shocked to find out that only $1,200 separated his salary from mine. I sat at the bar stunned as hell and I got so upset that I excused myself and headed home for the night.

I spent the remainder of my weekend steaming and stewing in my own juices as his words continued to ring in my ear. I had no slight against Mike or any of the other guys, for I too would have accepted such an offer coming right out of college. The fact that he was a new hire and an unproven commodity paid essentially the same as I did not sit well with me. There was no way I was going to let this situation rest as my mind raced trying to come up with a means of letting my feelings known.

As always, I went to work early the following Monday morning, and I walked to Richards's office to see if he had arrived. He was sitting in his office as I asked him if he had time to speak to me. Neither one of us had yet to have our coffee, so we proceeded to walk to the cafeteria to discuss the matter at hand. I told him first of my conversation with Jerry months earlier when I asked him for a raise. I repeated Jerry's comments in regards to my being ineligible to receive either a promotion or a raise due to my occupying the position for less than a year.

I asked Richard if the information provided by Jerry in regards to the timeframes was correct. I also told him of the conversation I overheard in regards to what the company paid the new hires to come on board. He confirmed what Jerry stated as being the unwritten policy of the company. He had not seen anything officially stating the policy regarding multi-level promotions within the same calendar year. He was somewhat surprised of the small degree of separation in salary between the new college hires and myself. I said that this was a matter of both principal and selfish interests to me.

Memoirs of an imperfect man seeking inner peace through the life and light of Jesus Christ

I had proven my worth and value to the company being a major contributor to the bottom line. There was no way that a rookie whom I was also training receives the same pay as I. Richard was in agreement with my opinion, as he attempted to calm me down. I was so angry and upset that my voice began to get hoarse from the strain I placed on my vocal cords. I asked him what I should do about the situation and how I should approach it. He knew that there was no way I was going to let it go, so he told me to give him a day or so to think about it. He told me to go upstairs and continue to "put it down", to exhibit the same level of effort as I would typically exert. I trusted Richards's opinion and respected him more than anyone else within the company.

I agreed to give him time to come up with a suggestion. I was still upset and was somewhat aloof with my coworkers for the remainder of the day. Mike had come over to my cubicle wanting me to go to lunch with him, but I declined. I was already having a difficult time containing the anger I felt. I did not want to say or do anything to jeopardize the friendship I had with him. The human resources department at the company kept base salary information a closely guarded secret. The actual particulars regarding the performance appraisal process were also very nebulous and cloaked in an air of secrecy as well.

The fact that so much energy was expended by the company to keep the employee workforce in the dark in regards to salary information was an indication of its inequity and lack of fairness. I soon would come to understand why, as I became a victim of corporate salary compression. I was hired into the company with an associate's degree; my compensation fell at the very bottom of the wage scale. The subsequent merit increases I received the previous three years barely kept up with inflation and the cost of living. The company supposedly offered the new college hires salaries commensurate with the prevailing market rate for those with Bachelor's degrees.

Under the so-called pay for performance system, those who contributed the most towards the goals and objectives of the organization were to receive fair and just compensation. A salary band based upon the principle of the Bell Curve determined the pay scale for a given position. The salary band contained a minimum, midpoint and maximum level of compensation for each position. The distribution was shaped in the form of a bell, whereby a person with entry-level skills would be compensated at the lower end of the curve.

Supposedly, as the skills and experience of the individual increased over time, the compensation would raise along the curve. Each department received a portion of funds designated for annual merit increases. These too were distributed along the curve amongst the members of the department. There was not an objective means of weighing and accessing a predetermined value to the corresponding goals of the department.

These goals were identified in the annual management by objective (MBO) appraisal process. The methods by which the company tendered its initial salary offer to new hires were also purely subjective. There was no objective rhyme or reason to how the company chose to access the value of one new employee over another. The initial placement of an individual's base salary along the compensation band was purely arbitrary. The salary offered to prospective college hires came at the whim and wishes of the hiring supervisor or manager.

Salary compression exists when the pay scale of those recently hired into a company either matches or exceeds the midpoint level of compensation. This is the range typically where more experienced employee's salaries lie. The two worlds of both pay for performance and salary compensation collided whereby corporate compensation guidelines failed to address. To both offer a competitive wage to attract new hires as well as offering fair compensation to those whom actively contributed to the achievement of the goals and objectives of the company.

The following day as promised Richard stopped by my cubicle and invited me to go along with him for a walk outside. He suggested that I speak to Bob and approach the issue from a position of strength. I was not to discuss the fact that I knew how much any of the new hires made. I was to find out what detailed measures I could undertake to obtain a promotion and an increase in salary. I listened intently to Richards's words while at the same time I began to formulate the line of questions and responses in my mind that I would later pose to Bob.

 Richard insisted that I should take a very timid and passive approach, as to not let my anger show through in my conversation with Bob. Nothing seemed to make sense to me and being born under the sign of Virgo, perfection, attention to detail brings forth order; and my life was far from perfect. I strongly believed in the adage that there is a reason for everything and for everything there is a reason. Although I was very upset, I still looked at the situation from an objective and logical point of view. I needed to know by what objective reason and rational that my value to the company was equal to those of the new hires.

I told Richard that I would try, but I couldn't promise him anything, for I was willing to put my job on the line. Richard told me to prepare to hear what I did not desire to hear and to expect nothing. I was prepared for that, but I still wanted to hear what Bob had to say on the subject matter. I called Bob's secretary and set up a meeting with him after hours. I was not the least bit nervous as I walked into Bob's office and sat down at his conference table. He looked up from his computer screen with the same wide smile and jolly chuckle he had upon our first encounter.

I thanked him first for taking time from his schedule to speak to me, but I immediately dismissed with the pleasantries. He could tell by the look on my face that I had something serious on my mind. He initiated the conversation by telling me to be completely free to speak what was on my mind. I asked Bob specifically how long he perceived it would take before I became eligible for promotion to senior engineer. He did not hesitate in responding by saying that it would be at least another year or so before that would occur. I began to run down the list of accomplishments that I had achieved to date and I asked why I had to wait to be promoted. He started to go into a litany of excuses that my projects have yet to commence with the installation phase.

He acknowledged the quality and quantity of projects I had under my umbrella of responsibility. Until the installation and turnover of the projects were complete, he was of the opinion that I should have to wait. I stated that I had a problem understanding the logic behind his statement. I pointed out that the current state of my projects was in the same shape as those of at least fifteen other engineers. Most of which were of senior level status.

In addition, I also in a around about way let it be known that I knew there were some engineers who didn't have one major project on their schedule. With that being the case, how could it be that someone who lacked the same level of experience and workload as I made just as much money? He started to stutter and stumble a bit over his words, as he stated that he would not discuss anyone else's salary situation. I quickly replied that I did not come to his office to discuss the particulars of anyone else's situation. I stated that the specific criterion by which salaries and promotions meted out were fair game for discussion. I said that I was trying to find out exactly what I needed to accomplish to obtain what I righteously deserved.

I told him I could understand and comprehend how engineers who have been with the company ten or more years and produced a greater volume of work than I deserved higher pay. I was at a loss as to how someone could be hired at the same pay grade, having yet to produce one project, was beyond my level of comprehension. Bob was silent, as he began to take off his glasses and rub his face. This was his trademark reflex action when he became angry, frustrated or upset.

I just sat there in silence at that moment, gaining some measure of pleasure from watching him squirm. I then stated that I did not come to cause any trouble; all that I wanted was to be treated fairly. I was among the top five performers and in accordance to the numbers; I should therefore be eligible for a promotion. I told him I really liked my job and most everyone within the department, but I have a family to support. In all honesty, I literally could not afford to wait for tomorrow because the urgency I had was immediate.

I told him if you have already made up your mind that I must wait another year, there was nothing more that I could say. Bob said that he understood my pressing need, and even agreed to some measure on my points of view. When it came right down to it, I knew Bob had no plans to accommodate my request to receive a promotion. The meeting concluded by Bob telling me if I stayed on track with my performance, I could expect to receive a promotion within a year.

As Richard forewarned me, I expected nothing and received nothing. I felt somewhat relieved that I had the opportunity to get my point across. As it is when eating a lemon, I was left with a bitter taste in my mouth.

CHAPTER NINETEEN

As I would often do when I was troubled or concerned about something, I consulted my man Aubrey. We had discussed at length my situation whereby he too voiced the same level of concerns regarding the matter. I tried my best not to consider the issue of race in my assessment of the situation in which confronted me. Skin color was not the defining issue for me, but the color of money and the lack of it certainly were an issue. Aubrey saw this as but another example of life's trials and tribulations to be prayed on for resolution.

However, Aubrey was a realist as well, for he too saw the lack of color in the managerial ranks and felt the squeeze of salary compression. I trusted in God to make the way for me by clearing my path of all obstacles to the yellow brick road of opportunity. Although I trusted in Him, my trust in the company and those who managed its affairs was another question. From my vantage point, I saw nothing to gain by waiting for the company to have a change of heart or to become so enlightened. I followed the chain of command within the hierarchy as not to bruise tender feelings or egos, but my hands were still empty.

As we continued to speak about my dilemma, I brought up the issue of my performance appraisal. For the entire year, I literally worked my ass off from the moment I stepped through the office front door. Jerry had called me into his office and told me that he had some great news. He proceeded to sing my praise for the efforts I had extended on behalf of the department, and how amazed he was at my level of performance. Although he knew of my desire for a promotion, he offered his promise to be an advocate to ensure I would receive it the following year.

Jerry informed me that I would be receiving a performance rating of two, which meant that I met or exceeded the goals established for the year. Receiving a performance rating of one was the highest one could achieve. Jerry was smiling from ear to ear waiting for some type of response from me, but all I could do is stare back at him. As I have previously stated, promotions and raises were based upon subjective means not objective ones. Quantitatively speaking, there was no way he could deny my place in the top five percentile of performers among the entire department.

The numbers spoke for themselves, but because of my not being the most popular, I was given a consolation prize. I knew that within my heart of hearts I should have received the top rating, but also realized I was in no position to have it changed. It had been several months since my conversation with Bob, and my life again was pretty much stuck in a rut. I felt like the proverbial mouse on the treadmill, moving furiously but getting nowhere fast. All of that was about to change in ways I could never imagine in my wildest dreams.

Jerry had returned from his weekly staff meeting with Bob when he approached me asking that I stop by his office. I followed him wondering what I could have possibly done, having pretty much kept a low profile during the past several months. We both sat down and I braced myself not knowing what to expect as he then leaned over and slide a piece of paper in front of me. I picked it up at first thinking I was fired. As I continued to read, I discovered it was a job description.

I then ask Jerry why I was given the description as he then asked me if I was interested in being interviewed for the job. I sat there in a state of shock, as I then read the description in more detail. The position was located at the regional headquarters building outside of Indianapolis, and it was one level higher in pay grade. The job description was vague, as my thoughts immediately switched from one of surprise to one of suspicion. I asked Jerry why was I selected and who was the individual that expressed an interest in interviewing me?

Jerry said that he did not know who the individual was, as he was directed by Bob to forward the job description to me. I really became suspicious at that point as I told Jerry until I found out some additional information I could not give him a direct answer. He understood and suggested that I speak to Bob to find out if he could shed some light on the situation. I called Bob's secretary to see if he was in the office and had time on his schedule to meet with me. Bob overheard the conversation and told me to come down to his office.

I sat down as he looked at me and smiled like the Cheshire cat and started chuckling. He said that he knew why I was there, as he began to fill in the information gaps. A man contacted Bob by the name of Reid, who was the director of the network operations planning department for the entire Midwest region. He and Bob would sometimes play a few rounds of golf, and the two of them had developed a very good working relationship. One of his managers had an opening that he had been trying to fill for some time.

As I stated, I was very leery and suspicious from the onset as I listened to Bob put his spin on the situation. He recalled our conversation month's prior regarding my comments requesting a promotion. He also reiterated his subjective opinion that I was ineligible for promotion within his department for at least a year. He received this request and decided that this could be an excellent opportunity to accommodate my needs.

My stomach was jumping something fierce, but I could not distinguish whether excitement or an intuitive forewarning of pending danger was the source. My desire to make more money and move one step higher on the corporate ladder blinded my better judgment. I told Bob to make the necessary arrangements to set up an interview. It would be several weeks before the interview, which provided me with time to investigate the situation further. I found out the names of the individuals that I would be reporting to as I immediately began to perform a background check via my covert network resources.

After a few days had passed, I had received word that the manager of the group was once the president of the Ohio operations. The individual to whom I would directly report to was Jerry. I thought at the time it to be a good sign that I already worked for a man with the same name. I also found out through the grapevine that my old friend Ralph was hired into the same organization. I immediately called Ralph and after we caught up on old times, I inquired as to the character qualities of Jerry. Ralph told me he worked with Jerry ten years prior and although many years had past, his opinion of him was quite favorably.

Ralph believed Jerry to be an intelligent, fair and straightforward individual. Ralph had no qualms or reservations of working for him. Since I considered Ralph to be a person of the highest character, his words carried major weight with me. I spoke to at least a half a dozen other individuals including my friend and mentor Richard to find out as much as I could about Jerry. Outside of Ralph, no one knew anything about the man who could further vouch for his character. I do recall thinking to myself how strange that someone who worked for the company almost twenty years could leave such an untraceable trail.

I told Ralph about my interview for the open position, he was very excited and stated that he would speak on my behalf. I still pondered the reasons as to why I was chosen to receive an interview. My curiosity was peaked when I was told through the grapevine that I was the only one being considered for the position. As with all things, the truth would be revealed in time a few months down the line. I went home that evening and told Jill of the possibility of our relocating to Indianapolis. Jill knew how much I disliked living in Ft. Wayne. She was aware of my efforts to receive a promotion.

I did not share all of the particulars about the position, nor did I share my concerns and reservations either. During the years I was married to Jill, I could count the number of times I spoke of matters regarding my job. I kept my personal life separate from my career to the extent possible. Since Jill lacked experience in dealing with corporate life, I saw no value in sharing it with her. I lacked both faith and respect in her ability to deal with and comprehend the complexities I faced on a daily basis. Her job and concern was to keep the home front running smooth, I would contend with the rest.

The day had finally come as I woke up early to make the trek to the regional headquarters building. Any other occasion I would have been dressed to the nine, but I felt no measure of excitement whatsoever. I wore a wool sport jacket and pleated blue slacks. My face was unshaven and as I think back, it was as if I was purposefully doing what I could to sabotage the interview. My emotions were all over the chart, being more pensive and melancholy as I tried to pump up my attitude. I wanted to get out of Ft. Wayne in a major way, as well as to make more money. I desired to have the opportunity to move up the food chain but as the old saying goes, "Be careful of what you wish for because you just might get it."

Bob made it abundantly clear that my expectations would not be met in the near term. Although I was still unsure as to his motives, this was the only game in town and if I wanted to play I had to sit at the table. I had to play the game with the cards dealt and let the chips fall where they may. While I drove, time appeared to stand still as my mind was working to unravel the mystery and figure out the answer to the enigma. I finally arrived at the office complex, walking into the lobby and then called Ralph to escort me up. We gave each other a big hug and proceeded to walk upstairs. Other than the occasion months earlier when I had driven the distance to hand carry a high profile project through the approval process, this was only the other time I had been inside the building.

The atmosphere within the office had a far different feel to it, almost intoxicating. The best way to could describe it is the difference between living in an apartment or trailer home versus living in a high-rise or penthouse suite. As we walked, I looked at passers by wearing nicely tailored suits and dresses, whereby the individuals appeared to have more of a swagger to their stride. From the moment I walked through the door, I knew that I was no longer in the minor leagues. The regional headquarters building went by many nicknames such as the jungle, the shark tank, the snake pit and the heartbreak hotel.

There were almost as many people who aspired to make it into the hallowed halls as those were who despised and cursed its existence. As we neared the department, I put on my game face trying to look calm and aloof. Ralph introduced me to Paul, who I had periodically worked with back in Ohio. I was then introduced to Lori, Dave and Jewel who were analysts that reported to Jerry. Ralph proceeded to introduce me to Reid, the director of the department.

Reid was one of those down home Georgia good old boys, who spoke with a very thick southern accent. He was a very charismatic individual who reminded me of a snake charmer or used car salesman. He was married, but fancied himself as the consummate ladies man often grabbing the hands of females and planting a kiss upon them. In time, I would nickname him "Mr. Kissahand" for his abilities both in kissing hands and asses. He was most certainly skilled at playing the political game albeit obvious as he was in doing so. Although I did not come to find out this fact until months afterwards, I discovered that Reid craftily orchestrated my transfer to his department.

As the story was told, a conversation between Reid and RJ took place while reviewing the quarterly MBO results. A comment was made in regards to the need of filling two more slots whereby Reid stated he was lacking color in his department. As a means of fulfilling one of his EEO/AA objectives, he sought to hire anyone who would fit the bill. After one of the weekly budget meeting, he expressed his need to Bob and I was immediately considered. I was used as a pawn on the game board of affirmative action. Bob would achieve the objective of promoting a minority candidate as well as removing me like a splinter from his eye. Reid could then achieve his objective to add color to the ranks by providing the avenue to bring me into his department.

From my understanding, Jerry had no choice but to accept the situation and hire me into his group. It was a mere matter of formality of interviewing me to put forth the appearance of the process being fair and impartial. I had no prior knowledge of this situation at the time, but in time, all would be made clear. What I perceived as a bright shining future with sunny skies would eventually bring something far darker and wicked. After I met with Reid, Ralph had finally walked me over to Jerry's cubicle.

He was a tall gangly man in his mid forties, who also had a deep southern twang to his voice. He reached out to shake my hand as I stared into his eyes to catch a clue as to his level of sincerity. He had a deadpan type glance similar to that of a point guard on a basketball team. He looked straight through me as not to tip the direction of the impending line of questions he would pass towards me. During our conversation, I found out that he grew up in a small town twenty-five miles south of my hometown. He grew up poor working on the family farm, and passed his free time away playing basketball.

He was good enough to have gotten a partial basketball scholarship at some small college where he attained his degree. Jerry proceeded to go into detail regarding the position I was being interviewed for. As a regulated monopoly, the company was bound to adhere to certain accounting and financial rules mandated by the various state public utilities and the federal communications commission. The department's charter was to create and maintain capital depreciation and valuation rate studies the company was required to file.

The work entailed was similar to that of a life insurance actuary, using various aging methods and curve charts. These rates would be used to determine how rapidly the company could recoup the costs of its capital investments through the rates charged to the consumers. As Jerry spoke, his eyes gleamed with excitement as he spoke of the various activities entailed under the scope of the position. You would think that the national security or the survival of the company depended upon the efforts of his group. I feigned my expression of interest in the position, periodically nodding and replying with a few "oh really" and "my that sound interesting" comments.

I specifically asked him the type of training opportunities were available as well as the type of career growth accepting the position could lead to. I told him that since my initial hiring into the company outside of the few engineering courses I had taken, I had received minimal formalized training. What I had come to learn was through digging my way through technical manuals and journals and through the aide of senior engineers. He began to paint a colorful picture of the potential opportunities that could spring forth by working in his group.

He said that he fully supported his people, and he was a big proponent of ensuring that his department was well versed on the emerging technologies. He stated that he kept a large amount of funds in his training budget specifically to attend classes and training seminars. He also proclaimed that due to the important nature of the work, the opportunity for exposure to executive management was great. During rate filings, it would be required to give expert written and verbal testimony in support of the company's position. He went on to say that several individuals who held executive positions came from the department.

As he was speaking what measure of doubt and reservations I came in with soon disappeared. He was almost evangelical in his approach, extolling the virtues and preaching the gospel of the importance of his group. During our discussion, I saw no evidence that he harbored any ill will or malice towards me. I bought the story he told hook, line and sinker, as I began to superimpose my face into the picture he was painting. He put on a very convincing act, displaying all of the qualities that Ralph described to me. He then posed a few questions to me, asking the typical in regards to my marital status, future goals, and aspirations.

I had yet to have my first cup of coffee that morning, and asked him where the cafeteria was located. He too was in need of caffeine, so we got up and continued the conversation in route. He asked me what my opinion was thus far about the position, and I replied that it sounded great. He then asked me what I thought of Reid; I immediately chuckled and said he was something else. He put on a weak smile and proceeded to ask me why he should hire me. I responded by saying I could not think of one reason why you should not hire me. He stopped mid stride and looked over at me to see how serious the look was on my face.

I just looked at him and said that I had been asked that same question a dozen times in less than five years. For me it was all a matter of choice, whether or not you desired to have me as a member of your group. I went on to say that once I decided to accept a role or responsibility, I played my heart out and gave my best effort. I repeated the same line as I told my current supervisor Jerry a year and a half earlier. As long as I had the latitude and the support when needed, I would get the job done. As we approached the cafeteria, I ran into Bob who I had not seen since I left Ohio.

We embraced each other both being quite happy to see one another. He invited me to stop by his office before I left for the return trip home. Just as it was during my first arrival in Ft. Wayne years prior, I ran into several old friends and associates. I was feeling very much at home in this new environment as I began to ponder the infinite possibilities I could achieve. Jerry and I sat down to continue our conversation as I again focused on the potential of upward mobility. I made it quite clear to him that I desired to become an executive and I inquired as to what specific steps I needed to take to make it happen.

He paused for quite sometime, musing over my statement with an expression I can only describe as derisive. He rocked back in his chair placing his hands behind his head and said in a condescending tone that I had to perform many tasks prior to being considered for executive management. Because I only had an Associates degree, he stated that I needed to further my education. I would also have to perform my job duties to the satisfaction of both himself and Reid in order to receive nomination to the company's executive "fast track" training program.

I hung on every syllable he spoke, writing down on my notepad the very steps as he laid them out. The tones, mannerisms, and reflections he spoke reminded me of how a parent would speak to a child before the Christmas holidays would arrive. It was as though I was playing the role of Cinderfella as he played the part of the fairy godfather. What I observed at that moment I saw through my subconscious mind. My conscience mind neglected to pay attention to the subtle nuances and body language he displayed. I heard from him exactly what I wanted to hear; the steps in the process I needed to take in order to make my dream a reality.

Had I been in the mind state of true awareness, I would have seen that from the very onset Jerry was blowing smoke up my ass. In past discussions that I had with Richard and Bob, my friend from Ohio, both voiced the opinion that I should never reveal my lofty career ambitions. By virtue of the fact that I was a black man working in a company controlled by white men, honesty was a virtue I could not afford. Some of the white men, who were easily intimidated, controlled their world as well as those they chose to become a part of it. If I chose to reveal my true intentions, my decision could prove to be detrimental.

Bob believed that I should be aggressive in my pursuit but be discrete and covert by keeping my cards face down never showing my hand. His advice contrasted that of my other mentor Richard, who believed that I should be more passive and patient waiting for opportunity to present itself to me. I chose to ignore the advice that my wise elder statesmen shared with me. Out of the same blind arrogance, stubbornness, and naiveté I had from the very beginning. I was unwilling to cloak my true character and put on pretenses for anyone. I was going to keep it real and to hell with anyone who could not deal with my frankness and unwillingness to pull any punches.

That if I played by their rules of engagement and worked hard as Bill the college recruiter told me, the sky was the limit. In the face of already being denied a promotion I deserved, I still held on to Bill's words as though my very life depended upon them. Jerry and I concluded our discussion and we headed back upstairs in order that he could show me an example of the type of reports his group produced. Ralph poked his head around the corner of his cubical smiling at me as I was taken to a common area that contained the binders of the various reports. As I looked at them, I happened to cut a glance at Jerry as he leered back at me.

Upon my review of the documents, I stated that I did not foresee any difficulties in performing the tasks necessary. I asked to sit with Ralph for a while to get a first hand look of the process entailed to generate the reports. My main purpose in speaking with Ralph was to further investigate Jerry's character. I told Ralph of the conversations we had thus far. Although my first impression was less than favorable, I was of the opinion that I could work for him. I specifically asked Ralph to rate Jerry from one to ten on his level of honesty and his ability to trust him. Ralph without hesitation responded with a rating of nine, allowing room for improvement.

Ralph continued to praise Jerry, telling me that he had met his wife and kids and by all accounts, he appeared to be a good man. Ralph's word was gold bond with me, but as an added measure, I went to speak to my man Bob. After Bob and I caught up on old times, I too ask what he knew about Jerry. I spoke to Bob of the circumstances by which I came to be interviewed for the position. Working as an IT systems administrator, he on a few occasions had the opportunity to talk to him. He thought Jerry was self righteous, pompous and condescending hillbilly.

Outside of the professional setting, Bob did not consider Jerry as a person he would associate with. Bob was always cautious and growing up in Columbus; he too was familiar with the small town of Jerry's upbringing. The town had the reputation of being very backward, prejudice and very racist. Bob said if I decided to accept the position, to keep my eye on Jerry because he sensed something about him that just did not appear quite right. I thanked Bob for his advice and prepared for the drive back to Ft. Wayne. When I left heading back to Ft. Wayne, I was confident that I would be hired albeit for reasons yet to be revealed.

I was notified within the week that I was hired and was scheduled to report two weeks from the following Monday. I was not overjoyed about it to say the least, but I was relieved to be finally leaving Ft. Wayne and to be making more money. I immediately decided to buy a new car with the newfound wealth and began to work feverishly to wrap up my projects. Mike the new hire would be my replacement and I began to introduce him to all of my contacts and associates. I really like Mike and appreciated his humor and lighthearted approach to life. I also considered him to be a good man as we too discussed many issues along the color line.

I believed men of good will and character such as Mike could change the culture of the company from within. I was willing to bend over backwards to help him in anyway I could. I made sure that I completed my projects whereby all Mike had to do was oversee them to their conclusion. Just as I had done before, I walked around and said my good-byes to those I cared about. Aubrey and Richard had taken me out to lunch one afternoon. Richard knew the environment in which I was walking into far too well and expressed his concerns suggesting that I reconsider my decision. Aubrey was also concerned, but he knew of the financial strains I was under as well.

For me it was an issue of dollars and cents, and if I could not make dollars, it did not make sense for me to stay. I told them both about the mysterious circumstances by which the position arose was far from the ideal situation and somewhat questionable. Unless a miracle happened to occur, I had to accept the offer placed on the table. Richard as always wished me well and offered his support and advice whenever I needed it. Aubrey and I promised to keep in contact, as we would seek each other's council from time to time.

When I left Ft. Wayne, I did not look back and had no remorse or doubts towards my decision to leave. I went into my new occupation with my head up eyes forward and prepared to face whatever came my way. Little did I know I would be confronted with one of the greatest challenges I would face in my life. I would face trials that would test this mans soul, integrity, courage and self-respect that would leave long lasting effects. I reported to work first thing on Monday morning ready to lock and load. I was placed into a cubicle adjacent to Jerry's office that was piled with boxes full of files.

I spent the first two days cleaning out my area, and it would be at least three weeks before I would be given a phone and a computer. During that first three weeks, I had been pouring over the previously approved rate filings. I at first thought it was odd that my work area was in close proximity to Jerry when there were empty cubicles elsewhere. I also questioned why my office was not prepared and equipped before my arrival, but I just shrugged it off. I sat with both Ralph and Paul to learn how to operate and manipulate the various aging calculations programs used to develop the charts and depreciation rates.

The three of us became close friends as both Ralph and Paul were showing me around the building. They were introducing me to people who could be of assistance when it came time to gathering information. While giving me the grand tour, Ralph took me to the workout facility located next to the cafeteria. Ralph wanted to lose a few pounds and since I was overweight, Ralph convinced me to work out with him. I figured that since I was embarking on a new career I might as well attempt to look the part.

After the workday, I would go to the hotel to change clothes and travel around attempting to learn my way around the city. I was also seeking areas in which to relocate my family when the time came. Ralph tried to convince me to look for a home in his area, but the prices were out of my reach. The area was also predominately white, as I desired to be in a more diverse neighborhood. I had fresh memories of my childhood growing up fighting because of my skin color. I remembered how conflicted I was.

I wanted to make sure that Neeko and my sons yet to be born would grow up not having to go through such an experience. After a few weeks, I had found an apartment on the north side of Indianapolis to move into temporarily until we could find a house. Once I found the apartment, I then began efforts to relocate Jill and Neeko the following weekend. We spent the entire weekend unpacking and setting up shop to get the apartment in order.

The following Monday, we hit the street seeking to find Jill a new job located along the daily route to work. Jerry was very accommodating when it came to my work schedule, as I periodically would leave the office to take Jill for her scheduled interviews. In no time flat, Jill landed a job as a receptionist at an insurance company dealing in workman's compensation. Just like before, the location of her office was in the direction and en route to work. One morning after I had dropped her off and arrived at the office, Ralph had stopped by to see if I had yet made it in. As we proceeded to get some coffee, Ralph was discussing the possibility of going back to college to obtain his bachelors degree.

One of his neighbors enrolled in an accelerated studies program offered by Indiana Wesleyan University and spoke of it quite highly. The program was designed for working professionals who wanted to obtain a degree, but could not afford to take a leave of absence to attend college full time. The class size was between 20-25 students, with a part time instructor who worked full time in the profession involving the particular course of study. The curriculum was designed in an intensive accelerated format, combining both individual and group study assignments.

I remembered the conversation I had with Jerry and knew that in order for me to achieve my long-term goals that I had to obtain a minimum of a bachelor's degree. I spoke to one of my old coworkers back in Ft. Wayne who was halfway through the program to get his opinion and insight. He too spoke highly of the program and suggested that I enroll in it without hesitation. Ralph and another mutual friend named Bob and I decided to attend a seminar offered by the college. After listening to the pitch from the director of admissions, we all agreed that we would sign up and run the educational gauntlet together.

Each class module ran from six to nine weeks depending on the course, whereby classes were held either at a hotel or office complex. The program lasted eighteen months, with a few breaks added in the summer and winter semesters. With the number of hours we were required to work, the program fit perfect into our schedule. The classes would be held in one of our office building right located right across the street from where Jill's workplace was, which made the logistics perfect. Nothing was going to get in my way and I was willing to pull out all of the stops to move it on up like George and Wheezy on "The Jefferson's".

After a few months of intensive house hunting to no avail, we stumbled across an ad in the local newspaper. A building contractor had advertised newly constructed homes in the area and price range we were seeking. With the relocation expense check the company provided, we were able to put a down payment on a new house. It was financed under a "buy down" program whereby the mortgage payments were on a graduated scale.

The payments would increase annually over a four-year period then locked at a final rate. This would enable us to buy a home we could not have afforded otherwise. I was of the opinion that I could perform or exceed at the current level of work performance, and therefore did not foresee any impediments to making the mortgage payments. Jill and I signed the necessary loan paperwork to get the home construction project underway.

The area of the subdivision was nicknamed the "Golden Ghetto". This was due to the mix of African American and Jewish family dwellings in the area. Everything we needed was within a three-mile radius, and the commute to the job took approximately the same time as I had while living in Ft. Wayne. The schools within the Washington Township district had the reputation for providing a great education, which was of great importance to me. Once the loan was approved, the builder immediately got started on the house, as I would stop by every few days to check on the progress.

All was going according to plan synchronized like a fine timepiece. We finally closed the deal and moved into the house during the fall of September 1986. With the help of my friend Ralph, we moved our belonging out of the apartment and into a house of our own. As we were loading up the moving van, Ralph was more elated than I was as he expressed his happiness for us. He stated that God had blessed us and believed that our lives were heading in the right direction. For anyone viewing the situation from an outsider's perspective, all did appear to be heading in the right direction. In a short time, what appeared to be the right direction ended up by my taking a series of U turns down the road of no return.

CHAPTER TWENTY

My life was like a high-speed train, as I was working long days and going to school at night. With the busy and hectic work schedule I had, it became necessary that Jill learn how to drive a car. During lunch one afternoon, I had stopped by the bureau of motor vehicles and picked up a study manual for a learner's permit. Later that evening Jill saw it lying on the passenger seat, and began to smile, knowing that she would soon learn how to drive.

I started looking for a vehicle for her to drive and found a small Toyota Corolla and had it retrofitted with hand controls. We would get up early Saturday mornings and I would take her to one of the local middle schools so that she could get familiar with handling the car. After a week, we then drove around the neighborhood as she maneuvered the car around the twists and turns of the small narrow streets. Finally, on an early Sunday morning she got her first lesson driving on the I-465 expressway.

After approximately a month, she had mastered the skills necessary to take her driving test and ultimately passed on her first attempt. She was so happy and proud of herself, and with her drivers license she now had a new sense of independence and freedom. She could now go shopping, take Neeko to the daycare center, get to and from work, and become totally self-reliant. This also allowed me to spend more time studying and to work longer hours at the office.

Even with the amount of activity I was involved with, I was beginning to get bored and wanted to do something to get my juices flowing. The car I was driving I had for a little over a year, and its luster had long worn off. During a lunch break, I drove to a local dealership and saw a sports car that caught my eye. After taking it for a test drive, I decided to buy a 1988 Toyota Supra. This purchase would be the beginning of financial troubles for my family. The moment you drive any new vehicle off the lot, the value drops $3K-$6K.

I owed more on the car I was trading in than what it was worth, known in the industry as being "upside down". I rolled the difference owed into the purchase price of the vehicle, perpetuating the condition. Since childhood, my penchant for automobiles has been a personal weakness of mine. Growing up, Big Frank bought many cars that I fell in love with. I dreamed of the day that I too could buy nice cars and drive them about town. In time, my love for cars became a compulsive disorder I used to both alleviate my boredom and to satisfy my ego.

Similar to the eating compulsive disorder I had growing up; this one was far more expensive and destructive. The wanting and the urge to own a new car was as addictive as crack. The attention I would receive and the power I felt from behind the wheel was intoxicating. Once I satisfied the urge and took possession of the car, the effects were short lived. In my mind, the future was full of endless possibility and prosperity, and I had no doubt that I would achieve my career and financial goals. This would enable me to support my habit. My life and my world would soon turn upside down. I was awakened from my sleep by a late night phone call from my sister Monya.

I could tell from the sound of her voice that she had been crying, and I know something was seriously wrong for she was not in the habit of crying. She proceeded to tell me that she and my youngest sister had left home after an altercation involving our mother. She called to let me know of her whereabouts, and gave me the telephone number to contact her later. After I hung up, I immediately called my mother to find out what had happened. It had been over four years since Big Frank had passed away, and she had become involved with a man we knew little about. He had four daughters whose mother had passed away. They became romantically involved and in a few months had decided to marry one another.

Everything happened so fast that there was little time for anyone to adjust to the new living arrangements. We were respectful to those who were respectful towards us, respecting the property of others as well. One day upon coming home from school, one of his daughters had apparently helped her self to some of my sister's belongings. Words were exchanged and a fight broke out between both of my sisters and his daughters. Both my mother and their father had been out drinking and arrived home during this altercation, and all hell broke loose.

Not being of a clear and sober mind, further arguments and threats ensued. My sisters ultimately refused to stay in a house of chaos, and they left. As I tried to ascertain what happened, my mother told me that she did not owe me any explanations and refused to discuss them with me. I asked her to repeat herself, as my mother said that she was grown and refused to discuss the matter any further. I asked her if she was sure about her decision not to speak, and told me to leave her alone. By her own words, she sealed her fate with me, for I responded that from that day forward I considered her to be dead in my eyes. It would be almost five years before I would speak to her again.

I saw her statements and behavior as an act of disloyalty and betrayal towards my sisters and me. Throughout the years since our childhood, we had experienced the up and downs as so many families do. When she suffered, we suffered and as her children, stuck by her decisions in regards to the mates that she selected. In my opinion, blood was always thicker than the mud, and you never place anyone before the needs of your own family. In my mind, she could offer no excuse or justification that would satisfy me. For the circumstances that caused the fight to begin with spoke for themselves. I knew the character of my sister's; I also knew that each of them stated their desires to his daughters in regards to respecting their private property.

Double standards of behavior never set well with me. I, after having met his daughters, saw first hand the lack of respect they displayed. I was so angry and upset with her for placing them in the situation, then turning her back on them due to drinking too much. I cut her loose like a bad habit, and had no remorse in doing so. At the time, I was not the forgiving kind and once slighted, it would take an act of God Himself to bring forth a change of heart.

A year had quickly passed by, and I began to notice that the merits Jerry touted about the position had yet to materialize. I was bored, for there was nothing exciting about updating spreadsheets and creating report binders. In the year since I occupied the position, every seminar or industry trade show I had requested to attend were denied. The tasks given me were menial in nature, and I saw nothing remotely inherent within the context of the position I was sold on. I spoke to Ralph and Paul and asked them how many training seminars or trade shows they themselves attended; both replied with the same answer…none.

When I made mention of Jerry's promise of training, Paul raised his eyebrow in disbelief. Paul was Jerry's confidant, as he would often share his thoughts and opinions with him. Paul spoke of Jerry's displeasure of our draining his educational and training budget by attending college. I asked Paul why Jerry would become upset at our taking advantage of a company benefit. He at first hesitated, but then stated that Jerry believed it was a waste of time and money for the company to spend on my behalf. I sat there motionless as the brightest of lights flashed before my eyes. Ralph had a puzzled look on his face as well, trying to juxtapose in his mind that his ears were hearing.

My thoughts were running in reverse as I began to recall the various statements and conversations I had with him during the past year. Jerry tended to dominate the ensuing conversations that would occur when breaking for coffee or lunch. As he would offer his opinions or make some off color comments, I noticed how he would glance in my direction. If the conversation related to race, religion or politics you can bet he was always on the far right end of the spectrum. Most members of the group would sit in silence, laugh or affirm his statements, but not I. More oft than not, I was the lone voice of dissent quick to counter his opinions with facts that I could use to disprove his statements. I thought nothing of it, for all I saw it as nothing more than break room debate. However, for him it was far deeper than just idle conversation.

After listening to Paul, I decided that I no longer wanted to be a part of Jerry's group. After a year, I concluded that the opportunities he spoke of would not materialize. I saw no value in staying in a position that would not serve to meet my ends, so it was time for me to move on. I approached him early one morning and expressed to him my desire to transfer to another department. I made it clear that my decision had nothing to do with him or anyone else in the department. He just sat in his chair glaring at me in complete silence. He asked me if I had my eye on a particular position, and I responded no.

I had not pursued an interest in any job; I just knew that I no longer wanted to pursue this one. He then smiled and said that he was sorry that things were not to my liking, as he then began to make comments indicating his true sentiments. As he spoke his entire tone and demeanor changed, as he stated that he spent a considerable amount of money hiring me into the group. He then spoke of someone who had left his group the year before my arrival. The guy apparently received a promotion in another department. Jerry went on to say that this man did not deserve a promotion because he failed to measure up to his subjective based expectations.

He made it perfectly clear that he would die and go to hell before he would allow that to happen again. As I sat there and listened, all became quite clear to me. Jerry never intended to deliver on the promises he had spoken, nor in anyway be supportive of my interests. He would play the game with the cards dealt, but he would ensure that he played with a marked deck whereby he held all the aces. I was suspicious from the very moment the job interview was offered to me. He harbored great resentment towards being forced to hire me, and he also harbored some racist sentiments as well. There were several occasions when he made sly comments regarding the behaviors or mannerisms of blacks he disliked.

I let the first few of them slide, but as the pattern became more frequent and repetitive, I made sure to check him on every statement. I met his family once and saw how nervous his sons were in my presence. I am quite sure it was due to his voicing his sentiments about blacks within the home. From the very beginning, my spider senses were tingling and my inner voice was screaming to get off the train tracks. Looking back, I saw the contradiction in Bob's refusal to promote me from within the engineering department and his offer of a promotional opportunity outside of it. My need for more money superseded the need to being prudent in making such an important decision.

I like so many individuals tied my self-esteem, self-respect and self-worth to the value of a dollar. When I look back, the warning signs were flashing all around me but I was blinded by my ambition. I had struggled and fought my entire life for what measure of success I had achieved to date. I considered this a continuation of the ongoing struggle to achieve my goals in life. The only purpose for my being hired was to be the token minority, making it possible for Reid to check off the EEO/AA objective from his executive goals for the year. I smelled the smoke and felt the heat, ignoring all of the signals placed before me. I considered myself a street-smart fearless individual who could take on any challenge.

The mere fact that I spent so much time checking Jerry out and making so many inquiries should have been sufficient evidence that something was amiss. In spite of all that was going on around me, I continued to proceed forward. I had always believed that there was nothing to fear but fear itself and I refused to succumb to it. Where there is smoke, there is fire; I choked on the lies and watch helplessly as my career was burning up in flames. Only a fool goes in where others dare enter and choose to fight in a burning house. It was foolish of me to deny that something was amiss and not pay closer attention to my feelings.

The lack of sufficient funds was real and not imagined. I could not achieve my goals within the given timeframe. I looked at my situation in a logic progression of events based on the information given to date. By striving to be a top performer, I should gain both in financial and corporate status. Within my mind's eye, money was power and power was respect. It was not enough that I respected myself. I needed the respect of my peers and superiors as well. If I could perform superhuman feats, I would gain their respect and reach my career goals at the speed of light.

I failed to heed the clues of my environment to assist me in making a conscience based decision. I should have paid attention to the subtle cues and body language displayed by Jerry, to my first impressions of Reid. Because of ignoring those clues, I jumped on to the first train leaving the station. After we finished the conversation and I returned to my desk, my stomach was flipping like a fish out of water. I had asked Paul and Jewel about this guy Jerry referred to, and both said that there was no love lost between the two. Jerry's attitude towards me soon changed from the aloof and standoffish manner he often displayed to one of being brash and quite crass.

He gave me an assignment that entailed the update of valuation rate filing records, which were due for submission to the FCC. The rates were calculated using the consumer price index (CPI) and gross national product (GNP) indexes. I independently researched the rates and indexes at the local library. The fact that I spent so much time gathering information for term papers that I had to write, I could kill two birds with one stone. I spent over six weeks working on this project going through the slow, tedious and cumbersome process to run the aging programs.

The programs ran on an old Tandem computer through a dialup modem, and the output files were then stored onto a floppy disk. One afternoon while working out with Paul, he told me that Jerry was keeping a file on my work activities to build a case in an attempt to get me fired. I cannot say that I was overly surprised as Paul only reconfirmed my suspicions. Deep down I knew he resented me or anyone who dared disagreed with him. Paul knew the truth behind Jerry's animosities, but he would never reveal it to me. He warned me to be careful and to do whatever I could to get out.

Any position I would apply for outside of the department required that the hiring manager contact Jerry to confirm or deny my release from my department. My mind was racing trying to come up with ideas to thwart his attempts to fire me. The first move I made was to meet with Linda, who was the manager of the human resources department. I spoke to her for well over two hours as I laid out the course of events, as I then knew them. She had written down my statements word for word and advised me not to be confrontational in any way towards him. I also immediately made a phone call to Richard, describing the current state of affairs that I was confronting.

I gave him a blow-by-blow account of all that occurred between Jerry and me. He too advised that I keep my head down low, and that he would make a few calls on my behalf. Soon I began to notice how the other members of my group began to distance themselves away from me. People who before would stop by my office to engage in conversation no longer came by. With the exception of Paul, Bob and Ralph, the remainder of the group ostracized me. Ralph had a cookout one weekend at his home, and I pulled the guys aside.

I told them that I did not want to jeopardize them in any way by maintaining their friendship with me. I suggest that they should stay away from me while in the office, until I could find a way out. Each of them has families to take care of, and this was my fight. Ralph would not hear of it, for he believed that Jerry was not the type of person to hold grudges. Ralph believed that his faith in Jesus would protect us from harm. He said that no one would choose his friends or decide whom to keep company. I tried to convince him otherwise, but Ralph was a true blue friend to the very end.

When I arrived at the office Monday morning to complete the final phase of the project assignment, the data output files were gone. The data contained on both the hard drive and the floppy disks were missing. Six weeks worth work of effort was gone as I started to panic. My panic regarding the situation soon turned to anger. I marched into Jerry's office, told him the files were missing, and he responded smugly that it was just too bad. I knew he was the culprit and there was no way that I could reconstruct those records before the filing date.

I kept a hard copy of the reports I had completed to date, but a soft copy was also required as part of the filing. I did not bother to ask anyone of the whereabouts of the disks, for I knew who took them. I walked over to Reid's office explaining the situation requesting that he file an extension until I could rework the reports. I also told him about the conflict I had with Jerry, but at the time, he was unwilling to get involved. My nerves were on edge, and both my temper and patience became short as my attitude was in ready combat mode. My self-control was slipping away, as I focused my thoughts on finding a way out of the dilemma.

Between buying the cars, new furniture and other items for the house, we were knee deep in debt. The conflict with Jerry threatened to destroy all that I had worked to build. Everyday my anger towards him grew as I saw how he relished and savored the anguish he was putting me through. I would not give him the satisfaction of letting him know he was getting to me. There was one occasion he instructed me to deliver some information in the form of a memo to another group. He told me to write a disclaimer essentially stating that due to the fact he had not reviewed the information prior, he would not stand on its accuracy.

I refused to write it, and he included this incident in my personnel file as being insubordinate. One afternoon he had pulled me aside to talk and all but let me know he was going to fire me. He went on to say that he was disappointed in my work performance, and questioned the validity of the performance rating I had received before being hired into his group. He accused my previous manager of sandbagging my appraisal, and at that moment, I told him he could go to hell. At that moment, I felt the sudden urge to grab him around the throat and choke the life from him.

My thoughts were to kill him, to rid the world of one less worthless redneck. My right arm was shaking from the anger I had within and as I clenched my fist to hit him, Jill and Neeko's face appeared before me. They relied on me, and being that I was the one who chose to accept the transfer, they should not be made to pay the price for the decision I made. I wanted so badly to knock that grin from his face as I stood there and told him that his opinion meant nothing to me. To my detriment, I discovered that he was a liar and a sorry excuse for a man. I said that in the span of less than five years, I had surpassed what had taken him fifteen to achieve.

The truth was that he could not stand the fact that someone young gifted and black could do more than wash cars or take out garbage. I told him in any other place, he would be dealt with but in all honesty, he was not worth my time. I said that he could fire me, but that would change the fact that he was spineless. Whether a lie is in written form or spoken, it is still a lie. I said that he had to prove his claims against me in either case. He asked if I was threatening him, I replied that I do not make threats just state the facts.

I laughed in his face as I walked away and took the rest of the day off. God was certainly looking out for me, for as this confrontation was taking place, the wheels of motion were also turning. Richard was working behind the scenes unbeknownst to me to orchestrate an exit plan. He had been in conversation with both Linda and Reid acting as a mediator and guardian of my personal interest. He knew of my character, and had a long and lengthy discussion with Reid about the situation.

Reid and Richard played golf on many occasions, and frequently kept in contact due to the nature of their positions. Jerry had informed Reid as to his intentions of firing me, but failed to tell him the truth behind his decision. I had originally thought Reid to be an undercover racist and duplicitous in Jerry's actions as well. When Richard told me of his willingness to assist me in the predicament, I was caught by surprise. The time had come to submit my annual performance appraisal for approval. I made it clear to all involved that I would not accept any rendering of my performance by Jerry whose opinion was biased and far from objective.

I feared that if he made another off color remark that I could not contain myself. Therefore, I requested that my appraisal be given under the observation of the human resource manager. Jerry rated my performance with the lowest rating possible, with an indication of five, warranting dismissal. I of course disputed the rating having already written a three page objection letter. I refused to sign the performance review in protest and left the meeting. Richard had contacted me a few hours after my performance review and gave me some great news. He had worked out an arrangement to transfer me out of the group into a newly formed department led by Harry.

The particulars of the deal were that my performance rating be revised from a 5 to 4 and that I would have to sign the appraisal. This was my opportunity to start out with a clean slate. The group would be comprised of me, Chuck who was one of my associates I worked with from Ohio and a man by the name of Franz designated as the supervisor. Although I would not receive a raise that year, I retained my position level. I felt as though I was saved from the jaws of death, having dodged a barrage of bullets. I was well aware that my reputation was damaged, and I believed in time I could reclaim it through this opportunity given me.

The following day I signed the appraisal and made the rounds to thank Reid for what he did on my behalf. I sent Linda a bouquet of flowers to show my gratitude, and immediately called Richard. He spent so much time and effort pleading my case for he knew I was not guilty of anything that warranted being fired. Through his grapevine, he discovered Jerry's less than stellar quality of character and suggested to Reid that he should keep a watchful eye on him. Richard paved the way for me and threw me a lifeline to get out of a situation of my own creation.

He did not lecture me about my decision to accept the position as he knew that I was attempting to better my financial situation. There was no way I could ever repay him for what he did for me. The only thing he said was to make sure that if someone needed my help in the future not to hesitate to do so. My thoughts turned to Jerry and what if anything I should do in his regard. It is said that revenge is like ice cream; it is a dish best served cold and sweet. I was well aware that nothing good can come from evil intentions but the dark side of my nature was beginning to overcome me.

He attempted to destroy me and harm my family, but he grossly underestimated my resolve. Ignorance was the only crime I was guilty of, and he was far from qualified to pass judgment upon me. As he stood on the stool of his own self-righteousness, professing to be a Christian his actions proved otherwise. Paul and Bob were not religious by any means, but they were men of great character who actions spoke for themselves. Even Reid, who was a known womanizer, had more character in the shot glass he drank from than Jerry had in his whole body.

In the face of what they knew about my situation, they did not run and hide even after I requested that they do so. For each and every, one of them was true to themselves and that is a virtue that cannot be bought in any store at any price. The justice of the street can be quite cold and harsh, and I fought an intense battle within myself not to enact my own measure of it. This man attacked my character, intellect, and work ethic and disrespected me at every turn. I believed that I was letting him off the hook by not kicking his ass or hurting him through some other form of physical retaliation. It wasn't so much that I gave a damn about the opinions of others, but my ego and warped sense of honor wouldn't allow me to let it go.

To do so would be a sign of weakness on my part as I felt obligated to bring pain to his life in the same manner that he rained it down upon me. Ralph came to his rescue and told me to let go and let God deal with him. He said that if I were to hurt him that I may feel good about it in the heat of the moment, but in time, I would come to regret it. He said that I was a bigger and better man than he ever hoped to be, and that his jealousy of me would get the best of him.

Ralph told me to flip the script on him, and smile from ear to ear without saying a word. By doing so, he would die a slow death of many cuts far more painful than any physical harm I could cause him. I listened to my friend and heeded his advice as I then tried to convince Ralph to get out of Jerry's group. I knew that Jerry would attempt to bring his wrath and anger towards upon Ralph because he refused to forsake me.

In the months that followed my transfer from the group, my prophecies and worst fears were realized. Jerry began to run a smear campaign on Ralph's character and job performance. He gave Ralph assignments with vague instructions and no direction with unrealistic deadlines setting him up to fail at every turn. He would make disparaging comments in the presence of outsiders, damaging Ralph's reputation. We would discuss the matter after class and I felt so helpless.

I again went to Linda, and spoke to her at length about Ralph's dilemma. I compared the recent events I had undergone to that of Ralph's, hoping that she would intervene. I posed the question as to how could it be that his performance could fall so far so fast? I asked her if she found it strange that Ralph's performance during his entire career was consistent, now all of a sudden his performance was unsatisfactory. I used the paraphrase about the leopard not changing its spots, that as a rule we are all creatures of habit. So how could his performance drop from satisfactory to less than satisfactory in the blink of an eye?

I told her of my opinion that Jerry was retaliating against Ralph for his support of me. That he was guilty by his association with me, but my words ultimately fell upon deaf ears. The company under the cloak of the corporate restructuring activities occurring at the time supported Jerry's actions and fired Ralph. I was distraught and my mind was racked with guilt as I blamed myself for Ralph's job loss. There have been few times in my life that I was at a loss for words, but at that moment, I did not know what to do.

Ralph was one of the first people I had met at the company and one of the first to help me. It was Ralph that spoke so highly of Jerry; whose words convinced me to accept the position. I knew Ralph's wife and kids, and our families spent considerable time together. There were many days and nights I spent crying and asking "God, did this event happen"? My loyalties to Ralph and his plight were in direct conflict with my perceived sense of fairness and justice. I spent almost an entire year trying to prove my innocence towards the accusations rendered against me by Jerry.

I felt I was obligated to stand up and protest on Ralph's behalf. I was compelled and honor bound to address these concerns with Linda, but my efforts were not enough. That although the company chose to let Ralph go, that I would not let the issue die with him. My current state of affairs and standing with the company was in a weakened position. I still had a heavy debt load and a family to support. With my new job assignment, I had to perform, and could ill afford to slip in anyway. I could not concentrate or focus on anything and one evening I decided to pay Ralph a visit. I was lost in an ocean of guilt as my sense of what was right and wrong wore on my conscience.

As always, Ralph and his wife welcomed me with the biggest smile as my heart began to tear. As I sat, the weight of the guilt I was carrying broke me down as I began to cry. I apologized several times to both of them for I perceived that I was at fault for their plight. Ralph put his hands on my shoulders and told me I was not to blame for what Jerry had done. He said if he had to make the decision all over again, he would still have done the same thing. Ralph said that there was no way he would have allowed Jerry to coerce him in abandoning his friendship with me. If he were to have done so, how could he have then looked me in the eye and call himself a man?

The way Ralph viewed the situation; it was his duty to stand up as a Christian in the face of injustice. It was more important to him what God thought of him than what Jerry could ever do to him. As I listened to him with tears still streaming from my face, I asked Ralph what did he want me to do? I felt obligated and was willing to sacrifice myself in anyway as repayment for the loyalty he shown me in my hour of need. I stared at the floor as he lifted up my head and said that being his friend and being the person that I was payment enough.

Ralph told me that I should take the opportunity and make the best of it. He planned to fight his dismissal and hired an attorney. All he asked that if the case ever went to court that I testify on his behalf. I swore on my life that I would do anything that was required as he grabbed my hand to let me know everything would be okay. I finally gathered myself, gave Ralph and his wife a hug, and proceeded home.

The capacity of an individual's willingness to sacrifice themselves for the benefit of others is in my opinion, the greatest gift Jesus left to mankind. In the face of injustice, Ralph performed in the same manner as Jesus, being about their faith not just talking about it. They stood unwaveringly, lived up to the principles, and kept God's promise to help those in need to their own detriment. To profess one's faith or beliefs is one thing, but to live in accordance to them is a totally different experience. Until that moment, I had a very jaded opinion about those who profess their religious convictions. It mattered not the religion practiced for my opinion viewed those who spoke the game rarely played it. Throughout my life, I had witnessed those who would speak or sing Gods praise, but treat people far differently.

I would look around and observe people standing on the street corner castigating passersby preaching gloom and doom to the tops of their lungs. I knew many people who watched religious programs on TV, or listening to gospel radio programs bobbing their heads and "AMENING" to every word said. But as soon as the music stopped they went about their daily lives derailing, berating or casting judgment upon the action of others. I found myself distancing my feelings and emotions, and sometimes felt obligated to respond to those acting in such a manner.

Hypocrisy has never been a friend of mine, and I never respected those who lived their lives in direct opposition to what they profess, especially within the context of religion. There were many occasions when I came close to succumbing to my belief that the human race was not worth saving. That perhaps another wiping of the planetary slate was necessary in order for the human race to have a fresh start. In almost every instance when I entertained the thought of causing harm to another, God has placed people in my path to reroute my anger causing a change of heart.

Ralph was my guardian angel in human form that renewed my hope and restored my faith that the human race is not a lost cause. Ralph was one of less than a handful of individuals God sent to prevent me from becoming a coldhearted person. One of a select few sent to protect me, whether it was my spirit or my personal well being. I thought that after going through such an ordeal, that I had paid my penance. Little did I know that it was but a precursor of things to come that would put my faith to the ultimate test.

CHAPTER TWENTY ONE

The Christmas holidays had come again and after the tumultuous year I endured, I looked forward to going back to Ohio to spend time with the in-laws. The effective date for my new position would start in January. The holiday season was always a joyous time to be around my in-laws that I truly enjoyed, and I needed a break from the stress in a major way. During the days that led up to Christmas, every evening was a mini celebration. There would be food galore, as the family played cards or some board game throughout the night. Often times I would engage in sidebar conversations with my brother in laws Sam, Kenny, and LA.

Sam was Queen's husband and Kenny, who at the time was the boyfriend of Jill's sister Sandy, provided much in the way of comic relief. Both of them would have me choking, as they would crack jokes on any unsuspecting victim sitting at the table. It was during this particular holiday I would come to meet Jill's brother LA, who was the eldest sibling of the family. He was released from prison under the supervision of his parents. He sat on the living room couch observing the spectacle in his weakened condition. LA was very sick, inflicted with chronic emphysema requiring the use of oxygen to assist his breathing.

I would sometimes sit by his side and have some very deep discussions about the current events of the time. Back in the day, LA was involved heavily in the pimp and hustle game. He was an associate of Big Franks and he periodically would stop by our house. I vaguely remembered him, but he certainly remembered my family and me. He was a very wise and intelligent man, well read and well spoken. Upon meeting him, most would never suspect that he spent the bulk of his life incarcerated.

As we spoke, LA expressed on a multitude of occasions his deep regrets for the choices he made in life. He felt both guilty and ashamed that he let down his parents by choosing the lifestyle, which ultimately cost him his freedom. LA spoke of the scores of brothers and men he met while in prison that came from all walks of life. Some of the men came from stable families with every chance and opportunity to live a productive life, while some from birth had little chance at all. Nevertheless, both ended up in the same place due to the poor choices and decisions they made.

For all the time effort and energies put forth in the street game, most had little to show for it. Some committed murder, killing over trivial matters while others committed a range of felony offenses from armed robbery to rape. Just as the teenage boys I had met back in the day in Joliet, many of these men came from single parent households headed by their mothers. Just as their fathers abandoned them, many of these men fathered children that they too abandoned. As inmates, these men would not have the opportunity to see their kids or have the chance to play a positive role in the lives of their children.

Due to the choices they made, many of their families disowned them cutting off all ties. Life inside of prison walls was a daily act of survival, whereby those of strong mind or physical stature stood a greater chance of making it from day to day. LA said that he spent many hours in the library reading, or sitting with some of the wise men, he had met. As I listened to him, I thought what a pure waste of time, intellect and talent these men had but chose to use while engaging in criminal activities.

LA spoke of some inmates who attained multiple degrees through correspondence school who had life sentences rendered against them. Some of these men became deeply involved in the study of religion and philosophy to pass the time away. The educational opportunities attained while incarcerated, these men could have pursued as free men. They "got caught up" in the allure and grandeur of what they perceived the "fast life" would bring them. He told me that his mother often blamed herself for his misgivings.

LA deeply regretted the pain and disappointment he caused his mother. Nevertheless, there was no way to turn back the hands of time and reclaim lost opportunity. For his health was failing him as he approached the twilight time of his life on this earth. He was thankful and grateful for his family, because in spite of all that he had done they loved and cared for him just the same. He felt bad that he could not repay them for the debt he believed he owed to them. So many people fail to understand there is a price to pay for everything we do in life, and the price can be quite high.

To give and receive the gift of love costs nothing more than one being willing to extend to another the love one has within. We all tend to take the life God gives us for granted, being of the opinion that the physical form we have will live on forever. We can choose to do whatever we chose with the gift of life given to us. The hands of time will continue to tick by with each passing sweep of the secondhand. Living the good life goes far beyond the price of the clothes we wear, the cars we drive or the house we live in.

Just as quick as we are blessed to receive material wealth, it can be taken away in the blink of an eye. Whether by the so-called acts of God, money can flow through our hands faster than trying to grasp sand. The blind pursuit of it can become the root of our own evil ways and intentions. Thus choking out the life of those whose happiness is tied to the sole pursuit of the proverbial pot of gold at the end of the rainbow. LA discovered the hard way that time waits for no one and that all that glitters is not 24K gold.

The time had come to start my new job as Harry called me into his office for a one on one discussion. He welcomed me into the department expressing his long felt desire in having me as part of his group. He said that he did not care about the previous encounters I experienced, but wanted my assurances that I would not pose problems for him. I responded by telling him that I appreciated the opportunity he gave to me, and I would repay him through my efforts.

Harry then introduced me to two men whom I would come to respect a great deal. Dave was the supervisor of the technical support group, and a deacon and reverend of a Baptist church. Franz was the supervisor of the newly formed Standardization management group I was hired into. I also reunited with an old partner in crime by the name of Chuck. We formed the nucleus of the department, as we all were informed as to the scope of the tasks we had to perform. During the course of discovery, I had come to know Franz, Dave and other members of his group quite well.

I later found out that another partner in crime from the past reported to Dave.... Arnie. The Ohio State operations were in the midst of another restructuring and another round of corporate downsizing was in the making. The technical support group was being consolidated as well, but Arnie finagled some means of maintaining a remote office location. He was visiting with when I overheard his voice coming from Dave's office. I shouted "who left the gate open at the nut house?" as I proceeded towards him. He replied shaking his car keys "he who has the keys runs the nut house," laughing loud enough to wake the dead.

It was great to see my old friend again after so long. Dave began to educate me regarding the task force created to address ways of reducing the operating costs of doing business. During the discovery phase, the task force uncovered the fact that the company was spending hundreds of millions of dollars supporting the myriad of network equipment used. The outcome of the study determined that a decrease in operating expenses was possible if the numbers of vendors and suppliers were reduced. As part of the study, one of the findings was to select a primary and secondary vendor source for everything from paper clips to multi-million dollar fiber optics and telecom switches.

Our group's charter was to create the pilot program the other operating companies would later model. Using clean slate, we were given the flexibility and latitude to do what we saw fit. The goal of the first year was to create the processes and workflow necessary to ensure that 90% of all purchases came solely from designated primary or secondary vendor sources. Chuck would handle much of the day-to-day operations of receiving requests for new products, field trial requests, submitting product defect memorandums, etc.

Franz and I collaborated upon the creation of the various documents, practices, procedures and guidelines under the charter. Both of us knew quite a few people within the company, and these contacts would prove to be of great value. We also embarked upon a massive awareness training effort required to educate the workforce throughout the entire Midwest region. Franz immediately recognized that in order to accomplish the task that the directors and VP's had to buy off on the program. He and Harry hosted a meeting to give them some forewarning as to the nature and scope of what was expected. Mike, the director of the department kicked off the meeting stuttering and stammering his way through the presentation.

He was of Greek decent and having lived in the United States for almost 25 years, you sure couldn't tell it by his poor command of the English language manner in which he spoke. It never failed that this guy would jack up my name every time he spoke it. I began to wonder if he had Alzheimer's, for every encounter I had with him was as if we met each other for the first time. He fancied himself as a suave and debonair individual, and was aptly nicknamed "Zorba the Geek" due to his Barney Fife like demeanor. His hair style could have been titled "Gone with the Wind" as it stayed disheveled. The $1,000 the suits the man wore looked far better on the store mannequin than on him. I thought to myself if this was the best the company had to offer I surely had a chance to make it into the executive ranks.

During the kickoff meeting, the executive's were informed that their incentive bonuses would include the 90% standard purchase goals as per the year end corporate objectives. There was some measure of displeasure and grumbling in the crowd, but it was not as if they truly had a choice in the matter. Upon the completion of the draft guidelines, we agreed to provide their respective departments with awareness training. I was so excited to be involved in such an undertaking, to have a second chance to pursue my career ambitions.

I leaped right into the job without hesitation as we began to use our contacts to gather information to piece together the puzzle of how the current process worked. The task would be monumental, similar to herding cats. People like cats are creatures of habit and trying to get individuals to change the way they conduct their business was a difficult task to accomplish. The purchasing department was the repository and means by which all transactions occurred.

We recognized that the control valve and check point would have to occur within their group. Franz and I held many meetings with the manager of the group to gain a full understanding as to how information flowed in and out of the purchasing system. The system contained in excess of 100K different piece part items each that had to be categorized based upon the corporate standard approved vendor listing. There was no humanly way possible the two of us could have performed such a feat by any reasonable timeframe. Therefore, we decided to enlist the aid of members from Harry's technical support group.

We sorted the piece part database by equipment type and item class into more manageable sized system files. Subject matter experts (SME) assigned to cross-reference checks the items against the corporate database to verify whether the items met the new standard classification. One of the SME's over the outside plant product line was Lonnie, a tall middle-aged man who in every way typified the stereotypical view of a Texan. Due to a degenerative nerve condition, one of his legs lacked mobility whereby he was required to walk with a cane.

Lonnie was very likeable with charm whose persona like my middle school gym instructor Coach Carroll reminded me of John Wayne. I like him right from the start, as he would join us during our lunch or break sessions. As I spent more time with my crew, I discovered that each of them knew of me long before I made their acquaintance. My previous altercation with Jerry apparently had become common knowledge, as I was repeatedly questioned regarding the circumstances behind the conflict. It was refreshing to know that my sediments regarding him were dead on point, for many of the guys questioned the quality his character as well.

I had become quite close to Franz, Lonnie and Dave sharing much of my life's story with them. Lonnie and Franz were avid college basketball fans and both were very knowledgeable and intelligent on many subjects. Lonnie played sports in his youth and I could tell as he reminisced of days gone by. He would sometimes become solemn, making referencing to his physical condition that he felt less than whole. He often would comment that he felt sorry for his wife who he believed, was burdened and suffering in silence due to his condition.

I told him about my wife Jill and the congenital condition she endured since birth. I said that in no way did either she or I feel in anyway burdened. When you marry and commit to someone the deal was sealed from the moment the vows were spoken. There are no guarantees in life that we will become immune to struggle, trouble and strife. I said that although I had never met his wife, that I am quite sure that she loved him irrespective of his physical condition. I said, "Hell, I would have turned tail and run away the moment I saw your crazy ass!" as he began to laugh.

He commented that he thought that I was a special kind of guy, for taking on the responsibility of marrying a woman with both a child and a physical impairment. I did not feel special in the least for the decision I made to marry Jill was not based on true love. It was more the case that I felt obligated to her based upon the vows I spoke to her, not for the love of her. In a few short weeks, I would meet a man whom becomes one of my best friends prevented me from betraying those vows. Harry had announced a new member of the department transferred into the group from Pennsylvania, whose name was Brad.

During the course of my tenure with the company, I had heard Brad's name mentioned in several conversations. He was almost like a living legend by the way some of the Pennsylvania clique spoke of some of the wild and crazy antics he performed. Brad was a handsome guy whose looks were somewhat familiar to that of the movie star Richard Gere. He had deep-set brown eyes with black wavy hair with a smile and a charm that could put any female under his spell. He was a single man whose marriage fell into the abyss of divorce. His divorce resulted from his infidelity as he fell to the temptation of the multitude of advances from females he received on a daily basis. When Harry introduced us, it was as though I was reunited with a long lost brother.

As we began to converse, I had come to find out that our birthdays were weeks apart, he being a fellow Virgo. It was almost as though we were mirror images to one another, with the exception of our skin color. Our philosophies of life, our demeanor, and straightforward approach to dealing with people were just a few of the similarities we shared. He had a best friend whose birthday was the same day as mine, and in a short time, we were inseparable.

From the moment he stepped into the headquarters building, the women there were swarming over him like bees to nectar.

He had a non-chalet air about him self as cool as any brother I met from around the way. I cannot say that I ever observed him mistreating women in any way, but he certainly did not take much in the way of drama from them. The moment any female started to whine or complain, he dropped them like a bad habit. One of the first times we went out together was a graduation celebration with my classmates from the bachelor's degree program one Friday evening after work. When we stepped into the lounge, it was all eyes on us.

Just like metal to a magnetic, our table was filled with women and several of them bought us drinks. When my classmates entered one by one, the party really got lively as we danced and drank until the bar closed down. It was as though a sleeping giant had awakened within me, as the Mr. Hyde version of my persona came back to life. My attitude towards my marriage and women in general started to become more careless and flip. The allure of the nightlife and mingling with singles put me into a trance, and with the added attention Brad provided, I felt like a totally different person.

Brad and I each payday would have a standing date to party on Friday night. I would follow him to his townhouse where we would smoke cigars (a habit I never engaged in until my encounter with him) and prime ourselves through drinking. We fancied ourselves as the "Miami Vice" of Indianapolis whereby I was a large version of Rico Tubbs to his Crockett. We became very well known throughout the singles bars and lounges and all those whom we allowed to accompany us always had a great time.

I was eating up the attention I was receiving from females like a child with a happy meal. Whether on the job or at play, we both were getting major play from women. The temptation to succumb to the advances became harder and harder to fight with each passing day for me as I began to question whether I should maintain my marriage. Jill had not done anything at this point to warrant such a decision; it was the fact that my carnal lust was beginning to take over my better judgment.

One evening a group of us went out to one of the singles bars and after a few hours, Brad had noticed that one of the two waitresses serving us had been staring at me. I said that he was tripping and that she was probably looking at him, as was the case so often in his regard. About ten minutes later, she came over to our table and asked if anyone wanted something else to drink. As she took the drink orders, she told me that she knew what I wanted and she would deliver it to me personally.

I was speechless for this woman was drop dead gorgeous being of Hawaiian and African American descent with long black hair and a fabulous body. The guys at our table jaws dropped in unison as she walked away and turned back smiling at me. Brad laughed saying I told you so as I was trying to pull my tongue back in my mouth and heart back into my chest. When the waitress brought the drinks, she sat mine down in front of me having paid for it. She leaned over whispering having licked my ear saying that she liked me and passed along her phone number. The boys really started to clown me at that moment as I stared at the slip of paper.

My ego at that point was probably 10.0 on the Richter scale as I watched her walk away with the prettiest of smiles. I folded the slip of paper up and placed it into my wallet as the guys began to raze me to no end. The battle between my vows and my desires began that night, a war that I would wage for the next several years to come. I fought a continual battle to remain faithful to my marriage. I wanted to sleep with the waitress in a major way, but every time I would pick up the phone to call the number, I would freeze like an ice sickle. I would hear the wedding vows I spoke like a loud voice screaming in my ear and the word hypocrite flash before my eyes.

It was a though a floodgate opened, as I was being approached and receiving advances from females both at work and in the street. I never received this type of attention living the life of a single man. In all honesty, I still to this day do not understand the nature of the dynamics that were at work at the time. I recall one instance where I left a meeting and as I proceeded back to my office, a fine sexy female who worked in the finance department introduced herself. She had transferred from the Illinois operations and apparently had her eye on me as the result of one of her coworkers making mention as to how nice a guy I was.

She was degreed, and was two levels higher in pay grade than me. She just bought her own home, drove a BMW and had all the physical and intellectual attributes I loved in a woman. We spoke several times in passing, but I was unaware of her initial interest in me. One day upon coming back from lunch, she stopped me while Brad accompanied me as she asked what I was doing over the weekend. I responded that Brad and I were going to one of the singles clubs after work that Friday, and I would be attending the Black Expo downtown with my family the following day. She asked if I my wife was going to meet us at the club and I said no, as she smiled and responded that she would see us there later.

I was both flattered and awestruck with her direct and forward approach as Brad rocked back and looked at her as she left us standing there. Brad looked at me with the biggest grin and said, "DAMN!" then asked me what I was going to do if she offered to take me home. I said I would cross that bridge when I came to it, for I honestly did not know what I would do. As promised, she showed up with a few of her coworkers in tow and sat down at the table with us. She sat next to me and started asking me a load of questions in regards to how my marriage was going, what type of woman Jill was, etc.

She then asked what I thought of her and the possibility that I would consider having an extramarital affair with her. With out giving a second thought I initially planned to accept her offer. Before I could respond, Brad slapped me on the back and told me to head to the bar with him to get another drink. As we walked to the bar, he advised me to give serious thought to what I was about to do. He acknowledged the fact that she was a fine as hell and in any other circumstance; he would tell me to go for it. Brad shared his feelings of guilt about his infidelity, which caused the breakup of his marriage that he still carried with him.

He met Jill several times; he liked her immensely, and said that if I chose to have an affair that I might regret it in ways I could not imagine. He said that he loved the fun that I shared with him, but the single life was far from the glamorous life. He said that he was growing weary of the dating scene and the associated rituals and games that went along with it. Although he loved sex as much as anyone else did, he grew weary of the cycle of starting a new relationship to have it end. The consistent patterns of familiarity repeated as each one would start out in a blaze of passion and ends up burning out in a not so glorious flame. Brad had reflected upon his life and expressed the fact that he missed having a love in his life he could count on.

Brad suggested that I postpone giving her an answer until I was 100% sure that I was willing to throw away my marriage and not look back. When we arrived back at the table, she asked me to dance as Brad entertained her two friends. He winked at me and I nodded in affirmation to everything that he said to me. I told her that in any other place and time I would have not hesitated to be in the company of a woman such as her. Although I wanted to accept her offer, I needed to go home.

She hugged me and said she respected my decision, and if I changed my mind, I knew where to find her. This was one of the toughest decisions I had faced during my marriage to Jill. Had it not been for the advice given to me from my man Brad, my marriage would have probably hit the rocks far sooner than it eventually did. The atmosphere and high-pressure environment at the headquarters building seemed to lend itself to the type of infidelities and indiscretions that I myself contemplated. The perception of success tended to cloud ones better judgment, both to those seeking power and to those who had it.

The casualties and stakes in climbing the corporate ladder of success sometimes came at a high price. When the goals of money and material wealth are the sole motivating factor in ones life, many shall become involved in riskier behaviors in other areas in their life. The workplace affairs within the company resulted in broken marriages that ended in divorce. The air was thick with rumors abound with the talk of who was sleeping with who in the company. The president of the regional headquarters building was caught having sex in the sauna room with one of the area sales managers. His wife's father was a high-ranking official in one of the company's overseas subsidiaries.

When the word reached his father in law, the president was suddenly transferred and later forced to resign his position. Spending so much time in the company of people who were highly motivated and driven to live a life of excesses diluted my sense of reality and morality. For as much as I despised soap opera drama, I too was "caught up" in the hype of a lifestyle that proved to be so detrimental to so many. I was not the only one so affected, as I would later find out that Harry too became involved in an extramarital affair. Because of his involvement with a married woman, it would ultimately prove costly to me in ways I could never have imagined.

A few months had passed by and several individuals that I had come to know approached me about an idea that they were kicking around. My friend Bob and I were asked to participate in the first annual company party for the African American employees. Outside of personal friendship gatherings, there had never been an occasion whereby the minorities within the company were formally introduced. The individuals who came up with the event idea saw it as a means of providing the opportunity to network and connect with one another.

I thought it was a great idea whereby a formal meeting was held at the home of one of the sisters who worked in the IT department with Bob. My task as a part of the planning commit-tee was to locate a DJ and a place to host the event. News about the event began to spread like wildfire, but at the same time, the voices of discontent began to spread as well. There were a few minorities occupying senior management positions that felt uncomfortable and con-cerned about the opinions of their white superiors. One of the detractors was a black female named Peggy, who was adamantly opposed to any involvement with the function.

I did not know her personally but had observed her many times in the hallways of the office building. It was hard not to notice a black woman with platinum blonde hair. I nicknamed her "the chameleon", because her demeanor would change depending upon the color of the person to whom she spoke. The manner of her speech and the reflection of her tone would totally change as she went into her chameleon like act. Depending upon the color of her au-dience, she would either transform into the "down for the cause" sister or sweet Polly Anna pure bread.

She apparently had asked if anyone sought permission from the company to host such an event. Oh boy did the sparks fly because of her posing the question to those on the event committee. The party was a private function comprising people of color who chose to attend the event of their own free will. As the party took place over the weekend, no conflict of interest prevented the event from occurring. No company funds were used to host the event; therefore no justifiable reason existed to be concerned. She and a few others were afraid to jeopardize their positions by attending the function, so they decided not to participate.

Bob did not think much of her from the start but the moment she posed that question, he was too through. I immediately became very angry by the mere fact that she could even entertain such an idea. My thoughts went back to the days when people of color had no choice in the occupations they had access too. It was as though she was a so-called house Negro afraid of doing anything that would displease her master. She viewed the party gathering as some type of conspiratorial plot to overthrow the company. She felt obligated to run and go tell the master the slaves in the fields were conspiring to have a good time without prior approval.

My militancy and fierce sense of independence burned red hot. I said that it would be a cold day in hell before I would ask anybody for permission to do a damn thing. She was a prime example of the fact that growing older does not necessarily make one grow wiser. To be middle aged black woman, her level of maturity barely matched her shoe size. There was a hip-hop song popular at the time called "Ain't no future in your fronting". Simply put the phrase-translated means there is little value in faking and perpetrating your way through life. She was like so many people I had met in my life where appearances counted far more than substance.

 To this day, I fail to relate to her rational as to why she was so reluctant and recalcitrant in her opposition to participating in the event. Perhaps she liked being one of less than a handful of minorities who occupied upper managerial positions and loved the false sense of security she felt being in the less than 1% population. Perhaps she felt that her climb up the career ladder would somehow decelerate if more of her own kind made it into the executive ranks. Her game may have been good enough to fool those who didn't know any better. I believe that she feared that one of her own would see through the thin veil of marginal talent she had at her disposal and may expose her.

Her words fell on deaf ears as the party went on as scheduled in spite of her fears and concern regarding her career or employment status. The turnout was phenomenal as minority employees from across the country attended the function having the time of their lives. The Monday after, several of the committee members told me that she approached them sheepishly inquiring about the affair. Because of her actions, she essentially ostracized herself from the vast majority of those of us of African American decent within the company. I could not muster up one ounce of pity for her as she chose to sell herself short by attempting to sell us out for the sake of putting on pretenses and protecting her precious position.

The time had come whereby Franz and I were ready to take our show on the road. We finally completed the first draft version of our standardization procedures document and decided that while it was working its way through the approval process, we would commence with the awareness training. I had to come to grips with one of my greatest fears…the fear of speaking in public. Previously, I gave speeches in small classroom settings, as well as a DJ working the crowd behind the microphone.

Nevertheless, that was an act performed under the cover of strobe lights flashing in a dark crowded room, not in front of scores of people in broad daylight. The closer to the departure date for our road trip across the country approached, the more nervous I became. In order to meet the deadline we had to cover ten states within two months, requiring that we would have to split the territory in half. We decided to start the tour with two of the smaller state operations, allowing us to get into the flow of the presentation and hone it to a sharp edge before performing in front of a larger audience.

The first presentation was in Franz's home state of Illinois to ten groups spread across the state. Lonnie had accompanied us on this trip as an SME to address the local outside plant engineering department's questions and concerns. The night before the presentation, we ate dinner at a steakhouse located in the city of Champaign. I normally was quite talkative among the guys, but I sat silent terrified about the pending presentation I had to give. As I was staring outside into outer space, a waitress had approached the table to take our order.

Lonnie nudged my leg to snap me out of my trance, as I looked up and made eye contact with another very beautiful woman.

Deirdre was a tall young black woman attending the University of Illinois working part time to pay her way through school. As she began to take our orders, our eyes locked up fixated on each other the entire time. She finally asked me what I desired for dinner, and Lonnie said, "I don't know what he wants for dinner, but I know what he wants for dessert" as we all started laughing. I tried to hide my embarrassment, but I was truly taken by her intelligence, beauty and grace.

Deirdre asked me if I lived in the area and I said no. She responded "Oh, that's too bad so I guess dessert for you is out of the question" as she went to the kitchen to call in our orders. My ego received a much-needed boost at that moment, and all of a sudden, my fears just disappeared. Lonnie and Franz began to clown me about Deirdre interest in me as the laughter and lighthearted conversation helped to ease my mind. The following morning finally arrived, as I was amazingly calm about the ensuing ordeal. I read the presentation materials countless times to the point of having the information committed to memory. Franz would lead the seminar discussing the objectives of the standardization effort from the corporate perspective.

I began to discuss the details of how the new process affected the purchasing of materials for their respective departments. As I sat in the front row waiting for Franz to finish, I was mentally exciting myself to a fever pitch. I thought back to several sermons I had heard as a child in church or the pep talks I received from various people who were important in my life. As I stepped up to the front of the auditorium to start my presentation, it was as though I was having an out of body experience.

I proceeded to work my way through the overhead slides and at some point; I totally disregarded them and started to speak free styling and ad libbing my way through the remainder of the presentation. As I looked into the crowd and saw Franz and Lonnie, both were sitting in their seats with an expressionless look upon their faces. Upon completing my presentation, I had asked the crowd if they had any questions of me, they sat there in complete silence. I immediately became nervous, thinking that I had failed in my first attempt at speech making.

Before I sat down, one man raised his hand and said that he had attended more than a few presentations in his time. He proclaimed that this was one of the best he witnessed in many years. All of a sudden, other people in the crowd began to comment on how well I had presented the materials and spoke of their willingness to adopt the new standardization methods. Franz and Lonnie walked up to me and shook my hands, as both of them congratulating me on how well I had done. Lonnie said he felt as though he was attending an evangelical revival meeting, and he was ready to jump up on his one good leg and start testifying.

I was not aware that I reached the audience by the looks on the faces of the attendees. However, I apparently had won them over quite convincingly. Franz said that we had a winning recipe so we would adopt the same approach for every presentation going forward. As a DJ or master of ceremony (MC), it was my job to move the crowd and pump them up into a festive mood. I never considered that I had the innate ability within to motivate a crowd in any other fashion outside of a club venue. I was very proud of myself at that moment, having put my fears aside all at the result of a chance encounter with a pretty woman. I recalled a conversation that Dave and I had about God one evening after work regarding what he perceived our role in life was.

Dave believed that we all have a purpose in life not rigidly cast in stone; that the nature of life is more fluid, pliable and flexible. Dave said that based upon the specific needs at a given point in time, God would place people or situations in our life's path to fulfill those needs. Deirdre unknowingly instilled a sense of confidence within me that I was in need of at that particular moment in time. For the next two months, we continued to spread the corporate gospel in support of the standardization process.

I was thankful to been given the opportunity to travel down the road of redemption to clear my name and reputation. However, as Franz and I were traveling about performing our road show, the wheels of regress were turning against us. Two weeks had passed since we completed our world wind presentation tour was very well received throughout the company. Harry had received positive comments from the various departments in regards to our performance. The entire department had been working quite hard and Brad and I floated the idea of having a group party. We approached Harry with the idea, and he was all for it and gave us a $1,000 to make it happen. We found a local cater who would come on sight with a BBQ trailer and provide all of the trimmings for $500.

Brad and I used the rest of the funds to buy liquor and other items. The party was hosted at Harry's house on a Saturday night and was the talk for weeks before the event. With our reputations for being live wires, people outside of the department were asking Brad and me if they could crash the party. The party was for our group and the fact that Harry's was the host, we could not oblige the multitude of requests we received. Brad and I arrived early to set up the party and to meet the caterer.

When Brad and I arrived Elaine, the secretary to the director of the department welcomed us. I was very puzzled and glanced over towards Brad who was as surprised, as I was to see her. She began to engage in a series of small talk while we were getting things in order for the party. We went to the backyard area to start mixing up a cooler full of Long Island ice tea for the party. Harry was upstairs getting dressed as he shouted down to us to make ourselves at home. We again looked at each other as I asked him what he thought was going down, and he started to laugh saying he was clueless. As the day progressed, it became quite clear as to the true nature of what was going on.

When Harry finally came downstairs, I looked up and noticed Elaine gazing at him longingly. At first, Harry tried to play it cool and aloof trying not to be so conspicuous about their mutual interests in one another. As the sun was going down people began to arrive at the house as Brad and I were in the back sampling the long island ice tea we had collaborated in making. Dave and his wife had arrived as well as Franz and his spouse to the party. They too began to notice how playful and close Harry and Elaine appeared to be as Franz cut a glance at me raising his eyebrow. I had heard rumors over the last few months that Harry was seeing her on the side, but I was far too busy to get caught up in the hype.

As the evening continued, the party was in full swing as people were eating drinking and having a good time. Brad, Dave, Franz and I were discussing the situation with Harry, Elaine, and our particular opinions about what we were observing. Dave, being a reverend and deacon of the church was trying to be non-judgmental about the situation. He knew that Harry's marriage ended with a nasty divorce, and he had recently ended a relationship with his long time girlfriend. Dave was Harry's confidante and was privy to many areas of his personal life that he was not at liberty to share.

I previously knew of Elaine through the exploits of her husband, who was the director over the regulatory affairs department for the company. In my old position, I had worked with several of his staff whereby it was common knowledge of his reputation for sleeping and cheating around on his spouses. He had been married several times before, and I had come to understand that his marriage to Elaine came at the result of their having an affair while married to his previous wife.

Franz was a family oriented and religious man, and he had great reservations about what he observed at the party. I was quite surprised to hear his viewpoint was on the subject. Franz was of the opinion that as long as their affair didn't get in the way of conducting business, he didn't have a problem with it. This was one of the few times that Brad and Franz saw eye to eye on the same subject, as he too believed in the live and let live policy. On the few occasions I had witnessed affairs or relationships within the workplace, you could bet that drama would soon follow.

It's the nature of the beast where two or more individuals are involved in extramarital affairs that with almost 100% certainty people's emotions get in the way of their better judgment. I tried to be objective about the situation, but deep down I knew nothing but trouble would come because of their relationship. The laws of what goes around comes around definitely came into play in this situation for no matter how you sliced or diced it up, she was still a married woman. Her marriage to her husband came as a result of her involvement in an affair with him while he was married. The patterns of his behavior were carried forward into their marriage, so it should not have been any surprise to her that she could not covert him into a faithful man.

It was rather foolhardy on her part to believe that he would treat her any different than he did his previous spouses. In the same token, it takes two individuals willing to participant in an affair and she chose to engage with both her husband and Harry. It is said that once a cheat always a cheat and although her husband cheated on her with reckless abandon, two wrongs do not a right make. The vows and the marriage license carrying both their names bound them to each other. Like so many others, their words held no meaning and were as empty as the promises made to one another.

Many are of the opinion that crimes of passion have no victims, but I beg to differ. Her relationship with Harry affected more than just the two of them as it affected the entire group dynamic and in time would ultimately affect the remainder of my career with the company. The air was thick with rumors involving another corporate restructuring of great magnitude that would result in massive layoffs. The end of the year was soon approaching. The time to assess the goals achieved during the course of it came upon us.

I had no doubt that I would receive a glowing performance appraisal for my efforts during the year as I worked my ass off to get the standardization initiative off the ground. I was working 50 to 60 hours a week plus attending evening courses to obtain my masters degree. There was no way that I could be denied what I thought was due, but I would soon discover otherwise.

CHAPTER TWENTY TWO

Franz and I began to tally up the results to calculate the percentage of standard equipment purchases made by department and for the region as a whole. After a multitude of reiterations and recalculations, the region had achieved an 86% rating four percentage points shy of the goal of 90%. When we presented the findings to Harry, he stared at the report for a while and asked us to go back and recalculate the numbers again for accuracy. We told him that we had performed the calculations ten times, with four different people performing the calculations.

The ratings were accurate and the numbers added up therefore there was nothing served by going through the effort again. Harry had a scowled look upon his face and said that Mike would not be happy with the results. I said that we met the other goals as part of the initiative. The fact that we had less than a full year to put the program in motion, being four percentage points off was a monumental feat to have achieved in such a short timeframe. Harry rose up from his seat to present the figures to Mike for review, stating he would get back to us later on that afternoon.

When we left his office, I asked Franz what wrong with Harry. Franz told me for the first time that his relationship with Harry was less than stellar. I was taken aback, for I saw no evidence and had no clue that there were any animosities between the two of them. Franz had forewarned Harry weeks before our completion of tabulating the results that we may fall short of the goal. Harry had essentially told Franz that all of the goals would be met without question. As I sat and listened to him, I was in a state of shock and disbelief. I thought I knew Harry, as he was one of the very first people I had met when hired into the company.

He treated me well and always showed a measure of respect towards me. For years, Harry promised to hire me into his group when he had the chance to do so and he came to my rescue in my time of need. I was unprepared for his reaction, and became more alarmed as I heard from Franz the type of mistreatment he endured over the year. As promised, Harry called us both into his office later on that afternoon to discuss the matter. He said that after speaking to Mike, he wanted us to include two other categories into our figures that would take the rating over the 90%.

Franz and I just sat there and looked at one another in silence as he then asked Harry "are you asking us to lie"? Harry hesitated for a moment, and said, "I am not asking you to do anything, I'm telling you to add the two categories as Mike instructed". Time appeared to stand still for an eternity as Franz looked Harry in the eyes and told him that he would not be involved in falsifying any reports. He then looked at me, as I said that I would not do it either for the results were as clear as crystal. If we were to have fudged the numbers, anyone who took a cursory view could see the discrepancy in the figures.

The tension in the air was as heavy as concrete as Harry slammed the report down on his desk and told us to get out of his office. Franz was as red as a beet and my heart was racing as if I had run a marathon. We both walked out of Harry's office and made a beeline back to Dave office for consultation to find out what he knew of the situation. Upon our arrival, Dave saw the disturbed look on our faces and asked what was wrong. In order to have a measure of privacy, we all took a walk outside around the perimeter of the building to discuss the matter. After Franz clued him in on the discussion, Dave was both perplexed and at a loss for words. Dave was not aware of any information that gave any indication as to the trouble that we faced.

As the conversation continued, Franz shared the frustrations he had during the course of the year in attempting to gain Harry's attention regarding our efforts. We were pretty much left to our own accord to do what we saw fit, and received little guidance from Harry. As we proceeded to carry out what we perceived our responsibilities to be, Franz would attempt to communicate with Harry to get his input and to keep him informed as to our activities. In almost every instance, Harry would blow Franz off and become perturbed with him for approaching him. Harry didn't care to know the details about what we were doing, he just wanted results.

Dave suggested that we stay away from Harry for a few days and give him a chance to cool down. In the meanwhile, he would talk to him and find out additional details regarding the situation. This conversation happened on a Tuesday and when Thursday arrived, the bomb had dropped that there would be another company wide restructuring effort. The regional operations headquarters from around the country would be centralized and consolidated in Irving, Texas. The new centralized headquarters would be staffed by cherry picking the so called 'cream of the crop" from the various regional headquarters personnel.

As the news about yet another corporate restructuring effort was spreading, so were the concerns amongst our department. The performance appraisal took on an entirely greater level of importance now, for it would be the determining factor as to retain or release employees from the company. Franz and I faced a serious dilemma by our refusal to falsify the year-end reports. Our jobs and careers were now in jeopardy, and Harry had our lives and our fates in the palm of his hands. When I drove home for the weekend, my mind was in deep turmoil and confusion for I was lost and didn't know what to do or where to turn.

Again, I was caught up in a game of double jeopardy not of my choosing and dealt a hand I had no desire to play. I asked God what I could have possibly done to deserve the anguish I was going through. It appeared to me that no matter how hard I worked, how hard I tried to treat people right; my reward was to be paid in pain and disappointment. I began to question my own sense of right and wrong, for what was it about my character that Harry thought that I would be willing to lie for him? I held the naïve notion that by working hard to achieve the goals set before us, which my efforts would be repayment for the debt of kindness and the opportunity Harry provided to me. That wasn't enough for him, for he had something else in mind.

From the first moment we met year's prior when I was first hired, he portrayed an image of being a straight shooter and a man of character. How could I have been so wrong about Harry, especially when people such as my mentor Richard thought so highly of him? I placed my complete trust in Harry and thought that he was a stand up, honest man. Through the passage of time and circumstance, the true color of his nature had cast him in a totally different light. I felt like the biggest fool walking the face of the earth at that moment.

How could I have been so blind and stupid to have placed my faith and belief in the notion that all I had to do was work hard and play by the company's rules? To believe that if I followed the rules, I too could have a slice of the company's opportunity pie. Harry's loyalty was to himself, being of the opinion that I was obligated to do his bidding without question. Harry bailed me out and offered me a lifeline to escape from the bad situation I was in with Jerry. Nevertheless, as it turned out, Harry was no different from the rest, for his offer came with strings attached.

He was a self-serving, double-dealing and dishonest individual who was willing to compromise himself or any one else for a dollar. For the last two years I was embroiled in some type of conflict of diverging interests involving those for whom I worked. I began to wonder if the cost for maintaining my sense of morality and honesty came at too high a price. I began to second-guess myself as my mind overflowed with self-doubt and dismay. Perhaps I was the type that protests too much; that I should just go along with the flow and do what I was told without question.

It would have been much easier if I were to join the crowd, talk and walk in lock step. I could have followed the old adage "when in Rome…" acting in the same manner by lying, cheating and conniving people every step of the way up the ladder of success. When it came right down to it, I knew that if I went down that road there would be no turning back for me. As the saying goes: Power corrupts and absolute power corrupts absolutely. I had a small taste of what power and influence could do; I felt the rush I received from the attention I gained from women both in and outside of the company. It would have taken little effort on my part to succumb and fall under the influence of the elixir and the illusion that power held over men far stronger and wiser than I.

I knew myself well enough to know that I could not afford to emulate the majority of those within the company who occupied positions of authority. It was this same level of self-awareness that I chose not to get myself involved in the use of hallucinogenic or mind altering drugs. If I were to have allowed myself to drink from the challis with the state of mind I had at the time, I too would have probably wrought much pain and grief upon those I loved the most. With my short temper and the level of anger I had within me, I would have been more ruthless than Al Capone and as merciless as Genghis Khan.

God be with anyone who dare oppose me or choose to get in my way. I proceeded home and suffered in silence, spending every waking moment trying to find a way out of the predicament. Each day felt like an eternity and like a ghost, I floated in and out of consciousness. Looking back, I know now that I was on the brink of having a nervous breakdown. It was all that I could do to maintain a civil tongue, having the desire to curse and shout at the top of my lungs the hate and contempt that I felt towards Harry. The icing on the cake came when Elaine was chosen as the new standardization management administrator.

The position was the same level and salary grade that Franz held, with no supervisory responsibilities. In effect, our jobs were eliminated, but Chuck's position was kept intact. When Harry made the announcement, the silence in the conference room was deafening. Everyone sat in their chairs in a state of disbelief, as Franz and I looked at each other in affirmation to the blatant act of disrespect perpetrated upon us. I felt the anger welling up inside of me, as I immediately rose from my seat and left the room. At that moment, had anyone attempted to get in my way, I more than likely would have caused bodily harm.

As I went back to my office and sat in my chair gazing out of the window, I felt my sanity slipping away from me. The only qualifications Elaine could lay claim too related to the fact she was romantically involved with Harry. Chuck, Franz and I were the primary contacts of the standards group. All activities relating to the charter flowed through and performed by us. Elaine was not involved in the process whatsoever, lacking both in formal educational and technical experience. She was the department secretary, the only occupation she performed during her tenure with the company.

The more I replayed Harry's words repeatedly within my mind, the more upset I became. The multitude of hypocrisies in regards to corporate policy came into question. The entire hiring process by which the company operated during the restructuring effort became more dysfunctional than before. The methods used to hire promote or fire people were neither fair nor objective, and this situation made it quite evident. I knew that if I came equipped with the same level of experience and education as Elaine, the company would never have considered my application for employment.

As part of the restructuring effort, the creation of a formal job description for every position was required. Every job description comprised a list of minimum qualifications that an individual must satisfy in order to be considered. No one in the human resources department questioned her lack of qualifications, or the means by which Harry arrived at his decision. There was no check and balance in the selection process and consequently, inequities such as this occurred. As the rest of the department returned from the conference, I sat in complete silence. It was common knowledge throughout the department in regards to their romantic affair.

However, when Harry's personal affairs transcended into the workplace, I took his actions quite personally. He chose to have the affair; he chose to ask Franz and me to lie for his own personal benefit. His selection was self-serving in that he chose to hire Elaine out of spite for us, not out of concern for what was best for business. Elaine made it clear on many occasions that the only reasons she chose to work were to alleviate her boredom. Her income satisfied her desire to shop at will, beyond the spending allowance provided by her husband.

Having families to support, the requirement to work for both Franz and I was a necessity, not a luxury. Franz later stopped by to gauge my reaction to the announcement, but he could see the look upon my face. He knew that Harry had no plans to keep him as part of the group. Franz was as shocked and surprised as I was about Harry's blatant disregard for our efforts in his decision to hire Elaine. He also took the opportunity to inform me that he received confirmation that his job transfer was finally approved. His contact within the marketing department paid off, as he was able to obtain a lateral position making slightly more money. He told me that the following week would be his last, as he relished the opportunity to get away from a bad situation.

He asked me what I was planning to do that he was willing to give me a glowing reference. I was at a loss and simply told him I did not have a clue. Lunch was soon approaching, as Dave, Franz and Lonnie came to my office to requesting that I join them. After the ordeal, I lost my appetite and graciously declined their offer. I wanted to be alone in my thoughts and with the level of anger I had within, I thought it best to keep my distance. As Franz's last day in the group approached, my mood became more pensive and melancholy.

I was happy for him in that he was able to find another position and continue to take care of his family. I respected Franz for his steadfastness for enduring the level of mistreatment perpetrated against him. Franz was now gone; and I was left alone with no way out and nowhere to go. Categorized as an excess employee, my job function was placed into the "Dead pool". I immediately began to search for another job, sending out scores of resumes to prospective employers. I did not receive so much as an acknowledge post card for my efforts, as my quiet desperation turned to panic.

The "Dead Pool" was aptly titled as I felt like a fish swimming aimlessly waiting for my day of execution. For the next three weeks, I would come to work and sit in silence the entire day. Dave and Lonnie would periodically stop by my cubicle in an attempt to break through my silence to no avail. The wheels of change were rapidly spinning, as I received an unexpected telephone call from an old friend. Mike, my young protégé from Memphis State, called me at the request of the switching engineering manager.

Upon becoming aware of my situation through his network of connections, Bob was working behind the scenes to keep me employed. He had been in constant contact with both Dave and Franz, whereby Dave informed him of my decision to remain silent. Mike said that I had many friends in my corner and strongly advised me to allow them to help. As I listened to him, I fought back the tears as my voice began to crack in my attempt to respond. From the very onset, I prepared myself mentally for the worse case scenario. I had no idea that anyone was concerned with my plight, believing that I was truly alone.

In the same token, my level of distrust regarding Bob's motives was quite high. In my mind, I apportioned some measure of blame towards him for my plight. For it was Bob who denied me the promotion I sought and deserved, and his involvement brought forth the job offer from Reid. I thought he was involved in some sort of massive conspiracy against me for reasons only he knew. After composing myself, I told Mike that I appreciated his friendship and efforts to help me. I expressed my reservations about trusting anyone at this point, as he responded, "What do you have to lose by doing so?"

There was a moment of silence, which seemed to me to have lasted an eternity. The events of my life over the previous two years played before my eyes in fast forward, with a view from an outsider's perspective. As I watched this instant replay of events and characters, I was looking with the motive of assessing blame for my predicament. At first, I began to appoint blame towards anyone and everyone who crossed my path. It was so easy to point fingers, to cast blame for my plight as it provided me a fleeting moment of comfort. However, the point of Mike's question loomed unanswered.

When faced with a dilemma most always people tend to ask the question why, as if knowing the cause for the dilemma, the dilemma would somehow cease to exist. Some ask the question as a means of assessing blame that by doing so the problems they face will somehow disappear. Ultimately, asking or knowing why some event occurs will in no way prevent it from occurring. The individual will have to confront the problem, regardless of the motives, intentions, or causes behind the event.

If two people are involved in a vehicular collision, it becomes irrelevant to both parties why the accident occurred. Assessing blame in this case will only go to resolve who is financially responsible for damages, but both vehicles will still require repairing. In solving a crime of murder, knowing the motives behind it may provide for some measure of melodrama, but the murdered victim is still just as dead. The problems we face in life may not be as grave, but no one is exempt from experiencing struggle and strife. Life situations are far more complex than a TV crime drama, and few issues are resolved within an hour's time.

A valid reason to ask the question "why" would be if the observer studied recorded history or an event in their past in order to gain perspective regarding a problem in the present. Why has relevance if the observer's intent in posing the question serves to seek out commonalties or occurrences between past and current events. By studying past trends, one can find clues and potential remedies to problems encountered in the present. To look toward the past to find causes that may reduce the chance or opportunity to repeat negative consequences.

History is replete with examples of events whereby the actions and words of men and women alike repeat in a seemingly endless loop. If knowing why something occurs in and of itself had relevance, would not logic and reason dictate to the human race to consider a different course of action? The problems we all face in life serve a purpose to strengthen areas of our being where we are weakest. The resultant trials and tribulations provide the vehicle through which the strengthening of the mind, body, and spirit occurs. Even the most spiritually enlightened individual is not exempt from this process; for this is the game of life.

When faced with a dilemma, the series of choices presented before us will serve to either advance our personal growth, or retard it. Nothing in life stays the same for life is dynamic and fluid, not static and motionless. At the time Mike posed the question of what I had to lose by trusting him, I was not so enlightened. When it came right down to it, it was a pure waste of time for me to look backwards upon the events of the past. No greater purpose would be served through my efforts to cast blame upon someone else. For no matter how I perceived it, I was both responsible and accountable for my actions.

I still chose to accept the terms and conditions presented before me. At that moment in time of my life, my viewpoint and perspective were based primarily upon monetary or material loss or gain. The enlightened response would have been to say "nothing, for I have everything to gain. I could not see beyond my problems out of fear of what I could lose financially. When I finally decided to reply, I said that I could lose my job, my home or my car because that is what I deemed most important in my life.

I proceeded to go into a tirade regarding the turn of events that befallen me. After listening to my rants and raves, Mike in a calm voice told me he understood the reasons behind my anger. Mike also told me to look at the reality of the situation I faced as well. He said that no matter how unjust or unfair it was for Harry to hire Elaine, it was his choice to make. From a realistic perspective, both Elaine and Harry had their positions solidified; I did not.

Mike said I could choose to be angry and upset, but my being upset changes nothing. In light of the poor perception of my past work performance, Harry's credibility with the company carried far more weight than my own. If I chose to stay on the path I was heading, the unemployment line would be my final destination. Mike said that although I was within my right to be displeased with the situation, I should consider accepting the helping hand extended to me. Although I could not see it at the time, having a family to support was a blessing in disguise.

Having a family forced me to make decisions based on sound judgment and not acting on the emotions I experienced at the time. I told Mike to pass the message back that I would accept whatever assistance put forth on my behalf and I thanked him for being a friend in my time of need. A few days passed by and a department meeting was held to discuss the latest changes within the department. An individual from the California operations was appointed the new director of engineering, operations and planning. He made the announcement of a new manager was being brought into the department from the Illinois operations by the name of Don. I did not know him personally, but over the years I had come to hear about him through a few associates of mine who worked with him.

He had the reputation among his peers of "kissing up" to his superiors and playing corporate politics to the hilt. During my tenure with the company, I was told repeatedly that multi-level promotions within the same calendar year were against company human resource policy. With this appointment, this constituted the second promotion for Don, three levels higher than his previous position. When the announcement was made during the meeting of Don's selection, I asked the director what process and selection criterion he used to fill the managerial position.

The room went deafly silent as I could see the facial expressions of several of the department managers begin to distort and their eyes rolling into the back of their heads. The director froze like a dime store mannequin and stared towards me in a state of both disbelief and anger. He took my question as a challenge to his authority and questioning of his judgment by choosing to hire Don. The director face was as red as a hot house tomato, replied with a lame retort that corporate human resource procedures were utilized to fill the position. In other words, shut the hell up and be prepared to catch hell for posing the question in a public forum.

The following week I discovered that an interdepartmental transfer was in the works to place me within the engineering operations department as a capital budget administrator as a subordinate to Don. Because of my questioning of Don's selection, Don and I were at odds from the moment of his arrival. I was thankful on one hand that I still had the ability to bring home a paycheck and take care of my family, but the bitterness and anger I felt towards Harry consumed me. There were a few occasions whereby we would pass each other in the hallway.

He would grin at me as though as a means of acknowledging his perceived triumph due to my unwillingness to obey his orders to fudge the reports. One evening before heading home Lonnie stopped by my cubicle to discuss the latest series of events. Lonnie stated that he was somewhat surprised that I had accepted my current circumstances so well. I told him that not all was what it appeared as I was having a great deal of difficulty resulting from the lack of equity and fairness by the company's hiring practices. I told him that I was considering filing a grievance with the human resources against Harry and Lonnie asked, "What is stopping you from doing so"? I sat in silence for a moment and could not give him any excuse.

Lonnie stated that if I were to remain silent or were to take no action, then I essentially deserved what I received. I left the office and while driving home, I thought about what Lonnie said. I thought about all that I had been told over the years during my career about the various rules, regulations, procedures, requirements I had to follow in order to make it up the corporate ladder. As a result of Harry's actions towards me as well as what appeared to me a rather abrupt change in the rules of the game regarding promotional policy, I had to do something. So when I returned to work the following Monday, I made up my mind that I would file a grievance against Harry.

For the next three weeks, I began to write a historical account of the encounters I faced since joining the company. I painted a picture of how newly hired college employees whom I trained a few years prior, were promoted while I stayed at the same pay grade. I graphed my salary increases versus those of college hires, which indicated that many either made the same amount of money as I or in some cases, paid several thousands dollars more. I created a graph indicating the number of college graduates hired into the department during the previous five years tracking their promotions versus my own.

I indicated how my performance ratings tracked until my arrival to Jerry's department were favorable. I stated how Jerry's false accusations tainted my work record and thus impeded my ability for career advancement. By the time I completed my writings, I had compiled about ten pages of documentation I was sure would make my case. I proceeded to the office of the Vice President of Human Resources to discuss the matter at length. As I spoke, he began to jot down notes appearing to be interested.

After an hour passed by, I concluded my statements and forwarded the documentation I prepared for his review. He then told me that after a thorough investigation of my claims was completed, a follow up meeting would take place. When I left his office, I felt positive about the feedback I received and thought that through my actions, a fair and just decision was in store for me. During the next several months, Don assigned menial projects to me consisting of cleaning out the technical manual library, generating meaningless reports and other tasks more suited towards the clerical staff.

I knew Don was assigning these tasks as a means of forcing me to quit, but I surprisingly I kept my composure. Four months had past by since I filed my grievance and on an early Thursday morning, I noticed that as I proceeded to my cubicle, that several of the managers were whispering and staring towards me. I rose from my desk to get a cup of coffee and saw Harry and the department director Larry walking down the hallway with a look of sheer anger on their faces. I noticed that the two of them came from the office of the VP of Human Resources and I surmised that a discussion regarding my grievance had taken place. This occurred on a Wednesday and upon my arrival to the office the coming Friday, the manager of the human resources department called me to her office.

As I sat down, I noticed that her demeanor was somewhat disconcerting as she shuffled through a few file folders on her desk. She informed me that after a thorough investigation, there was no evidence of any discrimination or improper hiring practices pertaining to my case. As I listened, I noticed that she could not look me in the eye as my own eyes began to open. I knew there was no point in arguing the finding so I thanked her for her time and returned to my desk. As I proceed back to my desk, I thought to myself "How could such a decision be rendered with all of the supporting documentation I provided"?

Little did I realize at the time that this was beginning of another yet another series of disappointments I would encounter. A week past by as on the following Friday morning, Don came to my cubicle requesting that I meet with him. Don's facial expression and the trembling of his voice gave me an indication that something was amiss. We entered into a small conference room and as soon as he closed the door, my stomach began to rumble as though a million butterflies were inside. Don informed me that he was ordered to reduce the headcount within his department and as a result, I once again placed into the "dead pool".

I was in a state of shock and bewilderment and it required every ounce of inner strength I could muster to keep the tears from falling from my eyes. As I began to ponder what my fate would be, Don proceeded to tell me that I had an option. Bob, who was the engineering department manager I worked for in Ft. Wayne, offered to hire me back into his group. Don stated that over the weekend I should consider the offer and upon my return to the office the following Monday, to inform him as to my decision. In my state of bewilderment, I looked upon Don's face and saw the appearance of victory come upon him.

In a moment of pure clarity, the truth was revealed to me. Although the corporate restructuring effort was still ongoing, it had nothing to do with the elimination of my position. Revenge and retribution typically comes fast and swift as Larry, Harry and Don found a means of eliminating a great source of personal aggravation…me. In a calculated move, I was essentially check mated as a pawn on a chessboard. If I were to turn down the job transfer, I would have no legal grounds to file wrongful dismissal charges against the company as they offered a comparable position within the same pay grade.

If I accepted the position and attempted to file charges later, the corporate lawyers could state that company acted in good faith towards me by offering a job with no reduction in salary. In my pursuit of fairness and justice, I was unwilling to face the realities of corporate life that there are prices to pay in order to move up the ladder. One must be willing to sometimes compromise their morals, ethics, and integrity and be willing to follow those whose interests are 180 degrees in opposition to your own. I remembered the words spoken to me by Bill, the man whom interviewed me years prior upon my graduation from junior college.

He told me that if I worked hard and played by the rules, the skies were the limit. This statement was yet another fairy tale I chose to believe as Bill failed to tell me that the rules of the corporate game were situational, fluid, and rarely applied in a fair and objective manner. During my tenure, after spending hundreds of hours working overtime, pursuing my bachelors and masters degrees, hard work alone did not produce the promised fruits of promotion. Working hard in and of itself was no guarantee of upward mobility within the company. Because I was unwilling to laugh on demand, blindly accept orders without question or play corporate politics, there was a price to pay.

By failing to remain silent when an injustice was committed, there was a price to pay. Due to my failure to recognize the signs along the way, there was a price to pay. By failing to accept the cold, hard fact that if I chose to maintain my integrity, lack of upward movement would be the ultimate price I would have to pay. I chose to ignore the realities I faced on a daily basis and by doing so, I could not truly be comfortable with the choices I made. During that particular time in my life, I was spiritually void therefore, I found no inner peace or solace in holding stead face to my beliefs or faith within myself.

Don asked if I did not have any questions that I should I go home for the remainder of the day. I was speechless, as it felt as though I had a bolder lodged in my throat. We left the conference room and I proceeded to gather my things to head home. When I entered my car, I could no longer hold back the tears and began to cry the entire trip home. A solid day passed before I shared the news with my then wife. The level of shame, sadness, grief and anger I felt was so overwhelming no one could console me. Everyone knew of my disdain for Ft. Wayne, but I had a far greater difficult time in dealing with my intense feelings of failure.

With no other job prospects in sight, deep in debt and a family to support, I had no other choice than to accept the offer at hand. Such is the game of life that we all must play the game with the cards dealt, no matter how bad the hand may be. I dreaded going to work the following Monday morning, to face Don and all of those within the department who also knew the truth and my fate. I attempted to avoid Don as much as I could the entire day by visiting several associates of mine who worked in other departments to solicit their opinions regarding my plight. I finally mustered up the courage prior to heading for home to stop by his office to inform him of my decision to accept the position.

Don stated that I would report to my new assignment the following Monday, so I should wrap up my assignments to be handed over to another member of the group. For the remainder of the week, I sat in solitude as I began to pack up my belonging. A few friends would periodically stop by to attempt to cheer me up to no avail. Friday finally arrived as I gathered my belongings to take to my car. I stopped by Dave's office to say goodbye to him as he rose, gave me a hug, and told me not to despair for God was with me every step of the way.

Dave's words were of little comfort to me, but I appreciated his concern and thanked him for his friendship and support during my time of need. As I entered my car, the tears began to flow again as I thought that in less than four years, I have come full circle. As Sunday evening began to fall, the dread of my emotions began to overcome me the closer I came to Monday. The very city I despised and the career position I thought I would never see again, hit my ego and self-pride in the face with a force of reality I could never imagine.

I placed so much emphasis upon achieving my career goals; so intertwined with my self worth and dignity that I viewed my return to Ft. Wayne as abject failure. I now would face the same individuals whom a short time ago, I saw through the rear view mirror of my life. Besides facing death, to confront ones' inner demons is probably the most difficult things for a person to do. As I entered my car that fateful morning, my journey to self-discovery and spiritual awareness was just beginning.

I would encounter chain of events over the comings years that would forever affect my outlooks on religion, love, relationships as well as my personal relationship with God....but this is another story.

EPILOGUE

I started writing this book in November of 2001, two months after 9/11; an event, which has forever changed the landscape of life on planet Earth. Many of the issues and topics I have touched upon can be found on the stage of current world events. History is once again repeating itself as mankind stands on the brink of spiritual implosion and human destruction. Just as in the final days of the Roman Empire, uncanny similarities and conditions that exist today in the United States and elsewhere around the globe are strikingly all too familiar.

The Roman Empire was once considered as the lone world's military superpower. The Romans wielded great power and control over many continents including the natural and human resources of the lands they conquered. The Roman's representative form of government was one of the first republics created on the planet. This became the blueprint the founding fathers of the United States of America modeled the Constitution of this nation after. But the same cancers of greed, graft and corruption that ravaged and destroyed the Roman Empire has infected the body politic of the United States and many other world governing bodies as well.

The need exists for mankind to make a paradigm shift from the selfish, self-destructive and violent behaviors currently engaged to a more constructive way of living. The need exists for each and every individual to start using the power of their conscience mind in order to bring about the positive changes necessary for life to continue to flourish on this planet. The inner turmoil and external conflicts being experienced around the world is a prime example of the need for change.

Continuing to adhere and follow the biblical phrase of "An eye for an eye, a tooth for a tooth" will lead to the same outcome mankind have experienced countless times before. The nursery rhyme of the three blind mice or the story of the three monkeys who see, speak and hear no evil has become our reality. Those who occupy political, corporate or religious leadership positions are leading us down a blind path paved by our own apathy and contempt.

The mind of mankind has become disenchanted and the ears deafened by the siren song of resignation. People across the world continue to dance to the music being played over and over again waiting for someone else to change the tune. As a result, the human race have once again contributed in transforming the world's global economy and collective psyches into another Great Depression in more ways than one. The four horsemen of the Apocalypse have continued to plague the human race driving us closer to extinction. War, famine, pestilence and death have a tight grip around the throat slowly choking the life energy from this planet.

The escalation of age-old religious conflicts over rocks and dirt shows how little mankind has progressed spiritually; and how little human life is valued. The continuing war being waged for so called "Holy Land" between the Palestinian and Jewish factions in Israel; the conflict between Russia and Chechnya are but a few of the violent struggles occurring around the world in the name of freedom. The warring parties continue to rack up the body count to unbelievable amounts fanned by the flames of hate, selfishness and extreme ethnic and religious intolerance.

From the viewpoint of the casual observer, one would most certainly question the motives of the so called "freedom fighters". What type of freedom and quality of life does one expect to experience through the killing and murdering of innocent human being? What difference does a regime change make, when the conditions of ignorance, poverty and despair that fuels violence continue to exist? The global conflicts are based upon the collective series of choices and decisions manifested within the disturbed minds and troubled spirits of a people in dire need of healing.

The conflicts come as the result of repeating the same failed measures chronicled throughout the history of the human existence. The old adages come into play when those who fail to recognize the lessons of history are doomed to repeat its failures. Frederick Douglass stated long ago that "Power concedes nothing without a demand; it never has and it never will". The troubled times in which we live necessitate that new approaches to change the balance of power be enacted without resorting to the use of violence, murder and mayhem.

"We are troubled on every side, yet not distressed; we are perplexed, but not in despair". (II Corinthians 4:8)."

The lives of God's children whether Christian, Muslim, Jew, atheist, or agnostic are under assault. One can hardly turn a page in the local paper or listen to the evening news without witnessing some sort of calamity or distress. The news overflows with reports of natural disasters, crime, anarchy, riots, war, and famine resulting in massive loss of life and property. Our five senses receive a continual bombardment of negativity transmitted in 30 second sound bites made in rapid succession multiple times a day.

Couple this to the concerns of how one will pay the rent, buy food and clothes for the children adds to the emotional stress many people carry from day to day. The added anxieties of potentially being laid off or downsized threatens what little security a family has left after all the bills are paid. Life is stressful enough for those so blessed to have a job, a supportive spouse and family. Those less fortunate are literally fighting to survive in order to obtain the necessities of life.

To cope with the stresses of daily life, many turn to activities or behaviors that will worsen an already unstable situation. To make ends meet, some will engage in prostitution, selling drugs, or theft. To dull the pain, some may turn to alcohol, drugs, and extramarital affairs. Others will choose to bury themselves further in their career, believing that working longer hours will somehow secure their position. These actions may provide temporary relief, but the pain still remains long after the effects of the pain killers have worn off.

For those of us who have chosen the Christian life, our faith is our shelter from the turbulent, problematic storms of circumstances beyond our control. It is one thing for a believer to say "I accept Jesus Christ as my Lord and Savior", but to wear the cloak of Christ in our daily lives is far more difficult. For the moment, the choir becomes silent and the music stops, we all must face the problems of life once we step outside the doors of the church. The Christian lifestyle requires one to be prepared to live a life of service, sacrifice, and periodic suffering. It is relevant issue in the body of the church today, as each of us must call into question the strength of our own faith and conviction.

Far too many Christians treat God like a coat or cloak, to be put on in times of trouble or taken off to suit our own personal vices. By keeping our Holy cloaks of faith in the closet, we leave ourselves unprotected to spiritual, psychological and physical attack from a world fueled by fear and full of danger. The Holy Bible contains the blueprint and source "code" of faith for those of us who believe in the Word of God as delivered by our Lord Jesus Christ. Although the Word has been in the possession of the human race for thousands of years, many still fall prey to fear and negative influences of the world in which we live.

Jesus told us "Let him ask in faith, nothing wavering. For he that wavereth is like a wave of the sea driven with the wind and tossed (James 1:6)". The faith among the body of the church has become more like a tidal wave crashing upon the shores in the lives of many followers, leaving in its wake great doubt, fear and confusion. Proverbs 30:5 states "Every word of God is pure; He is a shield unto them that put their trust in Him". The Bible contains many scriptures relating to the issues of faith, doubt, fear, love, life and death.

Webster's dictionary defines faith as " the adherence to something to which one is bound by a pledge or duty; firm belief in the integrity, ability, effectiveness, or genuineness of some- one or something". The bible defines faith as " the substance of things HOPED for, the EVIDENCE of things not seen (Hebrews 11:1)".

Jesus tells us we are not to look at the things, which are seen, but at the things which are not seen. For the things which are seen are temporal (temporary); but the things which are not seen are eternal" (II Corinthians 5:7,18). Once a person chooses to become "born again" in the body of Christ, the individual enters a covenant with Him in accordance to the spoken Word. The "born again" Christian pledges by faith to give their life to the Lord. The Holy Spirit that resides within us leads the actions and deeds of the believer.

The book of Romans (8:13-14; 1:17) states "For if you live according to the sinful nature, you will die. But if by the Spirit you put to death the misdeeds of the body, you will live, because those who are led by the Spirit of God are sons of God. For therein is the righteous- ness of God revealed from faith to faith: as it is written, the just shall live by faith". These scriptures are profound and provide clues to unlock the secrets as to why so many live a life of despair and hopelessness.

Individuals who attend places of worship do so by a pure act of faith. In Exodus 4:1-4, Moses voiced his concerns to God that the children of Israel would not believe that He sent him to deliver them from the hands of Pharaoh. God instructed Moses to cast his rod upon the ground whereby the rod was transformed into a serpent, which Moses immediately fled from. In a pure test of faith, God then instructed Moses to extend his hand and pick up the serpent by the tail. Expert snake handlers know that in order to avoid being bitten, the best way to control a snake is by holding it at the back of its head.

To grab a snake by the tail leaves the handler most vulnerable prone to being bitten. Moses, having absolute faith and trust in God without hesitation, followed His instruction and upon grabbing the tail, the rod reappeared. Do you believe this scripture to be true? If the question were posed as to whether or not Jesus Christ existed, many so called Christians would respond with a resounding YES! If I were to ask self professed Christians if they believed Jesus Christ performed miracles, and died on the cross I would hear the same. In these instances, you are exercising faith in the Word for you are "walking by faith, not by sight".

The Bible states that we are to "walk by faith, not by sight", which works fine when dealing with those who are walking in the Spirit. But to have blind faith towards those who live in the flesh can be very dangerous and detrimental to one's health. It is fine to have blind faith in a loving God, but the individual best keep their eyes wide open when dealing with man. Many people are of the belief that God is akin to a genie that by the mere act of prayer alone one's wishes and desires shall be granted.

Prayer is all well and good, but the words spoken in and of them selves accomplish nothing. The scriptures tells us that "Faith without works is dead" but the converse also holds true that works without faith is dead and shall bear no fruit as well. It is amazing how so many are quick to believe in rumors and urban legends regarding issues they themselves have not witnessed. How so many people allow things of this world and circumstances observed daily to shake their faith in Him? Jesus tells us in Johns 10:9-11, "I am the door, by me if any man enter in, he shall be saved; and shall go in and out and find pasture.

The thief cometh not but for to steal, and to kill and to destroy. I AM come that they might have life more abundantly. I am the Good Shepherd; the good shepherd giveth his life for the sheep". Let's reflect for a moment; take a long hard look at yourself and the condition of the world in which we live.

When it gets right down to it, we lack confidence and trust in the covenant we each made with God. We do not firmly believe that the sacrifice of His Son Jesus Christ redeemed us for ALL of our transgressions. The scriptures clearly states "in whom we have redemption through his blood, even the forgiveness of sins" (Colossians 1:14). "For there is one God, and one mediator between God and men, the man Christ Jesus; Who gave himself a ransom for all, to be testified in due time" (1 Timothy 2:5-6)".

The dictionary defines Redeem as the following: 1 a : to buy back : REPURCHASE b : to get or win back 2 : to free from what distresses or harms: : to free from captivity by payment of ransom b : to extricate from or help to overcome something detrimental c : to release from blame or debt : CLEAR d : to free from the consequences of sin 3 : to change for the better.

" Whosoever shall confess that Jesus is the Son of God, God shall dwelleth in him and he in God; and we know and believe the love that God hath to us. God is love and he that dwelleth in love dwelleth in God and God in him (John 4:15-16)." He that loveth not knoweth not God; for God is love. There is no fear in love but perfect love casteth out fear because fear has torment. He that feareth is not made "perfect in love". (I Johns 4:8,18)

Some of us fear that the sins of our past will resurface and be made public, bringing forth shame and guilt. Some fear that their indiscretions were so grave that there is no possible way God would allow your entry into Heavens gate. The act of redemption for our sakes is the blood Jesus Christ shed and the sacrifice of His life to clear the debt incurred upon man by Adam and Eve upon eating from the tree of knowledge. Once a person has given their life to Christ, the deal is sealed in His blood and through God's love and grace.

For it is written "that you might believe that Jesus is the Christ, the Son of God; and that believing ye might have life through his name (John 20:31)". "Verily I say unto you, he that heareth my word and believeth on him that sent me, hath everlasting life. And shall not come into condemnation but is passed from death unto life (John 5:24)". Many individuals are consumed by guilt and holding onto issues from the past or present that prevents them from holding on to God's promise. You fear losing your house, losing your job, your car, your spouse, your children, or your own life. If one so blessed with worldly possessions has great anxieties over what has yet to occur, how will one cope with the actual event?

Adversity provides valuable lessons that you would have been too blind to see, too arrogant to believe. Trials and tribulations force you to accept change when you are too stubborn to do so any other way than by painful experience. When losing a job force you to make a change that you would never have had the courage to leave otherwise. When you trust in the Lord, He will lead you down a path towards a new opportunity, then trouble may be a most valuable experience! Sometimes, trouble awakens one to use the gifts God has given you that you have taken too long for granted.

When what you may perceive as a problem, creates an opportunity for you to think, meditate, read, write or pray, then trouble is really a friend when it comes knocking on your door. These are but a few examples of what Christ meant when he said, "Whosoever will save his life shall lose it. And whosoever shall lose his life, for my sake, will find it (Luke 18:33)." For the Lord gives all blessings and what the Lord gives us, can at the blink of an eye, be taken away. When you take the walk of faith, God will turn your cries and tears of sadness into smiles and tears of joy.

He did for Abraham, Isaac, Joseph, Moses, Job, David, Ruth, Jesus, Paul, for those willing to take the leap of faith. If one will surrender to the experience, great things can occur in your life as well. The focus upon losing worldly possessions rules dominion over the mind of many and produces fear within the body of the church today. All of the material possessions we desperately seek to hold on to started as a thought, or an idea. The mind is the creative engine for thought, which become "energized" in the form of electrical impulses (An electroencephalograph (EEG) is an instrument used to measure and display brain waves).

Thoughts are manifested into words in the "energized" form of sound waves (spectrum analyzer is an instrument used to measure and display sound waves). The instant one's words are released, a subsequent series of physical actions/reactions occur. This energy is transmitted outward to the universe with a power to attract like "energy" to the source.

One of the definitions of power is " to possess the ability to wield force, execute permissive authority, or substantially influence outcomes". Anything, which has power, has a source that creates it or means that produces energy. Therefore, if thought produces energy; if there is power contained in words in the form of sound waves, both which are measurable, means that their energy can thus be stored and therefore controlled. The scriptures tells us " Therefore I say unto you, what things so ever you desire when you pray, believe that you receive them and you shall have them (Mark 11:24)".

"Go thy way and as you believed, so be it done unto thee" (Matthew 8:13); "We having the same spirit of faith according as it is written, I believed; and therefore have I spoken. We also believe and therefore speak" (II Corinthians 4:13). Perception is reality and truth is relative; and what one believes to be true shall be made manifest into their experience. Therefore, if the power of a person's mind produce energized thought waves of loss or lack. If the person then verbalizes those thoughts, they shall attract more of the same into their experience. One should focus their minds through prayer and meditation. The Bible tells us "To be carnally minded is death; but to be spiritually minded is life and peace (Romans 8:6)".

"Death and life are in the power of the tongue: and they that love it shall eat the fruit thereof"(Proverbs 18:21). Therefore, if we focus our thoughts on Higher pursuits and be mindful of the words we speak, we all could live a more peaceful and joyful existence here on earth. It is far better to focus on God, singing songs of praise, and give thanks to Him than to utter cries of whoa. " I will cry unto God most high; unto God that performeth all things for me (Proverbs 57:2)".

The Lord tells us in Isaiah 26:2-4 "Open the gates that the righteous nation which keepeth the truth may enter in. Thou wilt keep him in perfect peace whose mind is stayed on thee: because he trusteth in thee. Trust ye in the Lord forever: for in the Lord JEHOVAH is everlasting strength."

As goes the song by New Edition, "sunny days everybody loves them, but can you stand the rain"? Who amongst you could have the faith of Job if circumstances beyond your control caused you to lose that which you value? Could you maintain your faith in the Lord if He took away that which you hold near and dear to your heart? Thomas Paine stated that "These are the times that try men's souls" and the troubled times in which we live is the manner by which life will test the faithfulness of us all. The chronicles of the life of Jesus show us that He faced continuous trials and tribulation and overcame them by His undying faith in the Father.

The scripture speaks to the issue in I Timothy 6:9-11 "But they that will be rich fall into temptation and a snare into many foolish and hurtful lusts, which drown men in destruction and perdition. For the love of money is the root of all evil: which while some coveted after, they have erred from the faith and accrued themselves with many arrows. But thou O man of God, flee these things and follow after righteousness, godliness, faith, love, patience and meekness. Fight the good fight of faith lay hold on eternal life whereunto thou art also called and hast professed a good profession before many witnesses."

In Matthew 6:19-21 Jesus also tells us "Lay not up for yourselves treasures upon the earth, where moth and rust doth corrupt, and where thieves break through and steal. But lay up for yourselves treasures in heaven where neither moth nor rust doth corrupt and where thieves do not break through nor steal. For where your treasure is, there will your heart be also". "I will give unto thee the keys of the kingdom of heaven and whatsoever thou shalt bind on earth shall be bound in heaven. Whatsoever thou shalt loose upon the earth shall be loosed in heaven (St. Matthew 16:19)."

The terrorist attack of 9/11 on American soil drives home this point. The terrorists struck at the "mind" of America, which they perceived to be in the halls of the White House and Pentagon. They attacked at the "heart" of where they perceived our national treasures to be buried. The World Trade Center and Wall Street are the cornerstones of what drives the global economy and the American way of life. I find it strikingly odd the dichotomy between the mindset of those of the Islamic faith and that of the Christian.

Many Christian believers are afraid, due to the uncertainties surrounding the issue of the afterlife. If a person becomes unsure of a thing, they begin to doubt; where doubt exists, fear creeps in to fill the void. One of the greatest fears most of us have is the loss of one's life or that of a loved one. The root of this fear comes as the result of not having faith that God will make good on His promise to secure our eternal resting-place in Heaven. "The Lord is not slack concerning his promise, as some men count slackness; but is longsuffering to us ward, not willing that any should perish, but that all should come to repentance" (2 Peter 3:9)."For he hath said, I will never leave thee, nor forsake thee" (Hebrews 13:5)".

Americans and those of other western nations possess a great deal of financial wealth and control much of material resources of the planet. The laws and politics, which govern the global economy, serve to protect the financial interests of those who control the wealth. However, as a by-product, a great deal of insecurity develops within those who control the wealth. The rich fear losing the power, influence and control the wealth produces. Therefore, weapons are produced, walls are constructed to protect the treasures that an individual or nation values.

The perspective of life and death is quite different from those of the Muslim religion. Most Muslims fear living a life through the lens of abject poverty as most lack the basic necessities of life. As the saying goes, the most dangerous person in the world is the person who believes he has nothing to lose. Need breeds discord; desperation sows the seeds of discontent. If a person has nothing to live for, life has no meaning or value. In the same manner that some Christians view non-believers as unrighteous infidels (II Corinthians 6 14-15), some Muslims hold similar belief towards those not of the Islamic faith.

I ask the question: If in the eyes of Muslims, non Muslims are infidels and Christians view non believers as unrighteous sinners, then where on earth shall one find the holy saints and righteous followers of God? Some fundamentalist Muslim clerics justify the killing of infidels as performing the will of God, by misusing the interpretation of the incomplete version of the following verse from the Quran. "Kill the mushriqeen (pagans, polytheists, kuffar or infidels) where ever you find them [Al-Qur'an 9:5]". Fundamentalist clerics as well as critics of Islam actually quote this verse out of context.

In order to understand the context, one must understand the historical perspective underlying the 9 Surah. During the times of Prophet Mohammed, great conflict existed amongst the tribes of what is now known as Saudi Arabia. The Muslims were at war with the mushriqs of Makkah. A temporary peace treaty spanning four months was offered to the mushriqs or infidels to make amends. Otherwise, the war would resume. The mushriqs ultimately violated this treaty.

The complete first verse of the 9 Surah begins "But when the forbidden months are past, then fight and slay the Pagans wherever ye find them. And seize them, beleaguer them, and lie in wait for them in every stratagem (of war). But if they repent and establish regular prayers and practice regular charity, then open the way for them: for Allah is oft-forgiving, Most merciful." [Al-Quran 9:1-5] Read in this context, one comes to a different understanding of the aforementioned scripture.

By using an incomplete translation of Surah Verse 5, fanatical Muslim clerics are able to indoctrinate suicide bombers to commit murder by declaring jihad against any non-Muslims. The highway to heaven and hell are paved by the "golden" intentions of men. The highway to heaven is paved in the gold of Gods eternal love for His children. The highway to hell is paved in fool's gold of mans ignorance and self-righteousness, which is again leading the human race down the path of death and self-destruction. Pyrite, known as "fool's gold" has the same glimmer and shine as the genuine article, but holds no value to the person who possesses it.

The difference between the wise man and the fool is the wise man knows that "all that glitters, isn't gold". A fool can justify in their mind anything they so choose; for what a fool believes, is just that…what a fool believes. A foolish person does not have the capacity or the desire within to question the validity of the information presented to them. If you cannot read or comprehend, your ability to discern the truth from the lies within are limited. You cannot change what you deny exists. I use a phrase quite frequently that if you want something different, choose something different. It is a very simple concept, but many choose not to place it into practice.

Knowledge is power and wisdom is knowledge applied. In order to harness the power of knowledge and wisdom, one must be able to see and discern the truth where it exists. If not, the mind is suspended in a state of ignorance, apathy, and docility. To know the truth sometimes requires that one be able to read between the lines in order to recognize the lies intertwined within the story line. In such a state, the individual will not easily be duped or deceived. For one shall see that what is portrayed as truth, is in actuality a lie in disguise.

The appeal to someone who looks towards receiving everlasting life where the sacrificial lamb shall receive seventy virgin wives, gold and riches untold, and rivers that flow with honey sounds great to a man who has nothing to begin with. This is how the radical sect of Islam is able to convince the hopeless to sacrifice their life in martyrdom. In their misguided state of mind, their faith leads them to believe that the true pathway to Heaven is secure by making the ultimate of sacrifices, giving ones life in act of martyrdom. It is this state of mind, which perpetuates the bloodshed, and loss of life in the Middle East all in the name of Allah.

Can you see the paradox here? The average Muslim has few worldly possessions, fears living, but has unyielding faith that his act of martyrdom will secure a place in Heaven through taking another's life. The average Christian, who has worldly possessions, values life, but fears death. For most do not firmly believe that a seat in the Kingdom of Heaven is secured. In either case, it is the degree of faith and trust in God that distinguishes the two and dictates the level of fear each of us must come to grips with.

Irrespective of the differences in religion, race, or nationality that divides us, Jesus told us in St Luke 6:35-36 "Love your enemies and do good and lend. Hoping for nothing again; and your reward shall be great. And ye shall be the children of the Highest for he is kind unto the unthankful and to the evil. Be ye therefore merciful, as your Father also is merciful." "Ye shall be hated of all men for my names sake. But he that shall endure unto the end, the same shall be saved (Mark 13:13)". Jesus knew that His followers would face trial and tribulation for spreading the Gospel.

A song written long ago by Simon and Garfunkel speaks the heart of Jesus love for His children allow me to repeat them to you:

When you're weary, feeling small,

When tears are in your eyes, I will dry them all;

I'm on your side. when times get rough

And when friends just can't be found,

I will lay me down like a bridge over troubled water

When you're down and out, When you're on the street, When evening falls so hard I will comfort you.

I'll take your part. When darkness comes and pains is all around,

Like a bridge over troubled water I will lay me down.

Sail on sadness, Sail on by. Your time has come to shine.

All your dreams are on their way, See how they shine.

If you ever need a friend I'm sailing right behind.

Like a bridge over troubled water I will ease your mind.

I will lay me down like a bridge over troubled water

I will ease your mind.

Allow God's love to be your bridge over troubled waters that shall bring peace to your mind and still your soul. "Be still and know that I am God...." (Psalm 46:10)". Instead, "allow the peace of God to rule your heart (Colossians 3:15)." Jesus gave each of us the key to have peace on earth and secure our place in Heaven. For what you lack within you shall go without. In order to have peace, we must live a life of peace. The scriptures tell us "If only you had paid attention to My commandments, your peace would have been like a river, your righteousness like the waves of the sea (Is. 48:18)."

Some may face the choice of Peter to either renounce one's faith in God in order to save their life or choosing to stand upon their faith and face death. If we truly believe, that Jesus is by our side in times of trouble. If we truly believe we shall stand by the right hand of Jesus in the afterlife, what is there to fear in this life? "Take heed to yourselves for they shall deliver you up to councils. In the synagogues ye shall be beaten; and ye shall be brought before rulers and kings for my sake for a testimony against them (Mark 13:9)". The day may come when every one of us will face a choice; to either stand strong upon our faith, or bow down to the pressures of outside forces controlled by those whose hearts are wicked and hold positions of power and authority.

Jesus tells us that "thou shall love the Lord thy God with all thy heart, and with all thy soul and with thy strength and with all thy mind and thy neighbor as thyself (St. Luke 10:27; St Mark 12:30)." The scriptures tell us in Romans 5:1-5 "Therefore being justified by faith we have peace with God through our Lord Jesus Christ. By whom also we have access by faith into this grace wherein we stand and rejoice in hope of the glory of God. And not only so, but we glory in tribulations also: knowing that tribulations worketh patience; and patience experience; and experience hope. And hope maketh not ashamed because the love of God is shed abroad in our hearts by the Holy Ghost which is given unto us."

One of the laws of physics state "A body at rest stays at rest; a body in motion stays in motion". For every action there is a reaction. Just as by dropping a rock or stone into a body of water, the ripples from ones actions move outward from the center in all directions. You can choose to respond to those who transgress against you in hate or retaliate in anger.

One must realize there is a far reaching relational cause and effect and subsequent consequence for each action and reaction. The Divine Law of Compensation states "For as ye sow so shall ye reap (Galatians 6:7)". Other familiar phrases such as "what comes around, goes around" and "the chickens come home to roost" reaffirm the relatedness of biblical truth to physical scientific laws.

All which occurs in life is based upon the principles of cause and effect, but few acknowledge this fact. The words and deeds of an individual, let alone a nation, cast a great shadow that ripples throughout time; actions which effects lives across generations. In the Book of Genesis (Chapter 21), God instructed Abraham to listen to the voice of his wife Sarah, to cast out Hagar and their son Ishmael. In verse 13, the Word states "Yet I will also make a nation of the son of the bondswoman, because he is your seed".

When Abraham banished Hagar and their son to the wilderness of Beersheba, with only one skin of water and bread, his actions planted the seeds of hate in the minds of both Hagar and their son. One can easily imagine the words spoken by Hagar to her son while traveling across the desert, as to the manner of treatment they received by the hand of Abraham. Both perceived Abraham actions as an act of malice that in their minds, would lead to their certain death. Does one believe Hagar's words spoken to Ishmael as they walked in the hot, desert sun regarding Abraham were of a kind and loving nature?

Abraham followed Gods instruction, but the Lord did not instruct him to act in such a malicious manner. The separation could have been handled in a far more kind and generous way. Abraham acted from the emotional displeasure by the joint decision he and wife Sarah made by using Hagar as a surrogate mother, not from a place of charity and compassion.

Thus, the seeds of hate sown over 6000 years ago, grew and in time, rippled throughout generations. As a result, the world has reaped the harvest of hate from some of the more extreme factions of the Islamic religion in the region now known as the Middle East. Far too many Imams, Reverends, Rabbis, Pastors and Preachers use their bully pulpit to condemn those not of the same faith. Throughout the recorded history of man, millions have lost their lives in the name of God and religion.

In their self-righteousness, the radical extreme fundamentalist groups within the body of the three major religions have sown the seeds of hate and discontent. Many shepherds have "fleeced" their flock and abusing their authority. Some are using the individual's weaknesses to create fear for their own personal gain. Some leaders foster an atmosphere of dependency to use their flock to live lavish lifestyles, erect temples, trophies, and monuments to revere and edify themselves, not God.

Jesus spoke of self righteous men as those "who outwardly appear righteous unto men, but within are full of hypocrisy and iniquity (Matthew 23:28)." As the hands of time turns, history tends to repeat itself. Our faith requires each of us to reach out to those in need, including those whom we consider as our enemies. God allows circumstances to develop around your life as a proving ground to give your faith opportunity to temper as the strongest steel. The "enemy" can come in the form of a stranger. On the other hand, the "enemy" could be a painful relationship with one's mother, father, sister, and brother, husband, wife, children, or coworker.

"Love your enemies, do good to them which hate you (Luke 6:27)". The scriptures tell us to "recompense to no man evil for evil; provide things honest in the sight of all men. If it be possible, as much as lieth in you, live peaceably with all men. Be not overcome of evil, but overcome evil with good (Romans 12:17-18, 21)". This is part of the promise each of us made when accepting Jesus Christ as our Lord and Savior.

Poverty has become a global cottage industry whereby trillions of dollars are made from the misery of those less fortunate. Global corporations exploit the plentifully cheap supply of labor that few benefit from. The manufacturing based economies of the western world have all but disappeared due to the transfer of that industry to the third world. The keepers of status quo see their bottom line threatened by those who are the advocates for the poor and the proponents of peace.

The mongers of hate and the industries that produced the instruments of war see their way of life threatened as well. If there was peace in the land, whom could they get to work the presses and plow the fields for pennies a day? If there was no one left to fight, who would purchase the weapons of war? The scriptures tells us that "Wisdom is better than weapons of war; but one sinner destroyeth much good (Ecclesiastes 9:18)". "For though we walk in the flesh, we do not wage warfare according to what we are in the flesh". For the weapons we fight with are not fleshly (carnal)". (II Corinthians 10:3-4).

For we wrestle not against flesh and blood, but against principalities, against powers, against the rulers of the darkness of this world, against spiritual wickedness in high places (Ephesians 6-12). In any nation, who occupies positions of power in "high places" as referred to in scripture?

How better off would the world be if the trillions spend on war were spent to feed, educate, house and clothe the neediest among us? How likely would a person with clean clothes, a warm house, and a full stomach become apt to listening to the rants and ravings of a mad man or follow a hate monger? How prone would a person be in falling prey to those who espouse killing, terrorism or war as a way of life?

History shows us that separation and divisiveness brings forth anarchy, war, discord, and chaos. Jesus was a threat to the status quo the Roman Empire state and the self serving hypocritical religious leaders of the time who supported it. Jesus knew what His ultimate fate would be for revering the love of God over the self-indulgence and reverence of men. How many people would continue on a journey knowing at the end of it, one would be ridiculed, tormented, and face an agonizing death? Jesus died because of speaking His truth, willing to sacrifice His life as a living example to mankind God's greatness and love for us all.

When faced with a crisis, most people tend to ask the question why, as if knowing the cause for the dilemma, the dilemma would somehow cease to exist. Why has relevance if the observer's intent in posing the question serves to seek out commonalties or occurrences between past and current events. By studying history, one can find clues and potential remedies to problems encountered in the present. The past has value in the context of providing an historical account of ones successes and failures. History serves the greater good if reviewed with the purpose of reducing the chance or opportunity to repeat negative consequences in the present or future.

Contrary to popular belief, it is not mutually exclusive to make a profit whereby the employee, the employer and the society at large can all benefit. Capitalism without a social conscience and a sense of morality will lead to a lack of confidence in the economy as well as those who participate in it. A system of free enterprise that functions on lies, corruption, and deception erodes the faith in the markets in which it operates. It is said that "he who tells a person who is starving, without shelter or self-respect to go in peace, is a thief and a liar".

The pathway to peace comes through inclusion of the poor, disenfranchised segments within a civilized society. To show love, caring and compassion for your fellow man. The time has come to sow new seed in the fertile soil of God's grace; energized by the light of God's love. For we all came from the same "dust of the ground; that God breathed life into the nostrils of man to become a living soul (Genesis 2:7)." The time has come to promote the shared values and beliefs that unify and highlight the similarities between the religions. The time has come for evangelicals to exhort that all men are brothers and all women are sisters.

Before Jesus was crucified, these words were spoken "Not for these only do I pray, but for those also who believe in me through their word, that they may all be one; even as you, Father, are in me, and I in you, that they also may be one in us; that the world may believe that you sent me. The glory which you have given me, I have given to them; that they may be one, even as we are one; I in them, and you in me, that they may be perfected into one;

that the world may know that you sent me, and loved them, even as you loved me(John 17:20-23).

No one religion has exclusive rights to God or His love for the Creator loves all of His children saint and sinner alike. Jesus tells us in (St Mark 12:29) "The first of all commandments is hear O Israel; the Lord our God is one Lord". The words of the Quran, Torah, and the Bible were inspired from the Divine Creator of all men to benefit the lives harvested from the seeds of Abraham. Each belief system contains the common thread of truth that we are to love one another, as we love God and ourselves.

The trademark of God's hand in the doctrines of man is reflected within The Golden Rule of all three faiths:

It is written in the Quran (Hadith, Muslim, imam 71-72):

"No man is a true Believer unless he desires for his brother that which he desires for himself. Allah will not be affectionate to that man who is not affectionate to Allah's creatures. Assist any person oppressed whether he is Muslim or non-Muslim." The Torah states (Babylonian Talmud, Shabbath 31a): "What is hateful to yourself do not do to your fellow man. This is the law: all the rest is commentary."

The Holy Bible states (King James St. Luke 6:31): "And as ye would that men should do to you, do ye also to them likewise." The Holy Scriptures tells us "For as the body is one, and hath many members, and all the members of that one body, being many, are one body: so also is Christ. For by one Spirit are we all baptized into one body, whether we be Jews or Gentiles, whether we be bond or free; and have been all made to drink into one Spirit (1 Corinthians 12:12-13)".

In St. Johns 14:1-3 Jesus tells us "Let not your heart be troubled: ye believe in God, believe also in me. In my Father's house are many mansions: if it were not so, I would have told you. I go to prepare a place for you. And if I go and prepare a place for you, I will come again and receive you unto myself, that where I am, there ye may be also." Many school children age tend to scoff and question the need for the study of history. History plays an important role in providing a track record of the accomplishments and failures of the human race.

The objective is to repeat the successes and build upon them keeping the momentum of man's spiritual progress moving forward. The failures are to be acknowledged and dissected to uncover the root causes, which gave rise to the historical conditions being reviewed. One needs to look no further than the recent demise of the dot.com industry. Tried and true business practices proven through out time was tossed out in lieu of many investors being caught up in the hype of empty promises contained on pro forma statements.

During the period of the 16th century in Holland, tulips were the hottest speculative product on the market and highly valued for their aesthetic beauty. The aristocracies of the time coveted them for their beauty and were willing to pay a high price. People began to plow the fields and plant tulips in great quantity with the hopes of getting rich quick. The laws of supply and demand quickly turned the dream of quick riches into the harsh reality that timing is everything. As the market became flooded with tulips the prices began to fall drastically. Many people soon discovered the hard way that all good things come to an end. American history is replete with examples of those that took the path of least resistance and got caught up in the wave of so called "irrational exuberance".

The California Gold Rush of 1859 was another example of greed and dreams of riches run amok. Ivar Krueger known as "The Match King" controlled two-thirds of the worlds match market during the 1920's. Through an elaborate pyramid organizational structure and a labyrinth of accounting manipulations, he was able to bilk millions of people of their hard earned cash. Similar methods were used during the recent collapse of the Enron Corporation. This goes to show that there is not much new under the sun, which hasn't occurred in the human experience at least once. In this case, the lesson to be learned if something sounds too good to be true, it probably is.

The current uncertainty of the world's economy can be partly attributed to the rise of corporate greed and corruption and the rise of distrust of the financial institutions on Wall Street and similar foreign stock exchanges. The world's economy is intertwined and global in reach, what infects one market affects all markets. Time has now shown that the run up of US corporate debt and federal government budget deficits fueled the economic and financial successes of the 1980s and 1990s. The excesses of the previous two decades have materialized at the dawn of the new millennium replete with financial and corruption scandals too numerous to count.

One plus one no longer adds up to two, as the math taught by the nations most prominent business schools has now become as fuzzy as truth, honesty and integrity are virtues no longer practiced by many business executives. Accounting firms overflowing with MBA's practicing the latest in creative financing aided these companies in duping the investment public out of billions of dollars. Accounting firms such as Arthur Anderson aided and abetted Enron in one of the most malicious cases of theft and embezzlement ever committed. A fair exchange is no robbery and in this life if you want to dance, you've got to pay the band.

There is a price to be paid for what we do as individuals and as a society at large. Greed is the breeding ground for corruption in any society but once again, lines of distinction are drawn based upon which side of the economic strata one belongs to. An individual, who chooses to rob a bank and is then caught, is subjected to serving 15-25 years in prison. But if a corporation or white collar criminal embezzles millions or billions of dollars from a company, those who perpetrate the act will be treated far differently.

In America, if the bank robber happens to be a person of color or poor white trash, the measure and type of punishment doled out from the so-called justice system will be far harsher. The perpetrator's of white-collar crime will either not receive prison time or will have their sentence drastically reduced. Why the difference in treatment? Because justice is no longer blind or just for as with everything else, it too has become a commodity to be sold or bartered to the highest bidder. Money is power in any society and the more of it one has, the more influence one has in buying favor and access to benefit themselves.

Big business uses their money to buy influence in the political machinations of government to ensure that laws and regulations are constructed to benefit their bottom line. A recent example is the current rash of reports from the backing dating of stock options, to the safety of prescription drugs such as Viox and Celebrex. The Food and Drug Administration receives hundreds of millions of dollars from the major pharmaceutical corporations, which also contribute a great deal of campaign contributions to politicians through highly paid lobbyists. The pharmaceutical industry has flourished into a multi billion dollar business fueled by the insatiable need of consumers to sedate themselves literally to death.

But in the same token, the US government spends billions of dollars around the world to fight the so-called war on drugs. The hypocrisy of the government handing down stiff prison sentences to those found with "illicit" illegal drugs such as marijuana makes one wonder. If the drug cartels who traffic in cocaine and heroin contributed millions of dollars to politicians in the same manner as pharmaceutical companies, would the heads of the various world's law enforcement agencies continue to pursue them?

The taxing agencies of many governments charged with assessing and collecting revenues from it citizens will expend no effort to audit and seize property from working class people. The exact opposite occurs when it comes to dealing with large multinational corporations. Some corporations don't pay one dollar of income tax due to the structure of the tax laws crafted, bought and paid for by political action committees. The very complex structure of the tax laws has created cottage industries within the fields of law, finance, and accounting. Each feeding from the trough created by politicians and funded by those industries to perpetuate their existence.

These acts have been committed by executive officers and boards of directors of companies such as Enron, Xerox Tyco, Vivendi and WorldCom. The shoe box and shell game accounting methods also exists within the budgets of state and federal government. Those involved in such crimes find out very quickly that once a lie is told, it must be perpetuated. The illusions must be maintained at any price, whereby honesty and the truth are the first items to be marked down and discounted. But what are the perpetrators of corporate larceny and embezzlement to fear?

Such actions in the past were typically rewarded with light jail sentences as CEOs leap from the burning flames of the corporations they helped to destroy. They pulled the ripcord on their golden parachutes with financially lucrative back dated stock options, with multi million dollar separation packages in tow. Some are allowed to retain some portion of the funds looted from the company coffers or stolen from the shareholders wealth. In most instances, these corporate crooks were aided by those willing to cast their morals aside for a few dollars more. "Mine was not to question why, mine was but to follow the orders and guidelines given by my superior" was the excuse many used to justify their actions.

Left in the wake of this sea of corruption are millions of people who have lost their jobs and seen their retirement accounts decimated. This is the same financial marketplace the current administration now plans to entrust trillions of dollars of public funds as part of the campaign to privatize the social security system. But this should come as no surprise to the observers of American history. For some of the same ingredients that led to the crash of 1929 and gave way to the Great Depression is coming to fruition today.

Trillions of dollars are run up in ever increasing deficit spending bills, but yet American citizens continues to suffer many of the same social problems that plagued it from the moments of this country's inception. The six degrees of separation between the corrupt acts committed within a so-called democracy versus a totalitarian dictatorship has become narrower. Wherever the conditions of ignorance, poverty and despair exist, this provides the fertile breeding ground for the various "ism" that cause friction and conflict to occur. In the presence of greed and need, conflict is sure to follow. You can bomb a nation into oblivion, but the seeds of discontent continue to grow long after the dreamer or the leader has died.

As a result of the attacks upon the World Trade Centers of September 11th, the United States led by President George W. Bush declared war against terrorism. As an extension of this effort, the Bush Administration declared Iran, Iraq and North Korea as part of an "Axis of Evil". This gave further justification by both the United States and Great Britain to initiate the war in Iraq. The premise was to eliminate weapons of mass destruction alleged to be in the possession of Saadam Hussein's dictatorship regime.

The U.S. congressional intelligence subcommittee investigations discovered that no weapons of mass destruction existed. This revelation came after the expenditure of hundreds of billions of dollars and thousands of lives lost. The administrations rational for starting the war was then changed as a cause to liberate the Iraqi citizens from the tyranny of a dictator. The US Middle East foreign policies over the last sixty years have negatively impacted the stability of the region. From the moment the United Nations governing council ruled to create the nation of Israel, conflict has been the order of the day.

US exercised its military might as the lone nuclear superpower to force the establishment of the Israeli territory surrounding East Jerusalem. The military and economic support given to the Shah of Iran as well as the continued support of the Saudi monarchy by both governments of the United States and Great Britain contributed to the "connecting the dots" which ultimately led hate filled terrorists to carry out the 9/11 disaster. The backing and subsequent reneging of US support to the Afghan mujahadeen rebel forces that fought during the ten year Russian occupation.

In addition, the United States failed to support the Iraqi opposition groups after the Gulf War of 1991 are but a few examples of the failure of Middle East US foreign policy. If the United States and world community were truly interested in the liberation of the Iraqi people, why didn't the world act in 1988 when Saddam ordered the genocide of over five thousand Iraqi Kurds? How many millions of Iraqi lives were lost and buried in mass graves that could have been spared had the world community acted earlier to remove a known mass murderer?

According to the records maintained by the Office of Management and Budgets, the U.S. has since 1977 allocated funds in excess of $9.3 trillion dollars for military, civil defense and domestic intelligence (FBI). This figure does not include funds spent by the CIA; NSA or dollars allocated for "Black Ops" projects. The money spent by the terrorists for the September 11th attacks was less than $1 million dollars. Look at this as if the situation was treated as a pure business investment opportunity. Company USA spent trillions of dollars to produce a national defense software product. The terrorist competition spent less than a million to hack their way through the firewall.

Not only did the competition hack through the firewall, but also slowed production by temporarily shutting down key portions of company USA operations. Now, who got the most bangs for their buck? How long would such a business stay in operation? The events of September 11th and history should teach us that no matter how high the wall we build or how wide the moat we construct we are not an island of one nation on this planet. The American as well as European nations have provided both economic and military support to prop up a multitude of puppet dictatorships and banana republics to keep the supply of cheap oil flowing.

How else can one explain the existence of generations of impoverished citizens within countries such as Nigeria, Argentina, Venezuela and Saudi Arabia whom collectively control and export more than sixty percent of the world's oil reserves? It is the leaders of these oil rich nations whom more oft than not reaps the financial benefits by pilfering the natural resources of the land. In a manner almost akin to paying retribution in a protection racket, the American, Asian and European nation's military and economic might are used to protect their respective nation's oil interests.

As long as the OPEC leaders continue to pay tribute and play ball, the U.S. and their European partners will continue to use their combined military might in order to protect the oil cartels. The banks and financial institutions of these wealthy nations are more than willingly to accept the billions of dollars deposited by those who control the oil revenues from the aforementioned oil producing countries. But in the end, the citizens and children who live in the oil producing nations are the ones that suffer the most and get the raw end of the deal. As stated previously, the most dangerous person in the world is the one who believes that they have nothing to lose.

The politicians and those who occupy leadership positions throughout the multitude of bureaucracies in government have shown the American public time and time again where their loyalties lie. The primary concerns of bureaucrats are to maintain the status quo. It is the members of Congress who enacted the tax rules and regulations the accounting and financial institutions used to commit the corporate frauds of the 1980s and 1990s. The focus is to pass laws under the cover of darkness to line their pockets from ill-gotten gains obtained from the myriad of special interest groups.

For the right price, corporations can buy influence to swing congressional votes in their favor. The focus of most politicians is not on serving or protecting the public interest or serving the common good, but in serving themselves. To think that by shifting around the same apathetic and pathetic individuals who were derelict in their duties for decades will bring forth change. One may as well believe in the tooth fairy. The representation of any government is a reflection of its citizenry. So what exactly does the citizens of a given nation see when they look into the mirror?

So many people speak with such self-righteous indignation towards the acts of injustice committed in other countries when the collective dirt on our own front porch is in dire need of sweeping. To put up such fervor in regards to the issue of the striking the words "under God" from the Pledge of Allegiance, when so few adhere to the words of God themselves. Diogenes of Sinope (c.320 BC) was a Greek philosopher perhaps the best renowned practitioner of the theory of cynicism. He pursued the idea of self-sufficiency; a life that was natural and not dependent upon the nonessential luxuries of civilization. Diogenes believed that virtue was better practiced through ones action's than by espousing empty rhetoric.

He protested most of his life against what he thought of as a corrupt society. He is said to have gone about Athens with a lantern in the daytime, claiming to be looking for an honest man—but never finding one. Today if Diogenes were chose any country and to roam the institutional halls of its government, one would seriously doubt that he would find the honesty he was searching for. In America, the base salary for the position of President is approximately $565,000, excluding other expenses and allowances entitled to support the office. What is the logical explanation as to why those seeking the office are willing to spend billions of dollars to campaign for a position which pays $565K?

It is because the financial rewards, power and influence one can wield from the Oval office is far greater and lasts long after one's term is expired. How can a political system whose body is riddled with the cancer of corruption be trusted with the welfare of its citizens? How can immoral and unethical individuals be trusted to be both fair and impartial? How free can the citizens of a corrupt nation truly be when conditions such as this exist? This is of special concern as both the executive and legislative branches of government are charged with the duty of selecting and confirming judicial court appointees.

The justices of the Supreme Court took the power of the vote from the hands of the citizens and made the selection for us. One of the greatest heists of the 20th century occurred when the Presidential election of 2000 was hijacked right before our very eyes. But yet there was no hue and cry made by the American people. No one for the exception of a select few seemed to care, as expediency superseded the sanctity of the election process and the Constitution. The most common prevailing opinion was "I don't care who wins, just hurry up and choose someone". Many people within the United States of America suffer from a severe case of acute attention deficit disorder which is taken advantage of by both Democrats and Republicans alike.

During the 2004 U.S. Presidential election, the truth once again took a back seat for millions of undecided voters whom ultimately re-elected George W. Bush. What is far more disturbing is that the so-called religious based "Moral Majority" constituency provided the margin necessary to reelect Bush to the White House. But many felt compelled to reelect George Bush based on his claims and the self righteous opinions of those which support him, that the decisions made as President were approved by a higher authority.

I beg to differ, for if our motives were pure and our concerns for the welfare of the Iraqi people genuine, the outcome would be far different. "Do not be deceived, God is not mocked; for whatever a man sows, this he will also reap (Galatians 6:7). For God is not a God of confusion but of peace, as in all the churches of the saints (I Corinthians 14:33)." It matter not to many American citizen's that the nation's economy and America's respect around the world has diminished. It mattered not that weapons of mass destruction were never found nor human rights violations were committed by some members of the U.S military in Iraq and Afghanistan.

In the 2004 presidential elections, both the Bush and Kerry campaigns pandered to the fear of many constituents of another terrorist attack upon America whereby the Bush campaign's ability to play up the "fear factor" ultimately won out. Not since the end of the American Civil War has this nation experienced the level of societal division and polarization as exists today. The US media has helped to foster this great divide by promoting the use of phrases such as left versus right, liberal versus conservative, red states versus blues states, etc. This has an overall effect of pandering to the extreme viewpoints of those on either end of the societal spectrum.

Most individuals lack the ability to see and to focus on any one issue let alone the myriad of issues that plague our planet. It has been reported that the campaign advertisements used during both the 2000 and 2004 US Presidential elections were targeted to appeal towards an audience with an eighth grade education. The quality of information available has become diluted and watered down into 30-second sound bites lacking both substance and content. The MTV generation seems to regurgitate on anything requiring any measure of lucid thought, desiring the news format in the same manner that it does its music.

To gyrate to and sing songs for the simple minded, as talent and originality has given way to sampling, sameness and uniformity. The crowd doesn't care to know or want to see the truth regardless of "whatever" goes on around them. Most are quite happy and content to watch the latest dirt or listen to the latest gossip about their favorite movie star or sports figure. Until the tragic events of 9/11, most were concerned only with trivial pursuits. The color of one's hair or nails, or how loud the music sounded from the trunk of ones car has taken precedence over what is going on in ones own backyard. Many prefer to live a life full of insane melodrama and strife in lieu of sanity and serenity.

The multimedia global conglomerates, whose members sit on the boards of directors of Fortune 500 corporations, slash and cut budgets allocated for investigative reporting. Journalists, who choose to operate outside of the purview of the political circle of their superiors, can find themselves looking for a new line of work. Those journalists who choose to ply the trade within many Third World governments can find that seeking the truth can cost them their lives. The American democratic system of government that million's have fought and died to protect has become a corrupt system of kleptocracy.

The constitutional freedoms we have enjoyed are slowly being eroded under the guise of protecting the security of the homeland. The application of justice and the rule of law have two faces; one for those that have financial means to buy favor from the judicial system and the other for those who don't. The devil be damned and God be with you if you so happen to be one of those who don't. The elected leadership of every nation that has attempted to adopt the democratic system of government from Mexico and India to the Philippines has become rotten to the core. In Nigeria where corruption within the government is so widespread and systemic, some of the citizens of the country practice fraud on a daily basis to make ends meet.

The "419" is a local code word based on a legal statute which supposedly prohibits the commitment of various overseas schemes to dupe unknowing foreigners from sending money via wire transfer to invest in bogus oil distribution ventures. The children of the global community have come under attack from many sources. The recent shootings at Virginia Tech, the October 2004 Beslan Russian massacre of over 350 children by terrorists as well as the Jonestown, Guyana mass suicide of 1978 is the latest example of how the warped ideology of one man can destroy the dreams of the innocent.

The seemingly never ending news reports of child abuse by parents, priests and other predators are as common as a cold. Children are left in the back seats of hot cars in the summertime, while their mothers shop or get their hair done and nails manicured. There are some that take better care of and have more concern for the welfare of a stray cat or dog than for the life of a child.

It appears that the value of life for the world's children is dropping faster than a tech stock on the NASDAQ. When all that a person holds sacred and true falls down around them, nothing is left but despair. When all that you hold near and dear to your heart has failed you, the effects upon the mind and spirit can be very devastating. In the song "If I Ever Lose My Faith In You" by Sting, the lyrics speak to such feelings and emotions:

You could say I lost my faith in science and progress

You could say I lost my belief in the holy Church

You could say I lost my sense of direction

You could say all of this and worse, but

If I ever lose my faith in you

There'd be nothing left for me to do

Some would say I was a lost man in a lost world

You could say I lost my faith in the people on TV

You could say I'd lost my belief in our politicians

They all seemed like game show hosts to me

No matter where one turns, the social fabric and spiritual glue which binds the human race together is being ripped and torn apart at the seams. There are almost 6 billion people on this planet, 90% of who have a belief in a higher power. But most just pay lip service to their faith and few have been willing to practice the more loving and compassionate tenants of their respective religions. For a people so conflicted emotionally and spiritually, it does beg the question as to why?

The libraries and book stores are filled with books about religion, relationships, spirituality which provide billions of dollars for the publishers and authors alike. But with the wealth of information abound to improve the quality of ones life, billions of people still live in misery and despair. Far too many see what is going on around them and are overwhelmed, frozen in a state of disbelief, denial, apathy and complacency. Many individuals just go through the motions, attending religious services and the like. But the moment one exits their place of worship, most are no better off spiritually than before they entered.

Most hold on to the belief the mere act of giving their tithes and donations is sufficient enough. Some turn blind eyes to those in need altogether, that is the extent to which they display their charitable ways. Some may choose to give to ease their conscience or to relieve their guilty feelings for acts of injustice perpetrated towards their fellow man. Most do not inquire as to what the charitable organizations or church leadership does with the monies given. Very few people question those accountable and responsible for the funds to ensure that those in need benefit from the charity given.

So let's keep it real as to who needs the money and for what purpose. God does not need money or mansions; for diamonds and gold are the idol material trappings of man. Those who profess to speak the word of God out of one corner of their mouth but yet abuse the power of their position to purchase expensive clothes, corporate jets, luxury automobiles and expensive jewelry with the donations given help no one but themselves. Until recently, I as well as many others held a great misconceived notion as to the true meaning of faith is as described in the Holy Books of the world religions.

Faith is the operating system or transmission medium by which that in the spiritual realm of God is made "real" and manifested into the physical realm of man. This transfer is executed by virtue of speaking the word of God through one's mouth as well as believing that what is spoken or asked for from God has already provided by the Creator. An example of this indicated in the Book of Genesis, that when God created the universe He uttered the words "Let There Be Light" and the sun appeared in the heavens. Through the life of Jesus Christ, He provided many examples in Scriptures of using His knowledge and belief in the Faith Operating System.

Jesus was able to walk on water, resurrect Lazarus, turn water into wine by knowing that every aspect of God's relative universe, exists and is stored in His Heavenly warehouse within the spiritual realm of the absolute. Christ held universal knowledge such as the law of gravity; therefore, He could appear to defy gravity. By knowing the laws of physics, Jesus could manipulate matter by speaking aloud, He could manifest and control that which He knew exists. He was thus able to work what many perceive as "miracles" on earth. The primary difference between Jesus and the rest of mankind is that Jesus level of spiritual awareness and faith in God's purpose for His life was superior to the average believer.

The Creator has given to each of us the means to summon the power of the universe to bring forth into our reality that which we desire to experience. In order to be truly committed to practicing one's faith requires one under go a change of heart or in other words, becoming truly aware of the power of the Holy Spirit within us. A person who is both hungry and thirsty can pray for food and water. But if one is unwilling to get up and pick the fruit from the trees growing around them, all that remains are the hunger pangs. Those who follow the tenets of Judeo-Christian and Islamic faiths believe that one day Jesus will return for the Day of Judgment.

If Jesus were to return at this very moment and pose the questions" What has the human race accomplished in remembrance of Me since my departure?" and "What have you done personally to show that My life, My time and My words was not wasted in vain upon thee"? I dare say that Jesus would be far from pleased and quite disappointed with the quality of responses He would receive. For well over 2000 years, the human race has had the opportunity to live life in accordance to His words. Why would Jesus believe after so much time has passed, that mankind would be any more prone to act differently upon his return? The spirit of Jesus lives in the homeless man; the poor woman or the hungry child you step over or drive by on your way to prayer or worship.

Christ Spirit dwells within the person you ignore or disrespect at work or sitting on the seat next to you on a bus or train ride home as well. Jesus spoke to those who profess to be His disciples "Then shall he answer them, saying, Verily I say unto you, Inasmuch as ye did it not to one of the least of these, ye did it not to me" (Matthew 25:45). Those who profess to believe in the words of Jesus, the book of Moses and the teachings of Mohammed have sat on their collective behinds for far too long. Each religion professes that their belief system is the only one so-called true religion.

That somehow they and they alone have exclusive rights to God's love and favor. To justify their position, some proclaim and profess to be waiting upon the return of the Messiah to lead them to the Promised Land. Others seek to become the catalyst of bringing forth Armageddon as written in the Book of Revelations. The scriptures clearly state that the "chosen" ones of this world are the poor and the needy." For you always have the poor with you, but you will not always have me (Matthew 26:11)". "Hearken, my beloved brethren; did not God choose them that are poor as to the world to be rich in faith, and heirs of the kingdom which he promised to them that love him? (James 2:5)".

If God desired the human race to experience one religious belief system and an androgynous physical appearance, would He not through the initial creation of the universe have done so? For the Creator has let it be known from the very beginning of time that His love for us is eternal, everlasting and unconditional. We as individuals have turned our backs to God and to each other, but the Creator has never forsaken and turned His back towards us. God designated the human race as the primary caretakers of the planet Earth.

This planet is the land promised to ALL of us, so it is quite foolhardy to expect to be delivered elsewhere at this place in time in HIStory. This is especially true with the track record we've accumulated thus far. Suppose you were to give your child a house to live in, periodically stopping by to pay them a visit. Upon your visits, you discover that your child is slowly but surely destroying the house you gave them brick by brick.

Would you give them another one to destroy? We have not yet proven ourselves worthy of moving onto the next level of our spiritual enlightenment. We will remain in spiritual stasis repeating the same failed attempts until we collectively decide we are ready to move forward together. Many men and women throughout history have attempted to lead us to the path of spiritual enlightenment. The impediment to our spiritual progression had not been due to the lack of leadership, knowledge or wisdom. The true cause is due to the lack of willingness to follow the leads God has given us along the way thus far.

As with clothing, no one size truly fits all. Therefore, if the religious system one practices does not bring the inner peace, love and serenity then it is incumbent on the individual to take an honest assessment of them selves. God helps those who help themselves, so why put off tomorrow what you can do today? There is nothing preventing or stopping you from treating your fellow man with kindness and respect. A kind word and a smile cost you nothing. What has the human race been waiting for that could have been accomplished thousands of years ago?

Billions of people are walking around in the dark unnecessarily searching to find the light of truth. The truth is out there for all to see. But you can't see the light if you are blinded by willful ignorance, and walking about with your eyes closed. If one must be led, follow the dictates of your heart and lead yourself in the direction the Holy Spirit compels you to go. Why must a disaster or calamity such as the recent occurrence of Hurricane Katrina, the 2004 Asian Tsunami or the Virginia Tech massacre take place before the people of the world come together to give the love, charity, care and compassion to those in need? Why must we wait for the loss of a family member or close friend to come together in a time of sadness instead of sharing the love and happiness while all are alive and well?

Individuals such as Oprah Winfrey, Aga Khan, Warren Buffet, Bill Gates, Ted Turner, and Angelina Jolie are shining examples of individuals with great wealth who give of their time and money to help those most in need of it.

Through both our collective inaction, irreverence and intolerance, Armageddon as referred to in the Book of Revelations is slowly but surely becoming a self-fulfilling prophecy. Many people claim to have grown weary of the greed, corruption, poverty, misery and plight that exist across this planet. Saying so doesn't make it so. If this is truly the case, then it is incumbent upon us to change the conditions in which we live. This situation is a prime example of the need for the citizens of this planet to entertain the thought of introducing a new way of living.

In America, it has become abundantly clear that the politicians of both the Democratic and Republican parties lack the moral and ethical foundation necessary to serve the needs of the American public. The sole purpose of government is to serve the needs of the people. Every institution of government whether local, states or federal is failing miserably to satisfy the pressing needs of society. These institutions are failing because we have come to accept these failings and settling for less than We the People deserve. The Democratic and Republican parties have become like a worn out pair of shoes.

The souls of its conscience have holes in it; the uppers of its integrity are held together with duct tape and Elmer's glue. They no longer fit on the feet of this once great nation nor serve the purpose for which they once stood. But We the People continue to hold on to these worn out shoes out of fear of change and a warped sense of loyalty to a way of life that no longer exists for sentimental reasons. The time has come whereby We the people must take back our nation and uphold the original intent, premise and promise contained within the Constitution and Bill of Rights.

It is the ultimate in hypocrisy to hold up our system of government as a shining example of virtue for the world to follow. If the United States intends on offering the glass of democracy for the world to drink from, let us offer it a clean one. Now more than ever, those eligible to vote must discern every spirit and adhere to the words of Jesus Christ to "Take heed that no man deceives you" (Matthew 24:4). The two major political parties in America use various "divide and conquer" methods to mobilize their base. These methods have worked in the past, but the country has paid a very high price as a result. It matters not whether the snake is a black mamba or a king cobra, its venom is just as deadly to those bitten by it.

We the People must not fall into the trap of the rat race ran on the track of corruption. Many individuals and families are riding the cycle of despair on the road towards the ditch of poverty, peddling hard but getting nowhere fast. "I returned, and saw under the sun, that the race is not to the swift, nor the battle to the strong, neither yet bread to the wise, nor yet riches to men of understanding, nor yet favour to men of skill; but time and chance happeneth to them all" (Ecclesiastes 9:11). As the 2008 Presidential election quickly approaches, be keenly aware and well informed as to the character of those whom you cast your vote for. This time, leave nothing to chance; let your vote count for those you can truly count on.

This time, do not allow your emotions over hot button issues to overrule your better judgment. Do not be misled by negative campaign ads or slogans that rhyme; or superficial catch phrases which may sound good to the ear, but ultimately leaves us empty handed. Take a long hard look at yourselves and the current conditions which surround you. Cast out those who speak with forked tongues, who cut deals under the cover of darkness at the people's expense. Cast your vote for those that will serve us, not the special interests groups or the rulers of principalities and powers in high places. The time is now for the citizens of this nation to use the power of the vote to bring about the positive changes necessary to improve the quality of life for the common good the community.

There is a quote by Charles Morgan Jr. that states "It is not by great acts but by small failures that freedom dies. The sense of justice dies slowly in a people. They grow used to the unthinkable, and sometimes they may look back and even wonder when things changed. They will not find a day or a time or a place. Justice and liberty die quietly, because men first learn to ignore injustice and then no longer recognize it". In short, it is time to throw away these worn out shoes and replace the existing lineup we have fielded. The nation needs new players of God's conscience willing to truly serve the needs of the public.

Unless the collective will of the public changes, we can expect more of the same from the current lineup of bureaucrats and politicians. The same can be said of the leaderships of the various governmental bodies represented by the United Nations as well. The UN has existed for over sixty years and for the hundreds of billions of dollars spent, the human condition on this planet has changed very little. Although sovereign nations bear the ultimate responsibility for the welfare of its citizen's, the UN charter states that when those which govern a nation are unwilling or unable to protect their citizens, the UN community of nations are to step in to support the people of a troubled nation.

After the Holocaust, the world said "never again" would the world stand idly by and allow the act of genocide and mass murder to go unchecked. From the killing fields of Cambodia to the ethnic cleansing of Muslims in Bosnia, the acts of genocide went unchecked. In 1994, the world community stood by and watched the genocidal killing of millions of Rwandan men, women and children. As the members of the UN general assembly and Security Council debated and produced meaningless reports on the conflict, people continued to die. Now in 2007, the same tragic events are reoccurring in the Darfar region of the Sudan. Once again the UN member nations stand idly by and debate whether or not the killings taking place before their very eyes constitutes genocide.

It is time for the creation of a New World order, but not in the sense of those opined by the conspiracy theorists. I do not speak of a New World order whose goal is to control and direct every facet of our lives through some elite governing body. The order in which I speak of is one whereby those of us who live on this planet can do so in peaceful coexistence. In the 1950's science fiction movie "The Day the Earth Stood Still", mankind was given a choice. Mankind could choose to either work towards living in peaceful coexistence with other members of the universe or being annihilated.

The premise of the choice offered was made by an intergalactic governing body who viewed the human race as a scourge and a cancer threatening to spread its violent ways through out the cosmos. If mankind were faced with such a choice today, I am afraid we would be signing our own death certificates by virtue of our collective actions and decisions. It is time to get back to basics and to take ownership of our personal responsibilities to change things for the better. To acknowledge and confront the current realities which face us and be willing to put forth the effort required to transform the landscape and mosaic of our lives.

On a personal level, it is time to stop the excuse mongering and casting of blame towards others for the current conditions one may face in life. What was done in the past can not be changed, but how you choose to deal and cope with the legacies of the past are within your scope of control. You can acknowledge the effects of what has occurred and how it relates your current state of being. You can choose to live in the past and harbor hate and resentment. Or you can choose to deal with the pain and begin to heal yourself from within. You can choose to wallow in a pool of self-pity and guilt wrapping yourself up in the blanket of your own misery.

Or you can choose to start down the path of recovery by reclaiming your joy and happiness. In order to accomplish this task, requires that you are both completely honest with yourself and be willing to change and take control over your life. Take a long hard look at yourself to assess what your strengths and weaknesses are. Pinpoint and hone in on those areas within that require work. It takes far longer to construct a building or a house than it takes to tear one down. Realize that it took time for the current situation to manifest itself, and it will take time to determine the cause and create a remedy to resolve the situation one faces in life.

In dealing with others, think long and hard about the intent behind your words before you speak them out loud. Be sure of why you are choosing a particular course of action. Once you allow the words to fly from your mouth, there is no taking them back. If your intent is to cause harm, be prepared to receive the same in kind sometime down the line. For what you put out into the universe you are sure to get back in return. Seek to bring to another that which you desire to have yourself based on the principle of "Do unto others that you shall have done unto you". Do for another that which will be to their benefit and not to their detriment.

To those who choose to have children under their care be fully aware of the responsibilities you decide to take on. Far too many males and females choose to engage in promiscuous sexual activity. Living a carefree and careless lifestyle contributes to the detriment of the child and the society left to care for it. Far too many people don't give a first let alone a second thought to the enormous task of raising a child. This is especially so when those involved are caught up in the heat of their sexual encounter. Too many people view raising children as an unfair burden upon their personal freedoms.

If an individual is unwilling to accept the responsibilities inherent in becoming a parent, better think twice before getting into bed. If you lack the desire to nurture, guide, and teach a child to become a responsible, emotionally and spiritually balanced individual, do both the child yet born and society a favor and don't give birth to one. A male and female may choose to engage in having sex, but a baby born as a result of the act does not. There is nothing loving, Christ like or Godly about giving birth to a life, to then abandon or become derelict in protecting and caring for that life.

The nurturing of the child starts from the moment of conception. A loving mother will ensure not to consume anything or engage in behaviors that will cause harm or endanger the unborn child. A loving father will assist in providing for the needs of both mother and child to increase the chances of giving birth to a healthy and happy baby. To those parents who have turned over the reigns of control of their household to their children, it is time to take them back. When you choose to become a parent, it is a lifetime commitment.

Teach the children the meaning of self-respect, honor, and virtue and to value life in all forms. Show them the value for education and the importance of acquiring knowledge to seek the truth for themselves. The responsibility and role of any parent is to impart the shared knowledge and wisdom to the child for the benefit of future generations. Through continual higher learning comes an improved quality of life for both the individual and for the society at large. To impart to a child the manners and decorum of conduct within a civilized society is one of the primary obligations under the parental charter. To allow a child to be both unruly and disrespectful and destructive serves neither the child nor society.

There is not an equal peer to peer relationship between a parent and a child, but one of teacher, advisor and guide. As stated before, a child will have friends come and go their entire life but they only have one set of parents. It is the prime duty of the parental responsibility to assist the child in becoming independent thinkers of conscience. Until a child is capable of thinking and acting independently, it is the responsibility of the parent to make the necessary choices and decisions on their child's behalf.

It is time to bring back the reality whereby it becomes once again socially acceptable to promote more intellectual pursuits. Parents should demand that the school systems abolish the "one size fits all" approach to teaching. Teachers should use methods that combine the basics of reading writing and arithmetic with logic and cognitive thinking skills. Courses in ethics, world philosophies as well as foreign languages other than the mother tongue will also assist in improving the quality of life within a nation. This will enhance the ability of the child to engage in deep thought and reflection instead of shallow and contrite behaviors.

Although the parents of the child may choose to practice a given religious system, great care is required in this area as well. Great caution and care should be entertained to ensure technology is used as a learning tool, in order to safeguard against becoming overly reliant upon it. Artificial intelligence can never substitute nor replace genuine human thought, care and compassion. By nurturing a child's innate curiosity during the course of their spiritual development, allow the flexibility of choice to guide the child towards the system which bests suits their own spiritual needs.

There are many doors in Gods mansion and many spiritual pathways which lead to it; it is God who gave man free will to select which path of spiritual enlightenment to travel in life. These teachings, coupled with the morals hopefully imparted by the parents at home will provide a greater opportunity that these virtues will be passed on to the future generations. Consideration should be given to revamp the current system of education as well. By formulating the teaching curriculum to foster the natural God given talents and desires of the child will promote independent thinking.

When a child is taught to think instead of being shown how to become a proficient test taker, it is less likely that the society will succumb to the various "isms" which exist today. When a child is given the opportunity to hone their own natural skills and abilities, they are more prone to be happy and well adjusted adults. The citizens of this nation and those across the globe should no longer tolerate ignorance and abject stupidity as the social norm. We are all free to choose the manner of life we desire to live, as long as it does not infringe upon the rights of others.

 It is one thing to choose to become involved in antisocial or self-destructive behavior. But when these choices impact the quality of life of those who choose to live otherwise, the boundaries of personal freedom have been crossed. People disconnected as a result of living life in a dysfunctional societal system will ultimately become disenfranchised pawns to be exploited and manipulated by the system. Dysfunctional behaviors and attitudes that seek to destroy life will not add quality or redeeming value to it. Those who choose to engage in and promote criminal activity by glorifying violence as a desired lifestyle of choice restrict the personal freedoms of others.

It matters not whether the promoters come from the music industry, movie industry or those individuals living the so called "thug life" in the street. One does not have to become incarcerated in order attain a formal education. You do not have to sacrifice personal freedoms to reclaim your spirit. One does not require prison bars in order to "get right" with God because God is always right there with you. For those who claim they are "keeping it real" by virtue of their criminal or self destructive acts, it is time to bring forth and promote a new positive reality.

It is time to pull up the sagging pants and to put out the cigarettes and blunts. In lieu of throwing up gang signs, toss away the colors and throw up the signs of peace. It is time to put down the guns, the drugs and the forty ounces; pick up books instead to acquire knowledge and wisdom. It is time instead to look towards the heavens to lift up the inner spirit and seek out the truth of self for yourself. The life and deaths of both Tupac Shakur and Christopher "The

Notorious B.I.G." are recent examples of individuals whose life and deaths imitated art, and neither are no longer here to share their talents with us.

Those who choose to take on the leadership role be they women or men shall be of good conscience and integrity whereby hypocrisy has no place in their lives. Such men and women recognize they are role models and by virtue of their position, are willing to lead by example using high ethical and moral standards as their guides. For each recognizes that those blessed with power and wealth uses the gifts given with the greatest of care and responsibility. By choosing to wield them with the soft hand of benevolence in lieu of iron fist of malevolence, the greatest good is served with the least potential for harm.

People across all walks of life have the opportunity right now to make this world a better place in which to live. The events touted in the Book of Revelations are not the inevitable absolute fate of the human race. Before we can begin to change the economic, education and social issues which affect us all, we must find a way to change hearts and minds. There is a spiritual component linked to the economic and social problems we face which have gone unaddressed for far too long. These problems stem from an extreme case of self absorption and collective attention deficit disorder of epidemic proportions, manifesting itself within the social fabric of our communities.

Engaging in heated debate steeped in anger and hate leaves everyone out in the cold on the outside looking in. For every child who is left behind or who slips through the cracks within the fabric of society today, becomes the adult who smokes crack and climbs through the window to steal us blind tomorrow. For what happens to the least of us, affects the soul of us all. To remove the sight of rural blight and urban decay requires the restoration of hope and the renewal of the human spirit.

To continue to foster the notion that "it is not my problem" or the mentality of "not in my backyard" will only continue to perpetuate the mistrust and deep racial, religious and class divisions which separate and prevents us from uniting in common cause to move the global community forward. Who will stand up to fill the spiritual void, sucking the life like a vacuum cleaner from the lives of the masses which are in deep emotional crisis? As John Steinbeck's story goes" the best-laid plans of mice and men often go awry".

"For where there is no vision, the people perish (Proverbs 29:18)." In order for us to succeed, the various religious institutions must throw off their passive shackles. Church leaders and their members must become more actively involved in reaching out to those in needs; in healing hearts and broken dreams before we can transform the communities in which we live. Extreme cases call for extreme measures, requiring bold vision and innovative ideas to tackle the problems posed before us. We must tap the ideas of both the young and the old; the tried and the true as well as the untried and the new.

If we do not come together and cast aside our differences, we will have changes forced upon us in the near future far direr than what faces us in the present. We can choose to maintain hard line positions and opinions, but all that shall be produced are hard times and cold hearts.

We can choose to accept the same old lame excuses, blame and zero sum gaming approaches whereby we all end up with the short end of the deal. Until we are willing to acknowledge the truth, face facts and demand more from ourselves, nothing will change for the better.

Unless we are willing to deal with the sources, which produce the apathy, complacency, fear, hopelessness, selfishness and despair gripping so many individuals and families, no good will come from this endeavor. So what shall it be? Will we educate or incarcerate? Will we construct new affordable housing and schools to produce highly educated, tax and tithe paying citizens? Or continue to build bigger prisons that produce more hardened criminals and menaces to society? Everything in this life comes at a price; for the bill will always come due. It becomes just a matter of time and how high the cost our society is willing to pay.

It is time to end the bickering and divisiveness, which have infected the church body as a cancer. The time has come to build bridges between faiths and denominations Christian and non-Christian alike. Those of you who have committed yourselves to serving Jesus Christ are called to extend the hand, which holds the olive branch of peace. Take the first step by beginning the healing process within yourself. If you do not love yourself and harbor self-hatred, having a peace of mind is impossible. You can not give what you do not have. Believe that God has forgiven you, embrace and accept His forgiveness within your heart and mind.

Release the pains of yesteryear into the abyss. Instead of harboring hate and anger towards someone in the present, focus on the positive aspects and blessing you possess. In order to improve the quality of your life and those around you in the here and now, give God His due and give thanks. In closing, each of you has a choice to make. Will you choose to serve a nation, a state, a man or God? We can no longer afford to passively sit on the sidelines and ignore what is going on around us. Christ's church has no walls, knows no physical boundaries!

The farmer is to sow the seed, cultivate, and harvest the fruit or "gifts" in order to feed the mind, body, and soul of God's children. Far too many of His farmers are hoarding the fruit for themselves and in some cases, allowing the fruit to wither and die on the vine. The quality and number of masters sent forth is a key indicator of the works of a great teacher or master. God needs many shepherds who are strong in the Word with unshakeable faith, who are willing to be led and to depend upon Him.

This is the true mark of a Spirit led house of God, where the percentage of active disciples is greater than the number passive members. Any House of God led by the Holy Spirit, the rejoicing and praise comes through every disciples collective efforts in welcoming home the lost, tired and wearing sheep to receive Gods love in great abundance. We must reaffirm our commitment to spread Gods love and grace through His Word and by our treatment towards our fellow man.

"Be not conformed to this world: but by transformed by the renewing of your mind. That ye may prove what is that good and acceptable and perfect will of God (Romans 12:2)". Rest you mind and allow your conscience to be free, allowing inner peace to flourish through your faith in God. Allow His love to flow deep within the recesses of your soul. For this is the way we can have peace on earth by showing love, care and compassion towards our fellow man. The conditions chronicled in the Book of Revelations are manifesting into our reality. The fate of the human race is not lost, as the ending is not cast in stone.

God has given us the choice by virtue of free will to find solutions to treat the causes instead of the symptoms of the social ills which continue to plague the lives of so many on this planet. "For now the God of patience and consolation grant you to be likeminded on toward another according to Christ Jesus (Romans 15:5)". For the scriptures say "if you forgive men their trespasses, your heavenly Father will also forgive you (Matthew 6:14)." Forgive those who have caused you pain, hurt and disappointment in love and grace. "Bless them which persecute you: bless and curse not (Romans 12:14)."

For it is written that "if any man be in Christ, he is a new creature: old things are passed away. Behold all things are become new. All things are of God, who hath reconciled us to himself by Jesus Christ, and hath given to us the ministry of reconciliation (II Corinthians 5:17-18)". God is inviting you today to take this walk of faith. He makes a promise to protect and bless you and your family. You will have divine appointments and guides along the way. You faith will be strengthened and hope renewed as you look back and see evidence of His hand at work. You will be able to have an abundant life that you can call upon and tell your children and grandchildren.

Jesus told us "Be careful for nothing; but in everything by prayer and supplication with thanksgiving. Let your request be made known unto God. The peace of God which passeth all understanding, shall keep your hearts and minds through Christ Jesus. Those things, which ye have both learned and received, and heard and seen in me, do. For the God of peace shall be with you (Philippians 4:6-7,9)".

"Peace I leave with you, my peace I give unto you: not as the world giveth, give I unto you. Let not your heart be troubled, neither let it be afraid (John 15:27)". "Brethren, be followers together of me, and mark them which walk so as ye have us for an example (Philippians 3:17)".If you can not muster the strength within yourself to change, do so for the children and the generations yet born. They deserve a chance to grow up and evolve to live happy and peaceful lives.

Don't deny them the opportunity by destroying the planet and continuing our pathologically self-destructive ways. We each have a story to tell and a life to live, whereby each day is but another opportunity to add a line to the continuing chapter of mankind. But know that you are not alone in your endeavor, for God is the great Editor in Chief. We as His divine reporters can share the fruits of our knowledge for the benefit of our fellow men and women for generations to come. God has given each of us a blank notebook called LIFE to write our personal story.

You are the author, and have the power to edit and revise the screenplay as many times as necessary with the notebook of life given unto you. Whether you decide to write a drama, a war saga or a love story that has a happy ending the choice is purely up to you. In the end, only you can provide the answer to the question God asks of you "I See That You Are Down But When Are You Going to Get Up?"

I offer the following books, music and movies, which will provide insight to awaken the mind. Each work in its own way will evoke thought to those interested in seeking a greater understanding of the human condition. Art reflects life and provokes thought about the human condition and the plight that still exists on this planet. Through their craft, some artists offer solutions to improve both the personal and interpersonal relationships that affect us all. Pay close attention to the dialogue within the movie or the lyrics within the song for each provide clues and glimpses of the truth.

Suggested Reading by Author:

The Holy Bible

Dr. Brad Blanton- "Radical Honesty" and "Practicing Radical Honesty"

Arnold Brown and Edie Weiner-"Future Think"

Vincent Bugliosi's "The Betrayal of America: How the Supreme Court Undermined the Constitution and Chose Our President"

Deepok Chopra-"The Way of the Wizard" and "Ageless Body, Timeless Mind"

Copi and Cohen-"Introduction to Logic, 11th Edition"

Charles Dickens-"A Christmas Carol" and "A Tale of Two Cities"

Jeffery Furst-"Edgar Cayce's Story of Jesus"

Mark Forstater-"The Spiritual Teachings of Marcus Aurelius"

Andrew Hacker-"Two Nations Black and White Separate, Hostile and Unequal"

Alex Haley-"Autobiography of Malcolm X"

Eamon Kelly-"Powerful Times-Rising to the Challenge of our Uncertain World".

Bruce Lee: "Words from a Master" and "Striking Thoughts: Bruce Lee's Wisdom for Daily Living."

Suggested Reading by Author (continued):

Rabbi Michael Lerner-"The Left Hand of God"

William Lynch-"The Willie Lynch Letter and the Making of a Slave"

John R. MacArthur-" The Selling of Free Trade"

Dr. Phil McGraw-"Self Matters" and "Life Strategies"

Leonard Peikoff- "The Ominous Parallels"

Plato's-"The Apology" and the "Statesman"

Thomas Sugrue-"There is a River-The Story of Edgar Cayce"

The Ayn Rand Lexicon-"Objectivism from A to Z" and "The Virtue of Selfishness"

William Shakespeare-"Julius Caesar"

Ilyana VanZant-"One Day My Soul Just Opened Up"

and "Finding Yourself and the Love you Want"

Neal Donald Walsch- "Conversations with God" series

Dr. Cornel West-"Race Matters"

Gary Zukav-"The Seat of the Soul"

Suggested Movies by Title:

"A Bronx Tale"

"A Few Good Men"

"Angels with Dirty Faces"

"Bamboozled"

"Ben Hur"

"BoyzNTheHood"

"Bullworth"

"Deep Cover"

"Do the Right Thing"

"Fearless"

"Gladiator"

"Glory"

"JFK"

"Malcolm X"

"The Matrix" Trilogy

"The Lord of the Rings' Trilogy

"Network"

"The Passion of Christ"

"The Peaceful Warrior"

"On Any Given Sunday"

Suggested Movies by Title (continued):

 "Rosewood"

"Saving Private Ryan"

"Scheindler's List"

"Star Wars Trilogy"

"The Day the Earth Stood Still"

"The Devil's Advocate"

"The Long Kiss Goodnight"

"The Ten Commandments"

"V for Vendetta"

"Wall Street"

"What Dreams Come True"

 Suggested Music by Song Title:

"A Minute to Pray, a Second to Die" by Scarface

"All For The Money" by MC Eight

"Ball of Confusion" by The Temptations

"Be a Father to Your Child" by Ed OG and Da Bulldawgs

"B-Movie", "We Almost Lost Detroit This Time" and "The Revolution Won't Be Televised by Gil-Scott Heron

"Controversy" and "Sign of The Times" by Prince

"Choice of Colors" and "Brand New Day" by Curtis Mayfield/The Impressions

"Crack Killed Apple Jack" by General Kane

"Don't Believe the Hype" and "Cant Trust It" by Public Enemy

"Do G's Get to Go to Heaven?" by Richie Rich

"If I Ever Lose My Faith In You" and "Its Probably Me" by Sting

"Inner City Blues", "Mercy, Mercy Me", "What's Going On?" and

"Love" and "143" by Musiq SoulChild

"Trouble Man" by Marvin Gaye

"In the Ghetto" and "Who is God?" by Rakim/EricB

"Money" and "Just Another Brick in The Wall" by Pink Floyd

"My Mind is Playin' Tricks on Me" by The Gheto Boyz

"One Mic" by NAS

"Opportunity" by Bobby McFerrin

"Respiration" by Black Starr featuring Mos Def/Common/Talib Kweli

"So Many Tears", When My Homie Calls", "I Ain't Mad at Cha", "Dear Momma" and "Brenda Has a Baby" by TUPAC

"The Message" by Grandmaster Flash and the Furious Five

"The Prayer" and "Who We Be" by DMX

"The Soliloquy of Chaos" by Gangstarr featuring the Guru

"You Must Learn" and "Loves Gonna Get You" by KRS-ONE

Index

A
abuse: of children, 113–114, 166, 277; in relationships, 187–188, 189
adolescent relationships, 68–70; in neighborhood, 80; thoughts on, 84
adversity, 261
advertising, 276
advice: from author, 283; from coworkers, 194–195, 239; from Mike (coworker), 250–251, 252; from mother, 196; from Ralph (coworker), 228–229
Affirmative Action, 160, 161; role in, 214
affirmative action, 224
afterlife: fear of, 263
Aga Khan, 281
Al-Qur'an. see Quran
alcohol use, 58–61, 72–73, 182; at Bobby's house, 144, 169; first occurrence of, 58–61; in high school, 72–73; perspective on, 174–175; police and, 170; at softball game, 150
Andalusia, Alabama, 44–45
anger: early development of, 20–21; harboring, 90; at school, 49–50; as shoplifting cause, 26; toward "Big Frank," 124; toward grandfather, 24; toward mother, 39, 97, 223; toward neighbors, 29–30; toward Uncle Skip, 73–74; in workplace, 86–87, 226–227
Anita (girlfriend), 68–70
Annie (Bobby's mother): conversation with, 168, 169
apartment hunting, 201, 219
Armageddon, 280, 281
Arthur Anderson (accounting firm), 271
Aryanism: collectivism and, 52
Aubrey (friend): character of, 198; conversation with, 211; meeting, 198
automobile: purchase of, 221–222
"Axis of Evil," 273

B
banter, 66
Beslan massacre, 277

294

G

Galatians, quotation from: 6:7, 267, 276
Gates, Bill, 281
Genesis, 267, 279; quotations from: 2:7, 269; 21:13, 267
global conflicts: reconciliation and, 286–287; thoughts on, 258
goals: of department project, 246; at work, 202, 203
God, 259–260; conversations about, 243; as creator, 88–89; Earth as gift from, 280; free will and, 288; spiritual pathways to, 285; unconditional love of, 122–123
Golden Rule, The, 270
government systems, 52–53
graduation: high school, 75–77; joy and, 106; Junior college, 100, 104–105; Monya's, 148–149
grandparents: death of, 30–32; fraternal great-grandparents, 13; love from, 23; as parental figures, 13–15; trust in, 25
greed, corporate, 271–273
grievance: filing of, 253–254
guilt, 26–27
Gulf War or 1991, 273

H

happiness: poverty and, 100
Harry (coworker), 246–248
hate, 20, 73–74
heaven: thoughts on, 265
Hebrews, quotations from: 11:1, 259; 13:5, 263
high school: graduation from, 75–77; self esteem in, 54–55; starting, 45–47
honesty, 120–122; in marriage, 191; at work, 246–247
house: location of, 220; moving into, 220; purchase of, 220
house painting, 24
humor, 130–131
Hurricane Katrina, 280
hypocrisy, 230–231; in corporate policy, 249

I

"If I Ever Lose My Faith In You" (song), 277–278
ignorance: effects of, 255
Indiana Wesleyan University, 219–220
inequality, 115
infidelity, 165–166; of coworkers, 239; opinions on, 244–245; possibility of, 238–239; thoughts on, 165–166
initiative, in career, 203
injustice, 173–174
inner conflict, 184

police: corruption of, 173–174; racial issues and, 172; stopped by, 170, 171
police brutality, 173
politicians (United States): corruption of, 281; responsibility of, 281–282
poverty: in neighborhood, 79; social restrictions and, 79; thoughts on, 268; unhappi-
        ness and, 100
power, 248; definition of, 262; of knowledge, 265; money and, 272, 275; political,
        275
prayer, 260; faith and, 279
prejudices, 29–30; of coworkers, 161
Presidential elections: of 2000, Supreme Court and, 275–276; of 2004, 276
pride, 85, 96
prisoners, 233
pro-creationism, 81
projects (work), 206, 210; goals of, 246
promotion: discrimination concerning, 252–255; interview for, 189, 191–192
Proverbs, quotations from: 29:18, 286; 30:5, 259; 57:2, 262
Psalms, quotation from: 46:10, 266
public speaking: fear of, 241, 242; first experience, 242–243
punishment, 28; for cheating, 68
pyrite ("fool's gold"), 264

Q
Quran, 20; quotations from, 264; and "The Golden Rule," 270

R
race: first perception of, 20; opportunity and, 102–103. see also Racial issues.
racial issues: coworkers and, 224; discussion of, 92–93; in early America, 111–113;
        police and, 172; in workplace, 86–87
Ralph (coworker), 194, 219; advice from, 228–229; firing of, 229; loyalty to, 229
reconciliation: within church body, 286–287; individual, 288
redeem, definition of, 261
redemption, 261
relationship(s): abuse in, 189; adolescent (see adolescent relationships); with "Big
        Frank," 124; "Big Frank's" thoughts on, 98–99; commitment in, 167–168; with
        coworkers, 86, 111, 117, 126; dating, 147; female, 95; friends and, 185; infidelity
        within, 165–166; with Jill, 202–203; at Junior college, 104–105; of mother, 19;
        with siblings, 134–135; thoughts on, 168. see also Friendship(s).
religion: corruption in, 278; different forms of, 280; murder and, 173, 174; and "The
        Golden Rule," 270
relocation, 193; disappointment with, 79; to Fort Wayne, Indiana, 198
respect, 280; in career, 225; honesty and, 116; in neighborhood, 30; supervisors and,
        125–126; thoughts on, 87; toward "Big Frank," 27, 28; toward teachers, 47; to-
        ward women, 31

ISBN 142512041-5